New
Inside Out

Sue Kay, Vaughan Jones,
Helena Gomm, Peter Maggs
& Chris Dawson

Advanced

Teacher's Book

MACMILLAN

Macmillan Education
Between Towns Road, Oxford OX4 3PP
A division of Macmillan Publishers Limited
Companies and representatives throughout the world

ISBN 978-0-230-00937-0

Text © Ceri Jones, Tania Bastow, Amanda Jeffries, Sue Kay and Vaughan Jones 2010
Text by Helena Gomm
Photocopiable resource materials by Sue Kay and Vaughan Jones with Jon Hird
Language and cultural notes by Pete Maggs
Design and illustration © Macmillan Publishers Limited 2010

First published 2010

Note to Teachers
Photocopies may be made, for classroom use, of pages xxxvii–xliv, and 157–195
without the prior written permission of Macmillan Publishers Limited. However,
please note that the copyright law, which does not normally permit multiple copying
of published material, applies to the rest of this book.

Designed by 320 Design Limited
Page layout by Carolyn Gibson
Illustrated by Kathy Baxendale, Beach, Dave Burroughs, Peter Campbell, Ivan Gillet,
Ben Hasler, Ed McLachlan and Bill Piggins
Cover design by Andrew Oliver

The author and publishers would like to thank the following for permission to reproduce
their material: **Alamy**/Jeff Greenberg p185

These materials may contain links for third party websites. We have no control over, and
are not responsible for, the contents of such third party websites. Please use care when
accessing them.

Although we have tried to trace and contact copyright holders before publication, in some
cases this has not been possible. If contacted, we will be pleased to rectify any errors or
omissions at the earliest opportunity.

Printed and bound in Great Britain by Martins the Printers

2014   2013   2012   2011   2010
10   9   8   7   6   5   4   3   2   1

Contents

TEACHER'S NOTES

RESOURCE MATERIALS

Student's Book contents map

(WB) = **Workbook**. Each unit of the Workbook contains a one-page section which develops practical writing skills.

Introduction

Welcome to *New Inside Out!*

New Inside Out Advanced is the fruit of many years of teaching and developing materials for advanced levels in a variety of different contexts. Teaching advanced students is both challenging and rewarding: challenging because our students already know so much, but still have so much to learn; rewarding because our students contribute so much to the learning experience. We hope that *New Inside Out* Advanced will help you and your students make the most of the experience.

Advanced students have reached a point where they are competent, independent users of the language. They can cope easily and comfortably in a wide range of situations. The challenge for both students and teachers at this level is to find the continuing motivation to move forwards from competence to proficiency. In the spirit of the *New Inside Out* series, we believe that the key to this motivation lies in three main areas: engaging and stimulating materials, structure and support in exploring the nuances and subtleties of the language, and the opportunity to take part in real world tasks and personally relevant discussion.

Engaging content and stimulating material

Students learn best when they are engaged and stimulated. Learning becomes more efficient when the language is introduced in contexts that are memorable and relevant. In *New Inside Out* Advanced we have tried to provide a variety of texts and topics that provoke a real, personal response and offer a springboard for discussion and exploration. At all times we encourage the students to make links between the material on the page and their own lives and world views, bringing the language closer to the students and helping them become confident, proficient and successful users of the language.

Ceri Jones   *Tania Bastow*   *Amanda Jeffries*

Support and structure

Throughout the language learning process, students need support and structure; support when dealing with, and processing, new language forms and features, structure when they are being asked to produce the language in a communicative context. This is no less true at advanced levels, where the amount and variety of language they encounter can be overwhelming. They need to be given a framework for analysing the nuances and subtleties of the language, and for integrating what they already know with any new language they learn. They need opportunities to experiment with these new-found nuances in a controlled and comfortable environment and to manipulate them and make them their own. Likewise, when setting up a speaking or a writing task, advanced students still need time to gather their thoughts and give structure to their ideas before being asked to communicate them.

Real world tasks

New Inside Out emphasises output, producing and practising the language to achieve clear, attainable goals, whether that be telling a personal anecdote, writing a formal email, or responding appropriately to a request or complaint. In *New Inside Out* Advanced we use these goals to stretch and challenge our students, asking them to push themselves that little bit further, to strive to communicate as carefully and clearly as possible. We encourage them to make the best choice of words to express exactly the meaning and attitude they, personally, want to convey, choosing the most appropriate grammar, lexis and pronunciation at their disposal. In order for students to invest the effort required to reach these goals, it is important that the tasks we ask them to complete are real tasks, ones that they feel they can transfer into their own lives and worlds.

Components of the course

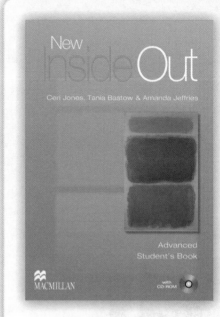

Student's materials

- Student's Book *see page viii–x*
- CD-ROM *see page xi*
- Workbook and Audio CD *see page xi*

Teacher's materials

- Teacher's Book *see page xii*
- Test CD *see page xii*
- Class Audio CDs *see page xii*
- DVD *see page xii*
- DVD Teacher's Book *see page xii*
- Website *see page xiii*
- *New Inside Out Digital see page xiii*

Student's materials A typical Student's Book unit (Unit 9)

A language menu at the beginning of each unit summarises the main teaching points.

Headings throughout the units provide clear information about what the students are studying.

Vocabulary is presented in context – in this case in a quiz focusing on students' sleep habits. Students are encouraged to examine new words in context and infer meaning. Practice activities expand the students' knowledge of selected lexical items and give them opportunities to use the vocabulary in meaningful exchanges.

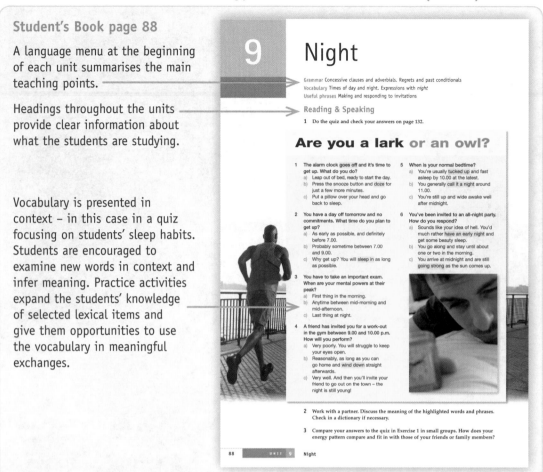

Motivating reading texts have been adapted from authentic sources to suit the Advanced level student. They have been selected not only for their language content, but also for their interest and appropriacy.

Glossaries give simple definitions for more challenging words in the text or, in this case, challenge students to explore new vocabulary items in the context of the authentic source material.

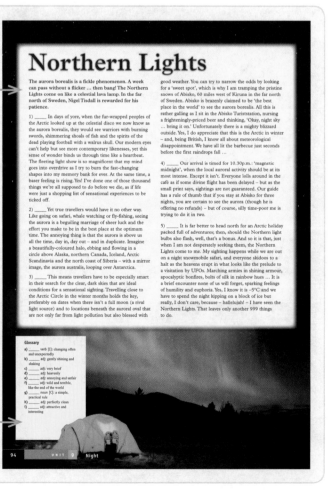

Student's Book page 92

New Inside Out Advanced is full of engaging material taken from modern authentic sources. As a first step, students are always encouraged to read or listen for meaning and enjoyment.

The listenings include several authentic recordings, as well as text specially written for language learning.

Pronunciation work on particular areas of sound, stress and intonation is integrated into every unit.

Students are encouraged to relate the topics to their own lives, views and feelings.

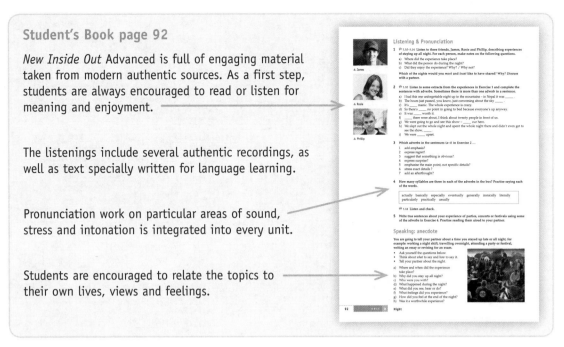

Student's Book page 95

New Inside Out Advanced includes an average of two grammar sections in every unit. Typically, these follow a three-stage approach.

1 Students 'notice' new grammatical structures that have been contextualised in the previous section. They focus on the way new language works.
   A brief summary of the grammar point is provided in the margin.

2 Language practice is designed to be realistic and meaningful.

3 Students use target language for controlled, personalised practice.

In addition, students are referred to the Grammar *Extra* pages at the back of the Student's Book for extended explanations and further practice.

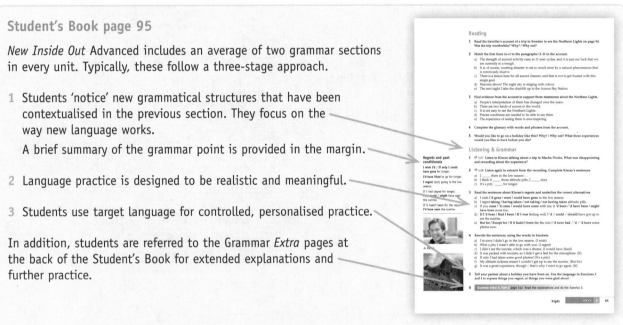

Student's Book page 96

Useful phrases gives students a portable toolkit of functional language. These sections are designed to be fun and engaging and the phrases are recorded on the Class CD.

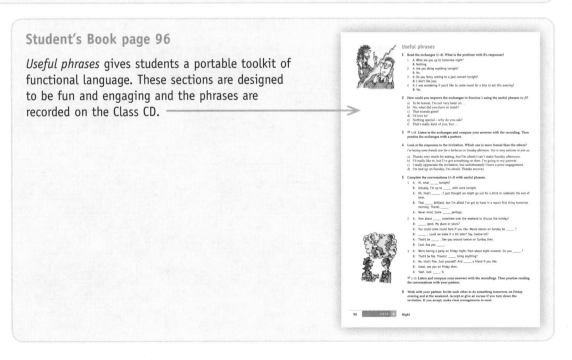

Student's Book page 97

The *Vocabulary Extra* pages at the end of units 1, 3, 5, 7, 9 and 11 explore key lexical areas such as collocation, lexical sets and in this case phrasal verbs. They provide students with detailed practice activities and help promote useful dictionary skills.

Student's Book page 109

The *Writing Extra* pages at the end of units 2, 4, 6, 8, 10 and 12 develop important writing skills in a variety of genres. They complement the complete self-contained writing course in the Workbook.

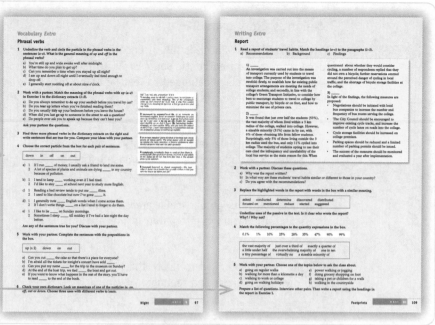

Student's Book page 98

There are four Review units in *New Inside Out* Advanced Student's Book. Each Review unit revises the new structures taught in the previous three teaching units.

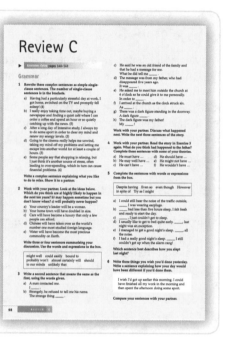

Student's Book pages 142 and 143

The Grammar *Extra* pages at the back of the Student's Book provide a summary of the new grammatical structures as well as extra practice.

CD-ROM

The CD-ROM in the back of every Student's Book provides a wealth of interactive practice activities along with integrated listening material contextualising the *Useful phrases*.

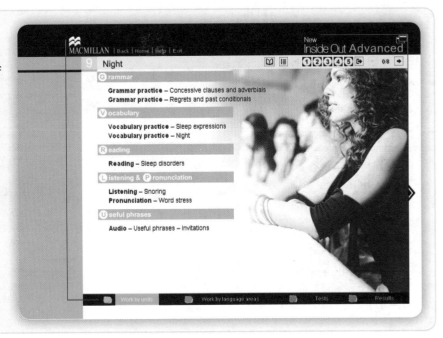

Workbook pages 52 and 53

The Workbook provides revision of all the main points in the Student's Book, plus extra listening practice, pronunciation work and a complete self-contained writing course. There are *with* and *without key* versions, and a story from *Horror Stories* (Macmillan Literature Collection) is included in the back of the Workbook.

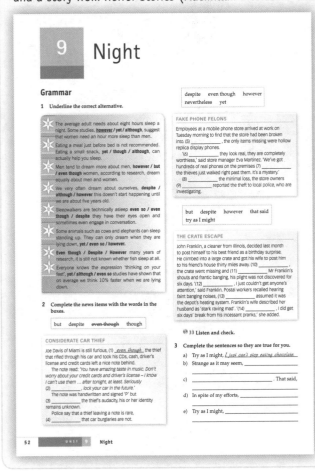

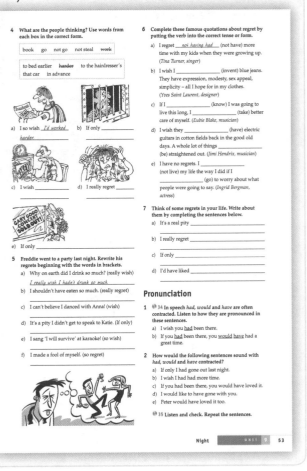

Teacher's materials

Teacher's Book

The 6-in-1 Teacher's Book contains:

- an Introduction
- Practical methodology
- Common European Framework (CEF) checklists
- complete teaching notes with answer keys
- a bank of extra photocopiable grammar, vocabulary and communicative activities
- a Test CD with word files that you can edit and the recordings of the listening test activities

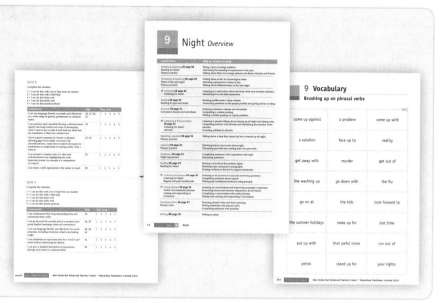

Class CD set

The Class CDs contain:

- the dialogues and listening activities from the Student's Book
- recordings of the pronunciation activities

DVD and DVD Teacher's Book

The DVD contains programmes which complement the topics in the Student's Book. There is a wide variety of formats including interviews, profiles, documentaries and video diaries. The DVD Teacher's Book contains related teaching notes and photocopiable worksheets.

Website

Visit www.macmillanenglish.com/insideout to find out more details about the course and its authors. The website provides downloadable resources and more information about *New Inside Out*.

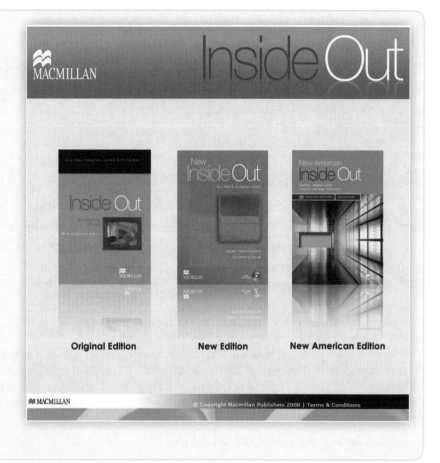

New Inside Out Digital

The evolution of the coursebook

Use *New Inside Out Digital* alongside the printed coursebook to enhance your experience in the classroom. It has been adapted to work on any interactive whiteboard or simply with a computer and a projector.

New Inside Out Digital offers a digital version of the coursebook with interactive tools and integrated audio and video. There is also a Teacher's Area which allows you to create and save your own material (slides, games, etc.).

Extra resources on *New Inside Out Digital* include: the Workbook answer key, Common European Framework checklists and the DVD Teacher's Book.

Practical methodology

Teaching advanced students

A student who has reached the advanced level is, by definition, a successful language learner. According to the Common European Framework (CEF), he or she is now a *proficient user* of the language and, having moved off the so-called 'intermediate plateau', is thus distinguished from an *independent user* (levels B1 and B2). The CEF descriptor for C1 is a useful summary of what a student at this level should be capable of:

Can understand a wide range of demanding, longer texts, and recognise implicit meaning. Can express him/herself fluently and spontaneously without much obvious searching for expressions. Can use language flexibly and effectively for social, academic and professional purposes. Can produce clear, well-structured, detailed text on complex subjects, showing controlled use of organisational patterns, connectors and cohesive devices. *

This level of competence may have been arrived at through prolonged instruction or prolonged exposure, or a mixture of both. Needs will vary. Some advanced learners will be extremely fluent but need to tighten up on accuracy, especially in written work. Others will demonstrate excellent grammatical accuracy but require coaching on how to make their English sound more fluent, natural or idiomatic. One thing is certain, they will all share a desire to continue improving and above all, not 'lose their English', an unfounded but understandable fear given the time and effort they have put in to become advanced learners in the first place.

In *New Inside Out* Advanced we've tried to balance the natural inclination to race ahead and learn more and more 'brand new' language with an analytical approach, which encourages students to notice more complex aspects of language they already 'know'. We believe that time spent learning more about 'half-known' words – things such as collocation, range, connotation and register – can help iron out any residual problems students may have without compromising a sense of progress and forward momentum.

In common with all the teaching materials in the *New Inside Out* series, there's a relentless focus on meaning. In particular, the aim is to help students make their own meanings in ever more communicatively competent and socially acceptable ways. This is built into every stage of the learning process. It's the core feature of *Inside Out* which helps students maintain their enthusiasm and motivation.

Right from the start

Every teacher has their own way of setting up their classroom, interacting with their students and conducting their lessons. Here are a few things that we've found useful to bear in mind.

The right environment

It's important to do everything you can to create a supportive learning environment. Start by memorising every student's name and learn as much information as you can about them. Make sure students learn each other's names too and that they all get to know things about each other early on.

Make sure you find time to 'chat' to individual students or small informal groups of students before or after class. More formally, it's a good idea to devote at least one lesson per term to counsel your students individually and discuss their progress.

Your classroom might be the only exposure to English that students get. Make that exposure as rich as you can by decorating the walls with maps and posters. Have several monolingual dictionaries available to refer to – a class set if possible. Also, try to have a selection of English books, newspapers and magazines lying around that students can pick up and browse before and after lessons. Here are some further ideas:

- Institute the 'Class Scribe' idea. One student in the class is given the role of recording any new language that comes up during the lesson that isn't necessarily the target language of that lesson. This unique record is then kept in a folder in the class and provides the teacher with valuable data for revision activities. The role of class scribe is rotated so that each student gets a turn at being responsible for recording the lesson. This shared responsibility can help promote positive group dynamics.

* Council of Europe, 2001. Common European Framework of Reference for Languages: Learning, Teaching Assessment p 24.

- Promote extensive reading. There's a large selection of readers available at the upper intermediate/advanced level: both simplified classics and original stories. Ask the students to always bring their reader to the lesson and occasionally set aside a ten-minute slot for them to talk about what they're reading. Alternatively, just devote ten minutes to silent reading. Most advanced students will feel confident enough to tackle unsimplified, original versions. This is fine, but make sure the students understand that it's much better to read and enjoy ten easy books than struggle through one difficult one. Get your students hooked on books!

- Promote content-rich websites in English, particularly news sites such as the BBC. Encourage them to sign up for free newsletters or blogs in areas that are of interest to them. The amount of free information in English that is available on the internet is virtually infinite.

The right learning skills

Students will always benefit from help with learning strategies. Here are some thoughts:

- Encourage students to ask questions about language. If you have created the right atmosphere in your classroom, then students will be more likely to take an active approach in their own learning and this is important. Students should never feel intimidated about asking questions.

- Spend time encouraging students to experiment with how they record words and phrases from the lesson. Make sure they note the part of speech – verb, noun, adjective, etc. Tell them to find a way of noting the pronunciation of the word, either using phonemic script or by developing their own system. Ask them to write complete personalised sentences putting the new word or phrase in a real context and thereby making it more memorable.

- A dictionary is a very important language learning tool and most students will have one. Usually students prefer a bilingual dictionary but at the advanced level they need to invest in a good advanced monolingual dictionary. The Vocabulary *Extra* pages at the end of units 1, 3, 5, 7, 9 and 11 in *New Inside Out* Advanced have been designed to give students valuable dictionary practice and make them aware of all the useful 'extra' information that is available in a good monolingual dictionary.

The right amount of practice

In our experience, the most successful lessons consist of a manageable amount of new input, and then a lot of meaningful practice. For this reason, we've tried to provide maximum practice activities in *New Inside Out*, both in the Student's Book and in the other supporting components. But there is never enough time in the lessons alone. Always set homework, even if it's just reading a chapter from a reader, and make homework feedback or correction an integral part of the lesson.

The top 10 activities for advanced students

These tried and trusted activities can be used as lead-ins, warmers, fillers, pair-forming activities, or for revision and recycling. Most of them require very little or no preparation and can be adapted to cover a wide variety of different language points. The emphasis is on vocabulary revision as we all know that it's only through repeated, systematic exposure to new words and expressions that students are likely to transform 'input' into 'intake'. You may be familiar with some of the ideas and others may be new. In any event, we hope they provide a useful extension to your teaching repertoire. They certainly get used and re-used in our own classrooms!

It's always useful to have a stock of small white cards and access to a collection of pictures. Magazine pictures are ideal, and can be filed in alphabetical order according to topics.

1 Board bingo

Aim

This activity is good for revising any type of vocabulary.

Preparation

Write down twelve to fifteen words you want to revise on the board. They could be words from last lesson, words from the unit you've just finished or a random selection of words covering the whole term.

Procedure

- Ask the students to choose five of the words and write them down. When they've done that, tell the students that you're going to read out dictionary definitions of the words in random order and that they should cross out their words if they think they hear the definition. When they've crossed out all five words, they shout *Bingo!* Make sure you keep a record of the word definitions you call out so that you can check the students' answers.

- If you teach a monolingual class, you could read out a translation of each word rather than an English definition. Alternatively, you could turn it into a pronunciation exercise by working on the recognition of phonemic script. Hold up cards with phonemic transcriptions of the words in random order. Students cross out their words if they think they've seen the corresponding phonetic transcription.

2 My criteria

Aim

This activity can be used to review almost any vocabulary.

Preparation

Choose up to ten words that you want to revise. You might want to start with recognisable lexical sets and then move onto groups of random words.

Procedure

- Write the words on the board in no particular order. Put the students in pairs or small groups. The activity consists of writing out the words in a specific order according to a particular criteria of the students' choosing. Each pair or group keeps their criteria secret. They then give their list to another pair or group who have to work out what they think the criteria is.

  For example, let's say you want to revise words for different types of shoe from Unit 10. You write eight items on the board: e.g. *clogs, flip-flops, sling-backs, slippers, slip-ons, stilettos, trainers, walking boots.* The students then rearrange the list according to a criteria that they have thought of. The criteria can be anything from 'alphabetical order': i.e. 1 *clogs*, 2 *flip-flops*, 3 *slingbacks*, etc., to 'useful': i.e. 1 *trainers*, 2 *slip-ons*, 3 *slippers*, etc.

- Sometimes the criterion clearly suggests only one possible order (i.e. 'alphabetical order'). If the criterion is 'useful' then the order of items might be open to debate. This is fine and can lead to some interesting discussion. To get the students used to this activity, in the first instance you might want to give them different criteria to choose from. Here are some more possible criteria for shoes: *expensive, fashionable, easy to find in shops, shoes I wouldn't be seen dead in.* Alternatively, you might want to give them just one criterion (one where the order is not obvious), and see if each group comes up with the same order.

- Here are some more ideas for lexical sets and criteria

  1 Stories (Unit 4, page 39)
  Possible criteria: long, interesting, spoken / written, child / adult.

  2 Phrasal verbs (Unit 9, page 97)
  Possible criteria: frequent, useful, largest number of meanings, most idiomatic.

  3 New words (Unit 11, page 117)
  Possible criteria: strange, useful to me, difficult to understand, likely to endure.

3 Category dictation

Aim

This activity can be adapted to review almost any vocabulary. It can also be used to review certain pronunciation and grammar points.

Preparation

Choose the language you want to review and devise a way of categorising it into two or more categories.

Procedure

- Write the category headings on the board and ask the students to copy them onto a piece of paper. Two simple categories is usually best. More than four can get complicated. Then dictate the words (10–12 maximum) slowly and clearly, and ask the students to write them down in the correct category.

  For example, you might want to revise names of different crimes from Vocabulary Exercise 1 on page 78. So, write the following on the board and ask the students to copy it down.

prison	fine

- Then dictate some crimes, e.g. *manslaughter, speeding, arson, shoplifting, burglary, embezzlement, libel,* etc. The students write down the words in the correct category according to how severe they think the crime is. When you've dictated 10 or 12 words, ask students to compare their lists. When they've done this, ask them to call out their answers and write them on the board in the correct category, so that they can check the spelling. In this particular case, students may not know the 'right' answer, i.e. whether the crime requires a custodial sentence or not. This doesn't matter as you could ask them to categorise the words according to their own opinion.

- Here are some more ideas for categories:

  1 Revise countable and uncountable nouns. (Unit 5, page 53)
  Suggested categories: *countable or uncountable.*

  2 Revise US/UK spellings. (Unit 5, page 55)
  Suggested categories: *same* or *different.* Read out same-sounding words, i.e. *centre, labour, colour, grey, blue,* etc., and students put the words in the appropriate column according to whether there is a difference in spelling.

  3 Revise collocations with *mind.* (Unit 6, page 63)
  Suggested categories: used as a verb or used as a noun.

4 Whose dialogue?

Aim

To imagine what people in pictures are saying to one another and to write a short dialogue.

Preparation

You will need a selection of eight to ten magazine pictures. Each picture should show two people who could be talking to one another. Try to get pictures of as widely varying contexts as possible.

Procedure

- Divide the students into pairs or small groups. Display the pictures on the board, on the wall or on the floor where everybody can see them. Ask each pair or group to secretly choose a picture, but without pointing or touching it. The students then write a short dialogue between the people in the picture they've chosen. When they've finished, ask them to act out their dialogue to the other members of the class without indicating which picture it's based on. The other students guess which picture the dialogue goes with.

- This activity is particularly suited to revising some of the functional language from the Useful phrases sections in the Student's book. You could write six or more useful phrases on the board and tell the students that their dialogues must include at least one (or two, or three) of them. The Useful phrases could be part of a recognisable set (i.e. Unit 5, page 54: *Could you give me a receipt?*, *I'm afraid it's still a bit pricey*, *Is that your final offer?*, etc.) Alternatively, they could just be random (i.e. *What a relief!*, *What I like about this is …*, *Would you mind lending me a fiver*, etc.)

- Alternatively, you could choose any ten to twelve words you want to revise and put them on the board. Then tell the students that they must include at least three (or four, or five) of the words in their dialogues.

5 Random letters

Aim

This activity is good for revising any type of vocabulary.

Preparation

None

Procedure

- Ask the students to call out any seven letters from the alphabet. (It doesn't have to be seven letters: anything between seven and twelve is fine.) Write the letters scattered on the board.

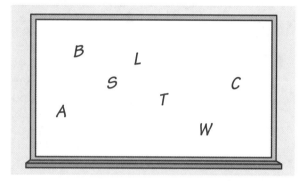

- Then ask the students in pairs to think of a word beginning with each letter on the board. The most obvious criteria is to revise words from a specific lexical set that you have taught recently. Alternatively, you could simply ask them for words they've noted down in lessons over the past two weeks.

- Another possibility would be to find the most interesting words they can from the Student's Book unit that you've just finished. If the lexical set you want them to revise is particularly rich, you could ask the students to think of as many words for each letter as they can in, say, three minutes: make it into a contest to find the most words.

- There are lots of possible variations using different criteria for words from the letters on the board. Here are a few:

  1 Use the same criteria as above, but ask the students to think of words ending with the letter on the board.

  2 Ask the students to write only nouns or adjectives or irregular verbs or some other part of speech.

  3 Ask the students to write only words with three syllables or words with the same vowel sounds.

  4 Ask students to write only words that start with the same letter in their own language or only words that start with a different letter.

6 Five favourites

Aim

This activity is good for revising any words learned recently.

Preparation

None

Procedure

- Students look back through their lesson notes for the last two weeks and select from the words they've recorded five words that they think are particularly useful. They compare their list with a partner and together they produce a common list of five words from the combined list of ten. To do this they'll have to argue for and against words on the combined list until they are both satisfied that they have the most useful five. If you wanted to continue the activity, you could then have each pair join up with another pair as a group of four and repeat the procedure. Depending on the size of your class you might continue until you had established a list of 'five favourites' for the whole class.

- The value of this activity lies in the students looking back through their notes, choosing the words and then arguing for them to be part of the combined list. The whole procedure gives them valuable repeat exposure to words recently learned.

- A possible extension activity after each pair has formed their common list of five words is to collect the lists and redistribute them so that each pair has a different list. The pairs then write a dialogue or short story incorporating the five words they have on the list they've just received. You could then ask them to read out their dialogues or stories and the other students guess what the five listed words were.

7 Crosswords

Aim

This activity is good for revising lexical sets and can help with spelling.

Preparation

Choose a lexical set you want to revise. For example: adjectives to describe conversations (Unit 1); different types of story (Unit 4); words on the topic of law (Unit 8), etc.

Procedure

- Students work in pairs. They'll need a piece of paper, preferably graph paper with squares on.

- Choose a topic, for example, *crimes*.

- Student A writes 'Across' words, and Student B writes 'Down' words.

- It's a good idea to provide the first word across, and make sure that it's a long one (e.g. *manslaughter*). Student B then adds another crime word down the paper from top to bottom. This word must intersect with the crime word written across the page.

- Student A then writes another crime word across that intersects with the word Student B has written down. Students continue taking it in turns to write in their words.

- Students build up a crossword until they can't think of any more crime words. (You could make it into a game by saying that the last person to write a crime word is a winner.) Note that students must leave one square between each word – this is why it's better and clearer to use squared paper.

8 Odd one out

Aim

This activity can be used to revise almost any language.

Preparation

Think of the vocabulary, pronunciation or grammar point you want to revise.

Procedure

- Write five words on the board and ask students which one is the odd one out. The students then explain why. This is usually relates to the meaning of the word.

in debt   thrifty   overdrawn   broke   in the red

- Here *thrifty* is the odd one out because it means being careful with money whereas the other words describe *not* being careful with money.

- You can use this format to practise and revise all sorts of things. The criteria doesn't always have to be meaning. Here are some examples:

  1 For British versus American English:
  sidewalk / curtains / diaper / candy / windshield
  curtains is the odd one out because it's more commonly used in British English (American English is *drapes*). The other words are more typically American English.

  2 For pronunciation stress:
  telepathy / technology / phenomena / subordinate / entertainment
  entertainment is the odd one out because the stress is on the third syllable. The other words have the stress on the second syllable.

  3 For connotation:
  slim / trim / skinny / lean / slender
  skinny is the odd one out because it has a negative connotation. The other words are all positive ways of describing somebody's build.

  4 For collocation: *do* or *make*
  sense / love / fun / business / war
  business is the odd one out because you use *do*. For the others you use *make*.

  5 For grammar:
  accommodation / furniture / equipment / information / business
  business is the odd one out because it can be countable. All of the other words are always uncountable.

- You should tell the students what the criteria is, for example 'think about connotation' or 'think about the spelling'. To make the activity a little more challenging, instead of writing the words on the board, you can dictate them. As a follow-up, ask the students to write their own odd ones out.

9 Making sentences

Aim

This activity is good for revising any type of vocabulary. It works best if the words are a fairly random selection and not part of a tight lexical set.

Preparation

Choose 12 words you want to revise and write them in a circle (like a clockface) on the board

Procedure

- Students work in pairs. They choose two or more of the words and try to make a sentence with them.

  Example sentences:

  The music is always blaring out *of my brother's* tacky *stereo.*

  The allegations *made by my* neurologist *were ridiculed in court by the* barrister .

  As he sat on the jetty *in his* flip-flops gazing *out at the ships moored in the bay, he decided that life wasn't so* dreary *after-all.*

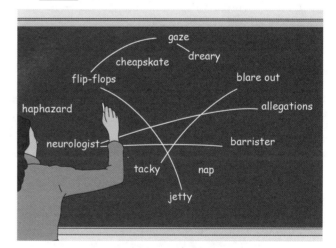

- The students then read out their sentences and you connect the words they have used on the board. You can correct the grammar as necessary or you can make it more difficult for the students by only accepting grammatically correct sentences. (You could make it into a game by saying that the pair who form the sentence including the highest number of words on the board is the winner.) It doesn't matter how bizarre the sentences are, the important thing is that students spend time looking at and remembering the vocabulary.

10 Spell check

Aim

To revise any vocabulary and focus particularly on spelling.

Preparation

Choose the words you want to review. They can be lexical sets or words at random. Eight to ten words is best.

Procedure

There are various different ways you can approach this, but the following four ways seem to work best:

1 The missing letter
   Student work in pairs. Write up the words with a letter missing from each one, e.g. *acommodation*, *commited*, *embarass*, etc. The students have to decide which is the missing letter in each case and rewrite the word correctly. Then give a definition.

2 The extra letter
   Students work in pairs. Write up the words with an extra letter in each one, e.g. *unfaithfull*, *occassionally*, *reccommend*, etc. The students have to decide which is the extra letter in each case and rewrite the word correctly. Then give a definition.

3 The wrong letter
   Students work in pairs. Write up the words with a wrong letter in each one, e.g. *sckedule*, *seperate*, *existance*, etc. The students have to decide which is the wrong letter in each case and rewrite the word correctly. Then give a definition.

4 Anagrams
   Students work in pairs. Write up the words as anagrams. The students have to unscramble the anagram and rewrite the word correctly. This is the most challenging version of 'Spell check', so it's best to give the students a clue, for example: 'these are all ways of describing settlements', e.g. *nowt*, *letham*, *pletroomis*, etc. (*town*, *hamlet*, *metropolis*): Then give a definition.

Anecdote tasks

New Inside Out Advanced includes a number of extended speaking tasks, where students tackle a longer piece of discourse. We've called these 'Anecdotes'. They are based on personal issues, for instance, memories, stories, people you know. When you learn a musical instrument, you can't spend all your time playing scales and exercises: you also need to learn whole pieces in order to see how music is organised. Anecdotes give students a chance to get to grips with how discourse is organised. We have found the following strategies helpful in getting our students to tell their Anecdotes.

1 Choose global topics that everybody can relate to

One of the main objectives of an Anecdote is to encourage students to experiment with and hopefully grow more competent at using language at the more demanding end of their range. It therefore seems only fair to ask them to talk about subjects they know something about. With familiar subject matter students can concentrate on how they're speaking as well as what they're speaking about. The five Anecdote topics in *New Inside Out* Advanced have been carefully selected to appeal to the widest range of students, whilst at the same time, fitting into the context of the unit.

Unit 2	Eating out
Unit 4	Telling a story
Unit 5	A purchase you made
Unit 9	A time you stayed up all night
Unit 10	A walk you have been on

As soon as you have got to know your students well enough, you'll be able to choose other Anecdote topics suited to their particular interests and experiences

2 Allow sufficient preparation time

Students need time to assemble their thoughts and think about the language they'll need. The Anecdotes are set up though evocative questions. Students read or listen to a planned series of questions and choose what specifically they'll talk about; shyer students can avoid matters they feel are too personal. This student preparation is a key stage and should not be rushed. Research, by Peter Skehan and Pauline Foster among others, has shown that learners who plan for tasks attempt more ambitious and complex language, hesitate less and make fewer basic errors.

The simplest way to prepare students for an Anecdote is to ask them to read the list of questions in the book and decide which they want to talk about. This could be done during class time or as homework preparation for the following lesson. Ask them to think about the language they'll need. Encourage them to use dictionaries and make notes – but not to write out what they'll actually say. Finally, put them into pairs to exchange Anecdotes.

A variation is to ask the students to read the questions in the book while, at the same time, listening to you read them aloud. Then ask them to prepare in detail for the task, as above.

Alternatively, ask the students to close their books – and then to close their eyes. Ask them to listen to the questions as you read them aloud and think about what they evoke. Some classes will find this a more involving process. It also allows you to adapt the questions to your class: adding new ones or missing out ones you think inappropriate. After the reading, give them enough time to finalise their preparation before starting the speaking task.

3 Monitor students and give feedback

It's important for students to feel that their efforts are being monitored by the teacher. Realistically, it's probably only possible for a teacher to monitor and give feedback to one or two pairs of students during each Anecdote activity. It's therefore vital that the teacher adopts a strict rota system, and makes sure that everyone in the class is monitored over the course of a term. Constructive feedback helps students improve their delivery.

4 Provide a 'model anecdote'

It's always useful for the students to hear a model Anecdote at some stage during the Anecdote task cycle. The most obvious model is you, the teacher. Students will enjoy hearing real stories from your own life experience. Alternatively, you might ask a teaching colleague or friend to talk to the students, or record one of them telling an Anecdote and play it back in class.

5 Repeat the same anecdote with a new partner at regular intervals

Consider going back to Anecdotes and repeating them in later classes. Let the students know that you're going to do this. This will reassure them that you're doing it on purpose, but more importantly, it will mean that they'll be more motivated to dedicate some time and thought to preparation. When you repeat the task, mix the class so that each student works with a new partner, i.e. one who has not previously heard the Anecdote.

In our experience, most students are happy to listen to their partner's Anecdotes. If, however, any of your students are reluctant listeners, you might think about giving them some sort of 'listening task'. Here are three examples:

- Ask the listener to tick the prompt questions that the 'Anecdote teller' answers while telling the Anecdote.

- Ask the listener to time the 'Anecdote teller'. In *Teaching Collocations* (page 91) Michael Lewis suggests reducing the time allowed to deliver the Anecdote each time it's repeated: for example, in the first instance the student has five minutes; for the second telling they have four minutes; and the third three minutes.

- Ask the listener to take brief notes about the Anecdote and write them up as a summary for homework. Then give the summary to the 'Anecdote teller' to check.

The pedagogic value of getting students to re-tell Anecdotes – repeat a 'big chunk' of spoken discourse – cannot be over-stated. Repeating complex tasks reflects real interactions. We all have our set pieces: jokes, stories. And we tend to refine and improve them as we retell them. Many students will appreciate the opportunity to do the same thing in their second language. Research by Martin Bygate among others has shown that given this opportunity students become more adventurous and at the same time more precise in the language they use.

You can also use the Anecdotes to test oral proficiency and thereby add a speaking component to accompany the tests in the Teacher's Book.

Key concepts in *New Inside Out*

The following excerpts are from *An A–Z of ELT* by Scott Thornbury (Macmillan Books for Teachers, 2006). They give clear authoritative definitions and explanations of some of the most important concepts in *New Inside Out*.

Scott Thornbury

Contents

Note: SLA = Second Language Acquisition

classroom interaction METHODOLOGY

Classroom interaction is the general term for what goes on between the people in the classroom, particularly when it involves language. In traditional classrooms, most interaction is initiated by the teacher, and learners either respond individually, or in unison. Teacher-centred interaction of this kind is associated with *transmissive* teaching, such as a lecture or presentation, where the teacher *transmits* the content of the lesson to the learners. In order to increase the amount of student involvement and interaction, teacher–learner interaction is often combined with **pairwork** and **groupwork**, where learners interact among themselves in pairs or small groups. Other kinds of interaction include *mingling* or *milling*. Pairwork and groupwork are associated with a more **learner-centred** approach. Rather than passively receiving the lesson content, the learners are actively engaged in using language and discovering things for themselves. The value of pairwork and groupwork has been reinforced by the belief that **interaction** facilitates language learning. Some would go as far as to say that it is *all* that is required.

The potential for classroom interaction is obviously constrained by such factors as the number of students, the size of the room, the furniture, and the purpose or type of activity. Not all activities lend themselves to pairwork or groupwork. Some activities, such as reading, are best done as *individual work*. On the other hand, listening activities (such as listening to an audio recording, or to the teacher) favour a *whole class* format, as do grammar presentations. The whole class is also an appropriate form of organisation when reviewing the results of an activity, as, for example, when spokespersons from each group are reporting on the results of a discussion or survey.

The success of any classroom interaction will also depend on the extent to which the learners know what they are meant to be doing and why, which in turn depends on how clearly and efficiently the interaction has been set up. Pair- and groupwork can be a complete waste of time if learners are neither properly prepared for it, nor sure of its purpose or outcome.

Finally, the success of pair- and groupwork will depend on the kind of group **dynamics** that have been established. Do the students know one another? Are they happy working together? Do they mind working without constant teacher supervision? Establishing a productive classroom dynamic may involve making decisions as to who works with whom. It may also mean deliberately staging the introduction of different kinds of interactions, starting off with the more controlled, teacher-led interactions before, over time, allowing learners to work in pairs and finally in groups.

collocation VOCABULARY

If two words *collocate*, they frequently occur together. The relation between the words may be grammatical, as when certain verbs collocate with particular prepositions, such as *depend on, account for, abstain from*, or when a verb, like *make, take*, or *do*, collocates with a noun, as in *make an arrangement, take advantage, do the shopping*. The collocation may also be lexical, as when two **content words** regularly co-occur, as in *a broad hint, a narrow escape* (but not **a wide hint* or **a tight escape*). The strength of the collocation can vary: *a broad street* or *a narrow path* are weak collocations, since both elements can co-occur with lots of other words: *a broad river, a busy street*, etc. *Broad hint* and *narrow escape* are stronger. Stronger still are combinations where one element rarely occurs without the other, as in *moot point, slim pickings* and *scot free*. Strongest of all are those where both elements never or rarely occur without the other, such as *dire straits* and *spick and span*. These have acquired the frozen status of *fixed expressions*.

Unsurprisingly, learners lack intuitions as to which words go with which, and this accounts for many errors, such as *You can completely enjoy it* (instead of *thoroughly*), *On Saturday we made shopping* (instead of *went*), and *We went the incorrect way* (for *wrong*). Using texts to highlight particular collocations, and teaching new words in association with their most frequent collocations are two ways of approaching the problem. Nowadays learners' dictionaries also include useful collocational information, such as the *Macmillan English Dictionary for Advanced Learners*.

communicative activity METHODOLOGY

A communicative activity is one in which real communication occurs. Communicative activities belong to that generation of classroom **activities** that emerged in response to the need for a more **communicative approach** in the teaching of second languages. (In their more evolved form as **tasks**, communicative activities are central to **task-based learning**.) They attempt to import into a practice activity the key features of 'real-life' communication. These are:

- *purposefulness*: speakers are motivated by a communicative goal (such as getting information, making a request, giving instructions) and not simply by the need to display the correct use of language for its own sake
- *reciprocity*: to achieve a purpose, speakers need to interact, and there is as much need to listen as to speak

- *negotiation*: following from the above, they may need to check and **repair** the communication in order to be understood by each other
- *unpredictability*: neither the process, nor the outcome, nor the language used in the exchange, is entirely predictable
- *heterogeneity*: participants can use any communicative means at their disposal; in other words, they are not restricted to the use of a pre-specified grammar item.

And, in the case of spoken language in particular:

- *synchronicity*: the exchange takes place in real time.

The best known communicative activity is the *information gap* activity. Here, the information necessary to complete the task is either in the possession of just one of the participants, or distributed among them. In order to achieve the goal of the task, therefore, the learners have to share the information that they have. For example, in a *describe-and-draw* activity, one student has a picture which is hidden from his or her partner. The task is for that student to describe the picture so that the partner can accurately draw it. In a *spot-the-difference* task, both students of a pair have pictures (or texts) that are the same apart from some minor details. The goal is to identify these differences. In a *jigsaw activity*, each member of a group has different information. One might have a bus timetable, another a map, and another a list of hotels. They have to share this information in order to plan a weekend break together.

Information gap activities have been criticised on the grounds that they lack **authenticity**. Nor are information gap activities always as productive as might be wished: unsupervised, learners may resort to **communication strategies** in order to simplify the task. A more exploitable information gap, arguably, is the one that exists between the learners themselves, ie, what they don't know – but might like to know – about one another (→ **personalisation**).

context LINGUISTICS

The context of a language item is its adjacent language items. In the absence of context, it is often impossible to assign exact meaning to an item. A sentence like *Ben takes the bus to work*, for example, could have past, present, or future reference, depending on the context:

> I know this chap called Ben. One day *Ben takes the bus to work*, and just as …
> Most days *Ben takes the bus to work*, but sometimes he rides his bike …
> If *Ben takes the bus to work* tomorrow, he'll be late, because there's a strike …

Likewise, a sentence like *You use it like this* is meaningless in the absence of a context. By the same token, a word or sentence in one context can have a very different meaning in another. The sign *NO BICYCLES* in a public park means something different to *NO BICYCLES* outside a bicycle rental shop. It is sometimes necessary to distinguish between different kinds of context. On the one hand, there is the context of the accompanying **text**, sometimes called the *co-text*. The co-text of this sentence, for example, includes the sentences that precede and follow it, as well as the paragraph of which it forms a part. It is the co-text that offers clues as to the meaning of unfamiliar vocabulary in a text. The *situational* context (also *context of situation*, *context of use*), on the other hand, is the physical and temporal setting in which an instance of language use occurs. The typical context for the spoken question *Are you being served?* is in a shop, for example. Both co-text and context influence the production and interpretation of language. **Discourse analysis** studies the relationship between language and co-text, including the way that sentences or utterances are connected. **Pragmatics** studies the relationship between language and its contexts of use, including the way meaning can be inferred by reference to context factors.

Various theories have been proposed in order to account for the ways that language choices are determined by contextual factors. One of the best known of these is Michael Halliday's **systemic functional linguistics**. Halliday distinguishes three variables in any context that systematically impact on language choices and which, together, determine a text's **register**:

- the *field*: what the language is being used to talk about, and for what purposes
- the *tenor*: the participants in the language event, and their relationship
- the *mode*: how language is being used in the exchange, e.g. is it written or spoken?

For example, this short text shows the influence of all three factors:

> Do u fancy film either 2nite or 2moro? Call me.

The field is 'making arrangements about leisure activities', hence the use of words like *film, 2nite* (*tonight*), *2moro* (*tomorrow*). The tenor is one of familiarity and equality (accounting for the informal *fancy* and the imperative: *call me*); and the mode is that of a written text message, which explains its brevity, its use of abbreviated forms (*u, 2nite*) and the absence of salutations. A change in any of these contextual factors is likely to have a significant effect on the text.

Language learners, it is argued, need to know how these contextual factors correlate with language choices in order to produce language that is appropriate to the context. One way of doing this is to ask them to make changes to a text (such as the text message above) that take into account adjustments to the field, tenor, or mode.

dynamics: group, classroom METHODOLOGY

Dynamics are the actions and interactions, both conscious and unconscious, that take place between members of a group, whether the whole class or sub-groups. Group dynamics are instrumental in forging a productive and motivating classroom environment. They are determined by such factors as: the composition of the group (including the age, sex, and relative status of the members, as well as their different attitudes, beliefs, learning styles and abilities); the patterns of relationships between members of the group, including how well they know each other, and the roles they each assume, such as group leader, spokesperson, etc; physical factors such as the size of the group and the way it is seated; and the tasks that the group are set, e.g.: Does the task require everyone to contribute? Does it encourage co-operation or competition? Are the goals of the task clear to the group members?

Ways that the teacher can promote a positive group (and class) dynamic include:

- ensuring all class or group members can see and hear one another, and that they know (and use) each other's names
- keeping groups from getting too big – three to six members is optimal
- setting – or negotiating – clear rules for groupwork, such as using only the target language, giving everyone a turn to speak, allowing individuals to 'pass' if they don't want to say anything too personal
- using 'ice-breaking' activities to encourage interaction, laughter, and relaxation
- ensuring that group tasks are purposeful, interactive, and collaborative
- personalising tasks, i.e., setting tasks that involve the sharing of personal experiences and opinions
- defining the roles and responsibilities within the group, and varying these regularly, e.g. by appointing a different spokesperson each time
- monitoring groupwork in progress, and being alert to any possible conflicts or tensions between members, and reconstituting groups, if necessary
- discussing the importance of groupwork with learners, and getting feedback on group processes

fluency SLA

If someone is said to be fluent in a language, or to speak a language fluently, it is generally understood that they are able to speak the language idiomatically and accurately, without undue pausing, without an intrusive accent, and in a manner appropriate to the context. In fact, research into listeners' perceptions of fluency suggests that fluency is primarily the ability to produce and maintain speech in *real time*. To do this, fluent speakers are capable of:

- appropriate pausing, i.e.:
  - their pauses may be long but are not frequent
  - their pauses are usually filled, e.g. with **pause fillers** like *erm, you know, sort of*
  - their pauses occur at meaningful transition points, e.g. at the intersections of clauses or phrases, rather than midway in a phrase
- long runs, i.e., there are many syllables and words between pauses

All of the above factors depend on the speaker having a well-developed grammar, an extensive vocabulary, and, crucially, a store of memorised *chunks*. Being able to draw on this store of chunks means not having to depend on grammar to construct each utterance from scratch. This allows the speaker to devote **attention** to other aspects of the interaction, such as planning ahead. Speakers also use a number of 'tricks' or *production strategies* to convey the illusion of fluency. One such strategy is disguising pauses by filling them, or by repeating a word or phrase.

Some proponents of the **communicative approach** re-defined fluency so as to distinguish it from **accuracy**. Fluency came to mean 'communicative effectiveness', regardless of formal accuracy or speed of delivery. Activities that are communicative, such as information-gap activities, are said to be *fluency-focused*. This is the case even for activities that produce short, halting utterances. Separating accuracy and fluency, and defining the latter as *communicative language use*, is misleading, though. There are many speech events whose communicativeness depends on their accuracy. Air traffic control talk is just one. Moreover, many learners aspire to being more than merely communicative.

Classroom activities that target fluency need to prepare the learner for real-time speech production. Learning and memorising lexical chunks, including useful conversational gambits, is one approach. **Drills** may help here, as will some types of **communicative activity** that involve repetition. Research has also shown that fluency improves the more times a **task** is repeated. Fluency may also benefit from activities that manage to distract learners' attention away from formal accuracy so that they are not tempted to slow down. (This has been called 'parking their attention'.) Some interactive and competitive language **games** have this effect. **Drama** activities, such as roleplays, recreate conditions of real-time language use, and are therefore good for developing fluency. Finally, learners can achieve greater fluency from learning a repertoire of **communication strategies**, i.e., techniques for getting around potential problems caused by a lack of the relevant words or structures.

focus on form SLA

When learners focus on form, they direct conscious attention to some formal feature of the language **input**. The feature may be the fact that the past of *has* is *had*, or that *enjoy* is followed by verb forms ending in *-ing*, or that adjectives do not have plural forms in English. The learners' attention may be self-directed, or it may be directed by the teacher or by another learner. Either way, it has been argued that a focus on **form** is a necessary condition for language learning. Simply focusing on the **meaning** of the input is not enough. Focusing on form is, of course, not a new idea: most teaching methods devote a great deal of time to the forms of the language, e.g. when new grammar items are presented. But the term *focus on form* captures the fact that this focus can, theoretically, occur at any stage in classroom instruction. Thus, **correction**, especially in the form of negative **feedback**, is a kind of focus on form. In fact, some researchers argue that the most effective form focus is that which arises incidentally, in the context of communication, as when the teacher quickly elicits a correction during a classroom discussion. This incidental approach contrasts with the more traditional and deliberate approach, where teaching is based on a **syllabus** of graded structures (or *forms*), and these are pre-taught in advance of activities designed to practise them. This traditional approach is called – by some researchers – a *focus on formS*.

frequency LINGUISTICS; SLA

The frequency of a word, or other language item, is the number of times the item occurs in a **text** or a **corpus**. Frequency data, derived from large corpora, provide valuable information for syllabus and materials designers. Nowadays, for example, compilers of learner **dictionaries** take frequency into account when deciding which words to include and which meanings of these words to prioritise, and the relative frequency of a word is usually indicated in some way. Word frequency is also a factor in judging the readability of texts. It has been estimated that around eighty per cent of any text consists of the two thousand most frequent words in English. (In this paragraph, for example, the figure is eighty-three per cent.) The most frequent words are **function words**, such as *the, of, in, and*, etc. Corpus research also provides frequency information about **grammar** items, but this has made less of an impact on teaching materials than has the research into word frequency. It has been shown, for instance, that simple verb forms are roughly twenty times more frequent than continuous ones (→ **aspect**). Proponents of a form of **lexical approach** argue that frequency should be a major priority when selecting items for a **syllabus**. This is because the most frequent words and structures in the language express its most frequent meanings. Frequency does not always equate with usefulness, however. Travellers know that it is often quite low frequency words, such as *toothbrush* and *bill*, that are of more immediate utility.

The frequency of an item in the input that learners are exposed to may also be a critical factor in the acquisition of that item. It has long been known that the more times a learner encounters a new word the more likely they are to learn it. (One figure quoted by researchers is that at least seven encounters over spaced intervals are necessary → **repetition**.) Now, scholars who subscribe to **usage-based acquisition** theories argue that acquisition is simply the result of exposure, over time, to language data (or 'usage'). From this data, regularities, or patterns, are abstracted using natural human processes of perception, pattern recognition, and association (→ **connectionism**). The more often a pattern occurs in the input, the greater the chance that the pattern will be observed and remembered. Indeed, the more or less fixed **order of acquisition** of grammar structures can be accounted for, at least in part, by the relative frequency of these items in naturally occurring input. The implications for teaching are that the learning of grammar and vocabulary might be speeded up by using texts that have a high frequency of occurrences of the target items. (The technique is known as *input flood* → **input**.) The 'frequency hypothesis' also justifies frequent recycling of recently taught items (→ **revision**).

function LINGUISTICS

The function of a language item is its communicative purpose. Language is more than simply **forms** and their associated meanings (i.e. **usage**). It is also the communicative **uses** to which these forms and meanings are put. These two sentences, for example, share the same forms, but function quite differently:

[in an email] *Thank you for sending me the disk.*
[a notice in a taxi] *Thank you for not smoking.*

The function of the first is *expressing thanks*, while the second is more like a *prohibition*. Likewise, the same function can be expressed by different forms:

[a notice in a taxi] *Thank you for not smoking.*
[a sign in a classroom] *No smoking.*

Thus, there is no one-to-one match between form and function. Assigning a function to a text or an utterance usually requires knowledge of the **context** in which the text is used. The study of how context and function are interrelated is called **pragmatics**.

Communicative functions can be categorised very broadly and also at increasing levels of detail. The 'big' functions, or macrofunctions, describe the way language is used in very general terms. These include the use of language for *expressive* purposes (e.g. poetry), for *regulatory* purposes (e.g. for getting people to do things), for *interpersonal* purposes (e.g. for socializing), and for *representational* purposes (e.g. to inform). More useful, from the point of view of designing language syllabuses, are microfunctions. These are usually expressed as **speech acts**, such as *agreeing and disagreeing, reporting, warning, apologising, thanking, greeting,* etc. Such categories form the basis of **functional syllabuses**, a development associated with the **communicative approach**. They often appear as one strand of a coursebook **syllabus**. Functions differ from notions in that the latter describe areas of meaning – such as *ability, duration, quantity, frequency,* etc. – rather than the uses to which these meanings are put.

One way to teach functions is to adopt a 'phrasebook' approach, and teach useful ways of expressing common functions (what are called *functional exponents*), such as *Would you like …?* (*inviting*) and *Could you …, please?* (*requesting*). More memorable, though, is to teach these expressions in the contexts of **dialogues**, so that the functional exponents are associated not only with common situations in which they are used, but with related functions (such as *accepting* and *refusing*). The term *function*, in contrast to **form**, is also used in linguistics, specifically with regard to the functions of the different elements of a **clause** (such as subject and object).

grammar teaching METHODOLOGY

Like the word **grammar** itself, the topic of grammar teaching is a controversial one, and teachers often take opposing views. Historically, language teaching methods have positioned themselves along a scale from 'zero grammar' to 'total grammar', according to their approach to grammar teaching. Proponents of *natural methods*, who model their approach to teaching second languages on the way that first languages are acquired, reject any explicit teaching of grammar at all. (They may, however, teach according to a grammar **syllabus**, even if no mention of grammar as such is made in the classroom.) This implicit approach is common both to the **direct method** and to **audiolingualism**. Through exposure to demonstrations, situations or examples, learners are expected to pick up the rules of grammar by **inductive learning**. At the other end of the spectrum, there are approaches, such as **grammar-translation**, that adopt an explicit and **deductive learning** approach. From the outset, learners are presented with rules which they study and then practise. Occupying a midway point between zero grammar and total grammar is the approach called **consciousness-raising**. Instead of being given rules, learners are presented with language data which challenge them to re-think (and *restructure*) their existing mental grammar. This data might take the form of **input** that has been manipulated in some way. For example, pairs of sentences, such as the following, have to be matched to pictures, forcing learners to discriminate between them, and, in theory, **notice** the difference (→ **noticing**):

The Queen drove to the airport.
The Queen was driven to the airport.

(This is sometimes called a *grammar interpretation task*, or *structured input*.) In order to do the task, learners have to process not just the individual words, but also their grammatical form. That is why this approach to teaching grammar is sometimes called *processing instruction*. There are other researchers who argue that it is by means of manipulating the learner's output, e.g. through productive practice, that mental restructuring is best effected.

The **communicative approach** accommodates different approaches to grammar teaching. Proponents of **task-based learning**, for example, argue that, if the learner is engaged in solving problems using language, then the mental grammar will develop of its own accord. However, advocates of the weaker version of the communicative approach (and the version that is most widespread) justify a role for the pre-teaching of grammar in advance of production. This view finds support in **cognitive learning theory**, which suggests that conscious attention to grammatical form (called **focus on form**) speeds up language learning, and is a necessary corrective against premature **fossilisation**. There is some debate, though, as to whether this form focus should be planned or incidental. Incidental grammar teaching occurs when the teacher deals with grammar issues as and when they come up, e.g. in the form of **correction**, or task **feedback**. In this way (it is argued) grammar teaching follows the learners' own 'syllabus'. Such an approach attempts to address one of the dilemmas of grammar teaching: the fact that the learner's mental grammar, and the way it develops, bears only an accidental relation to a formal grammar syllabus.

Nevertheless, the research into these different choices is still inconclusive. It may be the case that some items of grammar respond better to explicit teaching, while others are more easily picked up through exposure. There are also different learner types: some prefer learning and applying rules, while others are happier with a more 'deep-end' approach (→ **learning style**). Most current teaching materials hedge their bets on these issues. They offer both deductive and inductive grammar presentations, and opportunities for incidental as well as for planned learning.

learner-centred instruction, learner-centredness
METHODOLOGY

Learner-centred instruction aims to give learners more say in areas that are traditionally considered the domain of the teacher or of the institution. Learner-centred instruction is true to the spirit of progressive education, including the movement towards providing learners with greater **autonomy**. For example, a learner-centred **curriculum** would involve learners in negotiating decisions relating to the choice of syllabus content, of materials, of activity-types, and of assessment procedures. Learner-centredness also describes ways of organising **classroom interaction** so that the focus is directed away from the teacher, and on to the learners, who perform tasks in pairs or small groups. This contrasts with traditional, teacher-centred, classroom interaction. Some writers believe that the dichotomy between learner-centred (= good) and teacher-centred (= bad) is a false one. It might be more useful to talk about *learning-centred instruction*, i.e., instruction which prioritises sound learning principles. In a learning-centred approach there would be room for both learner-centred *and* teacher-centred interactions.

learning style PSYCHOLOGY

Your learning style is your preferred way of learning. This style may be influenced by biographical factors (such as how you were taught as a child) or by innately endowed factors (such as whether you have a 'good ear' for different sounds). Types of learning style are often presented in the form of polarities (some of which may overlap), such as:

- analytic versus global (or holistic) thinkers, i.e., learners who tend to focus on the details, versus learners who tend to see 'the big picture'
- rule-users versus data-gatherers, i.e., learners who learn and apply rules, versus those who prefer exposure to lots of examples
- reflective versus impulsive learners
- group-oriented versus solitary learners
- extrovert versus introverted learners
- verbal versus visual learners
- passive versus active learners.

Attempts have been made to group these polarities and relate them to brain lateralisation. So, a bias towards left-brain processing correlates with analytic, rule-forming and verbal learners, while a bias towards right-brain processing correlates with their opposite. A less binary view of learning style is that proposed by the psychologist Howard Gardner. He identified at least seven distinct intelligences that all individuals possess but to different degrees. These include the *logical/mathematical*, the *verbal/linguistic*, and the *visual/spatial*. Similarly, proponents of **neuro-linguistic programming** distinguish between different sensory orientations, including the *visual*, *aural* and *kinesthetic* (i.e., related to movement, touch). So far, though, there is no convincing evidence that any of these dispositions correlates with specific learning behaviours. Nor has it been shown that a preference in one area predicts success in language learning. In fact, it is very difficult to separate learning style from other potentially influential factors, such as personality, intelligence, and previous learning experience. Nor is it clear to what extent learning style can be manipulated, e.g. through **learner training**. The best that can be said is that, if the learner's preferred learning style is out of synch with the type of instruction on offer, then success is much less likely than if the two are well matched. This supports the case for an **eclectic** approach, on the one hand, and the individualisation of learning, on the other.

listening METHODOLOGY

Listening is the skill of understanding spoken language. It is also the name given to classroom activities that are designed to develop this skill – what are also called *listening comprehension* activities – as in 'today we're going to do a listening'. Listening is one of the four language **skills**, and, along with **reading**, was once thought of as being a 'passive' skill. In fact, although receptive, listening is anything but passive. It is a goal-oriented activity, involving not only processing of the incoming speech signals (called *bottom-up processing*) but also the use of prior knowledge, contextual clues, and expectations (*top-down processing*) in order to create meaning. Among the sub-skills of listening are:

- perceiving and discriminating individual sounds
- segmenting the stream of speech into recognisable units such as words and phrases
- using **stress** and **intonation** cues to distinguish given information from new information
- attending to **discourse markers** and using these to predict changes in the direction of the talk
- guessing the meaning of unfamiliar words
- using clues in the text (such as vocabulary) and context clues to predict what is coming
- making inferences about what is not stated
- selecting key information relevant to the purpose for listening
- integrating incoming information into the mental 'picture' (or **schema**) of the speech event so far.

Also, since listening is normally interactive, listeners need to be capable of:

- recognising when speakers have finished their turns, or when it is appropriate to interrupt
- providing ongoing signals of understanding, interest, etc. (*backchannelling*)
- asking for clarification, asking someone to repeat what they have just said, and repairing misunderstandings.

These sub-skills exist across languages, so, in theory, learners should be able to transfer them from their first language into their second. In fact, there are a number of reasons why this does not always happen. One is that speakers of different languages process speech signals differently, depending on the phonetic characteristics of the language they are used to. This means that speakers of some languages will find it harder than others to match the spoken word to the way that the word is represented in their mind. They simply do not recognise the word. Another problem is lack of sufficient L2 knowledge, such as vocabulary or grammar. A third problem is that learners may lack the means (and the confidence) to negotiate breakdowns in understanding. Finally, many learners simply lack exposure to spoken language, and therefore have not had sufficient opportunities to experience listening. These problems can be compounded in classrooms because:

- Listening to audio recordings deprives the learners of useful visual information, and allows the learners no opportunity to interact and repair misunderstandings.
- Classroom acoustics are seldom ideal.
- If learners do not know what they are listening for (in the absence, for example, of some pre-set listening task) they may try to process as much information as possible, rather than being selective in their listening. This can lead to listening overload, which in turn can cause inhibiting anxiety.
- Listening texts that have been specially written for classroom use are often simplified. But if this simplification means eliminating a lot of redundant language, such as speaker repetitions, pause fillers and vague language, the density of information that results may make it harder – not easier – to process.

For this reason, the use of audio recordings to develop listening skills needs to be balanced against the advantages of using other media, such as video, and face-to-face interaction with the teacher or another speaker.

Nevertheless, the use of audio recordings is an established part of classroom practice, so it is important to know how to use them to best advantage. The following approach is one that is often recommended:

- Provide some minimum contextual information, e.g. who is talking to whom about what, and why. This helps to compensate for lack of visual information, and allows learners to activate the relevant mental **schema**, which in turn helps top-down processing, including the sub-skill of prediction.
- Pre-teach key vocabulary: this helps with bottom-up processing, although too much help may mean that learners don't get sufficient practice in guessing from context.
- Set some 'while-listening' questions. Initially, these should focus on the overall *gist* of the text. For example: true/false questions, selecting, ordering or matching pictures, ticking items on a list, following a map.
- Play a small section of the recording first, to give learners an opportunity to familiarise themselves with the different voices, and to trigger accurate expectations as to what they will hear.
- Play the recording right through, and then allow learners to consult on the answers to the pre-set task. Check these answers. If necessary, re-play the recording until satisfied that learners have 'got the gist'.
- Set a more demanding task, requiring more intensive listening, such as listening for detail, or inferring speakers' attitudes, intentions, etc. If the recording is a long one, it may pay to stage the intensive listening in sections. Again, allow learners to consult in pairs, before checking the task in open class.
- On the basis of the learners' success with these tasks, identify problem sections of the recording and return to these, playing and re-playing them, and perhaps eliciting a word-by-word transcription and writing this on the board.
- Distribute copies of the transcript of the recording (if available) and re-play the recording while learners read the transcript. This allows the learners to clear up any remaining problems, and also to match what they hear to what they see.

The above approach can be adapted to suit different kinds of recorded texts and different classroom needs. For higher level learners, for example, it may be counter-productive to make listening *too* easy. The approach can also be adapted to the use of video, and even to *live listenings*, such as listening to the teacher or a guest.

meaning LINGUISTICS

Language consists of **forms** that express certain meanings. The study of meaning is called **semantics**. A basic principle in semantics is that the forms of a language are simply *signs* – they are arbitrary and bear no resemblance to the things that are *signified* by them. Thus the word *table* does not look or feel or sound like a table. Any other word, like *Tisch*, or *mesa*, or *tarabeza* (which all translate as *table* in their respective languages), would do as well. Learning a second language, then, is first and foremost a job of matching a whole new set of (arbitrary) forms to existing meanings. The teacher's job is to help in the matching process. In fact, establishing meaning is probably one of the most important functions of a language teacher.

Language teaching methods have evolved different approaches to dealing with meaning. Some, like the **direct method**, relied on visual aids, mime, and gesture, to convey the meanings of words and grammatical structures. Others, like **grammar–translation**, used translation. Either way, meaning is often elusive. The direct method approach, i.e., pointing to a real *table* and saying the word *table*, works well with words like table. But it works less well for an expression like *under the table*, as in *The deal was done under the table*. Here, the meaning is not literal but *figurative*, or *metaphorical*. Nor does a direct method approach deal well with the fact that 'table' is *polysemous*, i.e., that it has several meanings, one of which is a way of displaying information in rows and lines on a page.

Translation is equally problematic. It is easy enough to translate the literal meaning of words, i.e., their *denotations*. But it is less easy to capture a word's associations, often cultural, i.e., its **connotations**. For example, the English word *chuffed* translates as *contento* in Spanish, but this does not distinguish it from other words that are translated by *contento*, such as *happy*, *content* and *pleased*. It is not always easy to say what something means, e.g. by giving a definition. (Dr Johnson famously defined *network* as 'anything reticulated or decussated, at equal distances, with interstices between the intersections'.) For teaching purposes, it is often easier to say what something is *like* (using a **synonym**), what it is a *kind of* (using a **hyponym**), or what it is *not* (using an **antonym**).

motivation PSYCHOLOGY

Motivation is what drives learners to achieve a goal, and is a key factor determining success or failure in language learning. The learner's goal may be a short-term one, such as successfully performing a classroom task, or a long-term one, such as achieving native-like proficiency in the language. With regard to long-term goals, a distinction is often made between *instrumental motivation* and *integrative motivation*. Instrumental motivation is when the learner has a functional objective, such as passing an exam or getting a job. Integrative motivation, on the other hand, is when the learner wants to be identified with the target language community. Intersecting with these two motivational *orientations* are two different *sources* of motivation: *intrinsic* (e.g. the pleasure of doing a task for its own sake) and *extrinsic* (e.g. the 'carrot and stick' approach). Another motivational source that has been identified is success: experience of succeeding can result in increased motivation (called *resultative motivation*), which raises the question as to whether motivation is as much a result as a cause of learning.

Various theories of motivation have been proposed. Most of these identify a variety of factors that, in combination, contribute to overall motivation, such as:

- *attitudes*, e.g. to the target language and to speakers of the language

- *goals*, both long-term and short-term, and the learners' *orientation* to these goals
- how much *value* the learner attaches to achieving the goals, especially as weighed against *expectancy of success*; expectancy of success may come from the learner's assessment of their own abilities, and how they account for previous successes or failures
- *self-esteem*, and the need to achieve and maintain it
- *intrinsic interest*, *pleasure*, *relevance* or *challenge* of the task
- *group dynamic*: is it competitive, collaborative, or individualistic?
- *teacher's attitudes*, e.g. what expectations does the teacher project about the learners' likelihood of success?

As the last point suggests, teachers can play a key role in motivating learners, not just in terms of choosing activities that are intrinsically motivating, but in the attitudes they project. Two researchers on motivation offer the following advice for teachers:

> Ten commandments for motivating language learners
>
> 1. Set a personal example with your own behaviour.
> 2. Create a pleasant, relaxed atmosphere in the classroom.
> 3. Present the tasks properly.
> 4. Develop a good relationship with the learners.
> 5. Increase the learner's linguistic self-confidence.
> 6. Make the language classes interesting.
> 7. Promote learner autonomy.
> 8. Personalise the learning process.
> 9. Increase the learners' goal-orientedness.
> 10. Familiarise learners with the target language culture.

noticing SLA

If you notice a feature of the language that you are exposed to, it attracts your attention and you make a mental note of it. For example, a learner might notice (without necessarily understanding) the sign *Mind the gap*, repeated several times on a railway station platform. That same day, the learner hears the teacher say *would you mind* in the context of making a request in class. A day or two later, the same learner hears someone else say *I don't mind*. Each successive 'noticing' both primes the learner to notice new occurrences of *mind*, and at the same time contributes to a growing understanding of the use and meaning of *mind*. Proponents of **cognitive learning theory** believe that noticing is a prerequisite for learning: without it input would remain as mere 'noise'. The *noticing hypothesis*, then, claims that noticing is a necessary condition for acquisition, although not the only one. Some kind of mental processing of what has been noticed is also necessary before the **input** becomes *intake*, ie before it is moved into long-term **memory**.

Teachers obviously play an important role in helping learners to notice features of the language. They do this when they repeat words or structures, write them on the board, or even drill them. One way of increasing the chance of learners' noticing an item is to include it lots of times in a text, a technique called *input flood*. For example, learners read a text with the word *mind* included several times. They then categorise these examples according to their meaning. A set of **concordance** lines for a particular word can be used in the same way.

There is another type of noticing, called *noticing the gap*. This is when learners are made aware of a gap in their language knowledge. This might happen when they do a **dictation**, for example. When they compare their version with the correct version, they may notice certain differences, such as the lack of past tense endings, that represent a gap in their **interlanguage**. It has been argued that noticing the gap can trigger the **restructuring** of interlanguage. That is, 'minding the gap' leads learners to 'fill the gap'.

personalisation METHODOLOGY

When you personalise language you use it to talk about your knowledge, experience and feelings. Personalisation of the type *Now write five true sentences about yourself using 'used to'* is often motivated by the need to provide further practice of pre-taught grammar structures. But it is also good preparation for the kinds of situations of genuine language use that learners might encounter outside the classroom. These advantages are lost, though, if the teacher's response is to treat the exercise as *only* an exercise, and correct the learners' errors without responding to the content. The influence of **humanistic approaches** has given a fresh impetus to personalisation, both in terms of providing a more coherent rationale and suggesting a broader range of activity types. For a start (it is argued), personalisation creates better classroom **dynamics**. This is because groups are more likely to form and bond if the individuals in them know more about one another. And the mental and emotional effort that is involved in finding personal associations with a language item is likely to make that item more memorable. This quality is called cognitive and affective *depth*. Finally, lessons are likely to be more interesting, and hence more motivating, if at least some of the content concerns the people in the room, rather than the characters in coursebooks. On these grounds, some writers have suggested that personalisation should not be considered simply as an 'add-on', but should be the principle on which most, if not all, classroom content should be based. One teaching approach that is committed to this view is **community language learning**. In this approach, all the content of the lesson comes from the learners themselves. Personalisation is not without risks, though. Teachers need to be sensitive to learner resistance: learners should have the right to 'pass' on questions that they consider too intrusive. And teachers should be authentic in the way that they respond to learners' personalisations. This means that they should respond to *what* their learners are saying, not just how they say it.

practice METHODOLOGY

If you practise a skill, you experience doing it a number of times in order to gain control of it. The idea that 'practice makes perfect' is fundamental to **cognitive learning theory**. It is through practice that the skill becomes automatic. **Sociocultural learning theory** finds room for practice too. Performing a skill with the assistance of someone who is good at it can help in the **appropriation** of the skill. At issue, then, is not so much whether practice is beneficial, but what form it should take, when, and how much of it is necessary. In addressing these questions, it is customary to distinguish between different kinds of practice, such as *controlled practice* vs *free practice*, *mechanical practice* vs *meaningful/communicative practice*, and *receptive practice* vs *productive practice*.

Controlled practice is associated with the second P of the **PPP** instructional model. Practice can be controlled in at least two senses: *language control* and *interactional control*. In the first, the language that is being practised is restricted to what has just been presented (hence it is also called *restricted practice*). For example, if the first **conditional** has been presented, learners practise this, and only this, structure, and in a repetitive way, e.g. through a sequence of **drills**. Practice is also said to be controlled if the learners' participation is overtly managed and monitored by the teacher, such as in open-class work, as opposed to closed **pairwork** or **groupwork**. One reason for this degree of control is that it maintains a focus on accuracy, and pre-empts or corrects errors. *Free practice*, on the other hand, allows learners a measure of creativity, and the opportunity to integrate the new item into their existing language 'pool'. It is also less controlled in terms of the interactions, with pairwork and groupwork being favoured. Typical free practice activities might be **games**, **discussions** or **drama**-based activities.

Mechanical practice is a form of controlled practice, where the focus is less on the meaning of an item than on manipulating its component parts. Mechanical practice can be either oral or written: many traditional **exercises** are mechanical in this sense, such as when learners transform sentences from active into passive, or from direct speech into reported speech. The arguments in favour of controlled and mechanical practice have lost their force since the decline of **behaviourism** and its belief that learning is simply habit-formation.

Meaningful practice requires learners to display some understanding of what the item that they are practising actually means. One way of doing this is through **personalisation**. *Communicative practice* involves the learners interacting in order to complete some kind of task, such as in an *information gap* activity (→ **communicative activity**). Proponents of a communicative approach argue that it is only this kind of practice that is truly effective. This is because learners are not simply practising language, but are practising the behaviours associated with the language, and this is a pre-condition for long-term behavioural change.

Finally, some practice activities are purely *receptive*. They involve the learners in identifying, selecting, or discriminating between language items, but not actually producing them. Many **consciousness-raising** activities are receptive, on the grounds that learners first need to understand a new structure before they can properly internalise it. Receptive practice is also associated with comprehension-based approaches to teaching. *Productive practice*, on the other hand, requires learners to produce the targeted items (either orally or in writing), and is associated with output-based models of learning.

There is fairly general agreement nowadays that the most effective practice activity combines at least some of the following features:

- It is meaningful, which may mean that is personalised.
- It is communicative, thus it will require learners to interact.
- It involves a degree of repetition – not of the mindless type associated with imitation drills, but of the type associated with many games.
- It is language-rich, i.e., learners have to interpret or produce a lot of language.
- Learners can be creative and take risks, but support is at hand if they need it.
- Learners are pushed, at least some of the time, to the limits of their competence
- Learners get **feedback**.

pronunciation teaching PHONOLOGY

Pronunciation is the general term for that part of language classes and courses that deals with aspects of the **phonology** of English. This includes the individual sounds (**phonemes**) of English, sounds in **connected speech**, word and sentence **stress**, **rhythm** and **intonation**. These components are customarily divided into two groups: the *segmental* features of pronunciation, i.e., the individual sounds and the way they combine, and the *suprasegmental* features, i.e., stress, rhythm and intonation. **Paralinguistic** features of speech production such as voice quality, tempo and loudness, are also classed as suprasegmental.

Effective pronunciation teaching needs to consider what goals, course design and methodology are most appropriate for the learners in question. The goal of acquiring a native-like **accent** is generally thought to be unachievable for most learners (and perhaps even undesirable). Instead, the goal of **intelligibility** is nowadays considered more realistic, if less easily measurable. It is often claimed that suprasegmental features play a greater role in intelligibility than do segmental ones. Unfortunately, however, some of these suprasegmental features, such as intonation, are considered by many teachers to be unteachable. Moreover, learners intending to interact with native speakers may need to set different goals from those learners whose purpose is to learn **English as an international language (EIL)**. For this latter group, the so-called **phonological core** is a checklist of those pronunciation features considered critical for intelligibility in EIL.

In terms of the design of course content, a basic choice is whether the pronunciation focus is *integrated* or *segregated*. In an integrated approach, pronunciation is dealt with as part of the teaching of grammar and vocabulary, or of speaking and listening. In a segregated approach it is treated in isolation. A classical segregated exercise is the **minimal pairs** task, in which learners are taught to discriminate and produce two contrasted phonemes (as in *hit* and *heat*). There are doubts as to whether this item-by-item approach to pronunciation reflects the way that the features of pronunciation are interconnected. Nor does it reflect the way that they jointly emerge over time ('as a photo emerges in the darkroom'). A related issue is whether pronunciation teaching should be *pre-emptive* or *reactive*. That is to say, should pronunciation teaching be planned around a syllabus of pre-selected items, or should the focus on pronunciation emerge *out of* practice activities, in the form, for example, of **correction**? There is evidence that the latter approach is more effective than the former.

In 1964 the writer (and former language teacher) Anthony Burgess wrote, 'Nothing is more important than to acquire a set of foreign phonemes that shall be entirely acceptable to your hosts'. However, there is generally less emphasis given to pronunciation teaching nowadays. Indeed, some teachers are sceptical as to the value of teaching pronunciation at all. This view is reinforced by research that suggests that the best predictors of intelligible pronunciation are 'having a good ear' and prolonged residence in an English-speaking country. On the other hand, faulty pronunciation is one of the most common causes of misunderstandings. This is an argument for demanding higher standards than the learners can realistically achieve, in the hope that they will meet you 'halfway'.

reading METHODOLOGY

Reading is a receptive **skill**. But the fact that it is receptive does not mean that it is passive: reading is an active, even interactive, process. Readers bring their own questions to the text, which are based on their background knowledge, and they use these to interrogate the text, modifying their questions and coming up with new ones according to the answers they get. In order to do this, they draw on a range of knowledge bases. They need to be able to decode the letters, words and grammatical structures of the individual sentences – what is called *bottom-up processing*. But they also enlist *top-down processes*, such as drawing on **discourse** and schematic knowledge, as well as on immediate contextual information. Discourse knowledge is knowing how different text-types – such as news reports, recipes or academic papers – are organised. Schematic knowledge is the reader's existing knowledge of the topic. Reading involves an interaction between these different 'levels' of knowledge, where knowledge at one 'level' can compensate for lack of knowledge at another.

Readers also bring their own *purposes* to texts, and these in turn determine the way they go about reading a text. The two main purposes for reading are for *information* (such as when consulting a directory), and for *pleasure* (such as when reading a novel), although these purposes may overlap. Different ways of reading include:

- *skimming* (*skim-reading*, *reading for gist*): rapidly reading a text in order to get the *gist*, or the main ideas or sense of a text. For example, a reader might skim a film review in order to see if the reviewer liked the film or not
- *scanning*: reading a text in search of specific information, and ignoring everything else, such as when consulting a bus timetable for a particular time and destination
- *detailed reading*: reading a text in order to extract the maximum detail from it, such as when following the instructions for installing a household appliance
- *reading aloud*: such as when reading a prepared speech or lecture, or reading a story aloud, or an extract from the newspaper.

A reader's purpose usually matches the writer's intentions for the text. Readers seldom read telephone books from cover to cover, for example. Nor do they normally skim through a novel looking for names beginning with *Vron* .... In classrooms, however, texts are frequently used for purposes other than those for which they were originally intended. They are often used not so much as vehicles of information or of pleasure, but as 'linguistic objects', that is, as contexts for the study of features of the language. A distinction needs to be made, therefore, between two types of classroom reading: reading as *skills development*, and reading as *language study*. There is no reason why the same text cannot be used for both purposes.

Another distinction that is often made is between *intensive reading* and *extensive reading*. The former applies to the way short texts are subject to close and detailed classroom study. Extensive reading, on the other hand, means the more leisurely reading of longer texts, primarily for pleasure, or in order to accumulate vocabulary, or simply to develop sound habits of reading. This is typically done outside class, using graded **readers**, authentic texts, or literary texts.

A third important distinction is between testing reading and teaching reading. Traditional reading tasks usually involve reading a text and then answering **comprehension questions** about it. This is the testing approach. A teaching approach, on the other hand, aims to help learners to become more effective readers by training them in the *sub-skills* of reading, and by teaching them *reading strategies*. Some of the sub-skills of reading are:

- understanding words and identifying their grammatical function
- recognising grammar features, such as word endings, and 'unpacking' (or **parsing**) the syntax of sentences
- identifying the topic of the text, and recognising topic changes
- identifying text-type, text purpose, and text organisation, and identifying and understanding **discourse markers** and other cohesive devices
- distinguishing key information from less important information
- identifying and understanding the gist
- inferring the writer's attitude
- following the development of an argument
- following the sequence of a narrative
- paraphrasing the text.

Activities designed to develop these sub-skills include: underlining topic-related words; contrasting different text-types; comparing different examples of the same text type and identifying *generic* features; circling and categorizing discourse markers; identifying what the pronouns refer to; predicting the direction the text will take at each discourse marker; choosing the best summary of a text; putting a set of pictures in order; extracting key information on to a grid, writing a summary of the text, etc. *Strategy training* involves training learners in ways of overcoming problems when they are reading. Some useful strategies include:

- using contextual and extra-linguistic information (such as pictures, layout, headlines) to make predictions regarding what the text is about
- brainstorming background (or schematic) knowledge in advance of reading
- skimming a text in advance of a more detailed reading
- keeping the purpose of the text in mind
- guessing the meaning of words from context
- **dictionary** use.

There is some argument, however, as to the value of a 'skills and strategies' approach to teaching reading. Most adult learners of English come to English texts with already well-developed reading skills in their own language. They already know how to skim, scan, use context clues, enlist background knowledge, and so on. Theoretically, at least, these skills are transferable. What makes reading difficult is not so much lack of reading skills as lack of *language knowledge*. That is, learners lack sufficient vocabulary and grammar to unpack sentences, and they cannot easily identify the ways that sentences are connected. This can result in 'tunnel vision', with readers becoming distracted by unfamiliar words, at the expense of working out meaning from context. On the other hand, it can also result in an over-reliance on guesswork, and on superficial 'text attack' strategies such as skimming. This suggests that texts needs to be chosen that do not over-stretch learners' ability to read them fluently. At the same time, texts should not be so easy that learners can process them simply by skimming. It also means that tasks need to be chosen that both match the original purpose of the text, and that encourage learners to transfer their first language reading skills. Such tasks are likely to be those that motivate learners to *want* to read the text. This might mean activating interest in the topic of the text, through, for example, a pre-reading quiz. At the same time, classroom reading texts should be exploited, not just for their potential in developing reading skills, but as sources of language input. This will involve, at some point, detailed study of the text's formal features, such as its linking devices, its collocations or its grammar.

speaking METHODOLOGY

Speaking is generally thought to be the most important of the four **skills**. The ability to speak a second language is often equated with proficiency in the language, as in *She speaks excellent French*. Indeed, one frustration commonly voiced by learners is that they have spent years studying English, but still can't speak it. One of the main difficulties, of course, is that speaking usually takes place spontaneously and in real time, which means that planning and production overlap. If too much **attention** is paid to planning, production suffers, and the effect is a loss of **fluency**. On the other hand, if the speaker's attention is directed solely on production, it is likely that **accuracy** will suffer, which could prejudice **intelligibility**. In order to free up attention, therefore, the speaker needs to have achieved a degree of **automaticity** in both planning and production. One way of doing this is to use memorised routines, such as **formulaic language**. Another is to use *production strategies*, such as the use of **pause fillers**, in order to 'buy' planning time. The situation is complicated by the fact that most speaking is interactive. Speakers are jointly having to manage the flow of talk. The management of interaction involves *turn-taking skills*, such as knowing how and when to take, keep, and relinquish speaker turns, and also knowing how to repair misunderstandings.

For language learners these processing demands are magnified through lack of basic knowledge of grammar and vocabulary. For the purposes of most day-to-day talk, however, the grammar that is required is not as complex nor need be as accurate as the grammar that is required for writing. Nor do speakers need an enormous vocabulary, especially if they have developed some **communication strategies** for getting round gaps in their knowledge. A core vocabulary of 1000–1500 high-frequency words and expressions will provide most learners with a solid basis for speaking.

Activating this knowledge, though, requires **practice**. This in turn suggests that the more speaking practice opportunities that learners are given, and the sooner, the easier speaking will become. Speaking practice means more than simply answering the teacher's questions, or repeating sentences, as in grammar practice activities. It means interacting with other speakers, sustaining long turns of talk, speaking spontaneously, and speaking about topics of the learners' choice.

Approaches to teaching speaking vary. Traditionally, speaking was considered to be a by-product of teaching grammar and vocabulary, reinforced with work on **pronunciation**. This view has been replaced by approaches that treat speaking as a skill in its own right. One such approach is to break down the speaking skill into a number of discrete sub-skills, such as *opening and closing conversations, turn-taking, repairing, paraphrasing, interrupting*, etc. Another approach is to focus on the different *purposes* of speaking and their associated **genres**, such as *narrating, obtaining service, giving a presentation, making small talk*, etc. This approach is particularly well suited to learners who have a specific purpose for learning English. A third is to adopt a topic-based approach, where learners are encouraged to speak freely on a range of topics, at least some of which they have chosen themselves. This is the format used in many conversation classes. Typical activity types for the teaching of speaking include: **dialogues, drama** activities (including *roleplays* and *simulations*), many **games, discussions** and debates, as well as informal classroom chat.

task METHODOLOGY

A task is a classroom activity whose focus is on communicating meaning. The objective of a task may be to reach some consensus on an issue, to solve a problem, to draft a plan, to design something, or to persuade someone to do something. In contrast, practising a pre-selected item of language (such as the present perfect) for its own sake would not be a valid task objective. In the performance of the task, learners are expected to make use of their own language resources. In theory, tasks may be receptive or productive, and may be done individually or in pairs or small groups. However, in practice, most activities that are labelled 'tasks' in coursebooks involve production (either speaking or writing, or both) and require learners to interact with one another.

Tasks are the organising principle in **task-based learning**. In order to devise a syllabus of tasks it is necessary both to classify tasks, and to identify the factors that make one task more difficult than another. Different criteria for classifying tasks have been suggested. For example, tasks can be *open-ended* or *closed*. An open-ended task is one in which learners know there is no predetermined solution. It might be planning an excursion, or debating a topical issue. A closed task, on the other hand, requires learners to discover the solution to a problem, such as identifying the differences in a *spot-the-difference* task (→ **communicative activity**). Tasks can also be classified according to the kinds of operations they involve, such as *ranking, selecting, sorting, comparing, surveying* and *problem-solving*.

Factors which influence the degree of difficulty of the task, and hence which affect the grading of tasks, include:

- *linguistic factors*: How complex is the language that learners will need to draw on, in order to do the task? How much help, either before, or during the task, will they get with their language needs?
- *cognitive factors*: Does the task require the processing of complex data? Is the task type familiar to learners?
- *performance factors*: Do the learners have to interact in real time in order to do the task? Do they have time to rehearse? Do they have to 'go public'?

The term *task* is now widely accepted as a useful way of labelling certain types of classroom activity, including many which have a thinly disguised grammar agenda. But the concept of task is not without its critics. Some writers feel that the associations of task with 'work' undervalues the more playful – and possibly less authentic or communicative – types of classroom activity, such as games, songs and drama.

vocabulary teaching METHODOLOGY

Vocabulary describes that area of language learning that is concerned with word knowledge. Vocabulary learning is a major goal in most teaching programmes. It hasn't always been so. In methods such as **audiolingualism**, vocabulary was subordinated to the teaching of grammar structures. Words were simply there to fill the slots in the sentence patterns. The move towards *semantic* (i.e., meaning-based) **syllabuses** in the 1970s, along with the use of **authentic** materials, saw a revival of interest in vocabulary teaching. Subsequently, developments in **corpus** linguistics and **discourse analysis** started to blur the distinction between vocabulary and grammar. In the 1990s the **lexical approach** ushered in a major re-think regarding the role of vocabulary. This concerned both the *selection* of items (**frequency** being a deciding factor) and the *type* of items: **formulaic language** (or lexical chunks) were recognised as being essential for both **fluency** and **idiomaticity**. These developments have influenced the design of teaching materials. Most contemporary coursebooks incorporate a lexical syllabus alongside the grammar one. Recent developments in lexicography have complemented this trend. There is now a wide range of **dictionaries** available for learners, many of which come with sophisticated software for accessing databases of examples and collocations.

It is now generally agreed that, in terms of goals, learners need a receptive vocabulary of around 3000 high-frequency words (or, better, **word families**) in order to achieve independent user status. This will give them around ninety per cent coverage of normal text. For a productive vocabulary, especially for speaking, they may only need half this number.

Classroom approaches to achieving these goals include dedicated vocabulary lessons. Typically these take the form of teaching *lexical sets* of words (i.e., groups of thematically linked words) using a variety of means, including visual **aids**, demonstration, situations, texts and dictionary work. As well as the **meaning** of the items, the **form**, both spoken (i.e., **pronunciation**) and written (i.e., **spelling**), needs to be dealt with, especially if the words are being taught for productive use. Other aspects of word knowledge that may need to be highlighted include **connotation** and **style**, **collocation**, derived forms, and grammatical features, such as the word's **word class**. Vocabulary is also taught as preparation for listening or reading (*pre-teaching vocabulary*) or as a by-product of these skills.

It would be impossible, in class, to teach all the words that learners need. Learners therefore need opportunities for *incidental* learning, e.g. through *extensive reading*. They may also benefit from training in how to make the most of these opportunities, e.g. by means of dictionary use, note-keeping, etc. Some strategies for deducing the meaning of unfamiliar words will also help.

Amassing a fully-functioning vocabulary is essentially a **memory** task, and techniques to help in the memorising of words can be usefully taught, too. It also helps to provide learners with repeated encounters with new words, e.g. through the re-reading of texts, or by reading several texts about the same topic. Constant recycling of newly learned words is essential. One simple way of doing this is to have a *word box* (or word bag) in the classroom. New words are written on to small cards and added to the word box. At the beginning of the next lesson, these words can be used as the basis for a review activity. For example, the teacher can take words out of the box and ask learners to define them, provide a translation or put them into a sentence. The words can also form the basis for peer-testing activities, in which learners take a number of word cards and test each other in pairs or small groups.

writing METHODOLOGY

Like speaking, writing is a productive **skill**, and, like other skills, writing involves a hierarchy of *sub-skills*. These range from the most mechanical (such as handwriting or typing legibly) through to the ability to organise the written text and lay it out according to the conventions of the particular text type. Along the way, writers also need to be able to:

- produce grammatically accurate sentences
- connect and punctuate these sentences
- select and maintain an appropriate style
- signal the direction that the message is taking
- anticipate the reader's likely questions so as to be able to structure the message accordingly.

In order to enable these skills, writers need an extensive knowledge base, not only at the level of vocabulary and grammar, but at the level of connected discourse. This includes familiarity with a range of different text types, such as *informal letters, instructions, product descriptions*, etc. It follows that if classroom writing is mainly spelling- or grammar-focused, many of the sub-skills of writing will be neglected.

Nevertheless, the teaching of writing has tended to focus on the 'lower-level' features of the skill, such as being able to write sentences that are both accurate and complex, that demonstrate internal cohesion, and that are connected to the sentences next to them. This language-based approach is justified on the grounds that stricter standards of accuracy are usually required in writing than in speaking. Also, writing demands a greater degree of explicitness than speaking, since writers and their readers are separated in time and space. They therefore can't rely on immediate feedback in order to clear up misunderstandings.

By contrast, a text-based approach to teaching writing takes a more 'top-down' view. This approach finds support in **discourse analysis**, which shows that a **text** is more than a series of sentences, however neatly linked. Instead, texts are organised according to larger *macrostructures*, such as problem-solution, or definition-examples. Hence, learners need explicit guidance in how texts are structured. This typically involves analysing and imitating models of particular text types. For example, a business letter might be analysed in terms of its overall layout, the purpose of each of its paragraphs, the grammatical and lexical choices within each paragraph, and the punctuation. Each of these features is then practised in isolation. They are then recombined in tasks aimed first at reproducing the original text and then at producing similar texts incorporating different content.

This approach is called a *product approach* to the teaching of writing, since the focus is exclusively on producing a text (the product) that reproduces the model. By contrast, a *process approach* argues that writers do not in fact start with a clear idea of the finished product. Rather, the text emerges out of a creative process. This process includes: *planning* (*generating ideas*, *goal setting* and *organising*), *drafting* and *re-drafting*; *reviewing*, including *editing* and *proofreading*, and, finally, '*publishing*'. Advocates of a process approach argue for a more organic sequence of classroom activities, beginning with the brainstorming of ideas, writing preliminary drafts, comparing drafts, re-drafting, and *conferencing*, that is, talking through their draft with the teacher, in order to fine-tune their ideas.

The process approach to writing has a lot in common with the **communicative approach** to language teaching, and each has drawn support from the other. The communicative approach views writing as an act of communication in which the writer interacts with a reader or readers for a particular purpose. The purpose might be to ask for information about a language course, to relay personal news, to complain about being overcharged at a hotel, or simply to entertain and amuse. Thus, advocates of a communicative approach argue that classroom writing tasks should be motivated by a clear purpose and that writers should have their reader(s) in mind at all stages of the writing process. Such principles are now reflected in the design of writing tasks in public examinations, such as this one, from the Cambridge ESOL First Certificate in English (FCE) paper:

> The school where you learn English has decided to buy some videos in English. You have been asked to write a report to the Principal, suggesting what kinds of videos the school should buy. In your report you should also explain why students at the school will like these videos.
>
> Write your report.

The social purposes of writing are also foregrounded by proponents of a *genre-based approach*. **Genre** analysis attempts to show how the structure of particular text-types are shaped by the purposes they serve in specific social and cultural contexts. Put simply, a business letter is the way it is because of what it does. Advocates of genre-based teaching reject a process approach to teaching writing. They argue that to emphasise self-expression at the expense of teaching the generic structures of texts may in fact disempower learners. Many learners, especially those who are learning English as a *second* language, need a command of those genres – such as writing a CV, or requesting a bank loan – that permit access to the host community. A genre approach to teaching writing is not unlike a product approach, therefore. It starts with model texts that are subjected to analysis and replication. The difference is that these models are closely associated with their contexts of use, and they are analysed in functional terms as much as in linguistic ones. The genre approach has been particularly influential in the teaching of academic writing.

In reality, none of these approaches is entirely incompatible with any other. Resourceful teachers tend to blend elements of each. For example, they may encourage learners to 'discover' what they want to write, using a process approach. They may then give them a model text, both as a source of useful language items, and as a template for the final product. They may also provide exercises in specific sub-skills, such as linking sentences, or using a formal style.

The Common European Framework and *New Inside Out*

The Common European Framework for language learning

Introduction

The Common European Framework (CEF) is a widely used standard created by the Council of Europe.[1] In the classroom, familiarity with the CEF can be of great help to any teacher in identifying students' actual progress and helping them to set their learning priorities.

Students can use the descriptors (description of competences) at any point to get a detailed, articulated, and personal picture of their own individual progress. This is important, as no two language learners progress in the same way, and consequently it's always rather artificial to apply a 'framework level' to a class as a whole, or to a course or coursebook.

The European Language Portfolio is another Council of Europe project, designed to give every learner a structure for keeping a record of their language learning experiences and their progress as described in the CEF. Up-to-date information about developments with the CEF and Portfolio can be found on www.coe.int/portfolio.

The Swiss-based Eurocentres Foundation played a major role in the development of the levels and the descriptors for the CEF and the prototype Portfolio. The CEF descriptors, developed in a Swiss National Research Foundation project, were presented in clearer, simpler, self-assessment form in the prototype (Swiss) Portfolio. There are now dozens of different national versions of the Portfolio for different educational sectors, but the only version for adults is that developed from the Swiss version by EAQUALS (European Association for Quality Language Services) in collaboration with ALTE.[2] The descriptors used in this guide are taken from the EAQUALS/ALTE Portfolio. An electronic version that can be completed on-line can be downloaded in English or French from www.eelp.org. The EAQUALS/ALTE portfolio descriptors have been used in this guide, as they're more concrete and practical than the original CEFR descriptors.

1 Schneider, Günther, & North, Brian (2000): "Fremdsprachen können – was heisst das?" Zürich, Rüegger
North, Brian (2000): "The Development of a Common Framework Scale of Language Proficiency", New York, Peter Lang

2 EAQUALS is a pan-European language school accreditation body with over 100 full members. ALTE is an association dedicated to raising standards in language testing and encompasses the major European examination providers. Eurocentres provides high quality language teaching in countries where the language concerned is spoken. EAQUALS, ALTE and Eurocentres are the three NGOS advisers for language learning to the Council of Europe and all three implement the CEFR.

New Inside Out CEF checklists

New Inside Out Advanced is appropriate for students who can already communicate quite confidently in English in a good range of situations. They now need to focus on using language in a flexible and idiomatic way. They're learning to express their thoughts and intentions with precision, to use language skilfully to achieve exactly what they want to, and to build up their repertoire of expressions for specific situations. At this level autonomous study is very important, and students' success will depend greatly on the extent to which they read and speak English outside the classroom. By the time committed and enthusiastic students complete *New Inside Out* Advanced, however, they will be confident with most of the abilities described at the C1 level.

In order to help students and teachers assess progress, we have provided a list of C1 descriptors that may usefully be focused on whilst studying each of the units in *New Inside Out* Advanced. A reasonable ability with the B2 descriptors is presupposed at the start of the book. Students who have reached this level are often unclear about what their next priorities should be, and about exactly what they now need to work on in order to improve their English. A familiarity with the C1 descriptors can help students to set concrete goals and to approach their studies with the kind of attitude that will allow them to be successful. Every student learns differently, and at this level useful progress can really only be made towards personal objectives, so it is important the teacher supports students in taking responsibility for the process.

The level of ability suggested in a particular unit for a particular descriptor is given only as a guide, based on classroom experience, of what kind of progress it might be reasonable to expect to see from a 'typical' student. At this level of language learning, of course, there can be no such students, so variations from the levels indicated should not be taken as a sign that students are really doing either better or worse than an established norm.

In teaching a class of students at this level, meanwhile, it is necessary to choose materials that are likely to be of benefit to as many of the students as possible. The coursebook provides a framework for this purpose, and the descriptors for each unit can help the teacher to supplement the coursebook material constructively.

CEF Student checklists

Unit 1

Complete the checklist.

1 = I can do this with a lot of help from my teacher
2 = I can do this with a little help
3 = I can do this fairly well
4 = I can do this really well
5 = I can do this almost perfectly

Competences	Page	Your score				
I can follow extended speech even when it is not clearly structured and when relationships are only implied and not signalled explicitly.	5, 10	1	2	3	4	5
I can use language flexibly and effectively for social purposes, including emotional, allusive and joking usage.	4, 5, 8, 12	1	2	3	4	5
I can express my ideas and opinions clearly and precisely, and can present and respond to complex lines of reasoning convincingly.	5, 10	1	2	3	4	5
I can orally summarise long, demanding texts.	6	1	2	3	4	5
I can consistently maintain a high degree of grammatical accuracy; errors are rare and difficult to spot.	9, 11	1	2	3	4	5

Unit 2

Complete the checklist.

1 = I can do this with a lot of help from my teacher
2 = I can do this with a little help
3 = I can do this fairly well
4 = I can do this really well
5 = I can do this almost perfectly

Competences	Page	Your score				
I can understand a wide range of idiomatic expressions and colloquialisms, appreciating shifts in style and register.	14, 20	1	2	3	4	5
I can give clear, detailed descriptions of complex subjects.	16, 17	1	2	3	4	5
I can give an extended description or account of something, integrating themes, developing particular points and concluding appropriately.	18, 19	1	2	3	4	5
I can express myself in writing on a wide range of general or professional topics in a clear and user-friendly manner.	19	1	2	3	4	5
I can present points of view in a comment on a topic or an event, underlining the main ideas and supporting my reasoning with detailed examples.	23	1	2	3	4	5

Unit 3

Complete the checklist.

1 = I can do this with a lot of help from my teacher
2 = I can do this with a little help
3 = I can do this fairly well
4 = I can do this really well
5 = I can do this almost perfectly

Competences	Page	Your score				
I can use language fluently, accurately and effectively on a wide range of general, professional or academic topics.	26, 27, 29, 32	1	2	3	4	5
I can produce clear, smoothly-flowing, well-structured speech, showing control over ways of developing what I want to say in order to link both my ideas and my expression of them into coherent text.	30	1	2	3	4	5
I have a good command of a broad vocabulary allowing gaps to be readily overcome with circumlocutions; I rarely have to search obviously for expressions or compromise on saying exactly what I want to.	27, 33	1	2	3	4	5
I can present a complex topic in a clear and well-structured way, highlighting the most important points, for example in a composition or a report.	25	1	2	3	4	5
I can select a style appropriate to the reader in mind.	28	1	2	3	4	5

Unit 4

Complete the checklist.

1 = I can do this with a lot of help from my teacher
2 = I can do this with a little help
3 = I can do this fairly well
4 = I can do this really well
5 = I can do this almost perfectly

Competences	Page	Your score				
I can understand fairly long demanding texts and summarise them orally.	36	1	2	3	4	5
I can go beyond the concrete plot of a narrative and grasp implicit meanings, ideas and connections.	36, 39	1	2	3	4	5
I can use language flexibly and effectively for social purposes, including emotional, allusive and joking usage.	40, 43, 44	1	2	3	4	5
I can substitute an equivalent term for a word I can't recall without distracting the listener.	41	1	2	3	4	5
I can give a detailed description of experiences, feelings and events in a personal letter.	45	1	2	3	4	5

 New Inside Out Advanced Teacher's Book © Macmillan Publishers Limited 2010

Unit 5

Complete the checklist.

1 = I can do this with a lot of help from my teacher
2 = I can do this with a little help
3 = I can do this fairly well
4 = I can do this really well
5 = I can do this almost perfectly

Competences	Page	Your score				
I can read complex reports, analyses and commentaries where opinions, viewpoints and connections are discussed.	48, 52	1	2	3	4	5
I can give an extended description or account of something, integrating themes, developing particular points and concluding appropriately.	51	1	2	3	4	5
I can relate my own contribution skilfully to those of other speakers.	54	1	2	3	4	5
I have a good command of a broad vocabulary allowing gaps to be readily overcome with circumlocutions; I rarely have to search obviously for expressions or compromise on saying exactly what I want to.	46, 48, 51	1	2	3	4	5
I can consistently maintain a high degree of grammatical accuracy; errors are rare and difficult to spot.	47, 53	1	2	3	4	5

Unit 6

Complete the checklist.

1 = I can do this with a lot of help from my teacher
2 = I can do this with a little help
3 = I can do this fairly well
4 = I can do this really well
5 = I can do this almost perfectly

Competences	Page	Your score				
I can follow extended speech even when it is not clearly structured and when relationships are only implied and not signalled explicitly.	56, 60	1	2	3	4	5
I can extract information, ideas and opinions from highly specialised texts in my own field, for example research reports.	57, 58	1	2	3	4	5
I can understand long complex instructions, for example for the use of a new piece of equipment, even if these are not related to my job or field of interest, provided I have enough time to reread them.	57	1	2	3	4	5
I can read contemporary literary texts with ease.	61	1	2	3	4	5
I can read any correspondence with occasional use of a dictionary.	65	1	2	3	4	5

Unit 7

Complete the checklist.

1 = I can do this with a lot of help from my teacher
2 = I can do this with a little help
3 = I can do this fairly well
4 = I can do this really well
5 = I can do this almost perfectly

Competences	Page	Your score				
I can understand complex technical information, such as operating instructions, specifications for familiar products and services.	70	1	2	3	4	5
I can understand fairly long demanding texts and summarise them orally.	72	1	2	3	4	5
I can use language flexibly and effectively for social purposes, including emotional, allusive and joking usage.	76	1	2	3	4	5
I can give a clearly developed presentation on a subject in my fields of personal or professional interest, departing when necessary from the prepared text and following up spontaneously points raised by members of the audience.	75	1	2	3	4	5
I have a good command of a broad vocabulary allowing gaps to be readily overcome with circumlocutions; I rarely have to search obviously for expressions or compromise on saying exactly what I want to.	70, 72, 77	1	2	3	4	5

Unit 8

Complete the checklist.

1 = I can do this with a lot of help from my teacher
2 = I can do this with a little help
3 = I can do this fairly well
4 = I can do this really well
5 = I can do this almost perfectly

Competences	Page	Your score				
I can understand lectures, talks and reports in my field of professional or academic interest even when they are propositionally and linguistically complex.	79, 80	1	2	3	4	5
I can express my ideas and opinions clearly and precisely, and can present and respond to complex lines of reasoning convincingly.	80, 81, 83	1	2	3	4	5
I can use fluently a variety of appropriate expressions to preface my remarks in order to get the floor, or to gain time and keep the floor while thinking.	86	1	2	3	4	5
I can produce clear, smoothly-flowing, well-structured speech, showing control over ways of developing what I want to say in order to link both my ideas and my expression of them into coherent text.	81	1	2	3	4	5
I can write texts which show a high degree of grammatical correctness and vary my vocabulary and style according to the addressee, the kind of text and the topic.	87	1	2	3	4	5

 New Inside Out Advanced Teacher's Book © Macmillan Publishers Limited 2010

Unit 9

Complete the checklist.

1 = I can do this with a lot of help from my teacher
2 = I can do this with a little help
3 = I can do this fairly well
4 = I can do this really well
5 = I can do this almost perfectly

Competences	Page	Your score				
I can read contemporary literary texts with ease.	95	1	2	3	4	5
I can use language flexibly and effectively for social purposes, including emotional, allusive and joking usage.	88, 89	1	2	3	4	5
I can give an extended description or account of something, integrating themes, developing particular points and concluding appropriately.	92	1	2	3	4	5
I can relate my own contribution skilfully to those of other speakers.	96	1	2	3	4	5
I can produce clear, smoothly-flowing, well-structured speech, showing control over ways of developing what I want to say in order to link both my ideas and my expression of them into coherent text.	91, 92	1	2	3	4	5

Unit 10

Complete the checklist.

1 = I can do this with a lot of help from my teacher
2 = I can do this with a little help
3 = I can do this fairly well
4 = I can do this really well
5 = I can do this almost perfectly

Competences	Page	Your score				
I can understand a wide range of idiomatic expressions and colloquialisms, appreciating shifts in style and register.	101, 104, 105, 106	1	2	3	4	5
I can extract information, ideas and opinions from highly specialised texts in my own field, for example research reports.	100, 106	1	2	3	4	5
I can express myself fluently and spontaneously, almost effortlessly. Only a conceptually difficult subject can hinder a natural, smooth flow of language.	104, 105	1	2	3	4	5
I can consistently maintain a high degree of grammatical accuracy; errors are rare and difficult to spot.	103, 107	1	2	3	4	5
I can present a complex topic in a clear and well-structured way, highlighting the most important points, for example in a composition or a report.	109	1	2	3	4	5

Unit 11

Complete the checklist.

1 = I can do this with a lot of help from my teacher
2 = I can do this with a little help
3 = I can do this fairly well
4 = I can do this really well
5 = I can do this almost perfectly

Competences	Page	Your score				
I can without too much effort understand films which contain a considerable degree of slang and idiomatic usage.	111	1	2	3	4	5
I can keep up with an animated conversation between native speakers.	110	1	2	3	4	5
I can express my ideas and opinions clearly and precisely, and can present and respond to complex lines of reasoning convincingly.	117	1	2	3	4	5
I can relate my own contribution skilfully to those of other speakers.	116	1	2	3	4	5
I can write texts which show a high degree of grammatical correctness and vary my vocabulary and style according to the addressee, the kind of text and the topic.	114	1	2	3	4	5

Unit 12

Complete the checklist.

1 = I can do this with a lot of help from my teacher
2 = I can do this with a little help
3 = I can do this fairly well
4 = I can do this really well
5 = I can do this almost perfectly

Competences	Page	Your score				
I can extract specific information from even poor quality, audibly distorted public announcements, e.g. in a station, sports stadium etc.	118	1	2	3	4	5
I can write texts which show a high degree of grammatical correctness and vary my vocabulary and style according to the addressee, the kind of text and the topic.	120	1	2	3	4	5
I can use language fluently, accurately and effectively on a wide range of general, professional or academic topics.	120, 122	1	2	3	4	5
I have a good command of a broad vocabulary allowing gaps to be readily overcome with circumlocutions; I rarely have to search obviously for expressions or compromise on saying exactly what I want to.	121, 123	1	2	3	4	5
I can write formally correct letters, for example to complain or to take a stand in favour of or against something.	125	1	2	3	4	5

CEF Student checklists: Answer key

Unit 1

Competences	Page	Your score
I can follow extended speech even when it is not clearly structured and when relationships are only implied and not signalled explicitly.	5, 10	① 2 3 4 5
I can use language flexibly and effectively for social purposes, including emotional, allusive and joking usage.	4, 5, 8, 12	① 2 3 4 5
I can express my ideas and opinions clearly and precisely, and can present and respond to complex lines of reasoning convincingly.	5, 10	① 2 3 4 5
I can orally summarise long, demanding texts.	6	1 2 ③ 4 5
I can consistently maintain a high degree of grammatical accuracy; errors are rare and difficult to spot.	9, 11	① 2 3 4 5

Unit 2

Competences	Page	Your score
I can understand a wide range of idiomatic expressions and colloquialisms, appreciating shifts in style and register.	14, 20	1 ② 3 4 5
I can give clear, detailed descriptions of complex subjects.	16, 17	1 ② 3 4 5
I can give an extended description or account of something, integrating themes, developing particular points and concluding appropriately.	18, 19	① 2 3 4 5
I can express myself in writing on a wide range of general or professional topics in a clear and user-friendly manner.	19	① 2 3 4 5
I can present points of view in a comment on a topic or an event, underlining the main ideas and supporting my reasoning with detailed examples.	23	① 2 3 4 5

Unit 3

Competences	Page	Your score
I can use language fluently, accurately and effectively on a wide range of general, professional or academic topics.	26, 27, 29, 32	① 2 3 4 5
I can produce clear, smoothly-flowing, well-structured speech, showing control over ways of developing what I want to say in order to link both my ideas and my expression of them into coherent text.	30	① 2 3 4 5
I have a good command of a broad vocabulary allowing gaps to be readily overcome with circumlocutions; I rarely have to search obviously for expressions or compromise on saying exactly what I want to.	27, 33	1 ② 3 4 5
I can present a complex topic in a clear and well-structured way, highlighting the most important points, for example in a composition or a report.	25	① 2 3 4 5
I can select a style appropriate to the reader in mind.	28	1 ② 3 4 5

Unit 4

Competences	Page	Your score
I can understand fairly long demanding texts and summarise them orally.	36	① 2 3 4 5
I can go beyond the concrete plot of a narrative and grasp implicit meanings, ideas and connections.	36, 39	1 ② 3 4 5
I can use language flexibly and effectively for social purposes, including emotional, allusive and joking usage.	40, 43, 44	1 ② 3 4 5
I can substitute an equivalent term for a word I can't recall without distracting the listener.	41	1 ② 3 4 5
I can give a detailed description of experiences, feelings and events in a personal letter.	45	1 ② 3 4 5

Unit 5

Competences	Page	Your score
I can read complex reports, analyses and commentaries where opinions, viewpoints and connections are discussed.	48, 52	1 2 ③ 4 5
I can give an extended description or account of something, integrating themes, developing particular points and concluding appropriately.	51	1 ② 3 4 5
I can relate my own contribution skilfully to those of other speakers.	54	1 ② 3 4 5
I have a good command of a broad vocabulary allowing gaps to be readily overcome with circumlocutions; I rarely have to search obviously for expressions or compromise on saying exactly what I want to.	46, 48, 51	1 2 ③ 4 5
I can consistently maintain a high degree of grammatical accuracy; errors are rare and difficult to spot.	47, 53	1 2 ③ 4 5

Unit 6

Competences	Page	Your score
I can follow extended speech even when it is not clearly structured and when relationships are only implied and not signalled explicitly.	56, 60	1 2 ③ 4 5
I can extract information, ideas and opinions from highly specialised texts in my own field, for example research reports.	57, 58	1 2 ③ 4 5
I can understand long complex instructions, for example for the use of a new piece of equipment, even if these are not related to my job or field of interest, provided I have enough time to reread them.	57	① 2 3 4 5
I can read contemporary literary texts with ease.	61	1 ② 3 4 5
I can read any correspondence with occasional use of a dictionary.	65	1 2 ③ 4 5

Unit 7

Competences	Page	Your score
I can understand complex technical information, such as operating instructions, specifications for familiar products and services.	70	1 2 ③ 4 5
I can understand fairly long demanding texts and summarise them orally.	72	1 2 ③ 4 5
I can use language flexibly and effectively for social purposes, including emotional, allusive and joking usage.	76	1 2 ③ 4 5
I can give a clearly developed presentation on a subject in my fields of personal or professional interest, departing when necessary from the prepared text and following up spontaneously points raised by members of the audience.	75	1 2 ③ 4 5
I have a good command of a broad vocabulary allowing gaps to be readily overcome with circumlocutions; I rarely have to search obviously for expressions or compromise on saying exactly what I want to.	70, 72, 77	1 2 3 ④ 5

Unit 8

Competences	Page	Your score
I can understand lectures, talks and reports in my field of professional or academic interest even when they are propositionally and linguistically complex.	79, 80	1 2 ③ 4 5
I can express my ideas and opinions clearly and precisely, and can present and respond to complex lines of reasoning convincingly.	80, 81, 83	1 2 3 ④ 5
I can use fluently a variety of appropriate expressions to preface my remarks in order to get the floor, or to gain time and keep the floor while thinking.	86	1 2 3 4 ⑤
I can produce clear, smoothly-flowing, well-structured speech, showing control over ways of developing what I want to say in order to link both my ideas and my expression of them into coherent text.	81	1 2 3 ④ 5
I can write texts which show a high degree of grammatical correctness and vary my vocabulary and style according to the addressee, the kind of text and the topic.	87	1 2 ③ 4 5

Unit 9

Competences	Page	Your score				
I can read contemporary literary texts with ease.	95	1	2	3	④	5
I can use language flexibly and effectively for social purposes, including emotional, allusive and joking usage.	88, 89	1	2	3	4	5
I can give an extended description or account of something, integrating themes, developing particular points and concluding appropriately.	92	1	2	3	4	5
I can relate my own contribution skilfully to those of other speakers.	96	1	2	③	4	5
I can produce clear, smoothly-flowing, well-structured speech, showing control over ways of developing what I want to say in order to link both my ideas and my expression of them into coherent text.	91, 92	1	2	3	4	⑤

Unit 10

Competences	Page	Your score				
I can understand a wide range of idiomatic expressions and colloquialisms, appreciating shifts in style and register.	101, 104, 105, 106	1	2	3	④	5
I can extract information, ideas and opinions from highly specialised texts in my own field, for example research reports.	100, 106	1	2	3	④	5
I can express myself fluently and spontaneously, almost effortlessly. Only a conceptually difficult subject can hinder a natural, smooth flow of language.	104, 105	1	2	3	4	⑤
I can consistently maintain a high degree of grammatical accuracy; errors are rare and difficult to spot.	103, 107	1	2	3	4	⑤
I can present a complex topic in a clear and well-structured way, highlighting the most important points, for example in a composition or a report.	109	1	2	③	4	5

Unit 11

Competences	Page	Your score				
I can without too much effort understand films which contain a considerable degree of slang and idiomatic usage.	111	1	2	3	④	5
I can keep up with an animated conversation between native speakers.	110	1	2	3	④	5
I can express my ideas and opinions clearly and precisely, and can present and respond to complex lines of reasoning convincingly.	117	1	2	3	4	⑤
I can relate my own contribution skilfully to those of other speakers.	116	1	2	3	④	5
I can write texts which show a high degree of grammatical correctness and vary my vocabulary and style according to the addressee, the kind of text and the topic.	114	1	2	3	④	5

Unit 12

Competences	Page	Your score				
I can extract specific information from even poor quality, audibly distorted public announcements, e.g. in a station, sports stadium etc.	118	1	2	③	4	5
I can write texts which show a high degree of grammatical correctness and vary my vocabulary and style according to the addressee, the kind of text and the topic.	120	1	2	3	4	5
I can use language fluently, accurately and effectively on a wide range of general, professional or academic topics.	120, 122	1	2	3	4	⑤
I have a good command of a broad vocabulary allowing gaps to be readily overcome with circumlocutions; I rarely have to search obviously for expressions or compromise on saying exactly what I want to.	121, 123	1	2	3	4	⑤
I can write formally correct letters, for example to complain or to take a stand in favour of or against something.	125	1	2	③	4	5

New Inside Out Advanced Teacher's Book © Macmillan Publishers Limited 2010

1 Conversation *Overview*

Section & Aims	What the students are doing
Speaking & Vocabulary SB page 4 Fluency practice Adjectives describing conversation styles	Discussing relationships between people in photos. Catagorising adjectives used in conversations and matching them to the photos. Discussing recent conversations.
Listening & Vocabulary **SB page 5** Listening for gist Conversation collocations	Discussing what makes a good and bad conversation. Listening to conversations and matching them to questions. Completing extracts from conversations. Matching definitions to expressions.
Speaking SB page 5 Fluency practice	Talking about their last conversation in English.
Reading & Speaking SB page 6 Fluency practice Predicting and reading for gist	Discussing men's and women's conversation styles. Predicting the content of a book from the book cover. Discussing extracts from the book.
Vocabulary SB page 7 Word building	Matching vocabulary of personal values to definitions. Completing a table with noun, verb, adjective and adverb forms.
Speaking & Listening SB page 8 Fluency practice Predicting	Talking about typical complaints girlfriends and boyfriends make about each other. Listening to a conversation and matching extracts to speakers.
Pronunciation SB page 8 Intonation	Identifying angry tones from a conversation and practising conveying feelings by intonation.
Grammar SB page 9 Position of adverbials	Identifying different types of adverbials. Studying the implications of the position of adverbials.
Speaking SB page 10 Fluency practice	Discussing eavesdropping and accidentally overhearing people's conversations.
Listening SB page 10 Listening for gist and detail	Listening to conversations and identifying the dynamics displayed in them.
Grammar SB page 11 Aspect	Completing extracts from conversations. Identifying correct verb forms.
Useful phrases SB page 12 Useful phrases for opening conversations	Reading tips about starting a conversation. Matching the conversations to their situations. Matching conversation openers to their functions and responses. Discussing which conversation is the most successful. Practising starting a conversation.
Vocabulary *Extra* SB page 13 Multiple meaning and uses of common words	Discussing proverbs. Identifying the part of speech of the word *talk* in various sentences. Completing sentences and discussing idioms with *talk*.
Writing WB page 9	Writing a self-help tip sheet.

Conversation *Teacher's notes*

Warm up

Focus the students' attention on the photos and ask them in which situation they feel most comfortable: having an intimate chat with a close friend or talking in a large group.

Speaking & Vocabulary (SB page 4)

1

Pairwork. Focus the students' attention on the photos. Put them in pairs and give them time to talk about what they can see and to discuss the questions. Then have a feedback session with the class, getting as many different opinions as possible.

2

- Ask the students to classify the adjectives in the box according to the headings in the table. Allow them to compare their answers in pairs before checking with the class. You may need to point out that sometimes whether an adjective is positive or negative depends on one's personal viewpoint. Some people, for example, like having an *intense* conversation, while for others having this would not be desirable. The adjectives in the neutral category in the answers below could be either positive or negative depending on the circumstances. *Intimate* can be both positive and neutral.

- Students then add one or two more adjectives under each heading. Then compare their adjectives with their partner.

- Finally, ask the students to discuss in pairs which adjectives they would use to describe each of the conversations in the photos in Exercise 1.

> *Possible answers:*
> **Positive:** animated, hilarious, intimate, meaningful, stimulating
> **Negative:** boring, bizarre, frustrating, one-sided, pointless, predictable
> **Neutral:** in-depth, intense, intimate, lengthy

3

- Pairwork. Ask the students to work in pairs to answer the questions. Keep it light-hearted and make it clear that they don't have to reveal any information that they don't feel comfortable about sharing.

- Encourage the students to report back to the class on their discussions.

Listening & Vocabulary (SB page 5)

1

- Groupwork. Before putting the students into groups, go through the instructions with the class and make sure everyone understands that a *frustrating* conversation is one which leaves you unsatisfied, and that a *good conversationalist* is someone who is good at making conversation. (What they are expected to do here is not to explain the meaning of *good conversationalist*, but to discuss what qualities, skills and techniques a good conversationalist employs. If they miss the point, steer them towards doing this.)

- Encourage the groups to report back to the class on their discussions.

2 🔘 1.01–1.06

- Go through the instructions with the class and make sure they understand that they have to match each speaker with one of the questions from Exercise 1. Play the recording, pausing it after each speaker if necessary to allow the students to decide which question is being answered each time.

- Ask the students to compare their answers in the same groups they were in for Exercise 1. Encourage them to discuss whether the opinions expressed by the people on the recording were similar to their own.

- Only one of the speakers on the recording answers question c, so it might be worth spending some more time on this question and having a whole class discussion on whether being a good conversationalist simply means having something interesting to say or whether there are other factors at play, such as the ability to talk to anyone (no matter how boring or how different from you they are), the skill of being able to elicit good conversation out of other people and to make them feel important, the sensitivity not to dominate the conversation and the ability to steer a conversation subtly away from tricky subjects, etc.

> | Joanna – a) | Jessica – b) |
> | Mike – c) | Bryony – a) |
> | Phil – b) | Rafe –b) |

> 🔘 **1.01**
>
> Joanna
> *Well, I like to be able to take an active part, so it helps if there aren't some people who hog the conversation all the time, and also people need to have a sense of humour about things, I think, not to take things too seriously and you need a conversation that flows, so that you can ... well, you don't get stuck on one point.*

1.02
Mike

Um, a good conversationalist. I'd say it's someone who's, who's got a point that they want to put across during the conversation. Someone with something to say as opposed to someone who just talks endlessly about various subjects and doesn't engage in one particular subject, and I'd say it was someone who listens to other people as well, um, that's what I'd say.

1.03
Phil

When people aren't really interested in what you're saying, that's very annoying indeed. Also, people who interrupt you continually with grunts or opinions of their own or whatever, and also some people don't care about whose turn it is to talk, so they just, you know, butt in when you're in the middle of a thought and obviously, you know, when the topic's boring, that's very irritating. And sometimes, you know, the conversation goes nowhere, it's going nowhere, and that's, that is also extremely irritating.

1.04
Jessica

I really hate it when I'm with someone who just drones on and on in a conversation, and who doesn't give you a chance to speak at all. Oh, and I also really hate it when they just carry on and they don't care whether or not you are interested at all in what they're saying. They seem oblivious to how you're reacting to them. I hate that.

1.05
Bryony

Um, it's good when you're talking about things which you've got in common with the person you are talking to, like you're on the same wavelength and you can share the same tastes or experiences so you know where the other person's coming from. It's also nice if you can share a joke or a personal story or an anecdote or something like that.

1.06
Rafe

I can't stand it when you have to do all the talking yourself, when the other person's not responding. Or when they are responding, but it's with monosyllabic answers, you know, they're just going 'yeah', 'uh', 'hmm', and that's all you're getting back. And when you have to work to keep the conversation going. That's, that's really bad, when you're having to hunt around for things to say, because you're just not getting anything back.

3

Ask the students to complete the gaps. Play the recording again when they've finished for them to check their answers and hear the target expressions in context.

a) hog	d) butt in
b) flows	e) drones on and on
c) put across, something to say	f) on the same wavelength
	g) hunt around

4

Ask the students to work individually to match the definitions with the expressions in Exercise 3, but allow them to compare in pairs before checking with the class.

1 hunt around	5 on the same wavelength
2 butt in	6 put across
3 hog	7 flows
4 something to say	8 drones on and on

5

Pairwork. Put the students into pairs and ask them to decide which expressions they associate with which type of conversation.

Suggested answers:
a) hunt around
b) butt in, drone on and on, hog
c) flows, on the same wavelength, something to say

Speaking (SB page 5)

1

Pairwork. Go through the instructions and the questions with the class. Give the students time to think about their own answers before you put them into pairs to discuss the questions.

2

Have a feedback session with the class and get them to decide whose conversation was the most challenging and whose the most satisfying.

Reading & Speaking (SB page 6)

1

- It might be interesting to start this section with same-sex groups and then have mixed-sex groups for some of the later exercises.

- Put the students into groups and ask them to discuss the statements and how far they agree or disagree with them. Make sure the discussion doesn't become too heated and remind the students that they need to give reasons for their opinions.

2

- Focus the students' attention on the book cover. Elicit what Mars and Venus are (two planets, named after the Roman god of war and the god of love respectively). Put the students into pairs to discuss the questions. Give help with the vocabulary in the box in question c) if necessary.

- Encourage the students to report back to the class on their opinions and find out how much consensus there is. Take note of and perhaps draw attention to any gender differences in their opinions. If anyone has actually read the book, ask them to tell the class briefly about it and whether they enjoyed it.

John Gray

John Gray is an American relationship consultant and lecturer. He's the author of 16 books, including *Men are from Mars, Women Are from Venus*, which was first published in 1992.

3

- Pairwork. Think about how you pair the students up in this exercise. Would the students feel more comfortable in same-sex pairs? Would the results be more interesting if they were mixed sex but each read the text appropriate to their gender? Would it be more productive for them to read the text about their partner's gender?

- Ask one student in each pair to read each of the texts and make notes on their particular text.

Life on Mars
a) power, competence, efficiency, achievement, skills, results, doing things by themselves, autonomy
b) through success and accomplishment
c) objects and things; powerful cars, faster computers, gadgets, gizmos, new powerful technology

Life on Venus
a) love, communication, beauty, relationships, feelings, the quality of their relationships, living in harmony, community, loving cooperation
b) through sharing personal feelings, and talking and relating to one another
c) people and communication; sharing feelings

4

Allow plenty of time for the students to tell each other about their texts and to discuss the questions. Tell them to report back to the class on their discussion.

Vocabulary (SB page 7)

1

- Ask the students to complete the glossary.
- Then ask them to say whether the words were associated with men, women or both in the extracts.

---

a) skills (men)	e) satisfaction (men)
b) achievement (men)	f) fulfilment (both)
c) competence (men)	g) considerate (women)
d) efficiency (men)	h) value (both)

2

Ask the students to try to complete the table without using a dictionary. If they're tempted to put *compete* in the verb column for *competence*, point out that this verb has a completely different meaning.

Noun	Verb	Adjective	Adverb
skills	–	skilful/ skilled	skilfully
achievement	achieve	achievable	–
competence	–	competent	competently
efficiency	–	efficient	efficiently
satisfaction	satisfy	satisfied/ satisfactory/ satisfying	satisfactorily
fulfilment	fulfil	fulfilled/ fulfilling	–
consideration	consider	considerate	considerately
value	value	valued/ valuable	valuably

Vocabulary: word building

- Review some of the noun and adjective endings presented: -ment (indicates the result of an action *fulfilment*, *achievement*), -ence/-ance (*competence*), -cy (*efficiency*), -ion (*satisfaction*).

- Some other typical noun endings are: -ism (a belief in something, e.g. *optimism*), -ist (the person who believes, e.g. *optimist*), -ness (*goodness*); adjective endings: -ful/-less (*skilful*, note: double 'l' is dropped at the end of 'skill' and 'full'), *hopeless*), -able/-ible (*achievable*), -ing/-ed (*satisfying* (provides satisfaction), *satisfied* (receives satisfaction)).

3

Ask the students to complete the sentences. Then allow them to compare their answers in pairs before checking with the class. Note that there could be more than one answer for some of the gaps, Accept any answers that are grammatically correct and make sense.

---

a) consideration	e) achievement
b) fulfilling/satisfying	f) efficient
c) value	g) satisfaction/fulfilment
d) satisfied	h) skills

4

Ask the students to change the italic parts of the sentences in Exercise 3 to make them true for them. Then get them to compare their new sentences with a partner.

Speaking & Listening (SB page 8)

1

Groupwork. Put the students into groups. Again, you might consider whether this will work best with your students in single-sex or mixed-sex groups. Ask the students to brainstorm a list of complaints. In a class feedback session, get the groups to share their lists and then get the students vote on which ones are most commonly made about men and which about women.

2

- Groupwork. Put the students into two groups. If you have used single-sex groups up till now, perhaps change so that the students have a chance to think about the point of view of the opposite sex. You could also tell the male students to take the role of Suzi and the female students to take the role of Brian. With a very large class, make several groups, but when pairing the students up in the next exercise, make sure you have a Suzi and a Brian in each pair.

- Ask the groups to turn to page 128. Allow them time to read their information and discuss what they're going to say.

3

- Pairwork. Make pairs with students from different groups and ask them to act out the telephone conversation between Suzi and Brian. Telephone roleplays often work best if you seat the students back to back so that they can't see each other.

- As they work, go round monitoring and giving help where necessary. Take note of any particularly good conversations, which could be repeated for the class.

4 🌐 1.07

Ask the students to listen to the conversation and say how different it was from theirs.

🌐 1.07 (B = Brian; S = Suzi)

B: *Hello?*

S: *Hi, it's me!*

B: *Hiya! How are you doing?*

S: *Fine, a bit stressed out, had a hard day at work, you know, the usual.*

B: *Yeah, me too.*

S: *So, what about the film then? I just phoned the cinema to check the times and it's on at 7 o'clock and 9.30. Which do you reckon?*

B: *Listen, love, do you mind if we go another night? I'm tired, I just fancy a quiet night in, you know, bit of a veg on the sofa, watch some footie on TV.*

S: *But it's the last night. You said you really wanted to go!*

B: *Why don't you go with your sister? You said she wanted to see the film …*

S: *This is the third time you've pulled out. What's going on?*

B: *Nothing. I just don't fancy it tonight, that's all.*

S: *Come on, if there's something wrong, you can tell me. I'm not going to fly off the handle.*

B: *There's nothing wrong …*

S: *Yes, there is. You've been off for days. You don't talk to me, you don't want to see me.*

B: *That's not true.*

S: *Are you bored with me? Is there someone else? Have I done something wrong?*

B: *No, no, of course not.*

S: *You never used to shut yourself away like this, you used to want to spend time with me. What's changed?*

B: *Nothing's changed. Of course I want to see you.*

S: *But not tonight, eh? The football's more interesting, I suppose.*

B: *Oh, you know that's not true. It's just that I'm tired, that's all. It's been a hard day. I just need a quiet night in …*

S: *Alone!*

B: *Look, if it's that important to you, I'll come. What time did you say?*

S: *No, forget it! I wouldn't want you to go out of your way or anything!*

B: *Don't be like that. Come on, shall I come and pick you up?*

S: *No, forget it. I've gone off the idea. Let's just drop it.*

B: *Look, I'd love to do something tomorrow, yeah?*

S: *Whatever. Just please yourself. You always do!*

B: *Suzi, don't … Suzi. Suzi?*

5

Pairwork. Ask the students to discuss with their partner whether the extracts are from what Suzi said or from what Brian said. Play the recording again for them to check their answers.

---

a) Suzi   b) Suzi   c) Brian   d) Suzi
e) Suzi   f) Brian   g) Suzi   h) Suzi

6

This could either be done as a class discussion or you could put the students into pairs or groups, and then get them to compare their suggestions. You might like to get different suggestions from male and female students and see how they differ.

Pronunciation (SB page 8)

1

Pairwork. Put the students into pairs and ask them to read the extracts and discuss the questions. Check answers with the class and make sure the students understand sarcasm. Explain that someone's tone of voice will often indicate that they are being sarcastic.

---

a) no
b) by using sarcasm – saying the opposite of what she really means

---

Language note

Pronunciation: stress and intonation to sound sarcastic

This section focuses on ways of using stress and intonation to show annoyance through the use of sarcasm. It's important for your students to try to imitate as closely as possible the stressed words within the sentences to achieve their maximum effect. Bear in mind sarcasm will be much more familiar concept to some cultures than to others.

2 ⊕ 1.08

- Play the recording and ask the students to identify the differences between the normal tone and the angry tone.
- Check answers before asking the students to look at page 146 and find other phrases where the girl uses an angry tone of voice. When they've identified these, get them to practise in pairs.

> When people speak angrily, the words are stressed more strongly.

> ⊕ 1.08
>
> 1 But not <u>tonight</u>, eh? The <u>football</u>'s more interesting I <u>suppose</u>.
> 2 But <u>not</u> tonight, eh? The <u>football</u>'s more interesting I <u>suppose</u>.
> 3 No, <u>forget</u> it! I <u>wouldn't</u> want you to go out of your <u>way</u> or anything.
> 4 <u>No</u>, forget it! I <u>wouldn't</u> want you to go <u>out</u> of your <u>way</u> or <u>anything</u>!

Grammar (SB page 9)

Position of adverbials

1

- Pairwork. Explain that adverbials give extra information about a verb. Focus the students' attention on the examples in bold in the sentences in this exercise and point out that adverbials can be a single word or a phrase.
- Pairwork. Put the students into pairs and ask them to read the example sentences and match the adverbials in bold with their functions.

> 1 a) on his own,
>   d) dramatically, like an overgrown teenager
> 2 a) never
> 3 b) tomorrow
> 4 c) on the sofa
> 5 e) Frankly

2

- Read the example sentence to the class and point out the four numbered positions. Give the students time to think about where in the sentence they'd add the six adverbials in the list. Encourage them to experiment with the different positions, saying the sentence aloud each time in order to develop a feeling for what sounds right and what sounds wrong.
- Check answers with the class and point out that sometimes more than one position may be correct (though sometimes this changes the meaning as they will see in Exercise 4).
- Go through the information about adverbials in the margin. Get the students to say what the function is of: *at home* (place), *tomorrow* (time), *quickly* (manner), *to see us* (purpose), *every week* (time). Point out that several adverbials can be used in combination as in the last three sentences in the margin.

> a) when she was younger – 1, 4
> b) always – 2
> c) in secret – 3, 4
> d) only – 1, 2, 3
> e) from time to time – 1, 3̶, 4
> f) probably – 2
>
> One word adverbials are often used in position 2. Phrases are usually used at the beginning or the end of the clause.
>
> In the negative sentence *always* and *only* come between the auxiliary and the main verb – *probably* comes before the auxiliary.

Language note

Grammar: adverbials

An adverbial gives us more information about the manner, frequency, time or place of an action. Adverbial phrases most commonly occur at the end of sentences (although they can also be used at the beginning of a sentence, often for emphasis), while one word adverbs often occur in the mid-position (or, again for emphasis, at the beginning of a sentence).

Notice the adverbials in the example sentence:

She lived happily in Paris when she was in her early twenties.

In the sentence we can see that place adverbials (*in Paris*) usually come before time adverbials (*when she was in her early twenties*). Manner adverbials (*happily*) come before place adverbials. Single word adverbs of frequency usually occur between the subject and verb, while phrases relating to frequency (*now and then, from time to time*) are more usually found at the end of the sentence.

3

Give the students time to think about how they could make the sentence true for them. Remind them that they should add at least three adverbials to the sentence. Then ask the students to compare their sentences with a partner.

4

Read the example sentences to the class, using intonation to help demonstrate the difference in meaning between them. Ask the students to read the other pairs of sentences and to think about what the different meanings might be.

> a) 1 – I can't speak to her at all.
>   2 – I can speak to her, but not honestly.
> b) 1 – Previously I had wanted him to come to the meeting, but then I changed my mind.
>   2 – He came too late.
> c) 1 – I only get into arguments when I'm extremely angry.
>   2 – I often get into arguments – especially if I'm angry.

5

Go through the two questions and the example with the class, pointing out the adverbials in bold in the example. Ask the students to answer the questions for themselves, using at least five adverbials in their answers. Then tell them to compare their sentences with a partner.

6 Grammar *Extra* 1, Part 1

Ask the students to turn to *Grammar Extra* 1, Part 1 on page 134 of the Student's Book. Here they'll find an explanation of the grammar they've been studying and a further exercise to practise it.

1

Suggested answers:

a) I always watch TV for half an hour before going to bed. / I always watch TV before going to bed for half an hour. / Before going to bed every night I always watch TV for half an hour.

b) I worked late at the office every night last week. / Last week I worked late at the office every night. / Every night last week I worked late at the office.

c) Quite honestly, I love reading a good book more than anything else. / Quite honestly, more than anything else, I love reading a good book.

d) I probably won't do anything special tonight. / I won't do anything special tonight, probably.

e) I sometimes wish I had more time to do sport at the weekend. / I wish I had more time sometimes to do sport at the weekend. / Sometimes I wish I had more time to do sport at the weekend.

f) I dislike loud music particularly in public places. / I particularly dislike loud music in public places. / I dislike loud music in public places particularly.

g) I'll probably have time to do more sport once I finish my exams. / Once I finish my exams, I'll probably have time to do more sport.

h) I know I eat too quickly but I'm always in a hurry.

Speaking (SB page 10)

1

Read the two sentences to the class and ask them to decide what the correct options are. Ask them if they have two different words in their own language for these things.

---

a) eavesdropping   b) overhearing

2

Put the students into small groups and ask them to discuss the questions. If the students show particular interest in the topic, allow plenty of time for discussion. Ask a spokesperson from each group to report back to the class on their discussion.

Listening (SB page 10)

1 🔘 1.09–1.10

• Ask the students to look at the two photos and take in what they can see in them. Explain that they're going to hear two conversations and they must decide which conversation goes with which photo.

• Play the recording for the students to choose which photo goes with which conversation. Then focus attention on the questions and ask the students if they can answer them without listening to the recording again. Play it again for them to check their answers.

Conversation 1 – photo 1
a) They are friends.
b) They're talking about what happened to one of them.

Conversation 2 – photo 2
a) A businesswoman talking to a client.
b) The client is unhappy about a delay in receiving some kind of printed material.

🔘 1.09 (W1 = Woman 1; W2 = Woman 2)
1

W1: *I'd been waiting and waiting and waiting and, you know, I was beginning to think, like, you know, like, he wasn't coming or something …*
W2: *Why didn't you phone him … or text, text him … or whatever …*
W1: *Yeah, well, you know, I thought he might have got caught up at work or something and I didn't really want to … I didn't want him to feel … to think … you know, that I was like hassling him, you know?*
W2: *So, what did you do?*
W1: *Well, actually he phoned me! He'd been waiting for me … but in another restaurant … in another restaurant on the other side of town!*
W2: *What …?*
W1: *Turns out there are two Italian restaurants called Casa Mia, and neither of us had realised! I had no idea.*
W2: *Me neither!*
W1: *Yeah, and so, like, you know, neither of us had realised and we'd both, you know, thought of the other one and …*
W2: *So, what happened? Did you go to him? Did he come to you?*
W1: *He came to me. He was driving … he had his car … it was easier for him. He was really sweet about it actually, really, really apologetic and we …*

🔘 1.10 (W = Woman)
2

W: *Mmm. Yes, well … I'm just on the train actually. It's just coming into the station now.*
W: *What? Ah, yes, well …. We've been working on it all week.*
W: *Yes, yes, it's almost done.*

W: Yes, of course, we all understand how important it is and we've already completed the initial plans, we're just waiting for the final details to come through …

W: Yes, yes, of course, I'm sure we'll have finished by then …

W: What? Sorry? I can't hear you very well …

W: Yes, yes, don't worry. We're working on the final details now. We'll be sending it to the printer's this evening …

W: Yes, yes, this evening … or tomorrow morning at the latest …

W: Sorry, what's that? You said you'd been promised it by the end of last week?

W: I really don't think that's possible … You must have been talking to the wrong person … I mean, there must have been some kind of misunderstanding.

W: Yes, of course. I understand your concerns, and I'll make sure it gets done this evening.

W: Of course, absolutely. I'll be taking care of it personally. You can be sure of that.

W: Yes, yes, I'll be bring round later this evening. You can count on that.

W: Goodbye.

2

- Pairwork. Put the students into pairs and ask them to discuss the sentences. Play the recording again if necessary.

- Have a class feedback session to find out if everyone agrees. Then play the recording again to confirm the answers.

a) both	c) Conversation 2
b) Conversation 2	d) Conversation 1

3

- Pairwork. Ask the students to turn to the recording script and decide with their partner what the other person was saying. When they've finished, ask them to practise their conversations. Get some of the pairs to perform theirs for the class.

Grammar (SB page 11)

Aspect

1

Go through the information in the margin with the class. Then ask the students to work in pairs to complete the extracts. Go round checking that they're doing this correctly.

a) waiting, waiting, beginning, coming	f) completed
	g) finished
b) got	h) talking
c) realised	i) been
d) coming	j) taking
e) working	

2

Pairwork. If the students have difficulty with this, refer them to the margin where there are examples of perfect and continuous forms. As aspect is a difficult concept to grasp for many people, you could go through the Grammar *Extra* section on page 134 with them.

1 **perfect verb forms:** he might have got / neither of us had realised / We've already completed / we'll have finished / There must have been
2 **continuous verb forms:** I was beginning / he wasn't coming / It's just coming / I'll be taking
3 **perfect continuous verb forms:** I'd been waiting and waiting / We've been working / You must have been talking

Language notes

Grammar: aspect
Aspect refers to how an event or action is to be viewed with respect to time, rather than to its actual location in time. The aspect of a verb is determined by whether the action is ongoing or completed. Although all verbs in the past have already happened, aspect is used to emphasise whether the action was ongoing or completed at the time.

Grammar: continuous verb forms
The continuous is formed using the auxiliary *be* + *-ing* form of the verb.

I'm seeing them next week.
He will be arriving in an hour.
They were staying at the Continental.

The continuous aspect describes events in progress at a given point in time.

Grammar: perfect verb forms
The perfect is formed using the auxiliary *will have/ have/had* + past participle.

Tomorrow they will have been here for two weeks.
We've missed the bus!
I knew I'd seen her before.

The perfect aspect describes events completed before a given point in time.

Grammar: perfect continuous forms
The perfect continuous is formed using the auxiliary *will have/have/had* + *been* + *-ing* form of the verb.

This time next year we'll have been working here for 20 years.
They've been waiting for ages.
She'd been hoping Mark would be there.

The perfect continuous form describes events over a period of time leading up to a point in time. It's not clear if the action is completed, but it's not important. The emphasis is on the length of time the action has been in progress, not whether or not it has been completed.

3

Pairwork. Ask the students to work in pairs and to decide which option is correct in each sentence. Remind them to think about whether the action is completed or ongoing at the specified time.

a) 'd been waiting	d) 've already posted
b) have finished	e) 've been seeing
c) be putting	f) have left

4

Pairwork. Focus attention on the pictures and ask the students to work in pairs to think of suitable ways to complete the thought bubbles. Allow them to compare with other pairs before checking with the class.

a) 'd forgotten	c) haven't even got
b) 'm writing	d) 've only just arrived

5

Groupwork. Put the students into small groups and ask them to discuss the questions. Appoint a spokesperson in each group to report back to the class.

6 Grammar *Extra* 1, Part 2

Ask the students to turn to *Grammar Extra* 1, Part 2 on page 134 of the Student's Book. Here they'll find an explanation of the grammar they've been studying and a further exercise to practise it.

```
2
a)
1  have you been        3  've just arrived
2  've been waiting      4  were just getting /
                            'd just got
b)
5  have you been living / have you lived
6  must have been / must be
7  'll have been
8  are you moving
9  're moving / 'll be moving
```

Useful phrases (SB page 12)

1

Pairwork. Focus the students' attention on the tips for how to start a conversation. Ask them to work in pairs and to read the tips and answer the questions. Encourage them to report back to the class on what they decided. Write any useful language that arises on the board as they'll be asked to compare conversation openers on the recording in Exercise 3 to the ones they came up with here.

2 🌐 1.11

Tell the students that they're going to listen to four conversations and that they should match them to the four situations in Exercise 1. Play the recording, pausing it after each speaker to give the students time to decide which situation it represents.

1 c)	2 d)	3 b)	4 a)

🌐 1.11

1 (S = Sue; J = John)
S: *Hey, John! Fancy meeting you here! How are things?*
J: *Sue? What a surprise. I wasn't expecting to see you here. You look great!*
S: *Thank you! You too. So, what are you doing here? On holiday? On business?*
J: *Yeah, on business. I'm at the conference. I forgot you lived here now. I should have got in touch …*

2 (M = man; W = woman)
M: *Sorry, have you got the time?*
W: *Yeah, just a sec … it's ten past three.*
M: *Shouldn't the number three be here by now?*
W: *Yeah, but it's often a bit late …*
M: *Especially when there's so much traffic.*
W: *Yeah, it's really busy today, there must be something going on in town …*
M: *It's that new exhibition, probably, you know, the travel fair or something …*

3 (J = Jay; R = Ruban)
J: *Hi, you must be Ruben. I've heard a lot about you.*
R: *All good, I hope!*
J: *Of course. I'm Jay, by the way. I work in accounts.*
R: *Hi Jay, pleased to meet you. So, how long have you been here?*
J: *Feels like forever, no, only joking, about three years actually. Before that I was …*

4 (A = Alison; S = Sarah)
A: *Great party, isn't it?*
S: *Yeah.*
A: *So, how do you know Kim?*
S: *We work together.*
A: *Oh really? At the school? Are you a teacher too?*
S: *No, I'm the receptionist.*
A: *Okay. Um, Sarah, right?*
S: *Yes, how did you know?*
A: *Ah, well …*

3

Have a class discussion on whether the conversation openers follow the advice in the tips sheet in Exercise 1. Then ask the students to compare them with the ones they came up with. This will be easy to do if you wrote their suggestions on the board in Exercise 1.

a) yes	b) yes	c) no	d) yes

4

Do the matching part of this exercise as a class, then play the recording again. Put the students into pairs to discuss which responses they prefer.

1 c)	2 a)	3 d)	4 b)

5

- Ask the students to underline the questions in the recording script on pages 146–147.
- Ask them to discuss in pairs which conversation they think is most successful. Make sure they give their reasons.

6

Pairwork. This could be done as a competition to see which pair can come up with the most alternatives within a set time limit.

7

- Give the students time to prepare their conversation openers. Allow them to write them down if it helps, but discourage them from simply reading them out when they're doing the mingling part of the exercise.
- Get the students to mingle and practise starting conversations. Allow time for each conversation to develop before giving the signal to stop. Make sure they are moving on to new partners and starting new conversations with different topics each time.

Vocabulary *Extra* (SB page 13)

Multiple meanings and uses of *talk*

1

Pairwork. Ask the students to work in pairs, read the sayings and discuss the questions.

2

Pairwork. Ask the students to look at the list. You might like to explain that it is part of a concordance, a list of examples of speech and writing, which linguists use to determine how language is actually being used. Point out that the word the researchers are interested in appears in the middle (here it is *talk*) and that the surrounding words give the context for its use. (In a real concordance, the surrounding words do not normally form complete sentences.) Ask the students to identify the part of speech in each sentence.

> verb, verb, noun [C], noun [U], noun [C],
> noun [C], adjective, noun [U], noun [C],
> noun [C], adjective, verb, noun [U], noun [U]

3

- Pairwork. Ask the students to work in pairs to read the sentences in Exercise 2 again and discuss the questions.
- Ask the students to work individually to check their answers in their dictionary and then to find other words formed with *talk*.

> a) talk of the town = everybody was talking about her smooth talker = someone who is very charming and pays lots of compliments
> b) when someone is criticising someone else for doing something that they do as well

4

Ask the students to work individually to complete the sentences.

> a) talks   b) talkative   c) talking

5

Pairwork. Tell students to think about the answers to the questions, then to discuss their answers with their partner.

Further practice material

Need more writing practice?
→ Workbook page 9
- Writing a self-help tip sheet.

Need more classroom practice activities?
→ Photocopiable resource materials pages 157 to 159
   Grammar: *Do I know you?*
   Vocabulary: *Being a man*
   Communication: *Class Q & A*
→ The top 10 activities pages xv to xx

Need DVD material?
→ DVD – Programme 1: *My Girl*

Need progress tests?
→ Test CD – *Test Unit 1*

Need more on important teaching concepts?
→ Key concepts in *New Inside Out* pages xxii to xxxv

Need student self-study practice?
→ CD-ROM – Unit 1: *Conversation*

Need student CEF self-evaluation?
→ CEF Checklists pages xxxvii to xliv

Need more information and more ideas?
→ www.insideout.net

2 Taste *Overview*

Section & Aims	What the students are doing
Speaking SB page 14 Fluency practice	Matching people with different foods. Talking about themselves as if they were a food item.
Listening SB page 14 Listening for detail	Associating situations with particular foods. Listening and matching speakers to situations. Completing descriptions of foods.
Grammar SB page 15 Noun phrases; order of adjectives	Studying the structure and use of noun phrases. Identifying fact and opinion adjectives and studying the order of adjectives.
Reading SB page 16 Reading for detail	Answering questions on the introduction to a restaurant review. Doing a jigsaw reading and discussing shared information.
Vocabulary SB page 17 Describing places to eat	Teaching each other new words and writing sentences using them.
Grammar SB page 18 Fronting	Putting words in order to make sentences. Studying the effect of putting certain parts of a sentence at the beginning. Completing sentences.
Speaking: anecdote SB page 19 Fluency practice	Talking about the last time they ate out.
Writing SB page 19 A restaurant review	Writing a restaurant review.
Listening SB page 20 Listening for gist and for detail	Talking about typical national dishes and local specialities. Listening to people talking about their experiences eating abroad. Listing the food each speaker mentions, then discussing the diet.
Pronunciation SB page 20 Practising sounding more or less enthusiastic	Identifying stress in sentences showing enthusiasm or reservations.
Vocabulary & Speaking SB page 21 Words derived from *taste* and idioms with *taste* Fluency practice	Studying words derived from *taste*. Completing sentences and examining idiomatic sayings with *taste*. Writing a definition of good taste. Discussing whether certain behaviour is socially acceptable.
Useful phrases SB page 22 Useful conversational phrases for agreeing and disagreeing	Matching conversations to topics and people. Completing extracts with useful expressions. Categorising agreeing and disagreeing expressions according to strength. Listening to statements and agreeing or disagreeing with them.
Writing *Extra* SB page 23 Letter to a newspaper	Reading a headline and speculating about the story behind it. Reading a woman's comments in response to a newspaper story. Identifying expressions for agreeing and disagreeing. Writing a reply to the woman's comments.
Writing WB page 15	Writing a letter of complaint.

Warm up

Write *taste* on the board and ask the students what they associate with this word. They'll probably think of food. Find out what things they think taste good. Remind them that you also use *taste* to talk about other preferences, e.g. people's taste in clothes. Ask them how they decide if someone has good or bad taste.

Speaking (SB page 14)

1

- Focus attention on the photos of the people and ask the students to say what they think they are like.
- Go through the instructions and the choices with the class. Explain that 'If you were a food/animal/piece of furniture/sport/car, etc, what would you be' is a game that people sometimes play to convey the essence of their character through the type they choose. Make sure the students know all the foods mentioned.
- Ask the students to decide who gave each of the answers and to be prepared to give reasons for their choices. They can share their ideas in pairs first.
- Have a feedback session with the class before asking them to turn to page 128 to see if they were right. Ask them if they were surprised by the answers.

2

- Ask the students to decide what food they would be and to tell their partner. Encourage them to share any interesting ideas with the class.
- Alternatively, get each student to write on a piece of paper what food they'd be and why (they should not put their names). Collect the pieces of paper, number them and display them on the wall. Let the students mingle and guess who wrote each one. You can then have a vote on who they think it is. The person named can either confirm or deny it.

Listening (SB page 14)

1

- Go through the situations with the class, then put the students into groups and ask them to discuss what kind of food or drink they associate with each one. Remind them to give their reasons.
- Get a spokesperson from each group to report back to the class.

2 🌐 1.12

- Go through the questions with the class before you play the recording so that the students know what information to listen out for. Ask them to write the numbers 1 to 6 on a sheet of paper and make notes for the two questions beside the appropriate numbers.
- Play the recording, pausing after each speaker to give the students time to note down their answers. Allow the students to compare their answers in pairs or small groups before checking with the class. Note that the speakers don't actually name the situations, but there are clues in each speech that point towards a particular situation. You could ask the students to identify what these clues are.

> 1 b) cup of bitter coffee in a plastic cup and milk in plastic containers, a greasy burger on a plastic tray
> 2 d) salad, cheese, bread and a glass of wine
> 3 f) roast lamb with potatoes, peas and gravy
> 4 c) crunchy milk chocolate biscuits and coffee
> 5 a) strawberries and cream, chocolate and fruit
> 6 e) fish and chips, Chinese takeaway, convenience food

> 🌐 1.12
> 1   *b) waiting at bus station*
> *Erm, bitter coffee in a plastic cup and milk in plastic containers. Yeah, either that or a greasy burger on a plastic tray. Looks great in the picture but tastes disgusting and is definitely over-priced.*
>
> 2   *d) summer*
> *Erm … watermelon maybe, or strawberries … no, I know, big bowls of fresh salad with home-made dressing, served with cheese, bread and a glass of chilled white wine.*
>
> 3   *f) gran's house*
> *Roast dinners, you know, huge plates of roast lamb served with mashed potatoes and tiny, sweet green peas, and on top of it all, swimming in it, the best gravy you have ever tasted.*
>
> 4   *c) rainy days*
> *Crunchy milk chocolate biscuits dipped in coffee, curled up on the sofa watching your favourite film.*

> 5   *a) in love*
>
> *No food really, I mean, I associate it more with not being able to eat anything, well, at first at least … and later … maybe chocolate or fruit for some reason … I don't know, something like strawberries, yes, succulent sweet strawberries with fresh cream.*
>
> 6   *c) end of hard day*
>
> *I don't know, hot chocolate? Er, no, fish 'n' chips or a Chinese takeaway – or some kind of microwaveable convenience food that doesn't need any cooking.*

3

Encourage the students to try to do this from memory, but play the recording for them again if they need it and to check their answers.

> a) bi<u>tt</u>er coffee <u>in</u> a <u>pl</u>astic <u>c</u>up
> b) big bowls of <u>fr</u>esh salad <u>with</u> <u>h</u>ome-m<u>a</u>de dressing
> c) huge plates of <u>r</u>oast lamb <u>s</u>erved <u>with</u> <u>m</u>ashed potatoes
> d) the be<u>st</u> gravy <u>you</u> <u>h</u>ave <u>ev</u>er <u>t</u>asted
> e) <u>cr</u>unchy <u>m</u>ilk <u>ch</u>ocolate biscuits <u>d</u>ipped <u>in</u> <u>c</u>offee
> f) <u>s</u>ucculent <u>sw</u>eet strawberries <u>with</u> <u>fr</u>esh <u>cr</u>eam
> g) some kind of <u>m</u>icrowaveable convenience food <u>that</u> <u>d</u>oesn't <u>n</u>eed <u>any</u> <u>c</u>ooking

Grammar (SB page 15)
Noun phrases

1

- Focus attention on the photo and ask the students to decide which description fits it best.
- Have a class discussion of the coffee served in the students' country or countries and that are available where you are now.

> b) the espresso coffee that you can get in the bar round the corner

2

Draw the students' attention to the example noun phrases in the margin and go through the items in the list with the class. Ask the students to identify examples of each of them in the descriptions in Exercise 1. Then get the students to answer the questions underneath the list.

> 1   coffee
> 2   bitter, plastic, strong, black, hot, milky
> 3   vending machine, espresso
> 4   in a plastic cup, in the bar, round the corner, with two or three sugars, in a mug
> 5   that you can get in the bar round the corner
> 6   steaming in a mug
>
> Before the head: 2, 3
> After the head: 4, 5, 6

Noun phrases

A noun phrase is a phrase in which the head is a noun or pronoun. It can be pre-modified (with a determiner or article and an adjective, for example) or post-modified (with a prepositional phrase or relative clause).

pre-modification			head	post-modification
determiner	article	adjective	noun	relative clause
That's	*the*	*new*	*coat*	*that she got with the money*

3

- Put the students into pairs and ask them to put the words and phrases in the exercise in the correct order. Encourage them to read their phrases aloud to try to find what order sounds best. The correct order of adjectives will be addressed in Exercise 5, so don't spend too much time on this here.
- Ask the students to discuss whether they have any of these things for breakfast and get them to write complex noun phrases describing their favourite breakfast food.

> a) a cup of green tea with a slice of lemon
> b) creamy Greek yogurt served with nuts and dried fruit
> c) a pile of freshly-made pancakes dripping with maple syrup
> d) two rashers of bacon cooked to a crisp

4

Read the descriptions to the class or get the students to read them. Then have a class discussion on which appeals most to them right now.

5

- Tell the students to look back at the adjectives in Exercise 4 and answer the questions with regard to these adjectives.
- Focus attention on the section in the margin on the order of adjectives and the description of the onion soup. Get the students to match the adjectives there with the categories in this exercise. (e.g. *delicious* = speaker's opinion; *spicy*, *home-made* = ways it can be prepared; *onion* = basic ingredients).

> a)
> 1   *basic ingredients or qualities:* apple, lemon, Italian
> 2   *ways it can be prepared or served:* home-made, ice-cold, strong
> 3   *the speaker's personal opinion:* delicious, refreshing, strong, wake-me-up (with the last two there might be some discussion as to whether these are objective qualities or subjective opinions)
>
> b) The order is: speaker's opinion, ways it can be prepared or served, basic ingredients or qualities

Grammar: adjective word order

- You might like to explain that whenever we use more than one adjective to describe a noun, the order in which they are placed is more or less fixed (though there can be some variations).
  - size (*large, small*)
  - other qualities (*fresh, frothy, delicious*)
  - age (*old, new*)
  - shape/pattern/colour (*black, cream*)
  - origin (*Italian*)
  - material (*leather*)
  - type (*espresso*)

  So you could say: *A delicious fresh black Italian espresso coffee.*

- Although it's important to understand the order of adjectives, it's worth noting that native speakers would often precede a noun with just two or three adjectives and, on occasions, as many as four. A good rule of thumb is that adjectives expressing an opinion come before adjectives expressing a fact.

6

Tell the students to use the information they've learnt about the order of adjectives to complete the menu descriptions. Check answers before having a discussion about which dish they'd most like to try.

> a) a selection of delicious, local, French cheeses
> b) a bowl of tasty, piping-hot, clam chowder
> c) half a dozen exquisite, grilled, freshwater crayfish
> d) a mouth-watering, savoury, vegetable pancake

7

Ask the students to identify the two noun phrases in the sentence (the restaurant, food). Put them into groups and ask them to add further elements to the two noun phrases to make the sentence as long as they possibly can. Tell them they have three minutes to do this and the group with the longest sentence will be the winner.

Extra activity

Write the sentence *The girl was eating an apple* on the board. Divide the class into teams and get the teams to take turns reading the sentence aloud, each time adding an extra element to one of the two noun phrases. Each team should include the modifications made by the other teams. Set a time limit for them to discuss what they're going to add each time. Any team that cannot add anything or forgets any of the elements added previously is out.

8 Grammar *Extra* 2

Ask the students to turn to *Grammar Extra* 2, Part 1 on page 134 of the Student's Book. Here they'll find an explanation of the grammar they've been studying and a further exercise to practise it.

1
a) A battered old bike covered in rust.
b) An action-packed thriller with a great soundtrack.
c) A moving story about a man with no home.
d) A pair of black high-heeled shoes I wear to work.
e) An espresso in the Italian sandwich bar that makes the best coffee in the world. / An Italian sandwich bar that makes the best espresso coffee in the world.
f) A new seafood restaurant serving a wide range of Asian dishes / A new Asian restaurant serving a wide range of seafood dishes.

Reading (SB page 16)

Warm up

Ask the students to work in pairs and to tell their partner about their favourite restaurant. Keep the discussion fairly short as they'll have the opportunity to talk at length about the last time they ate out in the Anecdote activity on page 19.

1

Allow the students plenty of time to read the text and the questions. Point out that this is just the introduction to a restaurant review; they will be reading the rest of the review later.

> a) ten years ago
> b) located on a small island, access to the restaurant by boat, no advance bookings, only building on the island, limited menu which is different every day, only four tables, it was extremely cheap for such an excellent meal
> c) Students' own answers.

Cultural note

La Traviata /læ ˈtrævɪːætæ/
An opera by Italian composer Giuseppe Verdi, first performed in 1854. It is based on a novel by Alexandre Dumas, published in 1848.

2

- Pairwork. Put the students into pairs and ask them to discuss the questions.
- Encourage the students to report back to the class and make a list of their proposed changes on the board.

3

- Divide the students into two groups and get Group A to read the text on page 17 and Group B the text on page 128. Give them plenty of time to read, discuss and make notes on the items listed. Make sure every student in the group makes a copy of the group's notes.

- With large classes you could have several groups, but make sure there are an equal number of students in each group so that each A student can pair up with a B student in the next exercise.

> **Group A**
> a) The village had become a town. There was a new sign with the restaurant's name in lights. There wasn't any wine served from a barrel anymore
> b) The small bar had been replaced by a large, noisy one which was very busy and catered to more than the restaurant customers, everything looked very efficient.
> c) The small launch had been replaced by a large motor boat; the journey was quick, but the treatment was very impersonal. They were taken to the island by a smart boat crew rather than just by Marianne, and conversation was replaced by music.
>
> **Group B**
> a) There were lots more tables, with paper tablecloths rather than linen ones, on a large concrete terrace in the sun. There were lots of waiters running around. The waiters were aggressive and spoke English to them. There was a large kitchen with four chefs and the family were not there.
> b) The bread wasn't home-made and the squid was battered and served with chips. There was a fixed menu including ingredients which were not from the island.
> c) It had disappeared and been replaced by hotel rooms. *vegetable garden*

4

Pairwork. Put the students into pairs so that each student in each pair was in a different group for Exercise 3. Tell them to close their books and tell their partners about the changes to the restaurant that they read about. Encourage them to use their notes as a prompt, but not to simply read them out.

5

Pairwork. Keep the students in the same pairs and ask them to discuss the questions. Go round monitoring and giving help with vocabulary where needed. Encourage them to report back to the class on what they discussed.

Vocabulary (SB page 17)

1

- Pairwork. Put the students in pairs, making sure both students in each pair read the same section of the restaurant review.
- Ask them to follow the instructions, finding the target words in their text and discussing their meaning with their partner. Emphasise that they need to think about the best way to explain these words to someone who hasn't read the text.

> **Group A**
> blared out – played very loudly
> bobbing – moving gently up and down on water
> clientele – the customers of a bar, restaurant, shop or hotel
> exquisite – extremely delicate and well-prepared
> launch – a small, open boat
> pricey – expensive
> sped off – departed at speed
> thriving – very busy and successful
>
> **Group B**
> batter – a mixture of milk, flour and eggs used in cooking, especially to coat something which you are going to deep fry
> chug – to move slowly making a series of low sounds
> concrete – a material used for building
> entrepreneur – someone who sets up and runs businesses
> homely – simple and pleasant in a way that makes us feel comfortable and at home
> reverie – pleasant thoughts that help you forget what you are doing and what is happening around you
> satnav – a system for finding the best way to a place using satellite information, usually used in cars
> thrust – to put something somewhere with a quick, hard push

2

- Pairwork. Form new pairs, making sure that each student in a pair read a different section of the restaurant review. Tell them to take turns teaching their partners the words they looked at in Exercise 1. They should explain the meaning of the words and then, when they are sure that their partner has understood, ask them to write sentences using the new words.
- When both students have written their sentences, ask them to check their partner's work and make sure the words have been used correctly. Go round assisting where necessary.
- Check answers by having several students from each group read out their sentences.

Grammar (SB page 18)

Fronting

1

Encourage the students to do the reordering without looking back at the restaurant review. Do not alert them to the fact that in the text they are ordered differently from standard English word order.

Note: these answers show first standard English word order and then the order used in the restaurant review.

a) The family lived on the upper floors. / On the upper floors lived the family.

b) A large bar stood at the edge of the water. / At the edge of the water stood a large bar.

c) The opportunity to chat with Marianne was gone. / Gone was the opportunity to chat with Marianne.

d) The waiters ran between the tables. / Between the tables ran the waiters.

e) There was a basket on the paper tablecloth. / On the paper tablecloth there was a basket.

2

• Pairwork. Ask the students to look back at the review to check their answers.

• Ask them to answer the questions. When you're checking answers, tell them that standard word order is correct but explain that the word order here is used for special effect. Draw their attention to the further examples in the margin.

a) Students' own answers.

b) Subject and verb are inverted.

c) Sentence e – there

d) The effect is to emphasize the part of the sentence that is placed first and to create dramatic effect:

a) location – emphasizes the description of the place

b) location – see a)

c) the past participle, gone – emphasizes the change

d) the manner of running – emphasizes how busy they were

e) position – see a)

Language note

Grammar: fronting

When fronting, the speaker inverts the sentence and starts it with either a complement, object or adverb (for emphasis), reversing the subject and verb. It's a device used mainly by writers for dramatic effect. It isn't commonly used in everyday speech.

Compare:

(1) *The gaunt expression was gone. The lines under his eyes were gone.*

(2) *Gone was the gaunt expression. Gone were the lines under his eyes.*

3

Ask the students to work individually to rewrite the sentences, but allow them to compare in pairs before checking with the class.

a) Gone was the peaceful little restaurant we once knew.

b) In its place (there) was a modern monstrosity.

c) When exactly the change took place, we didn't know.

d) Above the restaurant lived the chef.

e) Down to the beach went the path lit by small twinkling candles.

f) Home we went, tired and hungry.

4

• Ask the students to complete the sentences with memories of a place from their past. Go round giving help where needed.

• Pairwork. Ask the students to compare their sentences and take turns asking for more information about any changes that have been made to the place. Encourage them to report back to the class on their discussions and get a few students to read their sentences to the class.

5 Grammar *Extra* 2

Ask the students to turn to *Grammar Extra* 2, Part 2 on page 134 of the Student's Book. Here they'll find an explanation of the grammar they've been studying and a further exercise to practise it.

2

a) Down came the curtains on her last act.

b) Gone had her long blonde locks.

c) In her eyes (there) was a special light.

d) Still intact was her youthful beauty.

e) Loudly rang applause through the theatre. / Loudly through the theatre rang applause.

f) No-one else was on the stage with her as she took her last bow.

g) What would become of her, no-one knew.

Speaking: anecdote (SB page 19)

For more information about how to set up, monitor and repeat Anecdotes, see page xx in the Introduction.

• Go through the instructions and the questions with the class. Give the students a minute or two to decide which restaurant they're going to talk about. Then ask them to look at the questions and think about their answers to them. Allow them to make notes of what they're going to say and how they're going to say it, but discourage them from writing a paragraph that they can simply read out. Go round, monitoring and giving help where necessary.

• Pairwork. Put the students in pairs and ask them to take turns to tell their partner about the last time they ate out at a restaurant. Encourage them to ask each other follow-up questions to get further information. Ask some pairs to report back to the class about what they found out.

Writing (SB page 19)

1

The writing of the restaurant review could be done for homework. Give the students time to think about what they're going to write and the language they'll need. Encourage them to make notes and to ask you for help with vocabulary. Remind them to decide what order to present the information in.

2

Ask the students to write their reviews. If you do this in class, go round giving help and advice.

3

Groupwork. Put the students into small groups and ask them to exchange their reviews. They could take turns to read their reviews aloud to the group. Ask them to guess what kind of person each review was written for. The student who wrote the review should say whether or not they are correct. Finally, encourage the group to decide which of the restaurants reviewed they'd like to go to.

Listening (SB page 20)

1

- Focus attention on the photos in the margin and ask the students to identify which countries the dishes shown come from (sushi – Japan; burger – anywhere, but perhaps the USA; tacos – Mexico). Then ask the students to say what dishes are typical of their country or countries. *Chinese or Thai?*

- Put them into groups and ask them to think of a typical dishes for as many countries as they can in three minutes.

2

Ask the groups share their lists of dishes with the class. Then discuss the three questions with the students.

3 🌐 1.13–1.16

- Explain that the students are going to hear four people talking about their experiences of eating abroad. Before they listen, make sure they understand that these aren't meant to be definitive descriptions of the local cuisine, but subjective opinions, which the students are free to disagree with if they wish.

- Ask them to write the names of the people on a piece of paper and note down next to each name whether or not they liked the food. Play the recording, pausing after each speaker to give the students time to decide if the speaker liked the food or not.

- Play the recording again and ask the students to note down next to each name all the food vocabulary the speaker uses. You may need to play the recording more than once and pause it between speakers to allow the students time to do this.

They all liked the food except for Bill.

Anne: hot, spicy, delicate, flavours, lemon grass, coconut, fish, soups, meat, big, fat, yellowish noodles, tubs of spices

Kim: hot, spicy, a huge helping of rice, sauces, balls of rice, leftovers

Bill: fried, cooked in pig's fat, cabbage, pickled, served with sour cream, bread – soft and tasty, scones, pastries, goulash, bean soups, paprika, spicy

Steve: seafood, shellfish, grilled green chili peppers, spicy, various different specialities

---

🌐 **1.13**
Anne

The food? Mmm, it's superb, really hot and spicy, but quite delicate too. Kind of like a cross between Indian and Chinese food but with its own special flavours too. They use a lot of lemon grass and coconut and a lot of fish. I really liked the soups. You can buy them from stalls on the corner of the street. You choose the meat you want in your soup and the kind of noodles – long thin white rice noodles, or big fat, thick yellowish ones, and there are these tubs of spices too, and you choose as much or as little of whatever you want. Then you sit there on the street, or in the market or wherever you are, and eat it. I had some for breakfast one day – it was great! Really great!

🌐 **1.14**
Kim

The food? Well, it took a bit of getting used to actually. I like hot, spicy food, but this was too much for me at the beginning. I reckon I built up a kind of immunity to it as time went by though and I got to like it by the end. It's nothing like the kind of food we get in restaurants back home. I loved the ritual of it, going to the small street cafés where they serve your food on a banana leaf. They wash the leaf and then serve a huge helping of rice right in the middle and give you generous helpings of all the various different sauces on offer that day. You don't get a knife and a fork. You eat with your right hand, making little balls of rice and then soaking up the sauce with these little balls – it takes quite a long time to get good at it. When you've finished, they bundle the banana leaf up with any leftovers and throw it out on the street, where the goats and cows eat them. I love that side of it too – nothing goes to waste!

🌐 **1.15**
Bill

The food? Well, to tell you the truth, I didn't really like it that much. It isn't the healthiest of diets. Everything is either fried or cooked in pig's fat and, hmm, I don't really like cabbage that much and that's a staple part of their diet, like a lot of places in Central Europe. It's usually pickled and served with sour cream – so, no, it isn't really my favourite. Having said that, there were some things I loved – the bread, for example, it's really soft and tasty, and so many different kinds, and the scones, and pastries too, are really good. And some of the soups, the various kinds of goulash – that's their national dish – and the bean soups are really delicious and the paprika makes them quite spicy – great on a cold day.

1.16

Steve

The food? It isn't particularly elaborate, but it's good. The seafood is especially good, and there's just such a variety, so many different kinds of shellfish, I wouldn't know the names for half of them in English. Another favourite of mine is the grilled green chilli peppers. They serve them up by the plateful to be shared between friends over a beer or two. There's always one that's so spicy it almost blows your head off. More than anything else I love the eating out culture. It's quite informal, you go to a bar and order huge platefuls of various different specialities and share them, everybody eating off the same plates. It's very sociable – a really nice social eating ritual.

4

Pairwork. Put the students into pairs and ask them to compare the lists of food vocabulary they made in Exercise 3. Ask them to discuss the questions. Encourage them to make a guess for each country before they look up the answers to the first question on page 128. Encourage the pairs to report back to the class on their discussion.

Pronunciation (SB page 20)

1 🔘 **1.17**

- Explain *reservations* (doubts about something). Ask the students to read the extracts and decide which of the words the speakers stressed to express enthusiasm or reservations. Encourage them to read the extracts aloud as they do this so they get a feeling for what effect stressing different words has on the meaning.

- Play the recording for the students to check their answers. Then play it again and encourage them to say the phrases at the same time as the speakers, copying their intonation.

> a) <u>Mmm</u>, it's <u>superb</u>, <u>really</u> hot and spicy …
> b) Well, it took a bit of getting used to <u>actually</u>.
> c) Well, to tell you the truth, I didn't <u>really</u> like it that much.
> d) … and hmm, I don't <u>really</u> like cabbage that much …
> e) … no, it isn't <u>really</u> my favourite.
> f) It isn't <u>particularly</u> elaborate, but it's good.

Language note

Pronunciation: intonation to show enthusiasm or reservation

In this section you hear people expressing enthusiasm by stressing key words with a rising tone, and people expressing their reservations by once more stressing certain words, but this time with a falling tone. The use of *really* to show enthusiasm is very typical and *not really, not particularly* and *actually* (at the beginning or end of a sentence) when expressing reservation.

2

- Go through the list of uses with the class and ask them to look at the words and sounds they underlined in Exercise 1. Play the recording again and ask them to match the stressed words and sounds to the uses.

- Point out that *really* can be matched with all the uses and that the intonation which is used when saying it has a profound effect on its meaning.

> a) Mmm, superb, really   c) really, particularly
> b) actually, really   d) really

3

Pairwork. Ask the students to discuss the questions and report back to the class.

> a) An enthusiastic tone rises, a reserved tone falls.
> b) Students' own answers.
> c) *Suggested answers:*
>   facial expressions, hand gestures, body language

4

- Pairwork. Read the original two dialogues to the class in a neutral tone. Then ask the students to discuss in pairs how they could be made to sound more enthusiastic or less enthusiastic. Point out that they can add words and sounds and use the other techniques they've just studied.

- Get them to practise saying the conversations aloud in their pairs, using the techniques they've decided on. Then ask them to perform them for the class.

Vocabulary & Speaking (SB page 21)

1

- Groupwork. Write the word *taste* on the board and ask the students to suggest some example sentences using it. Then put them into groups and ask them to answer the questions.

- Ask a spokesperson from each group to report back to the class on what they found out. You may need to feed in a few more *taste* words or idioms.

> *Possible answers:*
> a) taste buds, tasty, taster, (wine) tasting, tasteful, tasteless, tastefully, tastelessly, distasteful
> b) **adjectives:** good, bad, poor, impeccable, unusual, authentic, acquired, personal, questionable, bitter, sweet, real, fresh, nasty, sour, delicious, strong
>   **verbs:** acquire, develop, have, share, give, get, know, leave, linger
> c) Students' own answers.
> d) get a taste of your own medicine, leave a bad taste in your mouth, be in bad/poor taste, a question of taste, in the best possible taste, there is no accounting for taste, taste victory/defeat, a taste of freedom

Vocabulary: word formation and *taste* collocations

Taste can be the root word of two adjectives with different meaning: *tasteful* (+ -*ful*), which means showing good judgment about what is attractive or suitable, and *tasty* (+ -*y*), which means it has good flavour:

- *Tastefully, There's no accounting for taste* and *In poor/bad taste* are from the first meaning of *taste*.

- *Tasteless* and *an acquired taste* can refer to both meanings of taste.

- *Taste victory* (to experience victory for a short time), *give someone a taste/dose of their own medicine* (to treat someone in the same bad way that they've treated someone else) and *leave a bad/nasty taste* (often followed by *in your mouth* means you continue to feel unhappy or angry about it for a while*) refer to the 'flavour' meaning of *taste*.

2

- Ask the students to complete the sentences with the words and expressions in the box. Then allow them to compare their sentences with a partner before checking answers with the class.

- Have a class discussion on whether similar idiomatic sayings with taste are used in the students' own language(s).

a) tasty	f) of her own medicine
b) acquired	g) bad taste
c) tastefully	h) poor taste
d) share	i) accounting
e) tasteless	j) victory/success

3

- Pairwork. Ask the students to work together to write a short definition of good taste (remind them that the expression doesn't just refer to food).

- Get the pairs to read out their definitions to the class and have a vote on which one the students like best.

> *Suggested answer:*
> The ability to judge if something is good or bad in things like art, fashion and social behaviour.

4

Ask the students to work individually and to think about their own opinions on these things.

5

Pairwork. Put the students into pairs and ask them to compare their views on the things in Exercise 4. Ask them to discuss the questions and prepare to report back to the class on their ideas. Find out if the students think that age plays a large part in whether people find certain kinds of behaviour acceptable or not.

Useful phrases (SB page 22)

1 🌐 1.18–1.20

Go through the tasks with the class before you play the recording to make sure they know what to do. Then play the recording and ask the students to listen and note down their answers.

a) 1 c	2 a	3 b	
b) 1 b	2 c	3 a	

🌐 1.18 (J = John; M = Mrs Dersty)

Conversation 1

M: Hello?

J: Hello. This is accounts. Could I speak to Mrs Dersty?

M: Speaking.

J: I have your expense claim form here, but I'm afraid we won't be able to reimburse your dining expenses.

M: Oh, and why is that?

J: Because you could have used the company's dining facilities.

M: Yes, but it was a breakfast meeting with a client.

J: That may be, but it's company policy.

M: I think you'll find that it's only company policy if we're entertaining in-house guests.

J: I see. Well, we'll need to double-check that and get back to you.

🌐 1.19 (G = Girl; M = Mother)

Conversation 2

G: You bought strawberries?

M: Yes, what's wrong with that?

G: But they're out of season!

M: So what if they're out of season?

G: Well, apart from the fact that it doesn't help the environment, imported fruit doesn't taste as good.

M: That's a load of rubbish. These strawberries are absolutely delicious!

G: Yeah, but how much did they cost?

M: They were on offer.

G: Yeah, but they must have cost a fortune. Imported from Spain! What about the environment?

M: Okay, okay, I suppose you're right, it's not brilliant for the environment, but I couldn't resist them.

🌐 1.20 (A = Anna; B = Ben)

Conversation 3

A: I can't believe he got her a Hoover for her birthday.

B: Oh, I don't know. It's the thought that counts.

A: No! Come on! He couldn't have given it much thought, if that's all he came up with.

B: You gave me a drill on my last birthday!

A: So?

B: I rest my case.

2

- Pairwork. Ask the students to discuss in pairs what each pair of speakers is disagreeing about.
- Play the recording again for them to check their answers.

> 1 They're disagreeing about whether or not the woman can claim a business breakfast on expenses.
> 2 They're disagreeing about buying strawberries out of season.
> 3 They're disagreeing about whether a vacuum cleaner is a good birthday present.

3

- Ask the students to complete the extracts with the phrases in the box. Allow them to compare with a partner before checking with the class. You could play the recording again for them to check their answers.
- Point out that all these expressions are useful for agreeing and disagreeing – in English people rarely say simply *I agree* or *I disagree*; there are many different expressions and ways to signal agreement and disagreement.

> a) 1 That may be but
>   2 I think you'll find
> b) 1 That's a load of rubbish
>   2 I suppose you're right
> c) 1 Oh, I don't know
>   2 I rest my case

Language note

Vocabulary: *I rest my case*
I rest my case is an expression from the legal profession, used when a lawyer feels that there's nothing more to be said and he or she has argued the case sufficiently to win. In everyday speech, it's often used when someone in a disagreement says something which can be construed to support the other person's point of view. Here, the woman's response (*So?*) to the man's point that she gave him a drill for his last birthday indicates to him that she's in effect admitting that giving someone a tool as a birthday present is acceptable.

4

Pairwork. Ask the students to work with their partner and complete the table with the expressions from Exercise 3.

Language notes

Vocabulary: useful phrases – agreeing and disagreeing

- Other ways of showing strong agreement include: *I couldn't agree more* and *Exactly!* Other ways of showing strong disagreement include: *That's nonsense* and *Oh, come on! / Oh, come off it!*

- Agreeing or disagreeing reluctantly is as much about intonation as it is about the words used. Sounding hesitant or tentative will do the trick, even if you don't say anything – just make *mm* sounds.

> **Agreement**
> Strong: I know it's awful, isn't it?
> Reluctant: I suppose you're right.
>
> **Disagreement**
> Strong: That can't be. No way! That's a load of rubbish!
> Polite: I think you'll find …, That may be but …, Oh, I don't know.
>
> **Closing an argument**
> Polite: I rest my case.

5 🌐 1.21

Go through the instructions with the class before you play the recording. Get them to write the three categories on a piece of paper before they listen so that they only have to write the number of the speaker next to the relevant category each time.

> Uncertain – 1 (*Yes*); 4 (*No*)
> In total agreement – 2 (*Yes*)
> In total disagreement – 3 (*No*)

6 🌐 1.22

- Pairwork. Put the students in pairs and ask them to take turns being the person who responds to the sentences on the recording and the person who identifies the nature of the response.
- Play the recording twice so that each student in the pair has an opportunity to respond to the sentences.

> 🌐 1.22
> a) *The best way to eat fish is raw.*
> b) *French cuisine is the best in the world.*
> c) *People who smoke in restaurants are inconsiderate.*
> d) *If you want to get to the top, you have to start at the bottom.*
> e) *Life is too short to waste time worrying about what other people think.*
> f) *Travel is the best way of broadening the mind.*

7

Groupwork. Put the students in groups and ask them to discuss two or three of the statements from Exercise 6, using the useful phrases to agree and disagree with them.

Writing *Extra* (SB page 23)

Letter to a newspaper

1

Groupwork. Ask the students to work in groups. Tell them to look at the photos and discuss the questions.

2

Ask the students to read the headline and speculate on what the story might be about. Encourage the use of speculative language, such as *It might be … The school could have … Perhaps … Maybe …*, etc.

3

- Give the students time to read the text and ask them to say how they'd describe her reaction. Make sure they understand all the choices (moderate = not extreme; reasoned = sensible and logical).
- Elicit other possible adjectives from the class.
- Ask the students for their own reactions to the woman's letter and to the ban on baggy, ripped and super-skinny jeans.

> *Suggested answers:*
> c) and d)
> Other adjectives: pompous, disapproving, opinionated, frustrated

4

Ask the students to read the text again and look for examples of language used to convey the features listed.

Expressing agreement or approval:	It's good to see that … I'm really pleased to see I'm not the only one …
Accepting someone's arguments without necessarily agreeing with them:	I do, of course, respect … Having said that …
Expressing disagreement or disapproval:	I'm sick and tired of … I would draw the line …

5

Ask the students to add the new expressions to the table in Exercise 4.

Expressing agreement or approval:	I can sympathise with the view that … I couldn't agree more.
Accepting someone's arguments without necessarily agreeing:	Whilst not in total agreement with … There is no doubt some truth in … However, …
Expressing disagreement or disapproval:	I take exception to … I find it hard to believe that …

6

The letter writing could be done for homework and the results displayed in a future lesson for the other students to read. If you do it in class, go round giving help and advice. Encourage the students to use as many of the expressions in Exercises 4 and 5 as they can.

Further practice material

Need more writing practice?
➜ Workbook page 15
- Writing a letter of complaint.

Need more classroom practice activities?
➜ Photocopiable resource materials pages 160 to 162
  Grammar: *A bunch of partitives*
  Vocabulary: *Mineral or tap?*
  Communication: *Food for thought*
➜ The top 10 activities pages xv to xx

Need DVD material?
➜ DVD – Programme 2: *A favourite restaurant*

Need progress tests?
➜ Test CD – *Test Unit 2*

Need more on important teaching concepts?
➜ Key concepts in *New Inside Out* pages xxii to xxxv

Need student self-study practice?
➜ CD-ROM – Unit 2: *Taste*

Need student CEF self-evaluation?
➜ CEF Checklists pages xxxvii to xliv

Need more information and more ideas?
➜ www.insideout.net

3 City Overview

Section & Aims	What the students are doing
Listening SB page 24 Listening for specific information	Doing a quiz and listening to a radio programme to find out the answers. Replacing words in sentences with those used by a speaker.
Grammar SB page 25 Hedging	Studying hedging expressions. Rewriting sentences using hedging expressions. Listening to a discussion about a news story. Then writing the story.
Speaking SB page 26 Fluency practice	Discussing capital cities and the places where they live.
Reading SB page 27 Reading for gist and detail	Reading guide book extracts and identifying the places described. Discussing elements of descriptions that they like.
Vocabulary SB page 27 Describing cities	Matching adjectives to definitions. Finding adjectives in a text and identifying what they're describing. Matching halves of collocations and completing sentences with them.
Grammar SB page 28 Inversion after negative and limiting adverbials	Identifying adverbials with negative or limiting meanings. Rewriting sentences using inversion and matching places to the sentences.
Writing SB page 28 Describing a famous town or city	Writing a short description of a famous town or city in their country. Identifying the places described by other students.
Speaking SB page 29 Fluency practice	Discussing tourism posters. Listing possible tourist attractions and discussing the top three. Discussing a city in their country.
Reading & Vocabulary SB page 30 Reading for detail Words from the article	Reading an article about Leicester Square in London. Adding words and expressions to the article. Teaching each other some words from the article. Discussing nightspots.
Listening & Speaking SB page 31 Listening for detail	Discussing the dangers of city life. Listening to friends talking about the dangers of city life. Giving advice to people visiting their hometown or going abroad.
Pronunciation SB page 31 Intonation for adding emphasis	Completing extracts from a conversation with *just*, *really* and *actually*. Practising using *just*, *really* and *actually* with the correct intonation.
Useful phrases SB page 32 Useful conversational phrases for adding emphasis	Reading a blog about a building and discussing opinions. Matching language used for emphasis with rules. Adding emphasis to sentences and marking the main stress. Talking about buildings using emphasis.
Vocabulary *Extra* SB page 33 Lexical sets and collocations with *city* and *urban*	Using nouns and adjectives to describe photos. Studying words used to describe settlements of different sizes. Completing sentences with collocations.
Writing WB page 21	Writing a short article.

Warm up

Before the students open their books, ask them to call out the names of as many capital cities as they can in one minute. Write them up on the board, emphasizing the pronunciation and main stress. Then ask questions, e.g. *Which countries are they in? Which is the most polluted?*

Listening (SB page 24)

1 🌐 1.23

- Focus the students' attention on the photo and ask them where they think it is (New York). Tell them to do the quiz and then allow them to compare answers in pairs.

- Then play the recording for the students to check their answers. (Warn them that they're going to hear part of a radio programme in which the answers are given so they won't just hear the answers read out.) When you've checked answers, find out if the students were surprised by any of the information.

1 d)	2 a)/c	3 a)	4 b)	5 a)	6 d)

🌐 1.23 (M = Mike; S = Sue)

M: *Thank you John, and now it's back to the studio for the answers to last week's quiz. Sue?*

S: *Thanks, Mike. Hello, yes, and there are a few surprises in the answers this week. So, let's start with the first question, which I think held the biggest surprise for our contestants.*

According to data collected by the UN, 53% of the world's population live in cities, whilst 47% live in rural areas. In the EU the percentage of people living in urban centres rises to a staggering 74% and an even higher 87% in the USA. It would appear that there is a steady movement towards urban areas and that the proportion of city dwellers will continue to rise.

Although it may seem a fairly straightforward question to answer, there is still some discussion as to which is the world's largest capital. This is mainly due to the difficulty in deciding where the world's largest cities actually end as they all tend to be surrounded by a mass of satellite towns which all merge into one large agglomeration. If we take 'city' to mean a metropolitan area, then Tokyo, with a population of more than 32 million, is easily the world's largest capital city. Mexico City and Seoul both vie for second position with populations of just over 20 million.

Likewise, it is very difficult to tell which is Europe's noisiest capital, mainly as there don't seem to be any standardised noise pollution measurements across the countries of the EU, and very few exhaustive studies have been carried out. However, it is widely recognised that Athens is the European capital which suffers from the worst noise pollution levels. It's not known whether this information is based on popular opinion or on statistical data from the Greek authorities, although a recent government report seems to suggest that it's true. Judging from the entries we've received, this will come as quite a surprise to some of our listeners.

On to the fourth question. There is still some debate over this one. The Syrians claim that their capital city, Damascus, is the world's oldest city, though other Middle Eastern inhabitants would claim that their capitals are just as old. Sources seem to suggest that the Syrians are right and that their capital is indeed the oldest in the world, having been continuously inhabited since 5000 BC.

Question five was pretty straightforward. There is no doubt whatsoever about which of the world's capital cities is the highest. La Paz, in the Bolivian Andes, stands four kilometres above sea level.

And finally, the last question, again a fairly straightforward question. The first city to have reached a population of 1,000,000 was Rome, which had a population of over a million during the heyday of the Roman Empire in 133 BC. London reached the mark in 1810 and New York in 1875. Today there are over 300 cities in the world that boast a population in excess of one million.

So, the winners this week are, Jane Turbot from Whitstable in Kent, Carol Jackson from St Andrews …

2

Go through the sentences with the class and make sure that everyone understands that they have to find alternative words in the recording for the words and expressions in italics. Play the recording again. If the students are having difficulty, pause it after the answer to each question is given to give them time to write down their answers, and be prepared to play it several times.

a) would appear	d) not known
b) discussion	e) seem
c) widely recognised	f) no doubt whatsoever

1

Pairwork. Put the students into pairs and ask them to categorise the expressions. Explain that these expressions are *hedges*: words or phrases that are used to soften opinions and make statements less forceful or assertive. They're often used in newspaper articles. Go through the information on hedges in the margin, pointing out that there are various ways of making statements less categorical.

> a) no doubt whatsoever
> b) widely recognised
> c) would appear, seem, discussion
> d) it's not known

Language notes

Hedging
When you don't want to state a fact or opinion too categorically (if you're not sure you can prove that it's true), you can use a number of expressions that distance yourself from it. This is called hedging.

- **Hedging with verbs**
  You can use *appear (that)* and *seem (that)* to create a distance between yourself and what is said.
  It **seems that** *most people enjoy life in the country.*
  It **appears that** *older people like city life less than young people.*

- **Adding distance with *would***
  To add further distance you can use the modal verb *would*:
  It **would seem that** *there is less violent crime in the country.*
  It **would appear that** *life is less stimulating in the country.*

- **Hedging with the passive voice**
  You can use the passive voice of the verb to show that an opinion isn't necessarily your own:
  It **is widely recognised** *that people from the country are healthier than people who live in the city.*
  There **are not believed** *to be as many crimes in the country.*
  It **is not known** *whether people would consider changing their living circumstances.*

- **Hedging with noun phrases**
  You can also use the following noun phrases to hedge around a subject:
  There is little / no doubt that *the country offers a healthier lifestyle.*
  There is some doubt that *the country can manage its ever-expanding population.*
  There is little evidence of *the government's ability to manage change.*

2

- Focus attention on the results of the two surveys and give the students time to read them and take in the information. Then ask them to read the sentences and decide if they are true or false. They should correct any false ones they find.

- Check answers. Then ask the students to discuss whether they think the results would be the same in their country.

> a) False. Both surveys show that a significant percentage of people who live in the country would prefer to live in a city.
> b) False. The percentages quoted are reasonably significant (35% / 43%). It would be more accurate to say a significant number (more than a third) of people who live in cities would prefer to live in the country.
> c) False. The first report suggests that more than half the people who live in the country would prefer to live in the city.
> d) False. The second survey suggests that most people who live in the country are happy to stay there.
> e) ~~False~~ True. There is no evidence given in the surveys to back up this statement.

3

Ask the students to work individually to underline all the hedging expressions in the sentences in Exercise 2. Allow them to compare in pairs before checking with the class. Remind the students of the many different ways of hedging.

> a) It seems that
> b) it appears that
> c) seem to suggest
> d) would seem to show
> e) are not believed, there is little evidence

4

- Pairwork. Put the students into pairs and ask them to rewrite the statements using hedging expressions.

- Check answers by getting the pairs to read out their statements and then have a discussion on whether or not they agree with them.

> *Suggested answers:*
> a) It would seem that most young people prefer to live in large cities because of the job opportunities.
> b) There is little doubt that older people living on their own get very lonely in big cities.
> c) There is some discussion about whether people who live in the country are generally more healthy than city dwellers.
> d) It would not appear that life in the country is much less stimulating than life in a big city.
> e) It is generally accepted that there is far less violent crime in the country.
> f) There is little evidence that people suffer from sleep deprivation in big cities.

5 🌐 1.24

- Go through the instructions with the class, then play the recording. Ask them to take notes as they listen on the reasons young people prefer living in cities.

- Ask them to use their notes to make sentences giving the reasons.

> They prefer to live in a city because it's easier to find jobs; there's a better social life – nightlife, music, youth culture; there are more opportunities for continuing their education, facilities for their future families and there are better living conditions.

🌐 **1.24** (S = Sharon; D = Derek)

S: *Have you seen this? The article about that new survey …*

D: *Yes, I was reading it earlier. No surprises there, I don't think … seems pretty obvious to me. You don't need a survey to tell you that, do you?*

S: *Yeah, well, I don't know, I mean, it's not that simple is it? I mean, some people like living in the country …*

D: *Yeah, and you can see why; less stress, less traffic, less smog … but I don't think it's just a simple question of what you like, you know …*

S: *No, it's more like … well, it seems like it's a question of work and money more than anything else, I mean …*

D: *Yeah, it said that, didn't it? The main reason was that they couldn't find a job in the country …*

S: *Well, it doesn't say that exactly, but yes, it says it's, er, it's, you know, easier to find work in large cities and I reckon that's true. Don't you?*

D: *Yeah, but I don't think that's the main reason. I mean, it might be the main reason for older people … you know, no jobs, rural unemployment, whatever …*

S: *Yeah, there's a lot of that …*

D: *But it seems to be talking more about young people … I mean, the statistics here are referring to people under thirty and you know, I reckon that even if, even if there were plenty of jobs in the rural areas, well, they'd still go to the cities, wouldn't they?*

S: *Do you think so? Maybe you're right. Maybe it's more a kind of lure of the bright lights thing …*

D: *Yeah, you know, nightlife, music, youth culture in general …*

S: *Yeah, it says something about that, doesn't it? That bit where it talks about, what is it … 'leisure time activities' or something like that?*

D: *'Free time facilities'.*

S: *Yeah, that was it.*

D: *… pubs and clubs more like!*

S: *Yeah, and cinemas and exhibitions and stuff as well …*

D: *No, discos and the chance to meet other young people more like …*

S: *Yeah, okay, the social side of things, but it's important, isn't it?*

D: *Yeah, this survey seems to reckon it's the second most important factor, in fact, after getting a job. You know, if young people decide to leave their homes in the country, then they reckon the social side of things is the second most important thing they consider. What other things do you think they mentioned?*

S: *Oh, I don't know. Maybe they said there were more opportunities for continuing their education, like going to colleges and stuff. They might be thinking about facilities for their families in the future, like being near good schools and stuff. Um, what about better living conditions … more modern houses which need less work doing to them and stuff?*

D: *Yeah, I suppose they're all things you'd have to think about, aren't they?*

S: *Yeah, the survey makes quite a lot of sense.*

D: *Hmm.*

6

Pairwork. Ask the students to work together to write the story from the newspaper that the people in Exercise 5 were discussing. Remind them that they have a limit of 120 words. When they've finished, ask them to turn to page 129 and compare the story there with the one they've written.

7 Grammar *Extra* 3, Part 1

Ask the students to turn to *Grammar Extra* 3, Part 1 on page 136 of the Student's Book. Here they'll find an explanation of the grammar they've been studying and a further exercise to practise it.

> 1
> (Student's own answers.)

Speaking (SB page 26)

Pairwork. Put the students into pairs and ask them to discuss the questions. Encourage them to give reasons for all their answers and to report back to the class on what they discussed.

Reading (SB page 27)

1

Groupwork. Put the students into small groups and ask them to look at the guidebook extracts on page 26. Encourage them to discuss the clues and come to a consensus on which cities are being described. Tell them not to look at page 129 until they've discussed the texts fully. If they're still having problems, they can turn to page 129 for additional clues.

> 1 Madrid   2 Prague   3 Tokyo   4 New York

The Charles Bridge /ðə tʃɑːls brɪdʒ/
The Chales Bridge is a famous landmark in Prague, dating back to the 14th century. It joins Old Town with the rest of the city and was originally the only way of crossing the Vltava river. There are three towers along the bridge and around 30 statues.

Vltava /ˈvəltəvə/
The Vltava is the longest river in the Czech Republic (430 km) and flows south to north through the country (and the capital city, Prague) before merging with the Elbe in Mìlník.

Johann Wolfgang von Goethe (1749–1832)
/ˈjəʊhæn ˈvʊlfgæŋ vɒn ˈgɜːtə/
Goethe was a versatile and influential poet, novelist, playwright and philosopher, and is considered by many to be the father of modern German literature. One of his best known works is *Faust* (1808).

Kimono /kɪməʊnəʊ/
The kimono is a traditional garment once worn by men, women and children in Japan. It's now usually worn by women and children for special ceremonies.

2

Ask the students to read the extracts again and underline the information that helped them decide which city each extract is about.

3

Pairwork. Ask the students to discuss the questions and then report back to the class. When they discuss question a), make sure they understand that it's asking about the description that most appeals to them, not the city.

Vocabulary (SB page 27)

1

Do the matching part of the exercise first and check answers with the class. Then ask the students to decide which adjectives they'd use to describe the noun phrases in the box.

a) 1   b) 3   c) 6   d) 2   e) 4   f) 5

Possible answers:
Advertising campaigns: in-your-face
Coastal resorts: bustling, tacky
Collection of people: haphazard
Market: bustling
Plastic souvenirs: tacky
Scenery: awe-inspiring
Seaside postcards: tacky
Tower blocks: soaring
Tree tops: soaring

2

- Ask the students to find and underline the adjectives in Exercise 1 in the texts on page 26.
- Call out each adjective in turn and get the students to say what it is describing.

> awe-inspiring beauty
> haphazard modern development
> tacky tourist trap
> in-your-face experience
> bustling restaurants
> soaring office-blocks

3

- Pairwork. Encourage the students to do this exercise without looking back at the texts on page 26.
- When they've finished, get them to check their answers in the texts and then to explain the meanings.

a) to make way for the new	d) to live on top of one another
b) to work its magic	e) to put a finger on
c) to fall prey to	

4

Ask the students to put the phrases from Exercise 3 into the sentences. Allow them to compare in pairs before checking with the class.

a) to fall prey to
b) live(d) on top of one another
c) to put your finger on
d) work its magic
e) to make way for the new

5

Pairwork. Ask the students to work together to look at the sentences in Exercise 4 and decide if they know any towns or cities that fit any of the descriptions. They should then report back to the class on their suggestions.

Vocabulary: describing cities
You may like to mention some other adjectives you can use to describe cities, such as: *buzzing, cosmopolitan, funky, happening, romantic, soulless, thriving* and *vibrant*.

Grammar (SB page 28)

Inversion after negative and limiting adverbials

1

Pairwork. Focus the students' attention on the adverbials in the box and ask them to decide which have negative or limiting meanings. Remind them that adverbials give us more information about verbs and can be connected to place, time, manner, frequency, etc.

never, not a word, not until he'd finished, on no account, only after a long night, only after a long wait, only then, rarely, seldom, under no circumstances

2

- Ask the students to look at the pairs of sentences. Go through the questions underneath with the class.

- Focus the students' attention on the further examples of inversion in the margin. Tell them that this a structure primarily used in descriptive writing.

  a) Bs
  b) the subject and auxiliary verb are inverted (if there is no auxiliary, we use *do/does/did*).
  c) The effect is to bring about a change of emphasis.

Language notes

Grammar: inversion after negative and limiting adverbials

Sometimes you can put a negative or limiting adverbial in the front position in a sentence for emphasis. In this type of sentence the subject + auxiliary word order is inverted.

> I *have* never seen such breathtaking scenery.
> Never *have* I seen such breathtaking scenery.

The same happens with the verb *be*.

> It *is* not only the oldest building, but also one of the most beautiful.
> Not only *is it* the oldest building, it is also one of the most beautiful.

Negative adverbials

These are adverbial phrases that contain *no*, *not*, *never*, *never before*, *no sooner*, etc.

> **Not a word** did she say to anyone.
> **Never before** have I seen a more beautiful city.
> **No sooner** had I arrived **than** the doorbell rang.

Limiting adverbials

These are adverbial phrases that contain *only*, *only by*, *only then*, *only after*, *only when*, *only if*, or adverbials such as *seldom*, *little*, *rarely*, *barely*, *hardly*, etc.

> **Little** did they know that we were in the next room.
> **Only after** promising to be home before 11pm was she allowed out.
> **Barely** had I arrived **when** the doorbell rang.

3

- Focus attention on a) and point out that *You will rarely* has been inverted to produce *Rarely will you*, which emphasizes the rarity of seeing such a superb example. Ask the students to rewrite the remaining sentences, starting with the word or expression in brackets.

- When they've finished, write the answers on the board and get the students to check their sentences against the answers.

b) Rarely do I visit a city more than once, but this place is really special.
c) Never before had I seen anything so breathtakingly beautiful.
d) Only by wandering down its narrow side streets will you be able to experience the heart of this beautiful old town.
e) Only after you have spent an evening there will you begin to understand the special charm of this place.
f) Not until you climb to the top can you really understand exactly how beautiful the view is.
g) On no account should you leave the town without first tasting its famous local delicacies.

4

Pairwork. After the students have discussed the cities or villages to fit each sentence, feedback with the class.

5 Grammar *Extra* 3, Part 2

Ask the students to turn to *Grammar Extra* 3, Part 2 on page 136 of the Student's Book. Here they'll find an explanation of the grammar they've been studying and a further exercise to practise it.

2
a) Never before ~~I had~~ had I felt so happy.
b) Not until ~~had we~~ we had reached the top did we realise how far we had come.
c) Only once the show was over ~~we could~~ could we relax and enjoy ourselves.
d) Only after some years ~~I understood~~ did I understand how important that experience had been for me.
e) Not only did I want to do it again, ~~did I want~~ I wanted to do it as soon as possible!
f) Barely had I arrived when ~~happened the strangest thing~~ the strangest thing happened.

Writing (SB page 28)

1

Go through the instructions with the class and allow time for the students to decide where they're going to write about and what they're going to say. Make sure they don't write the name of the town or city and don't discuss their ideas with other students. You could set the writing for homework if you wish.

2

Groupwork. Put the students into small groups and ask them to take turns reading their descriptions to the rest of the group. The other students have to identify which place is being described and what clues helped them to decide. You could then display the finished descriptions for everyone to read and enjoy.

Speaking (SB page 29)

1

Groupwork. Focus attention on the posters and give the students time to look at them and take in what they see. Put them into small groups and ask them to discuss their answers to the questions. Encourage each group to appoint a spokesperson to report back to the class.

2

- Working in the same groups, the students make lists of things that would attract visitors to a city rather than the beach, the mountains or the countryside.
- Then get each group to choose their top three and then compare their choices with the other groups.

3

Put the students into new groups. In multinational classes, it would be easiest to have students from the same country working together. In monolingual classes the groups may have to discuss more than one city, with the student(s) from the relevant country supplying most of the information. Each student in the group should make notes as they'll all need the information for the next exercise.

4

Put the students into pairs. Make sure that each student is working with someone from another group. Ask them to follow the instructions and discuss their cities.

Reading & Vocabulary (SB page 30)

1

- Focus the students' attention on the photo of Leicester Square in London. Find out if anyone has been there.
- Ask the students to match the questions and answers. When you check answers, explain any difficult vocabulary, e.g. *brash* (offensively loud or showy), *sweaty* (hot and sticky) and *seething* (very crowded).

> a) 4   b) 3   c) 2   d) 1

Cultural notes

Piccadilly /ˌpɪkəˈdɪliː/
A street in London which runs from Hyde Park Corner to Piccadilly Circus. Famous landmarks include: The Royal Academy, Fortnum and Mason and The Ritz Hotel.

Covent Garden /ˈkɒvənt ˈgɑːd(ə)n/
A London district famous for its shops, theatres and street performers. Covent Garden was the site for London's largest fruit market until the 1970s.

Trafalgar Square /trəˈfælgə skweə/
Trafalgar Square, in the centre of London, commemorates the Battle of Trafalgar (1805), in which a Royal Navy fleet, led by Admiral Lord Nelson, defeated a combined French and Spanish fleet in the most significant battle of the Napoleonic

Wars. Nelson died late in the battle, after victory had been won. Trafalgar Square is now a popular site for tourists and for political demonstrations.

Dim sum /dɪm sʌm/
A Chinese meal consisting mainly of a variety of small dumplings, usually steamed or fried, and filled with meat, fish or vegetables.

2

- Go through the questions with the class to make sure they know what information to look out for as they read the article. You could ask them to speculate about what the answers might be before they read it.
- Ask the students to read the article and find the answers to the questions. Tell them to ignore the gaps. When you've checked the answers, deal with any vocabulary difficulties.
- Finally, ask the students who have been to Leicester Square to say whether the article matches their recollections of the place.

> a) buskers, artists painting cartoons and caricature, movie premieres, night clubs, cinemas, people-watching, eating out
> b) all kinds of people, locals, young people from the suburbs, people going to the cinemas, tourists, celebrities
> c) going to the Prince Charles cinema instead of the Empire, avoiding the restaurants in the Square, eating in Chinatown

3

- Ask the students to decide where the missing phrases should go. Allow them to compare their answers in pairs before you check with the class.
- Point out that *gawp* is another word for *see*, again conveying a sense of staring at someone in rather an impolite way.

> 1 g)   2 a)   3 c)   4 h)   5 d)   6 b)   7 f)   8 e)

4

Pairwork. Put the students into pairs and tell them to decide who will be A and who B. Tell them to turn to their respective pages and follow the instructions.

> **Student A**
> a) buskers – street performers such as musicians or actors
> b) check out – go somewhere to see what it's like
> c) eyeball (very informal) – stare intently at something
> d) gorge – eat a lot (it suggests overindulgence)
> **Student B**
> a) rant – to complain at length about a subject, usually angrily
> b) gawp at (informal) – to look at something in amazement
> c) handily– conveniently
> d) eateries – places where you can eat

5

Groupwork. Put the students into small groups and ask them to discuss the questions. Make sure every student in the group contributes to the discussion with information about their own habits and favourite nightspots.

Listening & Speaking (SB page 31)

1

Pairwork. Put the students in pairs and ask them to discuss the statement and make a list of the main dangers of city life. When they've finished, pool the lists to make one class list and put it on the board. You could then go on to encourage the students to discuss the dangers of traffic, pollution, loss of community, social isolation, etc. in a city.

2 🌐 1.25

Tell the students that they're going to hear two friends talking about the city they live in. Ask them to listen and make a note of whether they mention any of the dangers they listed in Exercise 1. Play the recording more than once if necessary.

> Dangers mentioned in the recording: muggings, pickpocketing on the underground, thieves carrying knifes.

> 🌐 1.25 (H = Helen; R = Robert)
>
> H: *Well, I don't really think it's particularly dangerous. Not any more than any other large city. You have to be sensible, take the normal precautions. I mean, I wouldn't walk down a street and stare at somebody and I certainly wouldn't walk home alone, and I wouldn't go down unlit alleys, you know, dark alleys at night, and obviously there are certain areas that you just know you wouldn't go into, but I think on the whole it's not a particularly dangerous city.*
>
> R: *Yeah, I think I agree, but, um, actually there have been a couple of stories in the papers recently about this spate of muggings that's been going on.*
>
> H: *Oh yeah, I read about that. Yeah, because they say things are changing and things are getting worse in the city. I did have a friend, actually, she was on the underground, and her wallet was snatched from her bag just as the train was coming into the station, and of course they got off straight away and there was absolutely nothing she could do about it.*
>
> R: *Well, I sympathise with her. I mean, I've seen that happen too, and, er, you've just got to watch it in a place like that, or like the street market. You've got to be really careful there because there is a big crowd and a lot of pickpockets, and they can steal something and run away.*
>
> H: *But I don't think it's really dangerous. They're not violent people, you just have to be sensible and keep your eyes open, and …*
>
> R: *Well, I don't know. This article I read they said that a lot of the thieves were carrying knives, which means if you resist then, er, you could get badly hurt, so that really makes you think, doesn't it?*

> H: *Hmm, I said it wasn't violent, maybe it is. I heard about a group of tourists the other day who were mugged. What do you do if you see something like that? You don't really know what's going on and you don't really want to get involved in case you get hurt.*
>
> R: *Yes. I think it's stupid to try and be a hero. I mean, you could get very badly hurt and all they want is just money. I mean, I know that is a terrible thing to say, but it's just money. It's not worth losing your life for.*
>
> H: *I suppose so. Apparently, these guys had a knife and they cut one of the women's handbags from her shoulder. I think she thought they were going to stab her husband actually.*
>
> R: *Did you hear if anybody was hurt at all?*
>
> H: *No, no-one was hurt. Apparently, the woman had had her passport stolen, and her travellers cheques taken, but the sad thing was that they had only just arrived and they didn't want to leave all their stuff in the hotel. They thought it was safer with them.*
>
> R: *Yeah, well, that's a problem with tourists though, isn't it? They're easy targets. They stand out in a crowd, thieves know they're probably carrying money and documents around, and they don't speak the language, and they're vulnerable, aren't they?*
>
> H: *Well …*
>
> R: *I mean, it happens to locals as well. There is a friend of mine who was jumped from behind, you know, and they got her bag and they ran away, and she tried to run after them but the thieves were too quick, obviously.*
>
> H: *Was she hurt at all?*
>
> R: *No, no, but she was really angry.*
>
> H: *Of course.*
>
> R: *She didn't lose anything really valuable so, um, she didn't report it to the police in the end, actually.*
>
> H: *I think she should have done that actually. I think it's quite important when something like that happens because it might be mild at the moment but they could get worse. I think they need to know if a crime's happened, actually.*
>
> R: *Yeah. Well, I mean, there should be more police around anyway, shouldn't there? There should be more police on the streets at night.*
>
> H: *I think you're right.*
>
> R: *You could be on main streets and there's nobody, just a police car driving up and down every now and again, would …*
>
> H: *You'd feel better protected I think.*
>
> R: *Yeah, and it would put the muggers and thieves off, wouldn't it?*

3

- Ask the students to compare their answers in pairs and then to discuss the questions.
- Play the recording again for them to check their answers.

> a) no
> b) don't stare at people, don't walk alone, don't walk down unlit streets

c) on the underground, in the street markets –
because there are crowds of people
d) bag snatching
e) the thieves cut the strap of one of the women's
handbags and ran away with the bag which
had her passport and traveller's cheques inside
f) Increase the police presence on streets.

4

Groupwork. Put the students into small groups and ask
them to discuss what advice they would give. Then ask
a spokesperson from each group to present their advice
to the rest of the class.

Pronunciation (SB page 31)

1 🌐 **1.26**

- Ask the students to complete the extracts, then allow
them to compare their answers in pairs.

- Play the recording for them to check their answers.
Then play it again for them to focus on the stress on
just, really and *actually*.

> a) just   b) Actually   c) just   d) really
> e) actually   f) just   g) really   h) actually

Pronunciation notes

Adding emphasis

- In this section, apart from a couple of sentences
where *just* means a short time before, *really,*
actually and *just* have no specific meaning. They
are there to add emphasis. In many cases *really*
could be replaced with *very*.

- The word *actually*, if put at the beginning or end
of a sentence and stressed deliberately, can mean
that you're contradicting what has been said.
A: *You were born in May, weren't you?*
B: *Actually, I was born in June. / I was born in June,*
actually.

2

- Ask the students to work in pairs to add the three
words to the conversations. There are several ways to
do this, so accept any reasonable additions,

- Get the students to practise the conversations and
then get some of the pairs to perform for the class.

> *Suggested answers:*
> a)
> So, what *actually* happened?
> Well, I was *just* coming round the corner when …
> *Actually*, it all happened *really* quickly.
> b)
> I wouldn't walk home that way if I were you.
> It's *really* dangerous.
> *Actually*, I walked home that way last night. It *just*
> took five minutes. I didn't look dangerous to me.

Useful phrases (SB page 32)

1

Focus the students' attention on the photos and ask
them to discuss the questions. Encourage speculation on
the use of the building without confirming or denying
any answers at this stage.

Cultural note

The GLA Building
The Greater London Authority (GLA) Building is
City Hall, home to the Mayor of London. It was
designed by Norman Foster and completed in 2002.
It is situated on the south bank of the River Thames.

2

Ask the students to read the comments on the blog and
decide if they agree with any of them. Then have a class
feedback session.

Cultural note

Tower Bridge /ˈtaʊə brɪdʒ/
Tower Bridge is a suspension bridge across the
Thames in London, situated next to the Tower of
London. It opened in 1894.

3

Focus attention on the rules in the margin. Ask the
students to look at the expressions in bold in the blog in
Exercise 2 and to match them to the rules.

> It does draw attention – 1
> What I like about it is – 2
> It did grow on me – 1
> The thing I like most – 2
> It's the location – 2

4 **1.27**

- Do the first one as an example with the class and then
ask the students to add emphasis to the remaining
sentences using the words given.

- Play the recording for them to check their answers.

> 🌐 **1.27**
> a) A: *Although I <u>really</u> didn't like it to start with,*
> *I <u>did</u> get used to it with time.*
> b) B: *It's the <u>design</u> I like best of all. It's <u>really</u> original*
> *and eye-catching.*
> c) C: *The thing I like <u>best</u> is the <u>simplicity</u> of the design.*
> d) D: *What people complained about <u>initially</u> was the*
> *<u>location</u>.*
> e) E: *One thing it certainly <u>does</u> do is <u>provoke</u>*
> *<u>discussion</u>.*
> f) F: *One thing it needs is a more <u>identifiable</u> shape.*

5

Play the recording for the students to listen and mark the stresses. Then play it again for them to listen and repeat. When they've done this chorally, ask for individual repetition of the sentences, and make sure they are also using stress and intonation for emphasis.

> (See answers underlined in Exercise 4.)

6

Groupwork. Focus attention on the photos. Ask the students to discuss in small groups which one they like best and why. Tell them to work together to write three sentences about the buildings using emphasis. Then get each group to read out their sentences to the class.

Cultural notes

The MI6 Headquarters /ði em aɪ sɪks hedˈkwɔːtez/
The MI6 Building at Vauxhall Cross on the River Thames in London is the home of the British Secret Intelligence Service. Designed by Terry Farrell and completed in 1995.

The Millennium Dome /ðə mɪˈlenɪəm dəʊm/
Completed in 1999 in time for London's Millennium celebrations on the Thames at Greenwich, the Dome's Millenium Experience was open to the public for the whole of 2000. In 2005, the Dome was renamed The O2 and redeveloped as a huge music and sports venue.

The Gherkin Building /ðə ˈgɜːkɪn ˈbɪldɪŋ/
The Swiss Re Building, or 30 St. Mary Axe, is known to most by its nickname The Gherkin. It was designed by Norman Foster and opened in 2004.

7

Pairwork. Ask the students to discuss the questions in pairs and then report back to the class.

Vocabulary *Extra* (SB page 33)

Lexical sets and collocations with *city* and *urban*

1

Focus the students' attention on the two photos and give them time to take in what they see. Ask them to think of two nouns and two adjectives to describe each one. Then ask them to compare their answers with a partner.

Cultural notes

Chonqing /ˈtʃʊŋtʃɪŋ/
Chonqing is situated in central China and has a municipal population in excess of 32 million. Construction in the city suggests it is growing at a rate of 140,000 square metres every day, while the population is growing by around 1,300 people a day.

Ny-Alesund /nuːˈɒləsuːnd/
Ny-Alesund is a settlement on the island of Spitsbergen in Norway. It has a population of around 35 (swelling to over 100 in summer), all of whom are research scientists.

2

Pairwork. Put the students into pairs and ask them to look at the words in the box. They should work together to decide on the meanings, using a dictionary if neither of them knows a particular word. Ask the students to answer the questions. Encourage them to decide on answers for all of them before checking in Section A.

> a) megalopolis, metropolis, conurbation, city, town/
>   satellite, outpost/settlement, village, hamlet
> b) (Students' own answers.)
> c) conurbation, megalopolis, metropolis, outpost,
>   settlement, satellite, hamlet

3

Ask the students to complete the sentences with suitable words in Section B, but encourage them to try to do it without looking at Section B first.

a) urbanisation	d) city hall
b) urban sprawl	e) urban renewal
c) citywide	f) cityscapes

4

Pairwork. Put the students into pairs and ask them to discuss the sentences in Exercise 3 and say whether they are true for their country or countries.

Further practice material

Need more writing practice?

→ Workbook page 21
• Writing a short article.

Need more classroom practice activities?

→ Photocopiable resource materials pages
    163 to 165
    Grammar: *Tale of two cities*
    Vocabulary: *Sentence halves*
    Communication: *City of dreams*
→ The top 10 activities pages xv to xx

Need DVD material?

→ DVD – Programme 3: *London's West End*

Need progress tests?

→ Test CD – *Test Unit 3*

Need more on important teaching concepts?

→ Key concepts in *New Inside Out* pages xxii to
    xxxv

Need student self-study practice?

→ CD-ROM – Unit 3: *City*

Need student CEF self-evaluation?

→ CEF Checklists pages xxxvii to xliv

Need more information and more ideas?

→ www.insideout.net

Review A *Teacher's notes*

These exercises act as a check of the grammar and vocabulary that the students have learnt in the first three units. Use them to find any problems that students are having, or anything that they haven't understood and which will need further work.

Grammar (SB page 34)

Remind the students of the grammar explanations they read and the exercises they did in the *Grammar Extra* on pages 134 to 137.

1

- This exercise reviews aspect from Unit 1. Remind the students to think of the viewpoint of the speaker to help them decide which verb form is needed.

- Check answers with the class before putting the students into pairs and asking them to talk about the last time they had to wait a long time for somebody.

> 1 been waiting
> 2 was getting
> 3 was he taking
> 4 Had something terrible happened
> 5 are protesting
> 6 closed
> 7 been worrying
> 8 gone

2

This exercise reviews position of adverbials from Unit 1. Remind the students that the position of an adverbial can sometimes affect the meaning of a sentence. Check answers with the class when the students have discussed in pairs the difference in meaning between the sentences.

> a) Sentence 1: The speaker has no real interest in going but may still go.
> Sentence 2: The speaker has no intention of going.
> b) Sentence 1: John has his phone number but no other contact information (address, etc.).
> Sentence 2: John is the only person who has his phone number.
> c) Sentence 1: The speaker did the work quickly and then got ready to go.
> Sentence 2: The speaker did the work and then quickly got ready to go.
> d) Sentence 1: It is the speaker's opinion that he won't apologise at all.

> Sentence 2: He may apologise, but he won't do it face-to-face; he might write a letter or send an apology from his company rather than from himself.
> e) Sentence 1: At first the speaker didn't believe him, but then changed his or her mind and started to believe him.
> Sentence 2: The speaker didn't believe him at all.
> f) Sentence 1: The speaker and Sam were the only people who went for a drink.
> Sentence 2: The speaker and Sam went for a drink but they didn't do anything else.

3

- This exercise reviews order of adjectives from Unit 2. Remind the students that there is a fixed order for different categories of adjectives.

- Check answers before asking the students to say whether they ever wear anything similar and to write a description of one of their favourite items of clothing to show to a partner.

> a) A beautiful silk shirt with a delicate floral pattern.
> b) A warm winter coat made of 100% lamb's wool.
> c) A scruffy old pair of running shoes covered in mud.
> d) Knee-high leather boots that my mother bought for me in Italy.
> e) An unusual hand-printed T-shirt with a picture of a cat.

4

- This exercise reviews fronting from Unit 2. Remind the students that this is a literary style and unsuitable for everyday conversation.

- Check answers before asking them to use the information to write a short newspaper story about Harry's disappearance. Check that they are using fronting appropriately.

a) Harry was his name.
b) His game was gambling.
c) Great were his losses.
d) His family were those who suffered most.
e) Gone was his car.
f) Where he had gone, nobody knew.

5

This exercise reviews hedging from Unit 3. There are many ways to do this. The answers here are suggestions. Put the students in pairs to discuss their statements.

Suggested answers:
a) It is widely recognised that life in some cities can be very dangerous.
b) It appears/seems that there are no job opportunities in small towns.
c) There is some evidence to suggest that capital cities are the best places to build a career.
d) There is little doubt that quality of life is more important than money.
e) Life in a small town is often believed/thought to be boring.
f) There is some discussion over whether people who live in the country live longer, happier lives.

6

- This exercise reviews inversion after negative and limiting adverbials from Unit 3.
- Check answers and then get the students to suggest what the question was and to write three more sentences. Accept any reasonable suggestions, serious or humorous.

a) 3   b) 1   c) 4   d) 2   e) 5
Will you marry me?

Vocabulary (SB page 35)

1

- This exercise reviews ways to describe conversation styles from Unit 1.
- Check answers with the class before putting the students into pairs to discuss whether they know anyone like the people described.

a) butting in, say
b) hog, drones on and on
c) flows, the same wavelength
d) hunt around, puts it across

2

This exercise reviews wordbuilding skills from Unit 1.

a) achievement	d) satisfaction
b) competently, efficiently	e) skilful, valuable
c) considerate	f) fulfilment

3

This exercise reviews expressions with *taste* from Unit 2.

a) 2   b) 4   c) 1   d) 3   e) 6   f) 5

4

This exercise reviews collocations and words for describing places from Unit 3.

1 b)   2 a)   3 c)   4 b)   5 b)   6 c)

Pronunciation (SB page 35)

1

Remind the students that the boxes show the syllables of a word and the large boxes indicate the stressed syllables. Here they are being asked to classify words according to how many syllables they have and where the main stress falls. Encourage them to say each word aloud to get a feeling for what sounds right.

2 ⊙ 1.28

- Ask the students to underline the stressed syllables in the words in the table. Then play the recording for them to check their answers.
- Play it a second time for them to listen and repeat.

1 and 2			
A: ☐☐☐	**B:** ☐☐☐	**C:** ☐☐☐☐	**D:** ☐☐☐☐
<u>a</u>tmosphere	ex<u>qui</u>site	<u>a</u>nimated	ef<u>fi</u>ciency
<u>in</u>tricate	ful<u>fil</u>ment	<u>awe</u>-inspiring	e<u>vo</u>cative
<u>mea</u>ningful	frus<u>tra</u>ting	<u>sa</u>tisfying	hi<u>la</u>rious
<u>re</u>verie	hap<u>ha</u>zard	<u>sti</u>mulating	his<u>to</u>rical

Further practice material

Need more classroom practice activities?
➔ Photocopiable resource materials page 166
   Board game: *Getting to know you inside out*
➔ The top 10 activities pages xv to xx

Need progress tests?
➔ Test CD – *Test Review A*

Need more on important teaching concepts?
➔ Key concepts in *New Inside Out* pages xxii to xxxv

Need student self-study practice?
➔ CD-ROM – *Review A*

Need more information and more ideas?
➔ www.insideout.net

4 Story *Overview*

Story *Teacher's notes*

Warm up

Ask the students to close their eyes and think back to their childhood and the stories that were told to them or read to them. Ask them which ones they remember most clearly and which ones they enjoyed most. Who were the main characters? Were there any stories that frightened them? Ask them to discuss this in pairs and report back to the class.

Speaking (SB page 36)

1

Ask the students to read the text and the six-word life stories on the right. Find out which one they like best and why. Ask them which ones they'd classify as optimistic and which ones as pessimistic. Find out if they have ever heard of six-word stories before.

Cultural notes

Ernest Hemingway /ˈɜːnəst ˈhemɪŋweɪ/ (1899–1961)
Ernest Hemingway was an influential American journalist and writer. He was awarded the Pulitzer Prize in 1953 for *The Old Man and the Sea* and the Nobel Prize in Literature in 1954.

Smith magazine
Smith Magazine was launched in 2006. It's an online magazine dedicated to the art of storytelling. Content comes mainly from contributors, who submit their own stories.

2

Go through the famous people with the class and make sure everyone knows them. Ask the students to match the people to the appropriate six-word life stories.

a) 4	b) 5	c) 1	d) 2	e) 3

Cultural notes

Bill Gates /bɪl ɡeɪts/ (born 1955)
Bill Gates set up Microsoft with his school friend, Paul Allen. In 1983, Microsoft created Windows operating system, which is used on most PCs around the world.

Gaius Julius Caesar /ˈɡaɪʌs ˈdʒuːliːʌs ˈsiːzə(r)/ (100 BC–44 BC)
A military and political leader, Caesar became consul of the Roman Republic in 49 BC. A group of senators led by Marcus Junius Brutus assassinated him on 15 March, 44 BC.

Dame Agatha Christie /deɪm ˈæɡəθə ˈkrɪstiː/ (1890–1976)
British crime writer, who 'keeps the reader guessing until the final page'. The names of her fictional detectives, Hercule Poirot and Miss Marple, are as famous as her own.

Martin Luther King, Jr /ˈmɑːtɪn ˈluːðə kɪŋ/ (1929–1968)
Martin Luther King was a Baptist minister and one of the leaders of the American civil rights movement. Inspired by Gandhi's success in India, he advocated civil disobedience to gain rights for the black citizens of the United States. He was assassinated in 1968 in Memphis, Tennessee.

Princess Diana /prɪnˈses daɪˈænə/ (1961–1997)
Princess Diana was married to Prince Charles, first in line to the British throne, from 1981 to 1996. The couple had two sons, William (born 1982) and Harry (born 1984). Diana was killed in a car crash in Paris in the early hours of 31st August 1997.

3

- Pairwork. Ask the students choose different famous people and to work together to write six-word life stories for them. Remind them that, like newspaper headlines, the stories don't have to be complete sentences and minor words can be left out.

- Put each pair with another pair. Ask them to take turns to read out their stories and to guess whose they are.

Reading (SB page 36)

1

- Write the name Michael Jackson on the board and ask the students to tell you everything they know about him. Write their ideas on the board.

- Explain that an obituary is a description of a person's life which is published after their death. Give the students plenty of time to read the extract from Michael Jackson's obituary. Ask them to see how many of the facts they suggested are mentioned in it.

Cultural notes

Elvis Presley /ˈelvɪs ˈprezliː/ (1935–1977)
An American singer, musician and actor, Elvis Presley became an international star in the 1950s and 1960s, with recordings like *Jailhouse Rock* (1957), *It's Now or Never* (1960) and *Suspicious Minds* (1969). In 1977, he died of a heart attack at the age of 42.

Frank Sinatra /fræŋk səˈnɑːtrə/ (1915–1998)
American singer said to be one of the most popular and influential in the 20th century. His best-known songs include *Strangers in the Night*, *My Way* and *New York, New York*. He also acted in several films including *High Society* (1956).

The Beatles /ðə ˈbiːtəls/
Paul McCartney, John Lennon, George Harrison and Ringo Starr formed the band the Beatles in Liverpool, England. The Beatles became the most famous pop group of the 1960s and Paul McCartney and John Lennon wrote some of the best-known songs in rock and pop music, including *Yesterday*, *Hey Jude* and *Let it Be*. The Beatles broke up in 1970.

Bob Dylan /bɒb ˈdɪlən/ (born 1941)
Bob Dylan was an influential American musician. He became the voice of a generation during the 1960s with his folk-styled protest songs, which chimed perfectly with both civil rights groups and anti-war demonstrators of the time.

The Rolling Stones /ðə ˈrəʊlɪŋ stəʊns/
English rock band, often referred to as 'the greatest rock and roll band in the world'. The band was formed in 1962 by Brian Jones, Mick Jagger and Keith Richards. They've released 29 albums, and had 37 top ten singles, including *Satisfaction*, *Honky Tonk Woman* and *Brown Sugar*.

J.M. Barrie /dʒeɪ em ˈbæriː/ (1860–1937)
Scottish author and playwright. Best known for his 1904 play *Peter Pan, or The Boy Who Wouldn't Grow Up* and follow-up stories about Peter and Wendy.

Peter Pan /ˈpiːtə pæn/
A character created by J.M. Barrie. Peter Pan was a mischievous boy who refused to grow up. He could fly, lived on a fantasy island called Neverland and was the leader of a gang called the Lost Boys. In Barrie's works, Peter Pan meets Wendy Darling and her brothers and takes them to his world, where they encounter fairies and pirates.

Neverland Ranch /ˈnevələænd rɑːntʃ/
The home of singer Michael Jackson from 1988 to 2005, named after the fantasy island of Peter Pan. Neverland Ranch was also a private amusement park and featured a Ferris wheel, bumper cars, pirate ship and many more rides and sideshows for his young guests.

Graceland /ˈɡreɪslænd/
The home of Elvis Presley in Memphis, Tennessee. After his death, Graceland was opened to the public and has now become a place of pilgrimage for Elvis fans around the world.

Bel Air /bel eə/
A district of the City of Los Angeles, California, Bel Air is a residential area. Most of the properties are hidden from view behind tall gates and trees, and are desirable residences for the rich and famous.

2

Pairwork. Ask the students to discuss in pairs whether the statements are true or not according to the obituary. Remind them to find evidence.

> a) False. Only a handful of performers – Presley, Sinatra, the Beatles – could challenge Michael Jackson for the title of most successful popular music entertainer of all time.
> b) True. *Thriller*, his magnum opus, released in 1982, remains by far the bestselling album ever released.
> c) True. The appeal of his impossibly slick and electrifying song-and-dance routines transcended barriers of age, race, class and nationality.
> d) False. He did not react well to the relentless barrage of (frequently prurient) media attention which was generated by success on such a grand scale.
> e) True. He was known to have had a nose job and a cleft put in his chin …. As he got older, though, his features became oddly contorted.
> f) False. The singer's death came only weeks before he was due to begin an unprecedented series of 50 concerts in London

3

Ask the students to complete the glossary with the words highlighted in the text.

> a) frail   b) dogged   c) slick   d) mainstream
> e) hype   f) reclusive   g) staggering
> h) allegations   i) unprecedented   j) erratic

4

Ask the students to discuss which six-word story describes Michael Jackson's life best and to give reasons.

Grammar (SB page 38)
The future as seen from the past

1

Focus the students' attention on the three extracts from the obituary. Read them out or get a student to read them. Answer the questions with the class, then draw their attention to the information in the margin and point out the different sections.

> 1 Extracts b) and c).
> 2 Extract a).
> The sentences are quite formal in register.

Language notes

Grammar: the future as seen from the past
There are a number of ways you can talk about the future as seen from the past. There are some events which you expected to happen and didn't. There are other events which you expected to happen and they did happen.

- **Events that took place**
  In a past sentence, you can use *would* or *was/were to* + infinitive to talk about the future.
  *They **would regret** that decision six months later.*
  *He **was to become** one of the most influential thinkers of his time.*

- **Events that did not take place**
  You can talk about events that didn't turn out as anticipated by using:
  was / were to have + past participle
  *She **was to have given** a speech, but was unable to attend the conference.*

- **Future plans in the past**
  You can talk about future plans in the past which didn't happen:
  (1) *was / were going to* + infinitive
  *I thought we **were going to see** a film.*
  (2) *had been hoping/thinking*
  *I **had been hoping** we could meet for lunch.*

- **Imminent events**
  To talk about something which was imminent (just about to happen), but didn't happen in the end you use *was/were on the point/verge of* + *-ing* verb or noun or *(just) about to* + infinitive.
  *He **was on the point of** retiring.*
  *In 2008, we **were on the verge of** a huge banking collapse.*
  *I was **just about** to call you.*

2

Ask the students to complete the sentences with suitable verb forms, expressing the future as seen from the past. Then ask them to say which events took place and which didn't.

> a) Jackson *was to/would suffer* from ill health at the end of his career. (Took place)
> b) He *was to have released* a new album, but he fell out with his business partner. (Didn't take place)
> c) The relentless media attention *was to/would cause* Jackson to become a reclusive figure. (Took place)
> d) Jackson *was to have retired* from his career after the series of concerts. (Didn't take place)

3

- Ask the students to choose the correct verb forms. Remind them that none of these events took place. Allow them to compare in pairs and then check answers with the class.

- Ask the students to compare the sentences with those in Exercise 2. Ask them which sentences are more formal. Then get them to identify which refer to intentions and which to imminent events.

> | | |
> |---|---|
> | a) to get | e) of winning |
> | b) to see | f) to buy |
> | c) to study | g) of giving up |
> | d) of going | h) to move house |
>
> The register is less formal.
> Intentions: a, b, d, f. Imminent events: c, e, g, h

4

Ask the students to complete the sentences and then put them in pairs to compare them. Ask several students to read their sentences out to the class. Get them to say if any of them are true for them.

> *Possible answers:*
> a) I was planning *to go to the concert*, but it was sold out.
> b) I was on the verge *of buying a new laptop*, but I decided it was too expensive.
> c) I had been hoping *to go to medical school*, but my grades weren't good enough.
> d) I was thinking *of going to the party*, but I was too tired.
> e) I was just about *to have supper*, when the phone rang.
> f) I was going *to have my nose pierced*, but a friend persuaded me not to.
> g) I was on the point *of accepting the job*, but I decided the salary was too low.

5 Grammar *Extra* 4, Part 1

Ask the students to turn to *Grammar Extra* 4, Part 1 on page 136 of the Student's Book. Here they'll find an explanation of the grammar they've been studying and a further exercise to practise it.

> 1
> a) 6   b) 5   c) 4   d) 3   e) 2   f) 1
>
> a) was about to go out
> c) had planned to retire
> d) was to have left
> e) weren't going to go
> 1 would go on
> 5 wouldn't be coming back
>
> *Suggested rewrites:*
> a) was on the point / on the verge of going out
> c) was going to retire
> d) had planned to / was planning to
> e) hadn't planned on going / weren't planning on going
> 1 were going to go on
> 5 wasn't going to come back

Vocabulary (SB page 39)

1

- Focus the students' attention on the two book covers at the bottom of the page and ask them what kinds of books they enjoy reading.

- Pairwork. Put the students into pairs and ask them to look at the different types of story in the box and to discuss the differences between them. Go round giving help where needed and then ask the pairs to report back to the class.

- Ask the students, in their pairs, to decide which type of story they'd expect each sentence to appear in.

anecdote: a story that you tell people about something interesting or funny that has happened to you – b)
fable: a traditional story, usually about animals, that teaches a moral lesson – f)
fairy tale: a traditional children's story in which magical things happen – a)
legend: an old story about famous people and events in the past – c)
myth: an ancient traditional story about gods, heroes and magic – h)
news story: an account of events in a newspaper report or news programme; an item of news – g)
short story: a short piece of fiction – e)
whodunnit: (informal) a story, usually about a murder, in which you do not know who committed the murder until the end. – d)

Language notes

Vocabulary: types of story

- Stories which are spoken and are short-lived are: *anecdotes, rumours, gossip, hearsay* and *jokes.*
- Stories which are originally spoken and then later written down (making them longer lasting) are: *fables, fairy tales, parables, myths* and *legends.*
- Typically written stories are: *novels, short stories, news stories / reports, (fantasy) epics* and *chronicles.*

2

Encourage the students to tell their partner about a story they've heard recently, saying what kind of story it is and giving as much detail as possible.

3

Focus attention on the definition of an *urban myth* in the margin. Make sure everyone understands it. Then ask them to read the urban myth on page 129. Have a class discussion on whether or not they believe it.

Listening (SB page 39)

1 🌐 1.29

- Ask students what types of fiction they like reading; detective novels, romantic fiction, science fiction, etc.
- Focus the students' attention on the photo of Simon. Tell them that they're going to hear him talking about his favourite story when he was a child. Ask them to listen and answer the questions.

> It is a fantasy story.
> He likes it because it's a powerful story and very exciting (a real 'page-turner'). He was totally engrossed in the story and thought it was very well-written and really magical.

🌐 1.29
Simon
Actually, this was my favourite book when I was a child. It's called the Lord of the Rings. *It's a real epic, it's a classic really – it was written for kids but actually lots of adults read it as well. It's massive, three books in fact, but such a brilliant read! It's set in a fantasy world called Middle Earth and it has fantasy characters like, erm, elves, and dwarves, and monsters and dragons, and all sorts of mythical creatures like that. And it tells the story of these creatures called hobbits, who are a bit like humans but not really humans. Er, the main character is called Frodo and he's the one who's got to get rid of the ring. Well, it's a very special ring that was crafted a long, long time ago by the Dark Lord, who is the villain of the story. And it's an extremely powerful ring, the ring of power you might want to call it, because everyone who puts it on becomes invisible. And, basically, this book is about their quest, the quest of the hobbits and their companions, to destroy the ring, because, um, if the Dark Lord gets hold of it, he can rule the world. Oh, and there's this other character called Gandalf, who is a wizard, and he's on the side of good, and he helps Frodo and his companions to vanquish the Dark Lord. And, well, anyway, they have all sorts of, kind of, adventures and there are lots of battles and stuff and, well, in the end Frodo throws the ring into a volcano and that's the end of the ring. Basically, it's about the battle between the forces of good and evil, and in the end, the good triumphs over evil. It's, um, a really powerful story, a real page-turner. You get totally engrossed in the story, it's so well-written, it's really magical. I couldn't put it down. It's been made into a film now, quite an epic actually, and very popular.*

2

- Pairwork. Put the students into pairs and encourage them to try to complete the sentences from what they can remember from the recording.
- When they've done all they can, play the recording again for them to check their answers. Then check answers with the class and explain any unknown vocabulary.

> *Suggested answers:*
> a) The story is set in a fantasy world called Middle Earth.
> b) The characters are elves, dwarves, monsters and dragons and all sorts of mythical creatures like that.
> c) It tells the story of creatures called hobbits, who are a bit like a humans but not really humans.
> d) The main character is called Frodo.
> e) The book is about the quest of the hobbits and their companions, to destroy a ring.
> f) The villain is the Dark Lord.
> g) They have all sorts of adventures and there are lots of battles.
> h) In the end the forces of good triumphs.
> i) You get totally engrossed in the story, it's well-written and really magical.
> j) Now the book has been made into a film.

3

Find out if anyone has read *The Lord of the Rings* or seen any of the three films that were made of it. Have a class discussion using the questions in the exercise.

Speaking: anecdote (SB page 39)

For more information about how to set up, monitor and repeat Anecdotes, see page xx in the Introduction.

- Go through the instructions and the questions with the class. Give the students a minute or two to decide which story they're going to talk about. Then ask them to look at the questions and think about their answers to them. Allow them to make notes of what they're going to say and how they're going to say it, but discourage them from writing a paragraph that they can simply read out.

- Pairwork. Put the students in pairs and ask them to take turns to tell their partner about their story. Encourage them to ask each other follow-up questions to get further information. Ask some pairs to report back to the class about what they found out.

Listening (SB page 40)

1

Pairwork. Focus the students' attention on the cartoons and the definition of *con*. Ask them to discuss what con they think the cartoons might illustrate and who is conning who. Get the pairs to report their ideas to the class.

2 🌐 1.30–1.33

Tell the students that they're going to listen to four people talking about what happened to them in the four situations illustrated in Exercise 1. Play the recording and then find out if any of the stories matched the predictions the students made in Exercise 1. Encourage the students to talk about any con tricks they know.

🌐 1.30 (F = Fiona; J = Jeremy)

1

F: So, have you ever been conned?

J: I'm ashamed to say I have actually, yes. Um, it was years ago. I was a student and I had a car, um, and it had a particularly distinctive sound about it, cos it was like a diesel engine and I wanted to get a different car, so I took it to a second-hand car salesman and he conned me into believing that the sound that the engine makes was in fact a fault and it was on its way out, and he said he would do me a favour by offering me a very small amount of money just to take it off my hands. And I remember at the time thinking, 'Is this really right?' and then I was kind of almost frightened to challenge him on it, and so I said, 'Okay, fine, yeah', and he gave me a very small amount of money for something that was in fact in perfect condition, and I could have got a lot more money for it at another time.

🌐 1.31 (M = Martin; J = Jennifer)

2

M: Do you have any experiences of being conned?

J: I do, actually, um, and this was at home. Someone knocked on my door.

M: Right.

J: A really nice lady. You know, very sort of young and bright and she said, um, 'Can you lend me £5 because I'm here to see my mum? She's not very well. I've run out of change.' Really, honestly I thought, gut feeling, yeah, she seems plausible. She said, 'I'll come back, I'll come back in twenty minutes and I'll pay you.' And so, yeah, I gave her the money. And I'm usually quite sort of, you know, you can see when someone's lying but this, this lady was really lovely. Very well dressed and …

M: How old was she?

J: Oh, she must have been about her early twenties and she ran off with my fiver and never came back. Absolutely unbelievable. I mean, I guess I was quite silly to have done that but she just completely conned me.

🌐 1.32 (M = Martin; A = Anne)

3

M: Do you have any experiences of being conned?

A: Yeah. Well, it's quite embarrassing actually. You know those phone calls you get and they say oh, you've won a holiday and all you need to do is answer a few questions.

M: Yeah.

A: So I answered a few questions about, you know, my ideal place to go and how much pocket money I'd need and how much … you know, all that kind of stuff and maybe have some extra money for … to buy some clothes and things like that, and they kept me on the phone for ages, and I was really excited and I put the phone down thinking I'd actually won a holiday, and then I didn't hear anything, and then I got the phone bill and it cost me £15 that phone call, so I didn't get the holiday.

M: How did you feel?

A: And I was gutted and felt quite stupid.

🌐 1.33 (G = Georgina)

4

G: Yeah, this is something that happened to me when I was living abroad and I was living in a flat and something went wrong with my loo, and so I got my boyfriend to get a plumber, to send round a plumber, and so the next day there was a knock on the door. This guy arrives and said, 'I'm a plumber.' So I said, 'right, come in, have a look, there it is', and he had a look at it and said, 'oh yes, you'll need a new something' – I don't know what it was –'but it'll cost you £20, um, so I can go off and get it now if you like' and so I gave him the £20 and, of course, never saw him again. And then that evening I said to my boyfriend, 'I don't think much of the plumber you sent,' and he said, 'What plumber? I never sent a plumber.' So what had happened, obviously, was that this guy was just coming round, knocking on doors and hoping to find someone gullible like me who'd hand over the money.

3

- Go through the questions with the class first, then play the recording again. Warn the students that the third speaker doesn't actually say why she believed the person on the phone, and the fourth speaker doesn't say how she felt about the experience. Note: *loo* is British English slang for *toilet*.

- When you've checked answers with the class, put the students into pairs and ask them to discuss what they'd have done in the situations described. Find out if anyone has actually had a similar experience or knows anyone who has.

a
a) The car salesman conned the speaker into believing that the sound that his engine made was a fault and the car was on its way out. He gave the speaker a small amount of money for something that was in perfect condition and the speaker could have got a lot more money for it at another time.
b) The speaker was almost frightened to challenge the salesman.
c) He felt ashamed (*I'm ashamed to say I have, actually.*)

b
a) A young lady knocked on the door and said she needed £5. She conned the speaker into handing over the money, and didn't come back.
b) The woman was very nice and very well dressed so she thought she would be honest.
c) She felt quite silly.

c
a) She got a phone call saying she had won a holiday and just had to answer a few questions. When she got the phone bill, she discovered the phone call had cost her £15.
b) The speaker doesn't say, but presumably she was excited at the prospect of a free holiday and didn't realise that she was paying for the phone call.
c) She was gutted (very disappointed) and felt quite stupid.

d
a) A plumber conned the speaker into handing over £20 to get a new part for her loo. He didn't come back.
b) Because she had asked her boyfriend to send a plumber round, and because she was gullible (easily tricked).
c) She doesn't actually say, but her use of the word gullible suggests she feels rather stupid.

Vocabulary (SB page 40)

1

Pairwork. Focus the students' attention on the phrases in the box. Ask them to think about what these expressions might mean and to try to use them to complete the sentences. Allow them to use dictionaries if they need to, but encourage them to think about possible meanings or functions first. When checking answers, make sure everyone has grasped the meaning/function of the phrases.

a) an old wives' tale
b) End of story
c) to cut a long story short
d) tales
e) a sob story
f) a cock-and-bull story
g) the story of my life
h) a long story

2

Pairwork. Ask the students to work in the same pairs and to match the phrases from Exercise 1 to the items in the list. When checking answers, ask the students if they can give examples of any of these things, e.g. an old wives' tale, a cock and bull story. Make sure that they know the difference between *my life story* (my autobiography) and *the story of my life* (used to express the idea that something bad keeps happening to you).

1 a)   2 f)   3 d)   4 e)   5 c)   6 h)   7 b)   8 g)

3

- Pairwork. Ask the students to follow the instructions. As they write their conversations, go round giving help where needed and making sure they include at least two of the expressions from Exercise 1.
- Get the pairs to take turns performing their conversations for the class, missing out the expressions. Ask the rest of the class to identify what the missing expressions are.

Pronunciation (SB page 41)
Weak and strong forms of auxiliary verbs

1 🔊 1.34

- Focus the students' attention on the extracts. Ask them to say them aloud quietly to themselves and to decide how the underlined words are pronounced.
- Play the recording for them to check their answers, and make sure all the students are certain about the pronunciation before moving on to questions b) and c). Ask them to discuss these questions in pairs and encourage them to try saying the words out loud to help them make their decisions.
- Focus the students' attention on the information in the margin, then ask them to practise saying the exchanges in pairs.

1 Q: So, **have** you ever been conned? /həv/
   A: I'm ashamed to say I **have** actually. /hæv/
2 Q: **Do** you have any experiences of being conned? /də/
   A: I **do**, actually. /duː/
a) 1 Q: So, have you ever been <u>conned</u>?
       A: I'm ashamed to say I <u>have</u> actually.
   2 Q: Do you have any experiences of being <u>conned</u>?
       A: I <u>do</u>, actually.
b) actually /ˈækʃəli/

Pronunciation note

Weak and strong forms of auxiliary verbs

- The weak form of the auxiliary is used in any question which begins *Have you …? (Have you ever been conned?)*, *Do you …? (Do you know any con men?)*, *Can you …? (Can you swim?)* or *Are you …? (Are you a plumber?)*. If the question in its entirety is *Have you? Do you? Can you? Are you?* the strong form is used.

- If an answer contains the auxiliary but isn't followed by a verb, the strong form is used. (*I have. We do. He can. They are.*)

- If an answer contains an auxiliary followed by a verb, the weak form applies. (*Yes, I have (I've) been conned twice, actually.*)

2 🌐 1.35

- Pairwork. Put the students in pairs and ask them to decide how the auxiliary verbs are pronounced in the four exchanges. Make sure they say them aloud as they make their decisions.

- Play the recording for them to check their answers, then ask them to practise the exchanges in pairs.

> a) A: So, <u>do</u> you … /də/
>   B: … I <u>don't</u>, actually. /dəʊnt/
> b) A: So, <u>are</u> you … /ə/
>   B: … I <u>am</u>, actually. /æm/
> c) A: So, <u>can</u> you … /kən/
>   B: … I <u>can</u>. /kæn/
> d) A: <u>Can</u> you … /kæn/
>   B: … I <u>can't</u>, actually. /kɑːnt/

3

- Ask the students take turns asking and answering the questions in Exercise 2 with their partner. Allow them to think of new questions to ask.

- Get the students to change partners and ask their questions. Go round making sure they are using weak and strong forms of auxiliary verbs appropriately.

Vocabulary & Speaking (SB page 41)

Deception and belief synonyms

1

- Remind the students of the stories about con tricks that they listened to. Elicit any useful vocabulary that they can remember about the subject of deception. Draw their attention to the list of deception and belief synonyms in the margin and see how many of these they know. Encourage the students who do know a particular word to explain it to the others.

- Ask the students to read the situations and complete the sentences with the words and phrases in the box. When they've finished, put them into pairs and ask them to discuss their answers.

> a) con   e) naïve
> b) fall for   f) sceptical
> c) plausible   g) fishy
> d) get taken for a ride   h) unfaithful

2

- Allow the students to work in pairs if they wish to decide which is the best alternative in each sentence.

- Pairwork. Ask the students to take turns asking and answering the questions in their pairs and then report back to the class on what they found out.

> a) gullible   e) two-time
> b) tricked   f) being taken in
> c) plausible   g) at their word
> d) made out   h) naïve

Reading (SB page 42)

1

Focus the students' attention on the cartoons in the margin on page 43. Find out how many students understand the jokes. Jokes don't improve by being explained, but if the students really don't get them, then explain that the first joke hinges on two different meanings of *doing*. In the customer's question, *What's this fly doing in my soup* means 'why is there a fly in my soup'. The waiter answers the question of what it is doing in the literal sense. He says that what it is doing is the breast stroke, a style of swimming. The second joke involves a play on the words *bean* and *been*, which are pronounced the same but have different spellings and meanings. Find out if there are similar jokes in the students own language(s).

2

Ask the students to read the extract and choose the best title. Check their answers and then answer any questions on vocabulary. Point out that in the first sentence 'the -ese' is used to refer to whatever nationality the speaker chooses to use in the sentence. Of course, this doesn't really work as there are few nationality words that end in -ese (Japanese, Chinese, Burmese, Portuguese, Nepalese) and the comment might be made about the English, the French, the Germans, etc.

> b) Humour across Frontiers

3

Ask the students to read the extract again and find evidence to support the statements.

> a) 'The -ese have no sense of humour'. Strictly speaking, this must be untrue, as all people laugh.
> b) The cleverest of French puns is lost on a Burmese.
> c) A Swiss friend of mine was offended by an earthy Spanish joke that had me in stitches.

d) It is certainly the case that there is such a thing as 'international' humour – that is to say, some types of humour and some jokes gain international acceptance.

e) Even in the area of international jokes, however, a distinct national flavour emerges.

f) This joke, which pokes fun at various national characteristics or weaknesses …

4

Ask the students to look through the article again to find the words to complete the glossary. Warn them that there are two possible answers for j). Tell the students to ignore the highlighted words for now.

a) dry	f) slapstick
b) humorous	g) gag
c) pun	h) poke fun at
d) earthy	i) punchline
e) have someone in stitches	j) hilarious, side-splitting

5

Pairwork. Put the students into pairs. Ask them to discuss the questions and report back to the class.

Grammar (SB page 43)
Discourse markers in writing

1

- Focus the students' attention on the examples of discourse markers in the margin. Point out that the parts with bold words are all possible endings to the sentence beginning *I love TV comedy shows, …* .

- Ask the students to look at the highlighted words in the text on page 42 and to match each one with a discourse marker in the box that has the same meaning or function.

> then – So
> in addition – too
> to be accurate – strictly speaking
> say – for example
> particularly – In particular
> in other words – that is to say

Language note

Grammar: discourse markers in writing
Discourse markers show us how the different parts of the text relate to each other. The discourse markers in this section are found in writing and can be used to give examples (*such as, including*), specify precisely (*namely, viz*), modify adjectives (*or at any rate, or at least*), intensify adjectives (*or even, not to say*), show difference (*on the other hand, by contrast*) and show similarity (*likewise, similarly*).

2

Do the first one with the class as an example and ask the students to look at the sentences with discourse markers in the text and in the margin, and to notice their positions. Ask the students to rewrite the sentences. Then check answers by getting several students to read out their sentences.

> a) So, why do different nationalities …
> b) Some writers, for example Oscar Wilde, are … / Some writers, Oscar Wilde for example, are …
> c) Many nationalities enjoy puns, the English in particular. / Many nationalities enjoy puns, in particular the English.
> d) What is universal about humour, then? / What, then, is universal about humour?
> e) The Americans … Europeans find it hilarious, too. / The Americans … Europeans, too, find it hilarious.
> f) Slapstick … In other words, I don't find it in the least amusing.

Cultural note

Oscar Wilde /ˈɒskə waɪld/ **(1854–1900)**
Irish author and playwright. Wilde was a Victorian celebrity as famous for his wit as for his writing. Amongst his most famous works are the novel *The Picture of Dorian Gray* and the plays *The Importance of Being Earnest* and *Lady Windermere's Fan*.

3

- Do the first one with the class, showing how the sentences differ in meaning. Ask the students to work individually to decide what the difference is between the remaining pairs. Then check answers.

- Ask the students to match the discourse markers with the ones in the box which have a similar meaning. You may need to explain that *or at any rate* and *or at least* are termed *hedges*: they qualify what has been said, narrowing the circumstances in which it is true, softening it or adding a note of hesitancy.

> 1a) gives an example of nationalities (and there are others).
> b) specifies precisely which nationalities (these and only these).
> 2a) modifies the idea of 'eccentric' with a less strong expression (slightly weird).
> b) intensifies the idea of 'slightly weird' with a stronger expression (eccentric).
> 3a) shows a difference.
> b) shows a similarity.
>
> or at any rate – or at least
> including – such as
> similarly – likewise
> viz – namely
> on the other hand – by contrast
> or even – not to say

4

Do the first one with the class. Point out that as *puns* and *jokes involving a play on words* are the same thing, we need a discourse marker that indicates that the same idea is being expressed in different words, i.e. *that is to say*. Ask the students to choose the best alternatives in the remaining sentences. Allow them to compare answers in pairs and check with the class. Then ask them to discuss in pairs whether the sentences are true for them or not.

a) that is to say	d) by contrast
b) in particular	e) namely
c) at any rate	

5 Grammar *Extra* 4, Part 2

Ask the students to turn to *Grammar Extra* 4, Part 2 on page 136 of the Student's Book. Here they'll find an explanation of the grammar they've been studying and a further exercise to practise it.

a) in particular	d) not to say
b) that is to say	e) So
c) or at least	f) including

Cultural note

Woody Allen /ˈwʊdiː ˈælən/ (born 1935)
Woody Allen is an American film director and comedian.

Listening & Speaking (SB page 43)

1 🌐 1.36–1.39

Remind the students that the *punchline* is the phrase or sentence in a joke which produces the humorous effect. It almost always occurs at the end of the joke and may involve a reversal of the expectations built up by the rest of the joke. Tell them that they're going to hear four jokes and that they should write down the punchlines. You may need to play the recording several times and pause between the jokes to allow the students time to write down the punchlines. Check answers and then ask them to say whether they got the jokes (i.e. if they understood why they are funny).

1 So he says, 'One idiot? I can see hundreds of them.' (He is the idiot driving the wrong way and everyone else is going the right way, but he thinks it is the other way around.)
2 'No, I've just graduated from medical school.' (The joke relies on the difference in meaning between the first 'Call me a doctor', which is a request to *fetch* a doctor because someone is ill, and the second which is a request to use the term *Dr* as part of someone's title.)

3 'Sorry, don't serve food.' (*We don't serve food* is a sign commonly seen in pubs which sell only drinks and no food items. What the barman says has two meanings: 1 This pub doesn't sell food and 2 We don't provide goods and services to customers who are themselves food items.)
4 'Got any nails?' The barman says no. 'Got any cheese?' (Here the punchline has two parts. The mouse's question 'Got any nails?' and the barman's negative response prove that the barman is in no position to carry out his threat of nailing the mouse to the bar. The mouse then knows it is safe to repeat its irritating 'Got any cheese?' question.)

🌐 **1.36**

So, there was this pensioner, right, and he was driving along the motorway, right, and he gets a call from his wife. Now, of course, he shouldn't pick up his phone, but he does. 'Take care,' she says, 'I've just heard on the radio that some idiot is driving down the motorway the wrong way.' So he says, 'One idiot? I can see hundreds of them.'

🌐 **1.37**

So, there's this businessman riding on the train after a hard day at the office, and this young guy sits next to him and says, 'Call me a doctor, call me a doctor,' the businessman says, 'Well, what's the matter, are you ill?' And the guy, the young guy says, 'No, no, I've just graduated from medical school.'

🌐 **1.38**

A sandwich walks into a pub and orders a pint of Guinness, and the barman says, 'Sorry, don't serve food.'

🌐 **1.39**

A: I've got one. A mouse goes into a pub and goes up to the barman and says, 'Got any cheese?' and the barman says, 'No, it's a pub, we don't sell cheese.' So the mouse goes 'Oh!' and scampers out. The next day the same mouse comes in the same bar. Goes up to the barman. 'Got any cheese?' And the barman says, 'Look, I told you yesterday this is a pub, we sell beer, we sell spirits, we don't sell cheese, okay?' The mouse goes 'Oh!' and scampers out. Next day, same mouse, same pub, comes in again, goes up to the barman and says, 'Got any cheese?' and the barman says, 'Look, I told you yesterday. If you come in here again, I'm going to nail you to the bar,' and the mouse goes, 'Oh!' and scampers out. Next day, same mouse comes into the pub again, goes up to the barman, 'Got any nails?' The barman says no. 'Got any cheese?'

B: I didn't get that at all.

2

• Go through the responses with the class. You may need to explain that *It leaves me cold* means that the person understands the joke but just doesn't find it funny, whereas *I don't get it* means the person doesn't understand the joke at all.

- Play the recording again, pausing after each joke for the students to make their own personal responses.

3

- Pairwork. Put the students into pairs and ask them to turn to the pages indicated, read their jokes and try to memorise them. Help anyone who doesn't understand the joke they've been assigned.
- Ask the students to take turns telling their jokes to their partners. Find out in class feedback how many people got the joke they were told.

Cultural note

Guinness /ˈgɪnɪs/
Guinness is a dry stout beer from the brewery of Arthur Guinness in Dublin, Republic of Ireland, first brewed in 1759. Its characteristics in the glass are a deep black body with a creamy white head of froth.

4

Have a class discussion of whether they think the jokes are funny or not. Find out if there are similar jokes in any of the students' countries. Then put them into pairs and ask them to tell each other jokes in English. If you spot any particularly good jokes being told, encourage the teller to repeat them for the class.

Useful phrases (SB page 44)

1 🌐 1.40

- Focus the students' attention on the picture. Tell them they're going to listen to a conversation between two friends which relates to it. Ask them to listen and note down their answers to the first question.
- Check answers and then ask the students to say whether anything like this has ever happened to them or anyone they know.

> a) When she was camping on a cliff, a wind got up, and started blowing harder and harder, and she realised that the tent was going to blow away. She then couldn't find her car keys and had to hunt for them.
> b) (Students' own answers.)

> 🌐 1.40 (W1 = Woman 1; W2 = Woman 2)
>
> W1: *I had a really scary experience when I went camping with my friend by the seaside. Actually, it was the first time either of us had been camping.*
> W2: *Really?*
> W1: *We pitched our tent right near the edge of a cliff so we had a beautiful view over the bay.*
> W2: *Oh, lovely!*
> W1: *But then during the night a wind got up, and started blowing harder and harder.*
> W2: *Oh no!*

> W1: *At first I thought we could just sleep though it but eventually I realised that the tent was going to blow away if we didn't act fast.*
> W2: *Oh, how scary! You must have been terrified!*
> W1: *So, anyway, we got up and started to pack our things up.*
> W2: *Right.*
> W1: *… and we were just about to start taking the tent down to pack it away in the car when I realised I couldn't find my car keys.*
> W2: *Oh, what a nightmare! That must have been awful!*
> W1: *So, I hunted high and low, and anyway, to cut a long story short, eventually found them lying on the grass outside the tent.*
> W2: *What a relief! I bet you were pleased!*
> W1: *Yeah, and fortunately we managed to get everything in the car before the rain started.*
> W2: *Oh, good!*
> W1: *But, all in all, it was a pretty horrendous night, and I don't think either my friend or I are in a hurry to go camping again!*
> W2: *I'm not surprised!*

2

Go through the useful phrases with the class. Then play the recording again and ask the students to number the phrases in the order they hear them. You may need to play the recording more than once.

> *Correct order: 7, 9, 3, 8, 5, 4, 6, 2, 1*

3

- Pairwork. Ask the students to look at the useful phrases in Exercise 2 and to try to remember what each was said in response to. Encourage them to try to do this without looking at the recording script. With weaker classes, elicit events from the class first and write them on the board. They can then put them in order and decide which response goes with which piece of information.
- Ask students to check their answers in the recording script. Then move on to the second part of the exercise and ask them to match the phrases with the things they express.

> a) the finding of the keys
> b) the fact that she and her friend are not in a hurry to go camping again
> c) the wind blowing harder and harder
> d) getting everything in the car before the rain started
> e) the fact that they started to pack up their things
> f) realising that the tent was going to blow away
> g) realising that the car keys were missing
> h) the beautiful view
> i) the fact that it was the first time she and her friend had ever been camping

a) *interest*: Right. Really?
b) *sympathy*: Oh, no! Oh, how scary! You must have been terrified! Oh, what a nightmare. That must have been awful!
c) *gladness*: Oh, lovely! What a relief! I bet you were pleased! Oh, good!
d) *agreement*: I'm not surprised. (This could be used in a number of situations but here it's for agreement.)

4 1.41

- Ask the students to match the phrases in the box to the categories in Exercise 3. Before playing the recording, ask them to try saying them aloud and to decide how they think they ought to be said.

- Play the recording and ask the students to say the phrases, copying the speaker's intonation.

a) *interest:* Uhuh
b) *sympathy:* Poor you! What a shame! How awful!
c) *gladness:* Lucky you! Oh, wow! Fantastic!
d) *agreement:* I don't blame you! Quite right!

 1.41

a) *Uhuh.*   f) *Quite right!*
b) *I don't blame you!*   g) *How awful!*
c) *Lucky you!*   h) *Oh, wow!*
d) *Poor you!*   i) *Fantastic!*
e) *What a shame!*

Language notes

Pronunciation: responding to a story

When using these expressions it's important to get the stress and intonation right.

- A rising tone with key words stressed expresses your interest or enthusiasm, while a falling tone with key words stressed shows an appropriate reaction to someone telling you of a situation in which there was a negative outcome.

- A falling tone without key words stressed usually expresses your lack of interest in the story or the outcome. If, for example, you don't stress the word *awful* in the reaction *How awful!*, you may end up sounding as if you mean the opposite, i.e. you really don't care.

5 1.42–1.46

- Ask the students to listen to the five stories and then have a class discussion of what happened in each one.

- Play the recording again and ask the students to make their own individual responses using appropriate phrases. They'll need to respond to the different parts of each story, not just the end. When they've done it once, play the recording again at full speed and ask them to respond as before.

1 The speaker lost her purse and couldn't pay for her meal. A stranger offered to pay for her, but she refused.
2 They had run out of money when travelling and were very hungry. There was a long queue for the last bus home but they managed to get the last two seats.
3 The speaker was too late to get tickets for the first concert, but phoned early for the second one and got good seats.
4 He tried to introduce a guy he knew to his girlfriend but he had forgotten his name. The guy introduced himself and spent the evening talking to his girlfriend.
5 The postman delivered an unexpected envelope containing a cheque for £5,000.

 1.42
1
So, anyway, I finished the meal and I called the waiter to pay the bill. And I opened my bag and, guess what? My purse wasn't there.

…

But you'll never guess what happened. This man at the next table leaned over and offered to lend me the money.

…

Obviously I said no. I mean, I didn't know him and it would just have been too embarrassing.

 1.43
2
We'd actually been travelling for two days but we'd run out of money. So I hadn't eaten for two days! I was absolutely starving!

…

It was the last bus home and there was a long, long queue. I was thinking, what if we don't get on? We'll have to spend the night in the bus station.

…

But, anyway, in the event, we managed to get the last two seats on the bus.

 1.44
3
I'd known about the concert for ages, it was one of my favourite groups playing. But for some reason I hadn't got round to phoning up for tickets. And when I did eventually phone, all the tickets had sold out.

…

But then, the next time they were playing, I phoned up well in advance of the concert date. And so this time we managed to get seats right in the front row.

 1.45
4
I was at a party with my girlfriend, and I saw this guy I'd known ages ago at school. And I was just about to introduce him to my girlfriend when I realised I'd completely forgotten his name.

…

Luckily I didn't have to introduce him though, because he immediately introduced himself.

…

Or perhaps it wasn't so lucky as it turned out … He spent the rest of the evening talking to my girlfriend!

🌐 1.46

5

I was sitting at the table, having breakfast, and suddenly there was this knock on the door.

…

It was the postman. He handed me an envelope which I had to sign for, because it was special delivery. And so I opened it and you'll never guess what was inside – a cheque for £5,000!

I remember – g)	went – j)
was – b)	crying – f)
asking – c)	carrying – a)
said no – i)	hurt – d)
took – e)	good – h)

4

Ask the students to complete the spaces in the text with the words and phrases given. Then read out the completed text (including also the words they substituted in Exercise 2) to show them how the addition of some more vivid language makes the story much more interesting.

1 b)	2 e)	3 g)	4 f)	5 c)	6 d)	7 a)	8 h)

6

- Preparation for this activity could be done for homework. If you do it in class, be sure to allow the students plenty of time to think up their anecdotes. Discourage them from just writing down their stories and reading them out.

- Pairwork. When the students are ready, put them into pairs and ask them to take turns telling their stories and responding to them. When they've finished, ask them how they felt about their partner's responses. Did they find it easier to tell a story when they got the expected response from a listener?

Writing *Extra* (SB page 45)
Descriptive narrative

1

Pairwork. Ask the students to think about their earliest memories and to tell a partner about them. Alternatively, you could ask them to do some preparation for homework.

2

Ask the students to read the text, ignoring the spaces and highlighted words for the moment. Then discuss as a class whether the ending is happy or sad.

> The ending is happy because the experience didn't put the writer off rollerblading, and he/she became quite good at it.

3

Focus the students' attention on the highlighted words and phrases in the text. Ask the students to replace them with the more vivid expressions in the box. Give them plenty of time to do this and allow them to compare in pairs before checking their answers.

5

- Go through the instructions with the class and allow plenty of time for preparation and writing. Get the students to do the writing for homework if there is not enough time in class. Remind them to use vivid expressions to make their stories more interesting.

- Ask them to swap stories with a partner and to make suggestions about how to make their partner's story more detailed and vivid. They could then rewrite their stories, incorporating any suggestions. Display the stories in the classroom for everyone to read and enjoy.

Further practice material
Need more writing practice?
→ Workbook page 27
- Writing a review.

Need more classroom practice activities?
→ Photocopiable resource materials pages 167 to 169
  Grammar: *A memorable day*
  Vocabulary: *Finding synonyms*
  Communication: *Early warning system*
→ The top 10 activities pages xv to xx

Need DVD material?
→ DVD – Programme 4: *The pedlar*

Need progress tests?
→ Test CD – *Test Unit 4*

Need more on important teaching concepts?
→ Key concepts in *New Inside Out* pages xxii to xxxv

Need student self-study practice?
→ CD-ROM – Unit 4: *Story*

Need student CEF self-evaluation?
→ CEF Checklists pages xxxvii to xliv

Need more information and more ideas?
→ www.insideout.net

5 Bargain *Overview*

Section & Aims	What the students are doing
Reading & Vocabulary SB page 46 Reading for detail Words and phrases for spending and saving	Doing a quiz about spending habits. Reading and discussing spending profiles and completing a glossary. Identifying odd words out. Writing sentences about spending habits.
Listening SB page 47 Listening for gist	Matching speakers to the questions they were asked. Making notes on what speakers say, then asking questions to a partner.
Grammar SB page 47 Prepositions in relative clauses	Studying formality and informality in sentences. Identifying defining and non-defining relative clauses. Rewriting sentences with non-defining relative clauses.
Reading & Vocabulary SB page 48 Reading for detail Spending and saving; phrasal verbs	Reading about a woman who tried to live on £1 a day. Choosing alternatives to complete sentences. Completing sentences and writing questions with phrasal verbs.
Listening SB page 48 Listening for detail	Listening to a radio programme about money-saving tips. Writing more tips to send to the programme.
Reading & Listening SB page 50 Reading for detail Listening for gist and detail	Reading tips on bargaining and identifying the false tip. Listening to people discussing bargaining and identifying the situation. Identifying errors in summaries.
Pronunciation SB page 50 Weak forms of common words	Identifying and practising saying stressed and unstressed words.
Vocabulary SB page 51 Words for *cheap* and *expensive*	Categorising phrases as *cheap* or *expensive*. Discussing register and connotations. Choosing the best alternative and completing tips on shopping.
Speaking: anecdote SB page 51 Fluency practice	Talking about a purchase they've made recently.
Reading SB page 52 Reading for detail	Reading about the Freecycle organisation and completing a glossary. Discussing recycling their possessions.
Grammar SB page 53 Articles	Studying the correct use of articles. Completing sentences. Crossing out inappropriate words in sentences.
Useful phrases SB page 54 Useful conversational phrases for negotiating, haggling, making a deal	Listening to a conversation between a customer and a market trader. Completing useful phrases for negotiating. Identifying problems, requests, proposals and agreements. Improvising conversations.
Vocabulary *Extra* SB page 55 British and American English	Identifying texts and sentences in British and American English. Giving equivalent British English words for American terms. Seeing how dictionaries distinguish between varieties of English.
Writing WB page 33	Writing a news story.

Bargain *Teacher's notes*

Warm up

Warm up

Write the word *bargain* on the board and see if any of the students know what it means. Ask if any of them have bought anything recently that they consider to be a bargain. Get them to describe it and how they felt when they bought it. Find out where they think the best bargains are to be had. Do they compare prices online to find the cheapest?

Reading & Vocabulary (SB page 46)

1

Pairwork. Ask the students to tell each other everything they've bought in the last twenty-four hours. If the students are relaxed talking about the subject, find out who has spent the most and the least in the last twenty-four hours.

2

Ask the students to do the quiz. Then ask them to compare their answers with their partner.

3

Ask the students to turn to page 130 to check their scores and read their spending profiles. Then discuss whether or not they think the profiles accurately reflect their spending habits.

4

Ask the students to complete the glossary with words from the quiz.

a) down-payment	e) slap-up
b) make do	f) shop around
c) bulk buy	g) impulse buy
d) play up	

5

Ask the students to choose the word or phrase in each group which has a different meaning. Allow them to compare their results in pairs. Let them check with a dictionary if necessary.

a) pay over the odds (to pay too much for something; the others mean to save money)
b) live within your means (not spend more than you can afford; the others mean to spend too much)

c) save up (to save money, usually for a specific purpose; the others mean to pay back money that you owe)
d) generous (to be willing to give things including money to other people; the others mean to be careful with your money and unwilling to spend it)
e) tight-fisted (to be mean with money; the others mean having little or no money)
f) extravagant (happy to spend money freely on expensive things; the others mean to owe money to the bank)

6

- Ask the students to write their sentences and give them plenty of time to do this (it could be done for homework). Give help where needed.

- Put the students into pairs and ask them to take turns reading their sentences to each other. The listening student should ask questions to elicit more details.

Listening (SB page 47)

1 🔊 **2.01**

- Go through the questions with the class and make sure everyone understands them. You may need to explain *impulsive shopper*: someone who buys things which catch their eye when they're out shopping rather than making planned purchases.

- Ask the students to write the numbers 1 to 6 on a piece of paper. Play the recording and ask students to note down the letter of the question next to it as they listen.

1 c)	2 f)	3 g)	4 h)	5 b)	6 a)

🔊 **2.01**

1
Ah, well bizarrely enough it's a department store. I just love the ease of being able to go in: do your food shopping, buy electronic goods, maybe buy some clothes and then I normally end up in the book section, and I'll buy some books that I probably don't need, but it's all under one roof, so it's absolutely perfect.

2
Oh, actually that's my responsibility. I don't like other people doing that for me, to be honest. I like to, you know, go and have a good look around and pick the produce that I really, really like the look of and the smell and all the rest of it, so er, yeah, I quite enjoy that. That's not one of my most painful chores.

3

It's going to be a house, which is a bit of a necessity. It will be lovely to unpack and spread my stuff around a few rooms. I know that it's going to cost a lot and organising finance is tricky, but a house is something I've always dreamt of having.

4

I have to say I'm really not. I like to consider everything I buy. Um, what I tend to do is I visit all the shops and I'll assess all the different prices, and perhaps some shops you might get additional things thrown in, for example. Inevitably, I end up going back to the first shop, probably because that's where I've asked all the questions and I feel a certain sense of customer loyalty perhaps, but I might check prices online, for example, and certainly do the rounds, but I like to put a lot of work in before I actually purchase anything.

5

Well, when I was much younger, I was shopping just before Christmas with my parents and I got separated from them, which was really scary at the time and, fortunately, I guess I knew to ask somebody at the counter and they put an announcement over the tannoy and, um, I waited there and was eventually reunited with my parents, but I remember it being quite traumatic and really, really scary.

6

Oh, my God – I love it. I mean anything and everything to do with shopping – I'm there. I mean, they call me the plastic bag lady because I'm constantly with bags, you know – down the high street. I mean, retail therapy, it's got to be the best thing for anyone.

2

- Play the recording again and ask the students to make notes on what the speakers say. Then as a class, discuss the speakers' answers to the questions.

- Put the students into pairs and ask them each to choose three of the questions. They then take turns asking and answering their questions.

Grammar (SB page 47)

Prepositions in relative clauses

It would be a good idea to do some revision of the rules for defining and non-defining relative clauses and relative pronouns before doing this section. (See Language notes on the right.)

1

- Focus attention on the pairs of sentences. Read them aloud or get a student to read them. Then ask the students to say which they think is more formal in each pair. You could point out that the formal sentences sound very stilted and that the use of *of which* and *of whom* is declining. Draw their attention to the final position of the particle *of* in the informal sentence a)1 and the position of *to* after the verb in sentence b)2.

- Ask the students to decide which of the sentences you could use *that* or *who* in.

> In the both pairs of sentences, A is more informal and B is more formal.
> *That* can be used in sentence A of both pairs. *Who* can be used in sentence A of the second pair.
> It's more common to miss them out when speaking.

Language notes

Grammar: relative clauses

Relative clauses describe or give information about the person or thing being talked or written about.

Non-defining relative clauses

- You use non-defining relative clauses to give extra, non-essential information about the person or thing you're talking about. You can also comment on the whole of the main clause.

- You always begin a non-defining relative clause with a relative pronoun and you separate it from the main clause with commas. Don't use *that* with non-defining relative clauses.
  *He works for Mike Jones, **who** I like.* (extra information about Mike)
  *He works for Mike Jones, **which** I like.* (comment on the whole of the main clause)

- Non-defining relative clauses can be formed with expressions like *many of / most of* and *all of* + *whom* or *which*. Compare the sentences:
  I bought lots of clothes. I don't like many of them.
  *I bought lots of clothes, **many of which** I don't like.*

  I saw lots of people at the party. I knew most of them.
  *I saw lots of people at the party, **most of whom** I knew.*

Defining relative clauses

- You use defining relative clauses to state exactly which person or thing you're talking about. When the relative pronoun is the subject of the relative clause, you must use *who, that* or *which*:
  *I like people **who** never let me down.*

- When the relative pronoun is the object of the relative clause:
  1) you can omit *who, that* or *which*: *Are you the person (that/who) I should talk to?*
  2) you don't need another object pronoun: *She got a new car that she's very proud of.* (NOT *… proud of it.*)

- Prepositions normally come at the end of the clause in informal written and spoken sentences. In more formal sentences they come before the relative pronoun – *who* becomes *whom* and *that* isn't used.
  Informal: *Are you the person **who/that** I should speak **to**?*
  Formal: *Are you the person **to whom** I should speak?*

2

Ask the students to rewrite the sentences to make them more informal. You may need to point out that you use the pronoun *where* rather than *which* for the first one. When you've checked answers, ask the students to say if the sentences are true for them and to discuss them with a partner.

a) The supermarket (<u>where</u>) I do my shopping <u>at</u> is very cheap.

b) I have a good friend (<u>who</u>) I like to go shopping <u>with</u>.

c) At the moment, there is nothing (<u>that</u>) I am saving up <u>for</u>.

d) I never buy clothes (<u>which</u>) I don't feel comfortable <u>in</u>.

e) Being tight-fisted is something (<u>that</u>) my friends would never accuse me <u>of</u>.

f) I can't remember the last person (<u>who</u>) I gave a present <u>to</u>.

g) The last thing (<u>that</u>) I wrote out a cheque <u>for</u> was very expensive.

3

- Focus the students' attention on the sentences. Read them out and ask the students to underline the relative clause in b).

- Make sure that the students understand the difference between a defining relative clause and a non-defining relative clause (see Language notes on page 49). Ask them to say whether the clause they underlined is defining or non-defining and how they know. You might like to ask the students if they can write a similar sentence about the clothes that includes a defining relative clause (e.g. *I've never worn most of the clothes that I bought in the sale.*). Put this sentence on the board and draw their attention to the differences in punctuation (no comma before the defining relative clause).

- Ask the students to say whether *which* can be replaced by *that* in this clause.

b) most of which I'll probably never wear
It is a non-defining: The students may identify the type of clause by the meaning and the fact that it is merely supplying additional information, not defining the clothes. However, the comma also identifies it as non-defining. We can only use *that* in a defining relative clause, so it cannot replace *which* here.

4

Do the first one with the class as an example and then ask the students to rewrite the remaining sentences. Note that for some of these sentences there's more than one answer. Go round giving help where needed.

a) I earn $200 a week, half <u>of which</u> I spend on rent. / I earn $200 a week, <u>of which</u> I spend half on rent.

b) I have several close friends, none <u>of whom</u> enjoys shopping. / I have several close friends, <u>of whom</u> none enjoys shopping.

c) There are several restaurants near my house, the nicest <u>of which</u> is beyond my price range.

d) My mobile phone bills, <u>of which</u> I got the latest last week, are quite high.

e) The people in my class, the majority <u>of whom</u> are students, can't afford to go out for a slap-up meal.

5

Ask the students to write true sentences with non-defining relative clauses about shops or restaurants in their neighbourhood. You may want to set a fixed number of sentences, at least three. Then put the students into pairs and ask them to compare their sentences.

6 Grammar *Extra* 5, Part 1

Ask the students to turn to *Grammar Extra* 5, Part 1 on page 138 of the Student's Book. Here they'll find an explanation of the grammar they've been studying and a further exercise to practise it.

1
a) Is that the book you were telling me <u>about</u> yesterday?

b) Who was that strange person that you were talking <u>to</u> on the bus?

c) What's the name of that restaurant that we went <u>to</u> with Bob?

d) <u>To</u> whom were you referring when you said some people have no idea how to behave?

e) Excuse me, <u>with</u> whom do I have the pleasure of speaking?

f) I spoke to a number of different people, many <u>of</u> whom I had never met before.

The last three are more formal.
Rewritten in a more informal style:
d) Who were you referring to when you said some people have no idea how to behave?

e) Excuse me, who am I speaking to?

f) I spoke to a number of different people, many who I'd never met before.

Reading & Vocabulary (SB page 48)

1

If £1 does not mean much to the students, convert it into their own currency or set it in context, e.g. a first-class stamp in the UK costs just over 40p, a cup of tea in a café about £1.20. Ask them to think about their answers to the questions and then discuss them with a partner. Then ask the pairs to report back to the class on their ideas and decisions.

2

Explain *economies* (here, ways of saving money). Ask the students to read the article and make notes on the economies the writer made in order to survive on £1 a day. Find out if any of these things are the same as the suggestions the students thought of in Exercise 1.

> She cut back on socialising (she turned down invitations to the pub or arrived late and drank water; she met her friends in parks with a flask of coffee and perhaps some doughnuts), food (she stored her food so it lasted longer, ate leftovers for lunch, used a wok because it took little oil, turned leftover vegetables into soup, picked free food from the countryside, ate samples from shops and buffet food at university lectures), entertainment (she got free cinema tickets from old newspapers and got free trial sessions at the gym and pool), clothes (she swapped clothes with friends and wore a second-hand dress to her brother's wedding), transport (she walked, cycled and hitchhiked), and life's necessities (she got free samples of shampoo and toothpaste from magazines and her hair was cut free by trainee hairdressers).

3

Ask the students to choose the best alternatives, but remind them that they need to give evidence from the text to support their decisions.

> a) wasted a lot of money (I squandered thousands, not on exotic holidays or expensive cars, but on the mundane items that we think we need: lunches out, coffees, toiletries and make-up, socialising, phone calls.)
>
> b) be able to buy a wedding present for her brother. (My brother's wedding was a year away and that was another incentive. I desperately wanted to save up and buy him something lavish.)
>
> c) were sceptical about her plan. ('A pound a day?' they spluttered, over their third glass of Merlot and bag of Doritos. 'Maybe in Bangladesh,' they scoffed. 'Maybe on food alone. But what about wine and phone bills? Coffee and make-up? Clothes and transport?')
>
> d) found alternative ways of socialising (… would turn up late and order a glass of water … I'd drag them to a bench in a park, with a flask of coffee and a rug – and a few doughnuts if we were lucky.)
>
> e) making economies (I became obsessed with food bargains and well acquainted with supermarket discount shelves. I resisted the urge to purge everything in my food cupboard in case it came in useful … became an expert at making perishables last … I'd gorge on tasters … I'd pick blackberries, apples and hazelnuts in the countryside.)
>
> f) changing her travel habits (buses – my previous staple – were too expensive, so I cycled or walked everywhere. (My main challenge, though, was getting around.)

> g) had changed her attitude to spending (… living frugally has become second nature to me. I think carefully before I buy a coffee or clothes and have eaten out only once. In fact, four months on, I probably still spend less than £5 a day.)

Language notes

Vocabulary: expressions for saving and spending money

As well as useful phrases like *save up*, *get by* (survive financially) and *cut back* (reduce expenditure), there are a number of idiomatic expressions connected to saving and spending money, which include:

I have to tighten my belt (I have to cut back)

We're living on a shoestring (we're living on very little money)

Save up for a rainy day (put money aside as an insurance should any unforeseen problems arise)

It cost an arm and a leg means it was expensive.

Daylight robbery means something is much too expensive (in your opinion).

(See Student's Book page 51 for expressions which mean *cheap* or *expensive*.)

Cultural notes

Merlot /ˈmɜːləʊ/
Merlot is one of the world's major grape varieties. It produces a medium-bodied red wine, which is characterised by its fruity flavour of plums or berries.

Doritos /dɒˈriːtɒs/
Doritos are flavoured tortilla chips, sold in packets.

Bangladesh /ˌbæŋɡləˈdeʃ/
Bangladesh is a densely populated country, bordered by India and Burma, with a traditionally high rate of poverty, although this has been improving in recent years.

Starbucks /ˈstɑːbʌks/
Starbucks is a coffeehouse chain, which was founded in Seattle, Washington in 1971. Starbucks now has more than 6,000 outlets around the world.

4

- Ask the students to complete the sentences without looking back at the text. The words they need are all particles missing from phrasal verbs and you might like to give them this clue. When they've finished, they can check with the text.

- When you've checked answers, ask the students to highlight the phrasal verbs in the sentence and to write three questions using three of them. Then put them into pairs to take turns asking and answering their questions.

> a) by   b) up   c) back   d) out of   e) in
> f) around

5

- First agree with the class what Kath Kelly's conclusions were. (Too many people are constantly in debt and are frightened of not earning enough to help them live within their means. However, there's a more satisfying way to live, and living frugally has many benefits including being in control of your life and learning a lot about yourself and others.)

- Then have a class discussion on whether they could do what she did and whether they agree with her conclusions.

Listening (SB page 48)

1 🌐 **2.02**

- Go through the instructions and the questions with the class. Then play the recording and ask the students to take notes of the answers to the questions.

- Check answers and then put the students into pairs to discuss what they think of the tips and whether they think they'd work for them.

---

a)
1 Cancel your gym membership and buy a bicycle.
2 Buy things in the sales whenever you can.
3 Stop buying designer label clothes.
4 Ask yourself 'Do I really need this?'

b)
1 You don't need to pay monthly subscription fees; you can buy a bike with the money you save and get your exercise for free; you can also save on train fares.
2 You can get things for half the price, and if you buy in bulk, you can also stock up on presents.
3 If you get your clothes at a market or in discount shops you'll save a lot of money.
4 You'll feel a lot happier, and a lot richer, when you get home. Plus the fact that your house won't be cluttered with stuff you're only going to give away or get rid of in a few months' time.

🌐 **2.02**

Presenter
Good evening and welcome to The Money Show, *the programme that helps you navigate the world of spending and saving, and manage your personal finances. Today we've asked you, the listeners, to write, email or call with your top tips for saving money or making it go further. The lines are open now on 0359-67678888, that's 0359-67678888, if you'd like to share your ideas.*

First off, we've had an email from Tony Price, who says: I've made huge savings by cancelling my gym membership. I found I was only going once or twice a week, which was not only making me feel guilty for not going more often, but was also costing me a fortune in monthly subscription fees. With all the money I've saved, I've bought a bicycle and now I get

my exercise for free. And on top of that, now that I'm cycling to work, I'm saving on train fares as well!

Thank you very much, Tony, for that idea. How to save money and get fit at the same time – can't be bad! And here's another idea from Gemma Banks. Gemma writes: It really makes sense to buy things in the sales whenever you can. Why pay over the odds when, if you wait for the sales, you can get it for half the price? And if you buy in bulk, you can also stock up on presents so you're never at a loss if you need a birthday gift for someone.

I agree, Gemma, in fact I can't honestly understand why anyone buys things at any other time. And talking of purchases, here's a tip from Penny Nowell, who writes: My top tip for saving money is to stop buying designer label clothes. My wardrobe used to be stuffed with top-of-the range clothes and accessories I hardly ever wore. Then a friend said to me, 'Face it, Pen – celebrities are given expensive clothes to wear – they don't actually go out and buy them. You're not a celebrity and never will be. How can you justify paying over the odds because a top designer has had his or her name sewn into the label? And can you honestly tell the difference between an exorbitantly-priced designer bag and one bought at a fraction of the price down the market? Get your clothes at a market or in discount shops and you'll save a fortune.

Thank you, Penny. So those of you with a penchant for upmarket clothes, take note – not sure I come into that category myself, though. And here's another money-saving idea from Paul Moore who's emailed us with the following suggestion: If you're an impulse buyer like me, my suggestion when you're waiting at the till with your new purchase is to count to ten and ask yourself 'Do I really need this?' The chances are the answer is no. Even if it's half price, if you don't need it, you're not saving money. So, put it down, walk away and believe me, you'll feel a lot happier, and a lot richer, when you get home. Plus the fact that your house won't be cluttered with stuff you're only going to give away or get rid of in a few months' time.

I like that suggestion, Paul. I'm sure we'd all be a lot happier if we could just be content with the bare necessities of life. And talking of bare necessities, here's a tip from Sally Richards …

2

- Pairwork. Ask the students to work with their partner and write a tip to send to a programme. Tell them to use the money-saving ideas listed, or their own ideas.

- Ask them to discuss their choices in pairs, explaining why this idea suits them best, what they do at the moment, how easy it would be to make the change and what they think the consequences would be.

- Get each pair to read out their tip to the class. Perhaps have a class vote on the most original, the most sensible, the most likely to succeed, etc. Encourage a class discussion of which ones would work and other ways to save money.

Reading & Listening (SB page 50)

1

- So far the students have talked about *a bargain* as something which can be bought at a good price. Here they'll encounter the verb *to bargain*, which means to negotiate a lower price from someone who's selling something. Make sure they understand the difference and find out if things are sold at a fixed price in their countries or whether bargaining is a common practice. If it is, find out in what circumstances it's acceptable and when and where it would be inappropriate.

- Ask the students to read the tips on bargaining which are aimed at people visiting a country where bargaining is the norm. Point out that one is false and they should try to identify which one this is.

> 'Avoid paying with small change, as this may annoy the seller. Larger denominations are preferable'. (The reverse is true.)

2 🌐 2.03

Go through the questions with the class so that they know what information to look out for as they listen. Then play the recording (more than once if necessary).

> c) both situations

> 🌐 2.03 (B = Bill; M = Marina)
>
> B: *So, have you got any experience of bargaining?*
> M: *Yeah, yeah, I have actually. I was in Turkey and I've got a bit of a passion for rugs, and I saw this kilim and I really liked it but it was way over-priced and er … but I got into this whole bargaining thing with this guy and because I, in a way, I kind of liked it – I mean, it was lovely, but I also didn't really want it and so because I didn't really want it, I just made up a price, you know, and really low. I started really low.*
> B: *Well, don't they say, go like a fifth of the price or something? (Yeah, that's right.) I mean, I know it's probably different in different countries but I know in Egypt they kind of literally go a fifth of the price, you know, and you think what, you're kind of insulting them but …*
> M: *But anyway, and so, because I didn't really care about it that much, there wasn't a huge emotional investment. I just, you know, I just made up a figure (Brilliant!) and, basically, we got it just above the figure that I had quoted.*
> B: *It's good fun though, isn't it?*
> M: *Yes and no. What about you?*
> B: *No, I really enjoy it. I think because they are so used to doing it, you know, in Turkey and Egypt and, you know, a lot of places other than England probably, and maybe America, I think they enjoy it. You know, they get a kick out of it and they know that they've got a margin that they can sell it at, and they try and get the most out of you, and I think it is a challenge for them, you know, and I've never left a bargain or a haggling situation not feeling happy and the seller not feeling happy. And that's always a good thing. You know, you go into a shop in this*

> *country and you know you've been ripped off but you still buy it because you want it or you need it.*
> M: *But, you know, I think at the moment you can actually bargain here as well.*
> B: *Do you think?*
> M: *Yeah, yeah, definitely.*

3

- Ask the students to read the two parts of the summary and then think back to what they heard in the recording to decide what the errors are.

- Play the recording again for them to check their answers. Then ask the students to rewrite the summary. Check that they do this correctly.

> Marina saw a rug in Turkey. She ~~really wanted it~~ didn't really want it and it was ~~reasonably priced~~ way over-priced but she decided to bargain for it. She ~~did not start~~ started by offering a very low price because she ~~was~~ wasn't afraid she might lose the rug. In the end, she was able to knock down the seller's price and bought the rug.
>
> Bill ~~does not like~~ likes bargaining. He believes that the sellers ~~do not~~ enjoy it ~~either~~ too. Generally, he has been ~~unsuccessful~~ successful in his experiences of bargaining when abroad. However, he feels that his experiences of bargaining in England have been ~~more~~ less successful.

4

Ask the students to discuss their experiences of bargaining in pairs and to be prepared to report back to the class on what they find out. If they are slow to start, you could ask them these questions: *Is it common practice to bargain in your country? Can you bargain in shops as well as markets? What if anything can you not bargain over?*

Pronunciation (SB page 50)

1

Ask the students to read the sentence in the margin and to think about how the red words would be pronounced. Ask them what sound occurs in these (the schwa) and whether these words are stressed or unstressed (unstressed). Point out that some parts of the words in black are bold. Ask them to practise saying the sentence aloud in pairs, stressing the sounds in bold.

> /ə/ – unstressed

2 🌐 2.04

Ask the students to say both sentences aloud so that they get a feeling for what sounds right. Ask them to say how *to* is pronounced in each sentence, then play the recording for them to check. Tell them that *to* is pronounced differently before a consonant and a vowel. Get them to say what the difference is.

| to drive /tə/ | a) /tə/ |
| to appear /tu:/ | b) /tu:/ |

3

Pairwork. Ask the students to take turns reading out the tips in Exercise 1 at the top of the page. Tell them to pay attention to their own and their partner's pronunciation of *to* and the weak forms and to correct it if necessary. Get several students to say the tips aloud to the class.

Vocabulary (SB page 51)

1

Focus attention on the words and phrases in the box and ask the students to try to put them into two categories: *cheap* and *expensive*. (Note: the exact meanings of the expressions will be explored in subsequent exercises.)

Cheap: affordable, budget, discounted, low-cost, no-frills
Expensive: daylight robbery, exorbitant, lavish, overpriced, a rip-off

2

Pairwork. Put the students into pairs and ask them to discuss the questions. They can use a dictionary if they are really stuck, but they should try to work out the answers for themselves. Give them the hint that more colourful or imaginative expressions are very often more informal. Get them to try to put the words into sentences to determine which ones cannot be used before a noun.

a) daylight robbery, no-frills, a rip-off
b) daylight robbery, exorbitant, overpriced, a rip-off
c) daylight robbery, a rip-off

3

• Ask the students to choose the best alternatives. Allow them to compare with a partner.

• Check that everyone has got a correct version before asking them to complete the sentences to make them true for visitors to their town or country. Put them in pairs to discuss their sentences. As they work, go round checking that they are pronouncing *to* correctly.

a) budget (*budget* just means cheap; *discounted* means reduced price, so it is more applicable to things like airline tickets for which there was a fixed price which has now been reduced)
b) lavish (*overpriced* is negative so it doesn't fit with a recommendation)
c) low-cost
d) exorbitant (*lavish* is not used for prices, but for things like services, meals, etc.)
e) affordable (*no-frills* is used for services rather than goods and could be ambiguous for clothes, which sometimes have frills!)

f) no-frills (you could use *discounted* for airline tickets but not the airline itself)
g) rip off (*daylight robbery* is never preceded by an article)

Speaking: anecdote (SB page 51)

For more information about how to set up, monitor and repeat Anecdotes, see page xx in the Introduction.

• Go through the instructions and the questions with the class. Give the students a minute or two to decide which purchase they're going to talk about. Then ask them to look at the questions and think about their answers to them. Allow them to make notes of what they're going to say and how they're going to say it, but discourage them from writing a paragraph that they can simply read out. Go round, monitoring and giving help where necessary.

• Pairwork. Put the students in pairs and ask them to take turns to tell their partner about something they've bought recently. Encourage them to ask each other follow-up questions to get further information. Then ask some pairs to report back to the class about what they found out.

Reading (SB page 52)

1

Discuss the proverb and any similar ones in the students' country or countries with the class.

People differ in what they love or hate.

2

Point out that the first part of the title is similar to the first part of the proverb they've just discussed. Ask them to read the article and think of a good way to complete the title. Accept any reasonable suggestions. Then have a class vote on the best.

Possible answer:
… is another man's treasure

3

Ask the students to read the article again and answer the questions with a partner.

a) To protect the environment.
b) By checking your emails or looking at messages posted online.
c) It helps to reduce the amount of rubbish being thrown away. It reduces the amount of raw materials that would be used to make a new item. The receiver has to pick the item up, so you don't have to go to any trouble to get rid of it. It's free and you don't have to give anything to the person you receive an item from.

eBay
Online auction website on which people can buy or sell goods.

Tucson /ˈtʌksʌn/
Tucson is an American city in the state of Arizona. It lies 100 km north of the U.S.–Mexico border.

The Salvation Army /ðə sælˈveɪʃ(ə)n ˈɑːmi/
The Salvation Army is a christian movement founded in the UK in 1865. Well known for its charitable work, the Salvation Army now operated in 118 countries around the world.

4

Ask the students to find words in the article to complete the glossary. Check answers with the class. Make sure the students realise that the use of *beauty* to mean advantage has nothing to do with physical beauty. It's often used to talk about a system or process that works well (*The beauty of it is that …*).

a) move over	f) missives
b) fads	g) rid themselves of
c) surplus	h) put yourself out
d) grassroots	i) unscrupulous
e) beauty	j) advocates

5

Pairwork. Ask the students to discuss the questions in pairs and encourage them to report back to the class.

Grammar (SB page 53)

Articles

1

Focus the students' attention on the email exchange. Ask the students to read it and identify the items that Harry is going to collect.

A sofa-bed, some bookshelves and a chest-of-drawers

2

• Focus the students' attention on the information on articles in the margin and go through it with the class. Then ask the students to decide which articles need to be added to the emails and where. Allow them to compare their answers in pairs before checking with the class.

• When everyone has a corrected version of the email exchange, ask them to do the second part of the exercise.

Hi. I have some furniture I need to get rid of (a sofa-bed, and some bookshelves) as I'm giving my bedroom a makeover. … Cheers, Mike.

Hi Mike
If the furniture is still available, … Could you give me some information about the sofa-bed? … Also, I'm in dire need of a wardrobe if you happen to have one. Cheers, Harry.

Hi Harry
… The sofa-bed is king-sized. Sorry I don't have a wardrobe but I do have a chest of drawers, if that's any use. You're welcome to come and collect the stuff if you have a van. Mike.

Hi – Yes, I'm still interested in everything, including the chest of drawers. I'll contact you again as soon as I've got hold of a van to pick the things up. Thanks a lot! H.

If something is unknown to the speaker, the listener or both, use *a(n)/some*. (*a sofa-bed, some bookshelves, a van*)
If something is known to both speaker and listener, use *the*. (*the furniture, the sofa-bed, the things*)

Grammar: articles
No article
You don't use articles with proper nouns such as places, people and companies.
Marc Goldstein is from Boston. He works for Reuters.
Exceptions are when the article is part of a name (*The BBC, The Rolling Stones*).
As the indefinite article means *one*, you don't use it with plurals or uncountable nouns. However, *some* can be used with both plurals and uncountable nouns.
He had some good ideas. / The bought some furniture.

Indefinite article *a/an* (introducing)
When you first mention new people, places or objects etc., the usual thing to do is introduce them:
She was wearing a beautiful dress from Italy.

Definite article *the* (referring/identifying)
When you identify something or refer to a specific thing, you use the definite article. This often happens for one of these two reasons.

1 **Back reference**
The jacket was made of soft leather.
The use of the definite article tells us we have already been introduced to the jacket.

2 **Shared knowledge**
As she drove down from the mountains, the sun was beginning to set over the ocean.
We are already familiar with mountains, the sun and the ocean.
In general statements you don't usually use the definite article with plural or uncountable nouns (*Ideas are food / Time is money*).

3

- Ask the students to write postings for Freecycle offering an item or items.

- Put the students into pairs and ask them to exchange their postings and write email replies. Encourage them to ask for further details about the items (colour, size, etc.), and to respond to any questions they're asked about their own items.

4

- Remind the students, if necessary, that in the first sentence *have dinner*, *have breakfast*, etc. are collocations that don't require any article because they refer to the meal in general. However, to talk about a special meal, an article is needed.

- Ask the students to complete the remaining questions and check answers with the class.

- Put the students into pairs and ask them to take turns asking and answering the questions.

> a) dinner, <u>a</u> special dinner
> b) train, <u>the</u>/<u>a</u> train
> c) <u>the</u> next long weekend, next weekend
> d) internet shopping, <u>the</u> internet
> e) north, <u>the</u> north
> f) <u>the</u> English, English

5

- Ask the students to cross out the words that aren't possible. If anyone is struggling, remind them to look at the sentences they've just written and those in the earlier exercises to find the answers.

- Check answers before asking the students to choose the alternatives that are true for them. Then put them into pairs to discuss their choices.

> a) meat (*meat* can't be used in a countable sense)
> b) work (we say *go to work*)
> c) supermarket (we say *at the supermarket*)
> d) business (we say *working in business*)
> e) music of Beethoven (we normally use *the* if the noun is qualified by *of*)
> f) people (we say *most people* because we are not specifying a particular group)
> g) the pasta (we don't use an article when talking about general likes and dislikes)

Cultural note

Ludwig von Beethoven /ˈlʊdvɪg vɒn ˈbeɪtəʊvən/ (1770–1827)

Ludwig von Beethoven was a German composer and pianist. In his late twenties, he began to lose his hearing and became totally deaf. Nevertheless, throughout his life he continued to produce masterpieces and he's widely regarded as one of classical music's greatest composers.

6 Grammar *Extra* 5, Part 2

Ask the students to turn to *Grammar Extra* 5, Part 2 on page 138 of the Student's Book. Here they'll find an explanation of the grammar they've been studying and a further exercise to practise it.

> **2**
> a) the/some, –   e) a, some, some
> b) a, the   f) –, –, some, some, the
> c) –, – /some   g) –, –, –, –
> d) the, the, the   h) the, a, some

Useful phrases (SB page 54)

1 🌐 2.05

- Focus the students' attention on the illustration. Ask them what the situation is (a woman is buying a vase from a market stall holder. The vase appears to be chipped, i.e. damaged but only slightly).

- Tell the students that they're going to listen to the conversation between the woman customer and the stall holder. Go through the questions, then play the recording and ask them to note down their answers.

> a) a marble vase
> b) She points out that it is chipped.
> c) She gets a reduction of 15 euros (reduced from 50 to 35 euros).

> 🌐 2.05 (C = Customer; M = Market stall holder)
>
> C: *Excuse me, how much is this vase?*
> M: *This one? It's 50 euros. Solid marble.*
> C: *Hmm. Yes, it's beautiful, but it's a bit more than I was prepared to pay. Could you give me a discount, do you think?*
> M: *Well, I suppose I could give you ten percent off. So, that would make it 45.*
> C: *Hmm. The thing is, it's a little bit chipped, here at the top, and I wanted to give it to someone, as a present.*
> M: *Well, I suppose I could knock off another 5 euros. But that's as low as I'm prepared to go. It's solid marble. Hand carved. You won't get another one like it.*
> C: *Yes, yes, I can see that, but I'm afraid it's still a bit above my price range. I think I'll leave it, thanks.*
> M: *Tell you what, you can have it for 35, and I'll throw in this little box as well.*
> C: *Oh, right. Is that your best price?*
> M: *Yes, I can't go any lower than that or I'll be giving it away.*
> C: *Okay, I'll take it. Thanks very much.*
> M: *Thank you. That's 35 euros, please. You've got yourself a bargain.*

2

Pairwork. Ask the students to work together to complete the useful phrases for bargaining. Play the recording again and then check answers.

3 🔘 2.06–2.08

- Go through the instructions and the questions with the class, then ask the students to read the first lines of the conversations and discuss their answers.

- Play the recording and ask the students to say whether they predicted correctly what would happen next.

1 a) Someone is looking at a room they want to rent.
  b) Someone is looking at a flat they want to rent.
  c) Someone is explaining to a teacher that they haven't had enough time to do an essay.
2 a) It's just that …
  b) The only problem is …
  c) the thing is…
3 (Students' own answers.)

🔘 **2.06** (F = Fiona; M = Man)

a)

F: Well, it's a lovely room, and the location is ideal. It's just that I was really looking for something furnished, particularly as the rent is rather high.

M: I see. Well, supposing I were to put in some furniture – say, a table and some dining chairs, a sofa, some cupboards. Would that help?

F: Well, that would be great, and, yes, I think that would solve the problem. So, I'll take it, then.

🔘 **2.07** (B = Brian; W = Woman)

b)

B: Yes, I really like the flat and I'm very interested. The only problem is, I don't have enough for a month's deposit at the moment.

W: Hmm. Well, I don't have any objections to deferring the deposit, as long as I get it, say, by the end of next month.

B: Well, that sounds like a good compromise. I'll have my pay cheque by then, so there shouldn't be any problems. Thanks very much.

🔘 **2.08** (P = Patrick; T = Teacher)

c)

P: I wanted to have a word with you about my essay. I know the deadline is the end of next week, but the thing is, I've had quite a lot to deal with recently. I was wondering if I could ask for an extension – say, an extra couple of weeks?

T: Well, in principle I'm prepared to grant you an extension, but the problem is, you've already had two extensions this year, and a fortnight is rather a long time.

P: Um, well, how would it be if I handed it in next Monday? I should be able to have it done by then, all being well.

T: Well, that seems like a good compromise, on condition that I have it on Monday morning without fail.

4

Ask the students to work individually to match the sentence halves. Check answers before asking them to say what each sentence expresses.

a) 6   b) 8   c) 7   d) 1   e) 3   f) 4   g) 2   h) 5

a) a request – e
b) a proposal – a, f, g, h
c) agreement – b, c, d

5

Pairwork. Put the students into pairs and get them to decide who will be A and who B. Ask them to turn to the pages indicated and follow the instructions. Go round taking note of any particularly good conversations that could be repeated for the class.

Vocabulary *Extra* (SB page 55)
British and American English

1

Pairwork. Ask the students to discuss the questions in pairs and to report back to the class. Ask them which variety of English they encounter most frequently through TV and the internet, as well as through personal contact with native speakers.

2

- Focus attention on the two adverts. Ask the students to read them and answer the first two questions.

- Check answers and then ask the students to examine the texts more closely and decide which is American English and which British. Ask them to underline the differences in vocabulary and spelling.

They are advertising a shopping website: shoppingexperience.com.

The blue advert is written in American English and the yellow one is in British English.
You can tell because of differences in grammar, vocabulary and spelling.

American advert	British advert
has gotten	has just got
a whole lot easier	so much easier
catalog	catalogue
mall	shopping centre
favorite	favourite
stores	shops
diapers	nappies
cell phones	mobile phones
baby strollers	prams
drapes	curtains
've gotten	've got
go downtown	go into town

Vocabulary: American and British English

- There are differences between British and American English both in terms of vocabulary and grammar. However, few of these cause any major problems of understanding between speakers of the two types of English. The differences are more a subject for curiosity than worry.

- At a time in our past when British English was adopting some characteristics of French court language, the English used by the Americans remained unchanged. So -re spellings (*centre*, *theatre*) in British English stayed as -er in America (*center*, *theater*). Likewise the British English use of *ou* (*favourite*, *colour*) remains *o* in North America (*color*, *favorite*) and *ue* at the end of words (*dialogue*, *catalogue*) is often dispensed with (*dialog*, *catalog*).

- In terms of vocabulary, in addition to the words given in the unit, students may be interested to learn the following differences:

American	British
gas station	petrol station
truck	lorry
sidewalk	pavement
freeway	motorway
two weeks	fortnight
pants	trousers

3

- Ask the students to work individually to decide how the words would be spelt in British English.

- Check answers and draw their attention to the spelling of *organize*. Point out that British English can use either z or s at the end of this word; American English uses only z in *ize* words.

centre	organise or organize
colour	pedalling
a driving licence	TV programme
grey	travelled

4

Pairwork. Encourage the students to discuss their ideas of what the differences might be before they check with the dictionary extracts.

5

Pairwork. Encourage the students to discuss who said the sentences and encourage them to come to a firm decision before you confirm the answers.

a) US (British English: *After I leave secondary school, I want to go to college / university in France.*)
b) British (US: *I went to a public school as my parents couldn't afford to send me to a private school.*)
c) US (British: *At college I studied maths, and got my degree last year.*)

d) US (British: *I use public transport because the cost of petrol is too high.*)
e) British (US: *We're hoping to go on vacation to Vancouver in the fall.*)
f) US (British: *The quickest way to the chemist's is to take the underground. It's only two stops away.*)

6

- Encourage the students to try this without looking in a dictionary. Most of the words are ones they'll already have encountered. Check answers before asking about the register of the words.

- Then put the students into pairs to discuss which of the sentences are true for them.

a) lift, first floor (There is a ground floor in British English so the first floor is one floor up from the ground.)
b) chips, crisps, sweets, biscuits
c) mum, a block of flats, (back) garden
d) At, go for a walk, cinema
e) queuing, angry, jump the queue or push in
f) wash my hands (N.B. *wash up* means wash the dishes in British English.)

7

Ask the students to check in their dictionaries and report back to the class.

Further practice material

Need more writing practice?

→ Workbook page 33
- Writing a news story.

Need more classroom practice activities?

→ Photocopiable resource materials pages 170 to 172
  Grammar: *Proverb auction*
  Vocabulary: *Communicative crossword*
  Communication: *Money talks*
→ The top 10 activities pages xv to xx

Need progress tests?

→ Test CD – *Test Unit 5*

Need more on important teaching concepts?

→ Key concepts in *New Inside Out* pages xxii to xxxv

Need student self-study practice?

→ CD-ROM – Unit 5: *Bargain*

Need student CEF self-evaluation?

→ CEF Checklists pages xxxvii to xliv

Need more information and more ideas?

→ www.insideout.net

6 Mind *Overview*

Section & Aims	What the students are doing
Speaking SB page 56 Fluency practice	Answering a quiz about the brain.
Listening SB page 56 Listening for specific information	Labelling photos of games. Listening to people talking about games. Identifying the question they were asked and making notes.
Reading & Speaking SB page 57 Reading for detail Fluency practice	Identifying words with negative connotations. Completing a text about brain training and discussing it. Doing a brain training quiz.
Reading SB page 58 Reading for gist and detail	Matching headings to extracts from a text. Reading extracts from a book and answering questions.
Vocabulary SB page 58 Verbs of seeing	Matching verbs to definitions. Matching *observe, recognise* and *see* to different meanings. Writing a paragraphs with *observe, recognise* and *see*.
Listening SB page 60 Listening for gist and specific information	Discussing questions on the senses. Listening to people and identifying which questions they answer. Making notes on their answers.
Grammar SB page 60 Verbs of the senses	Categorising verbs according to whether they're stative or dynamic. Completing extracts with sense verbs. Studying the use of modal auxiliaries with sense verbs.
Reading & Vocabulary SB page 61 Reading for gist Descriptive language	Matching mental problems with definitions. Reading a text about a problem dog and discussing the language used. Summarising the story in a factual account.
Grammar SB page 62 Participle clauses	Studying the form and use of participle clauses. Rewriting sentences. Adding *not* to sentences with participle clauses.
Vocabulary SB page 63 Collocations with *mind*	Studying collocations with *mind*. Matching *mind* collocations with definitions.
Pronunciation SB page 63 Word linking	Listening to a conversation and answering questions. Examining the way native English speakers run words together.
Useful phrases SB page 64 Useful conversational phrases for making appropriate requests	Identifying degrees of politeness and appropriate responses. Listening to conversations to identify how well the speakers know each other. Acting out conversations with different relationships. Practising different ways of making a request.
Writing *Extra* SB page 65 Emails making and declining requests	Reading emails to identify the sender and the requests. Examining ways to refuse requests and soften the tone of the refusal. Writing a reply to an email, refusing a request.
Writing WB page 39	Writing an informal email offering advice.

6 Mind *Teacher's notes*

Warm up

Ask the students to work in pairs and to write down five facts they know about the human brain. Ask them to put these aside and then come back to them after they've done the quiz. Find out how many of the facts they wrote down were mentioned in the quiz and if any were incorrect.

Speaking (SB page 56)

Ask the students to work individually to do the quiz. Encourage them to decide on their answers for all the questions and to compare with a partner before they turn to page 130 to check. Ask them to say which of the answers they found most surprising.

Listening (SB page 56)

1

- Pairwork. Focus attention on the photos and elicit that these all show games which require some kind of brainpower. Ask the students to label the games, and then decide which is the oldest and which the most recent. Allow them to work in pairs or small groups.

- Check answers and ask the students to say what the aim of each game is and which, if any, they enjoy playing.

> 1 Nintendo   4 crossword
> 2 Rubik's cube   5 chess
> 3 sudoku
>
> *From oldest to most recent:*
> chess (15th century)
> crossword (first crossword published in 1913)
> Rubik's cube (invented in 1974)
> Nintendo (first game console came out in 1977)
> sudoku (modern version invented in 1979)

Cultural notes

Sudoku /sʌˈduːkəʊ/
Meaning 'single number' in Japanese, Sudoku is a logic-based number puzzle in which players complete the missing numbers in a 9x9 grid so that only one number between 1 and 9 appears one time in each column/row.

Nintendo /nɪnˈtendəʊ/
Nintendo is a Japanese video game company. Since 1977 Nintendo has been producing home entertainment electronic equipment.

2 🔊 2.09

- Ask the students to read the questions. Then play the recording for them to match each speaker to one of the questions.

- Allow them to discuss their answers in pairs and then play the recording again for them to check.

> Speaker 1 – b   Speaker 3 – a
> Speaker 2 – d   Speaker 4 – c

> 🔊 2.09
>
> 1
> *Hmm, that's a difficult one. I think a crossword. Um, I don't think I've ever completed one, to be honest. And I've got a degree! Yeah, I mean, I've spent hours and hours … especially the cryptic ones – I always need help. But, um, you know, we get there in the end!*
>
> 2
> *Oh, I've got absolutely wonderful and clear memories of playing chess with my dad. I mean, we used to spend hours actually and, er, he taught me everything I know virtually and, and you know, I've gone on to play throughout my life and I find it a wonderful thing to pass on to my kids.*
>
> 3
> *I'm absolutely obsessed with Sudoku. I play it all the time if I'm on a train or a bus, or I can actually spend hours sitting at home doing it, it's quite sad!*
>
> 4
> *Well, I think those hand-held game things are just pointless. I mean, I don't see, I really don't see the point in them. People say, you know, it improves eye/hand co-ordination and all that kind of stuff, but I don't get it, I don't like them and I don't see how people can spend hours and hours playing them.*

3

Ask the students to listen again and make notes of what the people say. Allow them to compare their notes in pairs and ask them to discuss whether they agree or disagree with anything that was said. Encourage them to say what their own answers to the questions would be.

Reading & Speaking (SB page 57)

1

- Pairwork. Put the students into pairs and ask them to look at the box and discuss which words they think have negative connotations. Ask them to choose one word and to write a definition for it. As they work, make a note of which pair defines which word and try to ensure that each of the negative words is defined by at least one of the pairs.

- Call on various pairs to read out their definitions to the class, making sure that each word is covered. The rest of the class guess which word it is each time.

> *Words with negative connotations*: decay, decline, inactivity, lack, loss

2

- Ask the students if they know, or can guess, what *brain training* is (mental exercise which is supposed to keep your brain fit and improve your memory and your mental abilities, particularly as you grow older).

- Ask them to read the text and complete it with six of the words in the box in Exercise 1.

> 1 decline   2 inactivity   3 lack   4 decay
> 5 fit   6 training

3

Pairwork. Make sure the students understand the words in the box. Ask them to think about which ones best describe the article and to compare their choices with their partners. Then ask them to discuss the remaining questions.

> chatty, informal
> b) the editorial introduction to a magazine

4

- Ask the students to work individually to answer the quiz questions. Help them by telling them when the three minutes starts and finishes.

- When they've finished, tell them to turn to page 131 where they'll find some of the answers. Ask them to discuss in pairs how they did and whether this was better or worse than they expected. Find out if they enjoy doing quizzes like this.

Reading (SB page 58)

1

Pairwork. Ask the students to look at the book cover and the information underneath and to discuss the questions. They may be interested to know that a subsequent and similar book by Dr Sacks, *Awakenings*, was turned into a successful film starring Robert De Niro and Robin Williams.

2

Give the students time to read the four extracts on page 59. Then ask them to match a heading to each one. Give help with any difficult vocabulary but avoid discussing the highlighted verbs as they'll come up in the next section. Allow them to compare their answers in pairs before checking with the class.

> 1 The patient
> 2 The doctor's first impression
> 3 The doctor's examination
> 4 The diagnosis

3

- Pairwork. Ask the students to read and discuss the questions. Allow them to compare their answers with another pair before checking with the class. Give them plenty of time to use their imaginations in answering the last question before they turn to the file cards on page 131.

- You might like to ask the students to say which they think is the strangest case and whether the truth was any stranger than the ideas they came up with.

> a) His first symptoms were that he didn't recognise his students until they spoke to him and he mistook objects for people. He consulted an ophthalmologist when he developed diabetes. The ophthalmologist wasn't able to help.
> b) His eyes moved around; they didn't stay still and focus on the doctor.
> c) No, though he knew other people thought he didn't see normally and he knew he occasionally made embarrassing mistakes. He saw details but he couldn't put the details together to form a whole picture.
> d) (Students' own answers.)
> e) He told him to ignore the problem and concentrate on music, which is what he could do well and what gave him pleasure. Nowadays a doctor would probably prescribe a thorough brain scan and possibly surgery.
> f) (See answers in SB page 131.)

Vocabulary (SB page 58)

1

- Focus the students' attention on the highlighted verbs in the extracts on page 59. Point out that most of these words are to do with seeing or perception. Ask them to try to match the words with the definitions.

- Allow them to compare in pairs or small groups before checking with the class.

> | a) gaze | e) recognise |
> |---------|--------------|
> | b) observe | f) scan |
> | c) dart | g) examine |
> | d) take something in | h) see |

Vocabulary: verbs of seeing

- Ways of describing literally how to see something:
  Gaze means look at someone/something for a long time because you are interested or because you're thinking of something else.
  Gawp is to look at someone/something for a long time, usually with your mouth open, in a foolish way.
  Stare is to look at someone/something directly for a long time, which can be intimidating.

- Ways of looking at someone/something quickly:
  Glance (look at someone/something and then away again quickly).
  Scan (see Student's Book).
  Glimpse (to see something for a very short time, probably not completely).

- Ways of showing your disapproval:
  Glare (look angrily for a long time at someone).
  Frown (move your eyebrows down because you are angry or worried).
  Scowl and *glower* (look very angry).

2

Go through the sentences and the verbs in the list. Do the first one as an example and then ask the students to match the others. Allow them to compare in pairs before checking answers with the class.

a) 3	b) 1	c) 4	d) 2	e) 6	f) 5

3

Do this with the whole class. With multilingual classes, elicit several replies.

4

Pairwork. Ask the students to write their paragraphs, then tell them to exchange them with a partner. Go round, checking that they're using the words correctly.

Listening (SB page 60)

1

Pairwork. Ask the students to read the questions and to discuss their answers in pairs. Then ask the pairs to report back to the class on their discussions.

a) Traditionally, people speak of the five senses: sight, hearing, touch, taste and smell, but neurologists have identified many more, e.g., *thermoception*, the sense of heat (or its absence) *equilibrioception*, our sense of balance, which is determined by the fluid-containing cavities in the inner ear, *nociception*, the perception of pain from the skin, joints and body organs and *proprioception*, or 'body awareness'. This is the unconscious knowledge of where our body parts are without being able to see or feel them.
b) to f) (Students' own answers.)

2 ⊕ 2.10–2.14

- Go through the instructions with the class. Make sure that everyone understands that each speaker is answering one of the questions from Exercise 1. Ask them to write the names down, leaving space under each name to make notes for each person.

- Play the recording, pausing after each speaker to allow the students time to make notes. Play it more than once if necessary. Then ask the students to compare their answers with their partner, before checking answers with the class.

Mike – b, sight	Nick – b, touch
Maria – e, hearing	Petra – f, smell
Helen – d, smell	

⊕ 2.10

Mike

Mmm … sight I suppose. Yes, the most important one is sight I suppose … I mean, if you're blind, if you can't see, then although you can lead a full life and all that, I think it does make you more vulnerable, more dependent on other people, I don't know, for silly little things like, for example, like shopping in a supermarket or whatever, and I would really hate it if I couldn't see what things or people looked like … or the expression on a person's face when they're talking to you. I mean, you wouldn't even know if they were looking at you or whether they looked interested in what you were saying.

⊕ 2.11

Maria

No, I haven't, but I read this article about a man who'd gone deaf and then his hearing was restored to him, and he spoke about how isolating it can be if you can't hear. He said that you miss out on a lot of things, that although you can communicate fine when you need to, you miss out on the subtleties of a conversation, and the thing he missed most was humour … the humour in spontaneous conversation … because it all gets slowed down when you're signing. And he really missed listening to music, that was the worst part he said. That, and not being able to hear his wife's voice. And he said that it was really strange to start with when he regained his hearing. Everything sounded much louder. He said he actually misses total silence sometimes, just not hearing anything, and that it can be really relaxing.

⊕ 2.12

Helen

Um, I don't know … but maybe smell, I suppose … like someone can just walk past you on the street and you can catch the smell of their perfume and it reminds you really strongly of someone … or food … I can't remember where I was the other day, but I suddenly smelt the most wonderful cooking smells: coconut oil and eastern spices and it reminded me so strongly of my holidays in Thailand … I could see the palm trees, taste the food, feel the sun on my skin … yes, I think smell triggers the strongest, most vivid memories.

2.13

Nick

This may seem like a strange answer, but maybe touch … you know, the sense of touch … I think it's probably the one we take most for granted, being able to feel things and it's not, it's not, you know, a sense that's limited to one part of your body either – it's everything, every single pore, every single bit of your skin.
I remember seeing a documentary about a man who'd been born deaf and mute and had later lost his sight in an accident – he lived a full life – he was eighty-something and he still worked and even travelled. He just lived his life totally through his sense of touch. In this programme, they showed him visiting other people like him in Japan. It was amazing – they used an international signing language which was based on touch – they would touch each other and sign on each other's palms, and they could feel each other talking – and it showed them going to a drum concert, too – like a traditional Japanese drum concert – and they could feel the music, I mean, they could feel the vibrations of the drums, even though they couldn't hear them. It was just totally amazing.

2.14

Petra

Well, usually I'm renowned for my sense of smell! Sometimes I can smell things that no-one else notices. That can be good because I'm really sensitive to things like gas leaks and anything that smells bad … things like food that's gone off. My mum often asks me to smell meat or fish or milk or whatever to see if it's okay … but recently I've had quite a heavy cold and it's really affected my sense of smell. I mean, I can smell really strong things, like coffee or if something's burning in the kitchen, but I can't smell other things like perfume so I don't know how much to put on. And I really miss the subtler smells in the kitchen. It affects my taste too. Everything tastes so bland.

Grammar (SB page 60)

Verses of the senses

Oh, dear!

1

- Pairwork. Go through the instructions with the class and make sure they understand the difference between stative meaning and dynamic meaning. Draw their attention to the examples of verbs of the senses in the margin and the example sentences. In each pair of sentences, the first example demonstrates stative meaning and the second dynamic.

- Ask them to look at the verbs in the box and classify them according to whether they have stative or dynamic meaning or both.

> NO a) feel, hear, see, sense, smell, taste, touch ??
> NO b) listen, look, watch

it looks nice!

c) feel, hear, see, sense, smell, taste, touch – these verbs can be used with both a stative and a dynamic meaning, although the meaning can then change.

Language notes

Grammar: verbs of the senses

- To talk about ability or sensation the following verbs are used with a stative meaning (and are usually used with *can*, *could* or *be able to*): *feel, hear, look, see, sense, smell* and *taste*.

  *I **can see** her. Here she is.*
  *I **was able to taste** the ocean before I saw it.*

  Verbs with stative meanings are not usually used in the continuous form.

- To talk about actions the following verb can be used with a dynamic meaning: *feel, hear, listen, look, see, sense, smell, taste, touch* and *watch*.

  *Ben's **not feeling** well today.*
  *I'm **seeing** her tomorrow.*

  When using the sensory verbs in the continuous form, the meaning often changes (*How are you feeling today?* is a question asking about someone's health; *I'm seeing her tomorrow.* means 'I'm meeting her tomorrow', etc.)

2 **2.15**

- Do the first one as an example with the class, then ask the students to work individually to complete the remaining sentences. Remind them that they may need to modify the verbs. As they work, go round giving extra help where needed and making sure that the students are all forming their sentences correctly.

- Play the recording for the students to check their answers.

> a) can't see
> b) couldn't see
> c) can't hear
> d) listening, hear
> e) could see, taste, feel
> f) could feel, couldn't hear
> g) smells
> h) tastes

2.15

a)
… if you're blind, if you can't see, then although you can lead a full life and all that, I think it does make you more vulnerable …

b)
… I would really hate it if I couldn't see what things or people looked like …

c)
… I read this article about a man who'd gone deaf and then his hearing was restored to him, and he spoke about how isolating it can be if you can't hear.

d)

… he really missed listening to music, that was the worst part, he said. That and not being able to hear his wife's voice.

e)

… I could see the palm trees, taste the food, feel the sun on my skin …

f)

… they could feel the vibrations of the drums, even though they couldn't hear them.

g)

… I'm really sensitive to things like gas leaks and anything that smells bad …

h)

I really miss the subtler smells in the kitchen. It affects my taste, too. Everything tastes so bland.

3

Do this with the class, asking the students to look back at their completed sentences from Exercise 2 to find the answers.

> *can, could*; used with a stative meaning; *be able to*

4

Pairwork. Go through the instructions with the class, then do the first pair of sentences as an example. Then ask the students to discuss the differences between the remaining pairs of sentences.

> 1 A – *see* is a stative verb referring to ability to see
>   B – *see* is a dynamic verb meaning to meet someone socially (here it is not a verb of the senses)
> 2 A – *hear* is a stative verb referring to ability to hear
>   B – *hear* is a dynamic verb meaning that people have been telling the speaker things about the other person (here it is not a verb of the senses)
> 3 A – *feel* is a dynamic verb referring to a consciousness of one's state of health
>   B – *feel* is a stative verb referring to ability to feel
> 4 A – *taste* is a dynamic verb referring to the action of tasting
>   B – *taste* is a stative verb referring to ability to taste

5

- Go through the instructions with the class and ask them to work individually to make their notes. You might like to set a time limit in which they have to note down everything they can hear, smell and touch.

- Put the students in pairs or small groups to compare and discuss their answers.

6 Grammar *Extra* 6, Part 1

Ask the students to turn to *Grammar Extra* 6 Part 1 on page 138 of the Student's Book. Here they'll find an explanation of the grammar they've been studying and a further exercise to practise it.

> 1
> a) I can't see   e) watching
> b) Am I hearing   f) could always smell
> c) can you taste   g) 've heard
> d) listening to   h) can sense, 'm sensing

Reading & Vocabulary (SB page 61)

1

Groupwork. Ask the students to work in small groups to discuss the questions. Get a spokesperson from each group to report back to the class on any interesting information that came up.

2

- Explain that items a) to e) are the names psychologist give to various mental problems. Ask the students to match them to the definitions. Encourage them to try to work them out without resorting to dictionaries.

- Check answers and then ask the students which disorders they think are most common in humans and which in animals.

> a) 3   b) 2   c) 4   d) 5   e) 1
>
> It could be argued that all are common in both humans and animals, though c) and e) are usually associated with animals and b) is more commonly associated with humans.

3

Give the students plenty of time to read the case history and make their 'diagnosis'. They may decide that it isn't appropriate to ascribe any of these conditions to Willy and that he's just a destructive dog! (Be aware that in some cultures ascribing human traits to animals is not acceptable.) You might also elicit that it isn't a good idea to leave a dog in a car as they can die from heat exhaustion, and because bored dogs can become destructive when they need something to do.

> If anything, Willy may have been suffering from separation anxiety, made uneasy by the absence of his owner.

4

Pairwork. Ask the students to discuss the meanings of the expressions with a partner. Then check answers with the class.

a) a gentle, quiet animal
b) torn into small pieces
c) a short sleep
d) becoming quieter as he moved further away
e) unable to control his anger (in this context – obviously the emotion can vary)
f) people often see him

5

- The students could work on their summaries in pairs. You could have a competition to see who can get all the facts of the story in the smallest number of words.

- Get the students to compare their summaries with the original. Draw their attention to the various features of the writer's style, particularly the humorous and dramatic effect of understatement (*his new mode of transport had been completely remodelled; overcome with emotion*), and sarcasm (*an air-conditioning system had been thoughtfully provided by the removal of the windscreen; exhausted by all his hard work …*).

> *Possible answer:*
> Mr X left his dog alone in his van. The dog tore it up. When Mr X came back the dog ran away. Mr X chased angrily after him. The dog is still missing.

Extra activity

The facts of the story are quite simple and part of the humour lies in the exaggerated style. Ask the students to work in groups and to find examples of things that contribute to the humour.

> *Possible answer:*
> The story is told as if the writer believes that the dog was trying to be helpful in 'remodelling' the van. For example, the missing windscreen is described as a new air-conditioning system. The story is told consistently as if what took place was a good thing and that Mr X is pleased with his dog, when in fact he's very angry.

Grammar (SB page 62)

Participle clauses

1

- Focus the students' attention on the information and example in the margin. Ask the students to create three sentences by taking one clause from each box. Discourage them from looking back at the story on page 61 as they do this.

- Allow them to compare in pairs before checking answers with the class.

a), f), h) – Having left his trusty companion to keep an eye on the smart new van, Mr X returned from lunch to find that his new mode of transport had been completely remodelled.
b), e), g) – Waking up with a jump, Willy sat up to greet his owner and barked with excitement.
c, d) i) – Numbed by the efficiency of his new air-conditioning system, he's often spotted scouring the streets between deliveries, under the protection of a warm blanket.

Language notes

Grammar: participle clauses

- The action described in the main clause is usually a consequence of the action described in the participle clause.

Participle clause	Main clause
Meeting her for the first time,	*he understood why Rob found her so amusing.*
Wearied by a hard day's work,	*he poured himself a long, cool Martini.*
Having met him,	*I don't believe he deserves her.*

- A less literary alternative which shows the consequence clearly could be:
  He understood why Rob found her so amusing **when** *he* **met** *her for the first time.*
  He poured himself a long, cool Martini **because he was weary after** *a hard day's work.*
  I don't believe that he deserves her **now that I have met him**.

- *Not* always comes at the beginning of a participle clause:
  Not *discouraged by …,* **Not** *wanting to offend …*

2

Pairwork. Ask the students to discuss the questions and then get individual students to report back to the class on their answers.

a) present participle – b; past participle – c; perfect participle – a
b) a) Mr X b) Willy c) Mr X
c) 2 is more likely to be spoken; 1 was used in the text; *so* has been added

3

- Ask the students to work individually to rewrite the sentences.

- Allow them to compare answers in pairs before you check with the class. Make sure they punctuate their sentences correctly.

- Ask the students to say whether any of the sentences are true for them or anyone they know.

> a) Having finished university, I went on a long holiday.
> b) Living on my own, I don't really do a lot of cooking.
> c) Being on a diet, I don't eat sweets.
> d) Being tired after a long week at work, I like to spend the weekends relaxing.

4

Ask the students to read the sentence very carefully and to decide what word is missing and where it should go. Then tell them to check their answers on page 61 and explain that *not* goes immediately before the participle in participle clauses.

> *not*: and not thinking it necessary …

5

Pairwork. Ask the students to work together to decide if *not* is needed in each sentence and, if so, where it should go. Check answers with the class. Make sure in the last one that they don't try to put *not* before *Knowing*. Explain the difference in meaning that this would create.

> a) Not discouraged by the long climb …
> b) Not wanting to offend people, …
> d) Knowing that not arriving on time …

6

As the transformation is from written style to spoken language, it might be best to do this exercise orally, either selecting students to do each one or calling for volunteers. Alternatively, this could be done as pairwork, followed by a whole-class check.

> a) They weren't discouraged by the long climb ahead of them and they set off at dawn.
> b) They didn't want to offend anyone, so they decided to extend the guest list …
> c) When you have completed the form, please send it, with a photograph, to the address below.
> d) He knew that he'd make a very bad impression if he didn't arrive on time, so he …

7 Grammar *Extra* 6, Part 2

Ask the students to turn to *Grammar Extra* 6, Part 2 on page 138 of the Student's Book. Here they'll find an explanation of the grammar they've been studying and a further exercise to practise it.

> 2
> a) <u>Being</u> shy …
> b) <u>Having finished</u> university …
> c) <u>Impressed</u> by the publicity …
> d) Having <u>been</u> brought up …
> e) Finding <u>it</u> difficult …

Vocabulary (SB page 63)

1

Pairwork. You might like to set a time limit for the pairs to come up with as many collocations with *mind* as they can. Write the students' suggestions on the board and make sure everyone understands them all.

> *Possible answers:*
> at the back of my mind
> frame of mind
> have half a mind to
> set your mind on something
> have your mind on other things
> slip your mind
> cross your mind
> have an open mind
> blow your mind
> mind your own business
> don't mind me

Language note

Vocabulary: collocations with *mind*
The examples of collocations in this unit include a wide selection with the verb and the noun *mind*. In many cases the myriad meanings of *mind* can include *deciding, feeling, remembering, paying attention* and *thinking*.

2

- Ask the students to read the sentences and see how many of the collocations they listed in Exercise 1 they can find.
- Then read each sentence aloud in turn and ask the students just to identify when *mind* is a verb and when it is a noun. The meanings of the expressions will be explored in the next exercise.

> | a) verb | b) verb | c) verb | d) noun |
> |---------|---------|---------|---------|
> | e) noun | f) verb | g) noun | h) noun |
> | i) noun | j) noun | | |

3

- Ask the students to match the collocations in Exercise 2 with the meanings.
- Then ask the students to choose expressions they'd like to learn and to write new sentences using them.

> | 1 j) | 2 e) | 3 a) | 4 f) | 5 b) | 6 h) | 7 d) |
> |------|------|------|------|------|------|------|
> | 8 c) | 9 g) | 10 i) | | | | |

Pronunciation (SB page 63)

1 🌐 2.16

Focus attention on the illustration, then go through the instructions and the questions with the class so that they know what they're listening for. Play the recording for the students to listen to the conversation and note down their answers to the questions.

a) two brothers and colleague of the older brother
b) in a bar/pub; the atmosphere is generally relaxed – there is some tension between the two brothers – the two colleagues need to talk privately about a work issue

---

🌐 2.16

(A = Adam; B = Brad; D = Dylan)

A: Do you mind budging up a bit?
B: No, of course not.
A: Thanks. Dylan, would you mind not sitting there?
D: Why?
A: You're leaning on my jacket.
D: Sorry!
A: So, Brad, have you decided?
D: Decided what?
A: Mind your own business!
D: Oh, come on!
B: Dylan, would you mind getting us some drinks?
D: Yes, I would.
B: Oh, come on! It's just boring work stuff.
D: Oh, okay. I don't believe it for a second.
B: You know, I'll cover for you while you're away.
A: Would you?
B: Yeah, really, no problem.
A: Hmm, but what about Peter? Do you think he'll mind?
B: No, of course not. Mind you, Nicholas will.
A: Really, why?

2

- Ask the students to complete the sentences with collocations with *mind*.

- Play the recording again for them to check their answers.

a) Do you mind	c) Mind
b) Would you mind	d) Mind you

3

Play the recording again and ask the students to listen out for the underlined sections. Identify the sound and then get the whole class to repeat the expressions. Explain that native English speakers often run sounds together rather than pronouncing each one separately.

/ʤə/

Pronunciation note

Assimilation: final *d* before *you*
When two sounds join they can create a third. This is called assimilation. In this example we meet /d/ + /j/ = /ʤ/. This assimilation applies not only to phrases like *do you*, *would you* and *mind you*, but also within words like *education* /eʤukeɪʃ(ə)n/ and *gradual* /grӕʤuəl/.

4

Pairwork. Ask the students to discuss the questions and practise saying them out loud. Go round, listening and encouraging them to run the underlined sounds together.

Useful phrases (SB page 64)

1

Pairwork. Ask the students to look at the list of requests and put them in order of politeness/formality. When checking answers, note that the order given here is a suggested answer: there is room for discussion and it often depends on the context and the intonation as well as the actual wording of the request.

Suggested order: 8, 7, 1, 3, 5, 4, 2, 6

Language notes

Vocabulary: useful phrases – requests

- When making requests, generally speaking the longer the sentence, the more polite it sounds.

- Using an imperative either demonstrates a very informal request, dispensing with the usual pleasantries, or, if starting with 'Please …', brusque indifference from someone in an official capacity.

- Requests starting with *Would you …?* tend to sound more polite using a conditional voice to put a respectful distance between the person making the request and the recipient.

- When responding to a request, you can show polite reluctance by using these hesitation devices:
  Well …, To be honest …, To tell you the truth …, Actually …, etc.

2 🌐 2.17

- Ask the students to match the responses to the requests. Then allow them to compare in pairs but do not confirm answers at this point.

- Play the recording and ask the students to say if any of the responses seem inappropriate to them.

a) could match with: 1, 2, 3, 4, 6, 7, 8, most appropriate with 2
b) could match with all the requests, most appropriate with 4 or 8
c) 5
d) 1
e) 7
f) could match with 3, 4, 5, 6, 7 and 8, most appropriate with 6 – in a sarcastic tone
g) could match with 3, 4 and 8, most appropriate with 3
h) could match with either 1 or 4 – both appropriate

🔘 2.17

1   (M = Man; W = Woman)
M: *Do you mind if I smoke?*
W: *Er, I don't think you can here actually.*

2   (W = Woman; B = Boy)
W: *Okay if we pick you up at six?*
B: *I'm cool with that.*

3
A: *Would you mind lending me a fiver?*
B: *It depends.*

4   (G = Girl; B = Boy)
G: *Can I copy your homework?*
B: *Er well, to be honest, I'm not really comfortable with that.*

5
A: *May I have my book back, please?*
B: *What book?*

6   (M = Man; W = Woman)
M: *Give me a pen.*
W: *Anything else?*

7   (SA = Shop assistant; C = Customer)
SA: *Please sign here.*
C: *What do you mean, sign?*

8
A: *Would you mind awfully if I asked you to write that report again?*
B: *I hope you're joking.*

3 🔘 2.18

Explain that what the students heard in Exercise 2 were excerpts from conversations and that now they're going to hear the complete conversations. Go through the questions first so that they know what to listen out for, then play the recording. You may need to play it more than once.

1   no, probably acquaintances or strangers (in a children's playground), to be allowed to smoke
2   yes, making arrangements to pick someone up to go to the airport
3   yes, asking to borrow money to buy a train ticket
4   school friends or acquaintances, asking to copy another student/classmate's work
5   yes, asking for a book she lent her friend some time ago
6   yes, asking for a pen
7   no, shop assistant and customer, shop assistant asks the customer to sign a document
8   yes, boss and employee, asking the employee to change a report

🔘 2.18

1   (M = Man; W = Woman)
M: *Do you mind if I smoke?*
W: *Er, I don't think you can here actually.*
M: *Why not?*
W: *Well, I think it's a non-smoking area.*
M: *Huh. You can't smoke anywhere these days.*
W: *Mmmm.*

2   (W = Woman; B = Boy)
W: *What time does the plane leave?*
B: *At nine.*
W: *Okay if we pick you up at six?*
B: *I'm cool with that.*

3
A: *Would you mind lending me a fiver?*
B: *It depends.*
A: *On what?*
B: *On what you're going to spend it on.*
A: *The tube fare home.*
B: *I'll add it to your debt, shall I?*
A: *Yeah. Pop it on the tab.*

4   (G = Girl; B = Boy)
G: *Can I copy your homework?*
B: *Er, well, to be honest, I'm not really comfortable with that.*
G: *Oh, please. It's not as if anyone will know.*
B: *No, I'm sorry.*

5
A: *May I have my book back, please?*
B: *What book?*
A: *The one I lent you six weeks ago.*
B: *The one about the life and times of that guy …*
A: *Yes, that's the one.*
B: *Umm, yeah, sure.*

6   (M = Man; W = Woman)
M: *This one looks possible, two bedrooms, garden, lounge and kitchen, 125,000 pounds.*
W: *Where is it?*
M: *Southsea, and it's got a garage.*
W: *Make a note of the number.*
M: *Give me something to write on.*
W: *Here you are, write on the other side of this.*
M: *Give me something to lean on.*
W: *Use this.*
M: *Give me a pen.*
W: *Anything else?*

7   (SA = Shop assistant; C = Customer)
SA: *Please sign here.*
C: *What do you mean, sign?*
SA: *Well, if you want to go ahead with the purchase, you have to sign the contract.*
C: *Isn't that a bit excessive? It's only a toy.*
SA: *Not really.*
C: *Well, I think I'd better read it first.*
SA: *That's fine.*

8
A: *Hi there Mike.*
B: *Hello. What's the matter?*
A: *Would you mind awfully if I asked you to write that report again?*
B: *I hope you're joking.*
A: *No, I'm afraid I'm not.*

a) 1 you must be joking!
   2 we are unable to …
   3 I just can't
b) 1 why don't you try asking Izzy?
   2 Regrettably, However, it may be possible …
   3 I'm really sorry, Have you tried …?

4

- Pairwork. Put the students into pairs and ask them choose a situation from the pictures and act it out.

- Ask the students to change partners and choose another situation, this time, changing also the relationship between the speakers. Get the pairs to act out their conversations for the rest of the class to guess what the relationship is.

5

Groupwork. Put the students into small groups to discuss the questions. Then ask them to report back to the class on what they found out.

6

- Ask the students to write their requests and not to show other people what they've written. Make sure they choose six different ways to make their requests.

- Ask the students to stand up and mingle, taking turns to make their requests to as many people as possible and changing the way they make it each time.

7

Have a class feedback session in which the students discuss the questions in relation to their experiences of making requests in different ways.

Writing *Extra* (SB page 65)

Emails making and declining requests

1

Pairwork. Ask the students to read the emails and decide who the senders are and what requests were made of them. Get them to report back to the class on what they decided. Encourage them to say what clues they found to help them make their decision.

1 a) a friend; b) to look after a pet, probably a cat or dog as it needs a garden
2 a) train company customer services officer; b) a refund for a train ticket and expenses incurred when a rain was cancelled
3 a) a friend; b) to babysit

2

Ask the students to work individually to underline the phrases used to refuse and to soften the refusal. Then allow them to compare in pairs before checking with the class.

3

Ask the students to work individually to read the two emails. Give them plenty of time to do this. Ask them to think about which one they'd find most difficult to refuse and why. Have a class discussion of their answers.

4

Pairwork. Ask the students to work together to write a reply to one of the emails in Exercise 3. Remind them that they should try to work in some of the expressions they underlined in Exercise 2.

5

Get the pairs to exchange emails with several other pairs and answer the questions. Have a class vote on which was the most successful reply and which the most outrageous excuse.

Further practice material

Need more writing practice?
→ Workbook page 39
- Writing an informal email offering advice.

Need more classroom practice activities?
→ Photocopiable resource materials pages 173 to 175
Grammar: *Stative or dynamic phrases?*
Vocabulary: *Ways of speaking and looking*
Communication: *Memories*
→ The top 10 activities pages xv to xx

Need progress tests?
→ Test CD – *Test Unit 6*

Need more on important teaching concepts?
→ Key concepts in *New Inside Out* pages xxii to xxxv

Need student self-study practice?
→ CD-ROM – Unit 6: *Mind*

Need student CEF self-evaluation?
→ CEF Checklists pages xxxvii to xliv

Need more information and more ideas?
→ www.insideout.net

Review B *Teacher's notes*

These exercises act as a check of the grammar and vocabulary that the students have learnt in Units 4–6. Use them to find any problems that students are having, or anything that they haven't understood and which will need further work.

Grammar (SB page 66)

Remind the students of the grammar explanations they read and the exercises they did in the *Grammar Extra* on pages 136 to 139.

1

This exercise reviews the future as seen from the past from Unit 4. Check answers before putting the students into pairs to discuss whether they've ever been in a similar situation. Encourage them to report back to the class on any interesting stories.

> a) We were supposed to be going to the seaside, but the car broke down so we didn't go.
> b) I was going to do my homework last night, but I didn't feel very well so I went to bed early.
> c) We were due to leave at 8.30, but there was heavy fog and the plane was delayed by six hours.
> d) I was to have met the minister at the opening, but he was delayed at the last minute.
> e) We were on the verge of giving up hope when the rescue party arrived.

2

This exercise reviews discourse markers from Unit 4. Check answers, making sure the students understand the function of the discourse markers that complete the text. Then have a class discussion on whether or not they agree with the text.

> 1 for example
> 2 Similarly
> 3 such as
> 4 that is to say
> 5 at any rate

3

- Pairwork. This exercise reviews relative clauses from Unit 5. Put the students into pairs and ask them to discuss which is the correct alternative. Point out that sometimes both are possible. If necessary, go over the rules with them: *who* and *that* can both be used to refer to people. There are many places where *that* and *which* are interchangeable, but *that* cannot be used in a non-defining relative clause.

- Check answers before asking the students to discuss whether any of the sentences are true for them.

> a) that/which   d) that
> b) who   e) who/that
> c) which

4

This exercise reviews articles from Unit 5. Ask the students to work individually to put the articles back in the text. Then allow them to compare their answers in pairs before checking with the class.

> Are you <u>a</u> shopaholic? Think of your last trip to <u>the</u> shops or (<u>the</u>) mall. What did you buy? Did you take <u>a</u> list and buy only <u>the</u> things you came for? … <u>The</u> difference lies in your attitude to shopping. <u>The</u>/<u>A</u> compulsive shopper can't stop thinking about shopping. They think about it all <u>the</u> time and only really find relief when they are actually in <u>a</u> shop, choosing their next purchase. … It could be anything, <u>some</u> CDs, <u>a</u> new pair of shoes, <u>some</u> expensive make-up. … but <u>the</u> need to shop and <u>the</u> guilt are just the same

5

This exercise reviews participle clauses from Unit 6. Ask the students to work individually to match the sentences to the appropriate places in the text in Exercise 4. Check answers before the students underline the participle clauses and rewrite them as full clauses. Then ask them to compare with a partner.

> a) 2   b) 3   c) 1   d) 4
>
> a) Having bought their purchases home,
>   When they have bought their purchases home,
>   they'll hide them in the back of the wardrobe.
> b) Feeling guilty about the money they've spent,
>   Because they feel guilty about the money they've spent, they'll lie about the price. / They feel guilty about the money they've spent so they'll lie about the price.
> c) Finding pleasure in spending money,
>   Because they find pleasure in spending money, shopping soon becomes an addiction. / They find pleasure in spending money so shopping soon becomes an addiction.

d) Once addicted to shopping,
When they are addicted to shopping, they can spend hours at the mall, comparing prices and specifications. / They are/become addicted to shopping so can spend hours at the mall, comparing prices and specifications.

6

Pairwork. This exercise reviews verbs of the senses from Unit 6. Ask students to work in pairs and identify which sense is being used in each photo and what it is being used for.

1 hearing – the doctor is listening to the patient's chest – he can hear her heart beat
2 sight – the man looks like a scientist – he's looking for a solution to a problem
3 touch – the main is feeling his son's forehead to check if he has got a temperature

Vocabulary (SB page 67)

1

This exercise reviews expressions with *story* and *tale* from Unit 4. Check answers with the class and then get the students to talk about any similar expressions in their own language.

a) story   b) tales   c) story   d) story
e) story   f) story   g) story

2

This exercise reviews adjectives expressing deception and belief from Unit 4. Check answers before asking the students to do the second part of the exercise.

a) gullible   b) plausible   c) naïve
d) sceptical   e) trusting   f) fishy
g) unfaithful

3

This exercise reviews expressions to do with spending and saving from Unit 5. Check answers before asking the students to discuss in pairs whether any of the sentences are true for them.

a) slap-up   e) impulse buys
b) bulk buy   f) over the odds
c) down-payment   g) within your means
d) shop around

4

This exercise reviews phrasal verbs related to spending and saving from Unit 5.

a) by   b) up   c) off   d) up   e) back

5

This exercise reviews verbs of seeing from Unit 6. Check answers before asking the students to discuss in pairs whether or not they have done any of these things recently.

a) scan   b) dart   c) gaze   d) examine
e) recognise   f) observe

Pronunciation (SB page 67)

1

Remind the students that the boxes show the syllables of a word and the large boxes indicate the stressed syllables. Here they're being asked to classify words according to how many syllables they have and where the main stress falls. Encourage them to say each word aloud to get a feeling for what sounds right.

(See answers in Exercise 2.)

2 ⊕ 2.19

Ask the students to underline the stressed syllables in the words in the table. Then play the recording for them to check their answers. Play it a second time for them to listen and repeat.

1 and 2			
A: ☐☐☐	**B:** ☐☐☐	**C:** ☐☐☐☐	**D:** ☐☐☐☐
recognise	addiction	economise	competition
side-splitting	aggression	exorbitant	disappointment
sheepishly	eccentric	extravagant	observation
sympathy	emotion	necessities	superstition

Further practice material

Need more classroom practice activities?
→ Photocopiable resource materials page 176
   Speaking game: *Don't say it!*
→ The top 10 activities pages xv to xx

Need progress tests?
→ Test CD – *Test Review B*

Need more on important teaching concepts?
→ Key concepts in *New Inside Out* pages xxii to xxxv

Need student self-study practice?
→ CD-ROM – *Review B*

Need more information and more ideas?
→ www.insideout.net

7 Digital *Overview*

Section & Aims	What the students are doing
Speaking SB page 68 Fluency practice	Comparing and discussing mobile phones.
Reading SB page 68 Reporting verbs	Discussing the functions of mobile phones. Reading and discussing an article on the future mobile phones. Inserting missing sentences in the article.
Vocabulary & Listening SB page 70 Compound nouns Listening for gist and detail	Studying the structure of compound nouns. Matching compound nouns to definitions. Explaining technological words without using compound nouns. Identifying the features of a new mobile phone. Listening and numbering photos in order. Completing summaries with compound nouns.
Grammar SB page 71 Complex sentences	Studying the use of multiple clauses. Breaking complex sentences down into single clauses. Putting words in order to make sentences. Writing their own multi-clause sentences.
Pronunciation SB page 71 Words with unstressed syllables	Categorising words according to stress patterns. Identifying unstressed syllables.
Reading SB page 72 Reading for specific information Words and phrases to do with technology	Matching words with definitions. Predicting future technological developments and comparing it with an article about a scientist's predictions for the future. Discussing future developments, their likelihood and benefits.
Grammar SB page 74 Speculating about the future	Examining sentences using modals to make predictions. Identifying the position of phrases conveying degrees of possibility. Rewriting sentences, then making their own future predictions.
Listening & Vocabulary SB page 75 Listening for specific information Informal expressions	Listening to people talking about a gadget. Answering questions, then making notes on the arguments they hear. Studying the vocabulary used by the speakers. Discussing digital books.
Speaking SB page 75 Fluency practice	Discussing their top five scientific breakthroughs.
Useful phrases SB page 76 Useful conversational phrases for discussing implications	Discussing the implications of certain actions. Matching conversations to cartoons. Studying useful phrases for talking about making decisions. Discussing difficult situations and their implications.
Vocabulary *Extra* SB page 77 Acronyms and collocations	Matching acronyms used to talk about technology to their definitions. Matching devices to functions. Reading an article and identifying words that collocate with *digital*. Talking about the technology they use every day.
Writing WB page 45	Writing a discursive essay.

Establish the meaning of *gadget* (a small tool, machine or piece of equipment, often electronic). Ask the students to say how many gadgets they own or use every day. Start them off with a few examples: mobile phone, TV remote control, etc. Ask them to say which they couldn't do without.

Speaking (SB page 68)

Focus the students' attention on the photos. Ask them if either of the phones resembles their own. Then go through the questions with the class. Then put them into pairs and ask them to discuss them.

> a) the first is a basic model, the second is a PDA (a personal digital assistant) with a lot of extra functions
> b) the second, because it's a more complicated piece of technology
> c) and d) (Students' own answers.)

Reading (SB page 68)

1

Groupwork. Put the students into small groups and ask them to note down as many ideas as they can think of for each point. Make sure that everyone in the group has a copy of their list.

2

- Ask the students to read the article on page 69 and mark their lists according to whether they noted down the functions which are given in the article or not. Tell them to ignore the gaps in the article for the moment.

- Ask the students to work in pairs and to compare their notes and discuss the questions. Then ask them to report back to the class on their discussions.

3

Ask the students to read the sentences and decide where in the article they fit.

> a) 5   b) 3   c) 2   d) 1   e) 4   f) 6

4

Put the students into small groups to discuss the question and ask a spokesperson from each group to report back to the class on their opinions.

Vocabulary & Listening (SB page 70)

1

Pairwork. Put the students into pairs. Ask them to look at the compound nouns in the box and to match them to the two patterns: *adjective + noun* and *noun + noun*. When checking answers, draw the students' attention to the fact that most of these are written as separate words, though *voicemail* is one word.

> 1 adjective + noun: cellular coverage, central heating, mobile phone, remote alert, remote control
> 2 noun + noun: card reader, communication device, data network, evening meal, grocery shopping, home entertainment system, payment system, security centre, speech recognition, travel schedule, voice call, voicemail

Vocabulary: compound nouns

A compound noun is a noun made of two or more parts. Sometimes a compound noun can be written as one word, sometimes as two or more words and sometimes the parts are hyphenated. There is no rule to determine which way they are written and sometimes there is more than one acceptable way.

2

Ask the students to match the definitions to five of the compound nouns in Exercise 1. Note that there may be more than one answer for a).

> a) remote alert or security centre
> b) home entertainment system
> c) voicemail
> d) evening meal
> e) grocery shopping

3

- Pairwork. Go through the example with the class, and point out that as in the example and the definitions in Exercise 2, they shouldn't use either part of the compound noun in the explanation.

- Put the students into pairs and ask them to work together to write explanations of the remaining compound nouns in the box in Exercise 1. Check answers by having several pairs read out their explanations to the class.

4

Pairwork. Focus the students' attention on the photos and ask them to discuss in pairs what feature of the new phone they think each one shows. In a class feedback session, do not confirm or deny any answers, but see how many ideas the students came up with.

5 🔊 **2.20**

- Ask the students to listen to the recording and number the photos in the order they are described.

- Check answers and find out whether the students' guesses in Exercise 4 were correct or not.

Correct order: 2, 1, 3

Photo 2: The phone can be worn on the wrist like a bracelet. The earpiece is detachable.
Photo 1: The phone can be opened out to traditional phone size and shape.
Photo 3: It folds out further to become a keyboard.

🔊 **2.20**

This exciting new mobile phone prototype looks more like a piece of space-age jewellery than a phone. It's made up of two pieces: the wristband is the phone itself, whilst the silver hoop, which looks like it should be part of a pendant, is actually the earpiece. When used in this mode, the phone offers safe and easy hands-free voice calls, but it's also a great way of carrying your phone. You can't forget your phone when it's attached to your wrist! And the earpiece can be worn as a clip on your shirt or T-shirt.

When you're not wearing it around your wrist, it can open out into a fairly traditional phone size and shape with all the familiar features: keypad, camera, music player. The earpiece can be worn separately or clipped onto the phone and the phone brought up to your ear.

But possibly the most innovative features is the fact that it also folds out even further and the transparent touchscreen converts into a full size qwerty keyboard, or an interactive map.

6

- Ask the students to complete the summaries with the words in the box.

- Play the recording again for them to check their answers. Then discuss with the class what other features are mentioned.

---

1 wristband, earpiece
2 keypad, music player
3 touchscreen, keyboard

Other features: hands-free voice calls, interactive map

7

Pairwork. Ask the students to discuss in pairs which innovations they think would be most popular and to report back to the class.

Grammar (SB page 71)
Complex sentences

1

- Make sure everybody understands what a clause is: a grammatical unit containing a subject (explicit or implied) and which tells you something about the subject (this part is called the *predicate*). Focus attention on the information in the margin and point out that some sentences only have one clause; others contain multiple clauses. (See Language notes below.)

- Pairwork. Ask the students to look at the sentence from the article and to discuss in pairs how many clauses it has and what type the underlined clauses are. Check answers before asking them to break the sentence down.

The sentence has four clauses. The underlined clauses are main clauses.

a) It knows your travel schedule.
b) It checks for problems on the road.
c) It adjusts the time it wakes you up accordingly.
d) It gives you the best route into work.

Language notes

Complex sentences

- While a simple sentence contains just one clause, complex sentences contain a main clause and then one, two or several subordinate clauses.

  Simple sentence:
  It's the product of the future.

  Complex sentence:
  (Add a participle clause) *Outselling all others, it's the product of the future.*
  (Add relative clause) *Outselling all others, it's the product of the future (that) we've all dreamt about.*

- The subordinate clause gives more information about the main clause. Subordinate clauses can be participle clause, relative clauses and clauses starting with a linker (*because*, *as*, *and*, etc.).

2

Ask the students to compare the original sentence with their shorter ones. You could do this with the class and then discuss the advantages of the longer sentence.

> a) Because it knows … and adjust …
> b) and (it can) adjust
> c) giving you ….
>
> The longer sentence highlights the cause and effect relationship between the different pieces of information and allows for a complex concept to be expressed more economically.

3

- Ask the students to work individually to put the sentences in order.

- When you've checked the answers, ask the students to underline the main clauses. Discuss which feature they find most appealing with the class.

> (The main clauses are underlined in the answers below.)
> a) <u>I'd like to see a mobile phone that answers me</u> when I call it, maybe by beeping or whistling, to let me know where I've left it when I can't find it. / <u>I'd like to see a mobile that answers me</u> when I can't find it, maybe by beeping or whistling when I call it to let me know where I've left it.
> b) <u>My ideal phone would call me</u>, or text me, to remind me about important appointments, giving me the best directions to get there and making sure I'm never late.
> c) Because I use my phone in the car, voice recognition is very important for me, and <u>my ideal phone would be able to follow the instructions</u> I gave it without my having to press any buttons.

4

Allow plenty of time for the students to come up with ideas and to construct their sentences. Make sure there's also time for everyone to share their sentence with the rest of the class.

5 Grammar *Extra* 7, Part 1

Ask the students to turn to *Grammar Extra 7*, Part 1 on page 140 of the Student's Book. Here they'll find an explanation of the grammar they've been studying and a further exercise to practise it.

> a) Needing a new phone because someone had stolen mine, I went to the shop to buy a new one.
> b) There was a new PDA system that had some great features such as a built-in satnav system.
> c) Having thought about it for some time, I decided it was too expensive, so I bought a simpler model.
> d) Thinking about it again, I realised I just needed a straightforward phone to make calls and send messages.
> e) I'm happy with my purchase because, being smaller and lighter, it looks really good!

Pronunciation (SB page 71)

1

- Here the students are being asked to classify words according to how many syllables they have and where the main stress falls. Encourage them to say each word aloud to get a feeling for what sounds right and then add them to the table.

- Check answers before focusing on the schwa sounds above the unstressed syllables of the example word and getting the students to write the phonemic symbol for the schwa sound above the unstressed syllables in the other words.

A: □■□	B: ■□□	C: □■□□	D: □□■□
fa<u>mi</u>liar	<u>jew</u>ellery	tech<u>no</u>logy	inter<u>ac</u>tive
trans<u>pa</u>rant	<u>pro</u>totype	tra<u>di</u>tional	re<u>cog</u>nition

/ə/ /ə/ /ə/
A: fa<u>mi</u>liar, trans<u>pa</u>rent

/ə/ /ə/
B: jew<u>e</u>llery, prot<u>o</u>type

/ə/ /ə/
C: techno<u>lo</u>gy, tradition<u>a</u>l

/ə/ /ə/
D: int<u>er</u>active, re<u>cog</u>nition

2 🌐 2.21

- Play the recording for the students to check their answers to Exercise 1.

- Play the recording again so that the students can listen and repeat the sentences. When they've done this chorally, ask for individual repetition of the sentences and check that everyone is pronouncing the schwa sound correctly and placing the stress in the right place.

Reading (SB page 72)

1

- Explain *phenomena* if the students are unfamiliar with the word (plural of *phenomenon*: an unusual, significant or unaccountable occurrence; a marvel). Ask the students to match the phenomena with the definitions.
- Check answers and then have a class discussion of the questions.

> a) teleportation   d) invisibility
> b) force field   e) telepathy
> c) time travel   f) precognition

2

- Ask the students to read the article on page 73. Give them plenty of time to do this as it's quite complex and deals with some difficult concepts. Be prepared to answer questions on vocabulary.
- Discuss with the class whether Professor Kaku's ideas agree with the ideas they put forward in Exercise 1.

3

Pairwork. Go through the questions with the class and make sure everyone understands them. Then ask the students to discuss them in pairs, looking back at the article if necessary. Encourage them to report back to the class on their ideas.

> a) Class I impossibilities – likely to come true within a matter of decades or at most a century
> Class II impossibilities – may take centuries or millennia to perfect;
> Class III impossibilities – truly impossible
> b) Class I: teleportation, telepathy, invisibility, force fields
> Class II: time travel;
> Class III: precognition
> c) and d) (Students' own answers.)

4

Ask the students to complete the glossary, working in pairs if they wish.

> a) hierarchy   e) electrodes
> b) realisable   f) metamaterial
> c) millennia   g) wormhole
> d) MRI machine   h) unthinkable

5

- Groupwork. Put the students into small groups and ask them to discuss the questions. While they're doing this, go round, monitoring and giving help.
- Ask a spokesperson from each group to report back to the class on their ideas.

Grammar (SB page 74)

Speculating about the future

1

- Pairwork. Read the three predictions aloud, or get some students to read them. Ask the students to work in pairs, look at the words in bold and match them to the three categories.
- Check answers before asking them to make the sentences negative. Discuss the position of *definitely*. Then discuss which predictions they agree with.

> a) 3   b) 1   c) 2
> 1 Teleportation and force fields couldn't become scientific realities within decades.
> 2 Time travel definitely won't be possible in the future.
> 3 Telepathy, force fields and invisibility are not likely to become reality at some point in the future.
> *Definitely* comes after *will* but before *won't*.

Language notes

Grammar: speculating about the future

- As there is no future tense, talking about the future is often concerned with how sure you feel that something will happen, and modal verbs (*will, may, might, could*, etc.) play a huge part.
- Even though modal verbs give you a good idea of how likely someone sees a future event, you usually use adverbs (*almost certainly, definitely, easily, probably, possibly*) to modify your meaning. The adverb follows the modal verbs *will, may, might* and *could*:
  It will almost certainly happen within our lifetimes.
  However, the adverb comes before the modal *won't*:
  We definitely won't see teleportation for at least 50 years.
  (See Grammar Extra on page 140 for more information on this language point.)

2

- Go through the phrases in the box with the class and then ask them to say which could be used to replace *could, will definitely* and *are likely to*.
- When you've checked answers, draw their attention to the information in the margin about ways of speculating about the future.

> a) could: may, might
> b) will definitely: is bound to, is sure to
> c) are likely to: could easily, may very well, should, will almost certainly, will probably

3

- Ask the students to work individually to rewrite the sentences but allow them to compare in pairs before you check answers with the class.

- Ask the students to change any sentences they don't agree with (either by making them negative or substituting a different modal). Then put them into pairs to discuss their sentences.

- Have a class feedback session in which all the new sentences are shared.

> a) Computers <u>will definitely</u> become …
> b) A cure for cancer <u>is highly likely to</u> be within our reach … / <u>It's highly likely that</u> a cure for cancer will be …
> c) The Earth <u>is sure to</u> be destroyed by overpopulation.
> d) <u>We should be able to</u> engineer food crops …
> e) Men <u>will probably</u> soon be incubating babies …
> f) Low-lying countries like the Maldives and Mauritius <u>are likely to</u> be underwater … / <u>It's likely that</u> low-lying countries like the Maldives and Mauritius <u>will</u> soon be underwater …
> g) Organ donors <u>may</u>/<u>might</u>/<u>could easily</u> become things of the past …
> h) … computer whizz kids <u>are bound to</u> be travelling to India and China …

4 Grammar *Extra* 7, Part 2

Ask the students to turn to *Grammar Extra* 7, Part 2 on page 140 of the Student's Book. Here they'll find an explanation of the grammar they've been studying and a further exercise to practise it.

> 2
> a) may   d) that I'll be
> b) won't   e) I'm bound to
> c) should   f) certainly won't

5

- Groupwork. Put the students into small groups and ask them to make predictions. While they're doing this, go round monitoring and giving help. Encourage them to use a variety of ways for speculating about the future.

- Ask a spokesperson from each group to report back to the class on their ideas. Have a class vote on the most conservative prediction and the most outlandish (outrageous).

Listening & Vocabulary (SB page 75)

1 🔘 2.22

Focus attention on the gadget in the photo and ask the students to say what it is. Go through the questions and then play the recording and ask them to make notes of the answers. You may need to pause the recording at strategic points to allow them time to note down what the gadget can do.

a) It is an e-reader – an electronic reading device. It stores books, magazines, newspapers and other reading material and allows you to read it on a digital screen. It can automatically download the latest version of newspapers and magazines. The screen has no light and can even be read in strong sunlight.

b) The man is sceptical; he prefers reading a traditional paper book. The woman is very enthusiastic.

🔘 **2.22** (J = John; S = Sue)

J: *So, what trendy new gadget are you going to wow us with today, Sue?*

S: *Here it is, John, it's an e-reader – or an electronic reading device to give its full name.*

J: *Doesn't look very exciting to me. Give me a good old-fashioned paperback any day.*

S: *Ah, but this is so much more than a book. It's a thousand books, all stored in one small device. The e-reader is going to do for books what the iPod did for music. No more hunting around in bookstores, no more dusty bookshelves … books have gone digital. No more torn pages or newsprint stains on your fingers. All you need now is this – one small, slim gadget that you can fit in your pocket or bag and take with you wherever you go with all the books, newspapers, magazines and comics you could possibly ever need.*

J: *You've been reading too much hype! I bet you can't use it in the bath! And anyway, I love the smell of dusty old bookshelves – my house would look very bare without them …*

S: *Yes, but think of this, you're going on holiday, you're packing your bags, you've got to that point when you have to decide which books to take with you. How many can you fit in your luggage? Which one are you going to take on board with you? What if you don't like it? What if you finish it halfway through the journey and have nothing left to read except the in-flight magazine …*

J: *Horror of horrors …*

S: *Well, this is the answer. No more difficult decisions about which to take and which to leave behind. You can take them all with you … and if you need a map or a local guidebook when you're away, this little device connects to the internet and you can download everything you need, completely free of charge.*

J: *Yeah, but first you have to go hunting round to find an internet café or a wi-fi hotspot or whatever …*

S: *No, not at all … it uses mobile phone networks … and it automatically downloads the latest versions of newspapers, magazines and all your favourite blogs … anything you want to read really, it's there, at the push of a button.*

J: *Yes, but looking at a small screen like that for hours on end can't possibly be good for your eyes … I mean, it's like sitting in front of a computer for hours on end …*

S: Ah, but it isn't … there's no light on the screen, so no glare and very little eyestrain, no more than reading a normal paper book … you can even read it in strong sunlight … this is the shape of books in the future.

J: Yes, but it isn't a book. I'm sorry, but I really don't think any device, no matter how slick and quick and easy to use, can possibly replace a much-loved book.

S: Yes, yes, and when the first trains were built, nobody wanted to go on them because they thought the human body would be sure to explode if it travelled at over 40 miles an hour …

J: Yes, I know, I know, and no-one thought there'd be a market for personal computers back in the 1960s …

S: And think about the environmental impact – okay, so most of the paper for books is made from recycled wood pulp … but what about the costs of making the paper, printing the books and then shipping them all over the world? Not to speak of the mountains and mountains of newspapers trashed every single day … you know, it may not save the planet, but it'd definitely cut down on carbon gas production if we all gave up paper publications and turned to e-reading instead …

J: Mmm … I can see you're definitely sold on the idea … but do you think it'll survive a windy afternoon on the beach?

S: Why not give it a go? Have this one on loan for a week and we can talk about it again in the next programme … I'm sure it'll give you plenty to write about on your blog, which, by the way, you'll be able to read on your new e-reader!

2

Play the recording again and ask the students to make notes on the two arguments. Then check answers and discuss with the class who they agree with.

a) *In favour*: you don't have to go searching for books in shops, no more dusty bookshelves, the pages don't tear, you don't get ink stains on your fingers, you can take as many books, magazines and newspapers as you want with you wherever you go without worrying about the extra weight, you'll never be caught out with nothing to read, you can download useful information like maps and guide books from the internet, it uses mobile phone networks, not wifi, you can get the latest news wherever you are, the screen is easy to read, it's environmentally friendly, cutting down on paper and carbon gas production

b) *Against*: books are nice objects to possess and collect, they furnish your home, you can't read an e-reader in the bath, looking at a small screen is bad for your eyes

3

Read out each extract to the class and ask the students to say whether the man or the woman said these things. Then ask them to look at the words in bold and try to explain them.

a) man   b) woman   c) man   d) man
e) woman   f) man

a) wow = surprise and amaze
b) gone digital = converted to digital technology
c) hype = promotional information
d) slick = impressive and clever
e) trashed = thrown away as waste
f) sold on the idea = convinced about something

4

Groupwork. Put the students into small groups and ask them to discuss the questions. While they're doing this, go round, monitoring and giving help where needed. Then ask a spokesperson from each group to report back to the class on their ideas.

Speaking (SB page 75)

1

Groupwork. Put the students into small groups and ask them to discuss the questions. Ask them to make two lists with the breakthroughs in order of importance, with the most important at the top.

2

Ask a spokesperson from each group to present their lists to the class. Put all their suggestions on the board under two headings, *Past* and *Future*, so they can be used as material for the subsequent discussion. Discuss the remaining questions with the class, making sure that each group contributes ideas.

Useful phrases (SB page 76)

1

- Pairwork. Ask the students to discuss the future implications of each decision. Don't let them stray into which ones they're interested in doing; insist on a list of future implications. Then have a class feedback session.

- Ask the students to discuss their mode of decision making in pairs. Encourage them to report back to the class on what they found out.

2 🔘 2.23–2.26

- Tell the students that they're going to hear four conversations. Ask them to look at the cartoons and to speculate on what the conversations might be about. There aren't many visual clues, so accept any reasonable answers. The point is simply to get the students thinking about what these people might be talking about.

- Play the recording for the students to identify the decisions and match the conversations to the cartoons.

1 c (getting a tattoo)
2 d (going to university or doing some other four-year course)
3 b (resigning from a job)
4 a (accepting a promotion or a different post in the company)

🔘 **2.23** (C = Carla; B = Bette)

1

C: *I don't know if I want to do it … I mean, I do, but then …*

B: *Oh, come on, it's not such a big deal, is it? I mean, everybody does it …. even my mum's got one.*

C: *Yeah, but the thing is, once you've done it, there's no going back … You know, what's done is done and all that …*

B: *Ah, yes, sorry, I obviously hadn't thought through all the possible consequences. I mean, this could have a truly life-changing effect, couldn't it?*

C: *Oh, stop it! It's just that, you know, once it's there, I can't get rid of it, can I? Oh, and what if I decide I don't like it anymore?*

B: *Ah, well, you'll just have to live with the consequences, won't you? But no, seriously, I think it'll look really good. Go for it. Go on. You know you want to.*

🔘 **2.24** (M = Mrs Taylor; A = Austin)

2

M: *So, have you had a chance to think about it, then?*

A: *Yeah, but the thing is, I keep going round and round in circles …. I mean, you know, it's a big decision.*

M: *It certainly is. I mean, you know, it's the next four years of your life … and not only that … it will effect what choices you have afterwards as well … but remember, it isn't the end of the world if you start a course and then decide it isn't for you …. Lots of people change their minds, you know. I think you have to go for the choice that you feel happiest with now – what feels best for you at the moment.*

A: *Yes, I suppose you're right …*

🔘 **2.25** (A = Anna; R = Rachel)

3

A: *I've been thinking about what you said … you know … how I should stop dithering all the time … how I should learn to be a bit more assertive … stand up for myself and all that …*

R: *… and?*

A: *Well, I've made up my mind … I'm going to tell them tomorrow!*

R *You mean, you're actually going to hand in your resignation?*

A: *Yup, that's right! At long last!*

🔘 **2.26** (P = Peter; S = Stuart)

4

P: *It's a great honour … I'm very flattered that you think I'm capable … but I need time to think about it …*

S: *Look, why don't you sleep on it? Talk to your wife about it. You can let us know tomorrow …*

P: *Okay, thanks. I will. I'll call you first thing in the morning. Once I've had a chance to think it through properly … I mean, it really is a great honour… but, as you say, I need to talk to my wife about it.*

S: *That's fine … we understand. It's a big decision.*

P: *Okay, thank you. I'll call you in the morning.*

3

- Ask the students to match the extracts to the conversations.
- When they've finished, play the recording again for them to check their answers.

a) 1	b) 4	c) 1	d) 3	e) 1	f) 2	g) 4
h) 2	i) 1					

4

Ask the students to match the useful phrases in bold in Exercise 3 with their meanings.

a) not very important – 2
b) to consider something carefully – 1
c) a decision cannot be reversed – 3
d) to waste time being unable to make a decision – 4
e) to consider something carefully – 1
f) to waste time being unable to make a decision – 4
g) to postpone making a decision – 5
h) not very important – 2
i) a decision cannot be reversed – 3

5

- Pairwork. Put the students into pairs and ask them to decide who will be A and who B. Tell them to turn to their respective pages and follow the instructions.
- As they work, go round giving help where needed and encourage them to use the phrases in Exercise 3. Ask some confident pairs to perform their conversations for the class.

Vocabulary *Extra* (SB page 77)
Acronyms and collocations

1

- Pairwork. Ask the students to look at the acronyms and abbreviations in pairs and to answer the questions.
- Check answers with the class before asking them to match them to the definitions.

3G – 8	DVD – 4	GPS – 2	MP3 – 3	PC – 1
PDA – 6	PIN – 7	Wi-Fi – 5		

2

- Ask the students to match the gadgets and systems in the box in Exercise 1 to the tasks.
- Check answers and then have a class discussion of which the students use at least once a day and what for.

```
 1  3G, PC, PDA, Wi-Fi
 2  3G, PC, PDA
 3  3G, PC, PDA
 4  3G, MP3, PC, PDA
 5  3G, PC, PDA, PIN
 6  3G, DVD, PC, PDA
 7  3G, PC, PDA
 8  3G, DVD, PC, PDA, Wii
 9  3G, GPS, PC, PDA
10  3G, PC, PDA
```

3

Ask the students to read the article, find the difference between a digital native and a digital immigrant and decide which they are. Then put the students into pairs to discuss their answers.

A digital native is someone who has grown up with digital technology all around them; a digitial immigrant has learnt how to use digital devices as an adult.

4

Pairwork. Encourage the students to think of sentences which might contain the collocations in order to decide which ones are genuine collocations. They could also use an online search engine to research the possible collocations. Ask the students to discuss the questions, then to report back to the class on their conclusions.

a) friend, life, sleep (although all of these can be virtual)
b) digital banking – accessing banking services via a computer or mobile phone (the latter is also called m-banking)
digital broadcasting – digital TV and radio programmes
digital camera – these cameras take photos which can be seen immediately on a digital display screen and downloaded onto a computer
digital display – a screen which uses digital technology to display images and text
digital entertainment – books, films, TV and radio programmes, music and games which are produced using digital technology and can be accessed via computers, digital TVs and radios, DVD players, MP3 players and games consoles
digital images – images created using digital technology
digital learning – using computers and other digital applications in a learning environment, most commonly for distance learning via internet
digital library – books which are stored digitally and can be accessed via a computer
digital shopping – shopping online or on your mobile phone
digital technology – technology which stores information such as sound and pictures as numbers or electronic signals

digital thermometer – a thermometer which shows the temperature on a digital screen
digital TV – TV which uses digital technology
digital universe – all the information and services stored on, or powered by, digital technology
digital world – can be used with the same use as digital universe, but is also the name of a virtual world created by the Japaneses Digimon media franchise
c) the analogue version

Cyber: cyberbanking; cyber broadcasting; cyber camera – used as a product name; cyber display; cyber friend – friends made or found on the internet; cyber images, although not a compound noun is a common collocation; cyber is often used in the brand names of digital products and internet services, e.g. cybercamera, cyberbroadcasting, cyberlife, cyberworld are also registered products or companies.
E-: e-banking, e-broadcasting, e-library, e-shopping, e-learning
Online: online banking and online shopping are both common compound nouns.

5

Pairwork. Encourage the students to discuss the questions and to report back to the class with their ideas.

Further practice material

Need more writing practice?

→ Workbook page 45
• Writing a discursive essay.

Need more classroom practice activities?

→ Photocopiable resource materials pages 177 to 179
Grammar: *My future in a hat*
Vocabulary: *Give us a clue*
Communication: *Planet news*
→ The top 10 activities pages xv to xx

Need progress tests?

→ Test CD – *Test Unit 7*

Need more on important teaching concepts?

→ Key concepts in *New Inside Out* pages xxii to xxxv

Need student self-study practice?

→ CD-ROM – Unit 7: *Digital*

Need student CEF self-evaluation?

→ CEF Checklists pages xxxvii to xliv

Need more information and more ideas?

→ www.insideout.net

8 Law *Overview*

Section & Aims	What the students are doing
Reading SB page 78 Reading for detail	Identifying lawyers' blunders and deciding what they meant to say. Writing a title for an article.
Vocabulary SB page 78 Legal vocabulary	Categorising words according to meaning. Completing sentences with legal terms.
Listening & Grammar SB page 79 Listening for gist and detail Paraphrasing	Listening and identifying what crimes people are talking about. Paraphrasing what people say. Rewriting sentences about a court case and writing an account of it.
Speaking & Listening SB page 80 Fluency practice Listening for specific information	Ordering crimes according to seriousness. Listening to people talking about crime and punishments. Discussing punishment and deterrents.
Listening SB page 81 Listening for detail	Discussing their own experiences of crime. Listening to a woman talking about a crime and answering questions.
Pronunciation SB page 81 Elision and silent letters	Identifying silent and pronounced consonants in elided speech. Studying the rules for elision and silent letters.
Grammar SB page 82 Using modal verbs to talk about the past	Studying modal verbs to talk about the past. Rewriting sentences using appropriate modal verb phrases. Speculating on what might have happened in photos. Talking about the consequences of not having done things.
Vocabulary SB page 83 Collocations with *law*	Matching collocations with *law* to their meanings. Completing sentences with collocations. Talking about the use of metaphor.
Speaking SB page 83 Fluency practice	Discussing proposals for new laws. Discussing laws in their own country that they'd change or introduce.
Reading SB page 84 Reading for gist and specific information	Reading a legal anecdote and choosing a title for it. Completing a glossary of words in the story. Completing sentences with information from the story.
Grammar SB page 85 Inversion after *neither/nor, so/such*	Examining the position of the verb and subject after *nor, neither, so* and *such*.
Vocabulary SB page 85 Formal vocabulary	Completing newspaper headlines. Discussing stories likely to follow the headlines.
Useful phrases SB page 86 Useful conversational expressions for expressing surprise or disbelief	Listening to two colleagues. Identifying what news they're discussing. Completing the conversations with useful phrases. Listening to extracts from conversations, identifying the topics and noting down expressions of surprise or disbelief. Practising giving and responding to surprising news.
Writing *Extra* SB page 87 News stories	Examining the different treatments of a story by the press. Matching phrases with similar meaning. Rewriting a text in the style of a popular newspaper.
Writing WB page 51	Writing a short report.

Law *Teacher's notes*

Warm up

Focus the students' attention on the photo on page 78 and ask them to describe the man. They should discuss who the person is, where he is, what he's wearing and how they'd feel if they were about to face this man in court. Ask them why he's wearing a wig and gown (this is a tradition to give judges and lawyers an air of authority, to show the importance society attaches to what takes place in a court, and to contrast it with everyday life). Ask the students what clothes judges and lawyers wear in their own countries.

Reading (SB page 78)

1

- Explain *blunder* (a mistake, often one that causes amusement) and ask the students to read the text.

- Ask the students to decide what the lawyer in each case really wanted to say.

- Allow the students to compare their answers in pairs before discussing with the class. Ask them to say whether they found the blunders funny or not.

2

Pairwork. Put the students into pairs and ask them to think of a good title for the article. Get them to present their title to the class and have a vote on the best one.

> The original published title was: *Ask a silly question*. (Note, this is an example of the common practice of using a reference to a saying or proverb or just the first half of one as a title. The full saying in this case is *Ask a silly question, get a silly answer*.)

Vocabulary (SB page 78)

1

Go through the headings with the class and make sure everyone understands them. Then put the students into pairs and ask them to decide which heading each word in the box should go under. Ask them to add two words of their own to each category. Check answers and deal with any problems with vocabulary.

> Crimes: arson, embezzlement, libel, manslaughter, speeding

> Punishments: community service, fine, prison sentence, probation, solitary confinement, suspended sentence
> People: attorney, barrister, the accused
> Legal processes: award damages, cross-examine, return a verdict, sue, to sentence, weigh up the evidence

2

Ask the students to complete the sentences using the words and phrases in Exercise 1.

> | a) Libel | e) barrister |
> |---|---|
> | b) the accused | f) Community service |
> | c) sue | g) cross-examine |
> | d) weigh up the evidence, return a verdict | |

3

Ask the students to write three more gapped sentences, which can be completed with words and phrases from the box in Exercise 1. Allow them to use dictionaries if necessary. Then ask the students to exchange their sentences with a partner and to complete the ones they've received.

Language notes

Vocabulary: the law

- *Arson* is the crime of deliberately setting fire to property.

- *Embezzlement* means to obtain money dishonestly.

- *Manslaughter* means killing someone unintentionally (i.e. not murder).

- *Probation* is an alternative to prison for less serious and first offences, the offender has to fulfil certain conditions set by the court, such as living in a certain place, not going out at night, avoiding contact with certain people, etc.

- *Solitary confinement* isn't a punishment set by the courts, but a disciplinary measure used in prisons to isolate troublemakers; the offender spends a certain period of time alone in a cell with no contact with anyone else apart from prison officers.

- *Suspended sentence.* This punishment is a prison sentence set by the courts, but the offender doesn't actually have to go to prison if they stay out of trouble for a fixed period of time.

- *Award damages* means to set an amount of money that the offender has to pay the victim of the crime.

Vocabulary of the courtroom

Further vocabulary of the courtroom:

- Punishments: *a prison sentence* (a period of time in prison), *fine* (an amount of money you have to pay because you have broken the law), *under house arrest* (unable to leave your house, usually because you have committed a political crime).

- People: *defendant* (a person who has been accused of a crime and is on trial), *plaintiff* (a person who has brought a complaint against someone else to court), *eye witness* (someone who saw a crime), *expert witness* (someone whose expertise in their profession qualifies them to offer their opinion on the technical details of a trial), *the prosecution* (the lawyers in a court who try to prove that the defendant is guilty), *the defence* (the lawyers in court who try to prove that the defendant is not guilty).

- Legal processes: *to stand trial* (to be judged for a crime in the court of law).

Cultural note

There are two types of lawyers in the UK: *solicitors*, who prepare a case, and *barristers*, who use the information provided by solicitors to argue the case in court. The court is presided over by a *judge* and it's the judge who decides the sentence if the accused is found guilty. However, it's a *jury* of twelve ordinary people picked at random from the community who make the decision on whether someone is guilty or not, after hearing all the evidence put forward by the prosecution and defence barristers.

Listening & Grammar (SB page 79)

Paraphrasing

1 🌐 2.27–2.29

Play the recording and ask the students to listen to the three conversations and identify the crimes that the speakers are discussing. Check answers with the class and elicit any details the students can remember.

1 libel	2 speeding	3 embezzlement

🌐 **2.27** (D = David; M = Margaret)

1
D: So, have you spoken to Mike?
M: Yes.
D: And does he reckon you have a case?
M: Well, he says I certainly have a case but it'll probably cost me more than it's worth to take them to court. So, I'm not sure what to do.

D: Well, I think you should sue them, even if you only get minimal compensation. It's the principle that counts. People can't just go round spreading lies and rumours like that. What I mean is, you have to stand up for yourself, you know, show that it's important to you.
M: Yes, I agree. The only reason I'm hesitating is because I don't want any more bad publicity.
D: Well, it might not all be bad, and you know what they say, there's no such thing as bad publicity. But, if you want a second opinion, the best person to ask is Fred MacIntyre.
M: But, surely it's too late now, anyway? I mean, it's been almost three weeks since they published the article …

🌐 **2.28** (R = Rani; D = Daniel)

2
D: Well, I suppose what I should have said is 'Yes, officer. I'm sorry, but I was in a terrible hurry.'
R: But you didn't.
D: No, I tried to deny it, you know, make out that I couldn't possibly have been doing 100 miles per hour.
R: And?
D: And, he gave me an on-the-spot fine and said that if it happened again, I'd lose my licence.
R: Ooh, how much?
D: Fifty pounds.
R: Ooh!
D: That's a lesson I won't forget in a hurry!
R: What, don't lie to a policeman?
D: No, it's better to be late than fifty pounds worse off!

🌐 **2.29** (F = Fiona; D = Doug)

3
F: Yeah, being on the jury was a really weird experience.
D: How long did it last?
F: Ooh, a couple of weeks. It was fascinating, seeing how a court works, you know, how formal it all is and everything. We had to stay in a hotel overnight because we couldn't come to a verdict in one day. That was quite exciting.
D: Really? What was it for then? Murder?
F: No, nothing that drastic! It was your usual story of a guy setting up a company, borrowing money from banks, getting things on credit and then using the company money to buy himself and his girlfriend some nice treats, you know, a Ferrari, a Rolex …
D: A couple of diamond rings!
F: Exactly. But the main issue was that the accused used to be a local politician. Didn't you read about it in the papers? It was quite big news at the time.
D: Yeah, now you come to mention it, I do remember something … John Limes or something like that?
F: Yeah, John Limey.
D: And what did you decide?
F: Well, in the end, the verdict we returned was unanimous – guilty!

2

Ask the students to decide which sentences come from which conversation. Allow them to compare in pairs before checking with the class.

a) 3	b) 2	c) 1	d) 3	e) 1

3

Go through the examples on paraphrasing in the margin with the class. Point out that all three examples convey the same information. (See Language notes below.) Ask the students to paraphrase the sentences in Exercise 2 starting with the words given. Then put the students into pairs and ask them to compare their answers and identify any differences between their sentences.

---

1 We returned a unanimous verdict – guilty.
2 I won't forget that lesson in a hurry.
3 Fred MacIntyre is the best person to ask.
4 Seeing how a court works was fascinating.
5 They published the article almost three weeks ago.

Language note

Grammar: paraphrasing

Paraphrasing is saying the same thing in a different way. There are often several ways one can say the same thing. The differences depend on the situation (register) or on which part of the sentence you wish to place most importance (emphasis). This can be achieved by using the passive voice, participle clauses and, in certain situations, cleft sentences (see *Grammar Extra* on page 140 of the Student's Book).

4

- Do the first one as an example with the class, pointing out that there are several ways of doing this, some more natural sounding than others. Ask the students to rewrite the remaining sentences.

- You might like to ask the class whether they think this story is true. (It is highly unlikely as, although Welsh is an official language used in courts in Wales, an interpreter would always be present to translate into and out of English.)

---

a) 1 – It was in Wales that a recent case was held. /
   It was during a recent court case held in Wales …
   2 – Wales is where a court case was recently
   held. / Wales was the venue for a recent court
   case where … ?!
b) 1 – A Welshman who was accused of
   shoplifting stood in the witness box.
   2 – Accused of shoplifting, a Welshman stood
   in the witness box.
c) 1 – Defending him was a Welsh lawyer.
   2 – The lawyer defending him was Welsh.
d) 1 – 'May I speak to the jury in Welsh?' the lawyer
   asked the judge towards the end of the trial.
   2 – The lawyer asked the judge if he could
   speak to the jury in Welsh towards the end
   of the trial. / The lawyer asked the judge
   towards the end of the trial if he could speak
   to the jury in Welsh.

---

e) 1 – Not wishing to appear biased towards
   English, the judge agreed.
   2 – In order not to appear biased towards
   English, the judge agreed.
f) 1 – A verdict of not guilty was returned by the
   jury.
   2 – Not guilty was the verdict returned by the
   jury.
g) 1 – What puzzled the judge was (the fact) that
   the defendant was obviously guilty.
   2 – The defendant was obviously guilty, which
   puzzled the judge.
h) 1 – Not being able to speak Welsh, the judge
   hadn't understood what the lawyer had said.
   2 – As the judge didn't speak Welsh, he hadn't
   understood what the lawyer had said.

5

- Remind the students that the 'News in Brief' section of a newspaper is likely to be fairly formal in style. Ask them to write an account of the story in Exercise 4, using their sentences and making any changes or additions that they think are necessary.

- Then ask them to compare their accounts with the one on page 132 and discuss the differences.

6 Grammar *Extra* 8, Part 1

Ask the students to turn to *Grammar Extra* 8, Part 1 on page 140 of the Student's Book. Here they'll find an explanation of the grammar they've been studying and a further exercise to practise it.

1
a) It's grammar that's the most difficult aspect of
   learning a language.
b) Grammar rules are often made to appear more
   difficult than they really are (by grammarians).
c) The best way to learn grammar is by using and
   being exposed to the language
d) Having learnt my first language through
   exposure, I think it's the best way to learn a
   language.
e) It's a waste of time studying grammar rules and
   doing grammar exercises.
f) What helps me learn more efficiently is studying
   the rules of the language.

Speaking & Listening (SB page 80)

1

- Go through the crimes with the class. Either explain the ones they don't know or ask those students who know a particular word or expression to explain the meaning to the others.

- Ask the students to put the crimes in order of seriousness from most serious to least serious.

- When they've finished, ask them to compare their lists with a partner, decide what the punishment should be for each crime and report back to the class with their decisions.

2 🔘 2.30–2.35

- Ask the students to listen to six people talking about the punishments which they think are suitable for people guilty of some of the crimes in Exercise 1. Before you play the recording, go through the questions with the class so that they know what information to note down as they listen.

- Play the recording, pausing it if necessary to allow the students time to make notes.

---

1 a) littering   b) a fine
2 a) spreading computer viruses
    b) community service
3 a) shoplifting   b) therapy, counselling
4 a) tax evasion   b) a minimum of five years in prison
5 a) inciting violence   b) a long prison term
6 a) graffiti   b) no punishment – should be paid for their work

---

🔘 2.30   *littering*

1

Well, I suppose it's not really an offence is it, not, not a serious offence? I just think people do it without thinking. Um, they see other people do it so they do it themselves and then you end up with a really filthy street. People should think more about the environment, about their surroundings and perhaps rather than punishing them they should, they should have a deterrent fine or, or, you know, enough of a fine to make them think twice about doing it again, frankly.

🔘 2.31   *IT viruses*

2

Well, first of all, I think the damage these things do should not be underestimated. This is in no way a nuisance crime. It is extremely, extremely serious. It can have worldwide effects. It can lose businesses and individuals millions of pounds and I think the punishment should reflect this. It's a difficult one because I think perhaps prison is too harsh, but perhaps we should consider community service. I mean, a lot of these people that commit this kind of crime are obviously extremely talented, and have a lot of knowledge, and maybe that could be put to better use.

🔘 2.32   *shoplifting*

3

A: *I think it's really tricky because some people do it out of necessity. You know, a mum might do it for her children because she hasn't got a choice, but then some people just do it because others are. You know, they're copying their mates. No … no-one really gets hurt (True.) unless it's a, you know, very small company but, you know, no-one gets hurt. So, I … I think it's one of those things where if you are going to punish them – something a bit softer – you know, therapy, counselling, to try and find out why … why they did it in the first place.*

B: *Do you think that would work and stop it, do you?*

A: *I think it would help them, yes.*

petty crime

victimless crime

🔘 2.33   *tax evasion*

4

F: *Well, I … my main concern is that, you know, it's usually the super-rich who get away with this and, er, and because they are so wealthy they can employ, you know, excellent lawyers (Yeah.) and they, they just wriggle out of it. Now I think the crime, I think it's an enormous crime and I think it needs to be punished accordingly …*

M: *How do you mean?*

F: *Well, I think a minimum of five years really, I think so you know. Erm … because they are depriving people, you know, they're, they're depriving the country actually, of huge amounts of money by siphoning all this – you know, they're siphoning off their own wealth and I just don't think it's … I think it's a really serious crime.*

M: *Fair enough.*

🔘 2.34   *inciting violence*

5

M: *I think these guys are quite evil really, I mean, I think they're preying on innocent people and they're getting other people to do their dirty work by using the power of the word. I think they're quite low. I really think they need to be er … punished quite severely, myself.*

F: *And how? How would you do that?*

M: *Well, I mean, you know, a long prison term I … I think is the only way, really. Get them off the streets and then they … they can't continue to do it, can they?*

sentence

🔘 2.35   *graffiti*

6

M: *Well, I actually don't think it's a crime at all. To be completely honest, I … I love seeing it, I love seeing it. I've, you know, seen it all over the world. There's this place in Portugal where it's just everywhere and it's beautiful.*

F: *Really?*

M: *Yeah, and it brings the tourists in to look at it. You know, the locals love it, they add to it all the time. I mean, let's face it … it's artwork, it really is. It's street art and it's just beautiful and I mean, I don't think there should be any … any punishment. If anything, these people should be paid for decorating and making our streets look brighter and, yeah, a more interesting place.*

F: *Wow.*

3

Go through the questions with the class. Play the recording again. Then have a class discussion of the students' answers.

4

Groupwork. Put the students into small groups. Ask them to discuss the questions. Then appoint a spokesperson in each group to report back to the class on their opinions.

5

Pairwork. Put the students into pairs and ask them to
read the two cases and discuss the questions. Then ask
the pairs to report back to the class on what they decided.

6

Ask the students to turn to page 132 and read what
actually happened in these cases. Ask if they're
surprised by either of the rulings. Then discuss the
questions as a class.

Listening (SB page 81)

1

- Focus the students' attention on the photos and ask
  them to say what's happening in each one. (The first
  shows someone picking someone else's pocket and
  stealing their wallet; the second shows someone
  shoplifting, putting a CD in his inside pocket; the
  third shows someone breaking into a car.)

- Pairwork. Put the students into pairs and ask them to
  discuss the questions and report back to the class.

2 🌐 2.36

Go through the instructions and questions first, then
play the recording and ask the students to answer the
questions.

---

a) a brand new car
b) three teenagers who had broken out of a special
   school for young offenders
c) yes
d) she sued the boys' school

🌐 2.36 (T = Tim; A = Anne)

T: *Have you ever had anything stolen?*
A: *Er, yes, I have, a brand new car! I'd had it for just
   under a month.*
T: *You're kidding!*
A: *No!*
T: *You were insured, of course?*
A: *Of course, but the insurance company wouldn't pay up.*
T: *What do you mean, wouldn't pay up? I mean, a brand
   new car and you didn't insure it against theft?*
A: *Of course I did, and I was insured against theft …
   but they just didn't want to pay up. It was a bit of a
   complicated case … Fortunately, my boyfriend at the
   time was a lawyer so in the end, we managed to sort it
   out.*
T: *So, what happened then?*
A: *Well, you see, these three teenagers stole my car …
   they'd broken out of this special school for young
   offenders and well, it seems they wanted to run away,
   so they decided to pinch a car – my car! Anyway,
   while they were driving away they started arguing
   and drove the car straight into a tree.*
T: *Oh no!*
A: *The car was a write-off, a total write-off. I couldn't
   believe it when I saw it!*

T: *What about the kids?*
A: *Well, they weren't seriously hurt or anything,
   miraculous really, considering … but they got
   arrested, of course, and sent back to the school. I was
   just relieved I'd taken out insurance and I was already
   thinking I'd get another car with the insurance money
   … maybe buy a second-hand one this time and make a
   bit of money on the deal!*
T: *Sounds like a good idea … but they wouldn't pay up,
   you said?*
A: *Yeah, when I explained to the insurance company what
   had happened, they told me they would need to see my
   insurance documents. So, I went down to the garage
   where my car had been towed, only to find that all my
   documents had mysteriously disappeared from the
   glove compartment.*
T: *So, what did you do?*
A: *Well, I went back to the insurance people and
   explained the situation and they said it didn't matter
   because they had their own copy of the original
   contract and that anyway, I wasn't covered.*
T: *But didn't you say … ?*
A: *Well, I thought I was covered but they said I was
   insured against theft, but that the car had been found,
   so technically it was no longer stolen. The problem
   was that I wasn't covered for any damage incurred in
   the event of theft.*
T: *Surely they can't include such a ridiculous clause?*
A: *Well, apparently they can and they did. The box with
   this condition had been ticked. I hadn't read all the
   small print in the contract.*
T: *But why not? You really should have read it before
   signing it, you know. You were almost asking for
   trouble.*
A: *Thanks! Yeah, I suppose with hindsight I ought to
   have done, but I couldn't be bothered at the time.*
T: *But couldn't you have asked your boyfriend to check
   it over for you? He was a lawyer, wasn't he? Or you
   could have asked a friend.*
A: *Well, I suppose I could have done, but you know how
   these things are, they're standard forms so I thought
   I'd be all right. Anyway, I have no idea if I had
   actually ticked the box or not. I might have done but
   I didn't have my copy and so they might have simply
   ticked the box themselves to save them having to pay
   out the equivalent of £8,000.*
T: *They wouldn't have done that, surely? That's quite a
   serious accusation …*
A: *I don't know. They certainly could have done it if
   they'd wanted to.*
T: *It would have been far too risky, I mean, you might
   have found your copy of the contract.*
A: *Not if they had it.*
T: *What do you mean?*
A: *Well, the man who ran the insurance company office
   was the brother of the man who owned the garage
   where my car was towed. I reckon they must have taken
   it from the car, along with all the other documents.*
T: *That sounds too far-fetched, they wouldn't have dared
   do something like that, surely? I mean, I know you
   must have been upset at the time, and of course, you
   may be right … but they can't have just stolen the
   documents like that!*

A: I know it all sounds very improbable, but it all looked terribly suspicious at the time.
T: So, what happened in the end then?
A: Well, my boyfriend decided the best way to get the money back would be to sue the boys' school, which he did, and four years later we got the money back. Not that I saw much of it.
T: What, all swallowed up by the lawyers?
A: Yeah, my husband.
T: Oh, you married your boyfriend!
A: Yeah, to avoid the legal fees!

3

- Ask the students to decide whether the statements are true or false. Ask them to see how many they can do from memory before you play the recording again.

- Play the recording for them to check their answers. Remind them that they came across *fishy* in Unit 4. It's used to describe something that doesn't seem quite right, something one feels suspicious about.

a) false   b) true   c) true   d) false   e) true
f) true   g) false   h) false

4

Pairwork. Ask the students to discuss the questions in pairs. Encourage the pairs to report their conclusions to the class.

Pronunciation (SB page 81)

1

Pairwork. Put the students into pairs and ask them to discuss whether the underlined consonants are pronounced or not. Encourage them to say the phrases out loud to help them decide.

Language note

Pronunciation: final /t/ and /d/
When *have* is used either as a regular verb or as an auxiliary verb, *d* or *t* at the end of a word would be pronounced while the /h/ sound would be dropped. The difference being when *have* is used as an auxiliary verb, it takes the weak form /əv/, and when it's used as a regular verb, it's pronounced /hæv/.

2 ⊙ **2.37**

- Play the recording for the students to check their answers. Then play it again for them to listen and repeat.

- Ask the students to match the two halves of the pronunciation rules. Check answers and ask them to suggest examples of each rule from Exercise 1.

a) silent   e) pronounced/silent/silent
b) all silent   f) pronounced/silent
c) silent   g) silent
d) silent   h) both pronounced

a) 2 – a brand new car, second-hand, didn't want (*w* is a semi consonant), didn't matter, against theft, did you
b) 3 – said it, insured against, could have, asked a
c) 1– just didn't, want to, ought to

(Note: *I'd had* is an exception to rule b) – the *'d* is a word in itself and cannot be dropped.)

3

- Pairwork. Go through the questions with the class and then put them into pairs to discuss them.

- When you've checked the pronunciation, ask the students to discuss their answers to the questions. Encourage them to report back to the class.

a) it important – pronounced (see rule b)
   important to – t in *important* silent (see rule c)
   read everything – d in *read* pronounced (see rule b)
b) last time – t in *last* silent (see rule c)
   signed an – d in *signed* pronounced (see rule b)
   read it – pronounced (see rule b)
c) had to – d in *had* silent (see rule c)
   what for – t silent (see rule a)

Grammar (SB page 82)

Using modal verbs to talk about the past

1

- Pairwork. Ask the students to work together to decide which are the modal verbs. Check answers and draw their attention to the patterns with modal verbs in the margin.

- Then ask them to match the modal verbs they've underlined to the functions.

a) wouldn't – 1 (reporting the insurance company's statement: 'We won't pay up') or 3 (commenting on the insurance company's refusal)
b) couldn't – 1 (reporting her own disbelief) or 3 (commenting on her surprise)
c) should have – 3 (criticising her past actions)
d) ought to have – 3 (commenting on her own failure to read the contract)
e) couldn't – 3 (criticising)
f) 'd (would) – 1
g) might have – 2
h) wouldn't have – 3 (comment)
i) must have – 2
j) can't have – 2

Grammar: modal verbs to talk about the past

The modal verbs in this section all refer to the past.

- The first group consists of *could* and *would* (+ infinitive without *to*), which are used as the past forms of *can* and *will*.

- The second group is *should* and *ought to* (+ *have* + past participle). These modals are used to comment on or criticise a past event, e.g. *You should have told him what you thought of him.* The negative form of *ought to* is *ought not to* or *oughtn't to* (+ *have* + past participle). The question form is much more complicated and clumsy-sounding than *should*, so *should* is usually the modal of preference in questions. Compare: *Should they have done that?* with *Ought they to have done that?*

- The third group is used to speculate about a past event. *May*, *might* and *could* (+ *have* + past participle) can be used to tentatively speculate about a past event. *Can't* (+ *have* + past participle) is used to speculate with more certainty about an event that wasn't possible. *Must* (+ *have* + past participle) is used to speculate with more certainty about an event that was possible.

Note: You cannot use *can have* or *mustn't have* to speculate about the past.

2

Read the sentences out to the class or get several students to read them. Ask the students to decide which two sentences are incorrect and to correct them.

> a) and d) are incorrect.
> a) Anne <u>can't</u> have been very happy when she found her car had been stolen.
> d) Anne <u>must</u> have made a mistake about the insurance company.

3

Ask the students to rewrite the sentences using appropriate modal verb phrases. Allow them to compare their sentences in pairs before checking with the class.

> a) They must have stolen the documents.
> b) They may/might/could have changed the original contract.
> c) You shouldn't/oughtn't to have signed the contract without reading it first.
> d) You may/might/could have been wrong.
> e) The garage owner may/might/could have taken the documents. (*Could* is preferable here because it has the connotations of possibility.)
> f) The boys' parents wouldn't take responsibility for the boys' actions.

4

- Pairwork. Put the students into pairs and ask them to talk about what they think happened in the photos.
- Ask them to write sentences expressing what they think might have happened using the modal phrases listed. Encourage them to come up with imaginative explanations. Then ask the pairs to share their sentences with the class and have a vote on which explanation for each photo is the most imaginative and the most realistic.

5

Pairwork. Go through the instructions with the class, then put the students into pairs to discuss the things they didn't do. Encourage them to report back to the class on the things they didn't do and on how things would have been different if they'd done them.

6 Grammar *Extra* 8, Part 2

Ask the students to turn to *Grammar Extra* 8, Part 2 on page 140 of the Student's Book. Here they'll find an explanation of the grammar they've been studying and a further exercise to practise it.

> 2
> a) He must have forgotten his keys or something.
> b) The window may have been left open on purpose.
> c) The front door could have actually got stuck and he's climbing out.
> d) He can't have wanted to do it.
> e) I lost my keys once and couldn't get back into my flat.
> f) When I was a young kid, we used to leave the key under the doormat
> Sentences a–c refer to the picture

Vocabulary (SB page 83)

1

Focus the students' attention on the collocations with *law* in column a–i and ask them to try to match them to their meanings in column 1–9. Encourage them to do as many as possible without looking them up in a dictionary.

> a) 7   b) 2   c) 9   d) 1   e) 8   f) 6   g) 3
> h) 4   i) 5

2

Ask the students to decide which of the collocations in Exercise 1 best fits the gaps in the sentences. Allow them to compare in pairs before checking with the class.

> a) no-one is above the law   e) laying down the law
> b) law-abiding   f) a law unto herself
> c) in trouble with the law   g) my word is law
> d) take the law into my   h) by law
>   own hands   i) against the law

3

Ask the students to compare the collocations in
Exercise 1 with those used to talk about similar things in
their own language(s). Discuss whether they use similar
metaphors to talk about the law and if the laws are
treated like material objects.

Speaking (SB page 83)

1

Groupwork. Put the students into small groups and ask
them to read the proposals for new laws and discuss
them, saying which would affect them personally and
which they'd be in favour of. Get a spokesperson from
each groups to report back to the class on their ideas.

2

Ask the students to stay in the same groups to discuss
this question and report their conclusions to the class.

Reading (SB page 84)

1

Give the students plenty of time to read the anecdote
and then ask them to choose the best title.

> a) It pays to do your homework

2

Ask the students to complete the glossary. Point out
that the story uses quite a few formal words, possibly
because when people are talking about legal matters,
they tend to adopt a formal register.

> a) depicted   b) prominent   c) further
> d) to deceive   e) prior to   f) claimed
> g) severe   h) seeking   i) indulge in
> j) engaged   k) commenced   l) in due course

3

- Pairwork. Ask the students to work together to
  complete the sentences.
- In a class feedback session, get the pairs to read out
  their sentences to the class.

> *Possible answers:*
> a) Bruno was in court because he wanted to claim
>   compensation for a work-related injury.
> b) He was photographed in order to try to prove
>   that he was not actually seriously injured.
> c) The lawyer representing the insurance company
>   didn't know that Bruno had an identical twin
>   brother.
> d) When Bruno's brother walked into the
>   courtroom the lawyer felt very foolish.
> e) After the court case the two brothers went out
>   to celebrate / the insurance company fired their
>   lawyer.

Grammar (SB page 85)

Inversion after neither/nor, so/such

1

Ask the students to read the sentences and say which of
them come from the anecdote on page 84.

> Sentences b) and c).

2

Ask the students to look at the sentences in Exercise 1
again and to say what they notice about the position of
the verb and the subject after *nor*, *neither*, *so* (+ adjective)
and *such*. Draw their attention to the further examples in
the margin and point out that the change of position of
the subject and verb is called *inversion*.

> The verb comes before the subject.

> **Language note**
>
> **Grammar: inversion after *neither/nor, so/such***
> Inversion involves reversing the position of the
> subject and the verb, as happens when forming
> questions. The most common examples of inversion
> with *neither*, *nor* and *so* are:
>
> *A: I'm French. B: **So am I**.*
> *A: I don't like winter. B: **Neither/Nor** do I.*

3

Ask the students to rewrite the sentences in Exercise 1
using the words given, i.e. without inversion. When
you've checked answers, elicit which form is more
formal.

> a) He couldn't bend, move or walk very easily.
> b) He couldn't lift heavy objects or indulge in his
>   hobbies of gardening and tennis.
> c) His injury was so severe that he was practically
>   housebound.
> d) The nature of his injury meant that he could no
>   longer work.
>
> The sentences in Exercise 1 (with inversion) are
> more formal.

4

Ask the students to match the sentence beginnings and
endings.

> a) 3   b) 1   c) 2   d) 4

5

Ask the students to rewrite the sentences in Exercise 4 so
that they have inversion. Go through the example first
with the class, and remind them that they may have to
make some other changes.

a) They didn't release the prisoner, nor did they let the family see him.
b) He isn't young, nor is he good-looking, but he is very popular.
c) So happy were they with the results that they have recommended the company to all their colleagues.
d) Such an outcry was there over the new proposals that the government is having to reconsider its plans.

6

Pairwork. Explain that to invent a context for each of the sentences, the students have to think about the circumstances in which these sentences might be said or written. Ask them to work in pairs and to use their imaginations and invent possible situations for each of the sentences.

Vocabulary (SB page 85)

1

Ask the students to find suitable words to complete the newspaper headlines from the glossary they completed on page 84.

a) prior to   b) Severe   c) Prominent   d) depict
e) seeking   f) deceived

2

Pairwork. Ask the students to look at the headlines in Exercise 1 again and to decide which stories are about breaking the law (a, c and f, and possibly also d, depending on the privacy laws of the country). Ask them to think about what might have happened and to note down some ideas to share with the class. Then have a class discussion of any current news stories that involve the passing or breaking of laws.

Useful phrases (SB page 86)

1 🌐 2.38

- Tell the students that they're going to listen to two colleagues discussing some news. Go through the questions with them first so that they know what information to listen out for.

- When you've checked their answers, ask them to say what the two cartoons show (Bainbridge in his seemingly boring and respectable office life and his other secret life with sports car and house in the south of France, financed by embezzlement).

a) A colleague (Bainbridge) has been arrested for suspected embezzlement.
b) They're both surprised.

2

- Ask the students to read through the gapped transcript and to think of what the missing words might be before you play the recording again.

- Check answers with the class. Then ask them to say what all the missing phrases have in common (they are all expressions of surprise or disbelief).

- Get the students to try to explain what the four expressions in bold mean. Then ask if they have similar expressions in their own language(s).

1 Did I hear you right?
2 you've got to be kidding
3 You don't expect me to believe that
4 I never!
5 Who'd have thought it!
6 you never can tell

Wouldn't hurt a fly. = Would never be violent towards anyone.
Lives in the lap of luxury. = Lives a life of considerable wealth.
You can't judge a book by its cover. = Don't judge people by their appearances.
Still waters run deep. = Quiet people often have interesting secrets.

3 🌐 2.39

Ask the students to listen to extracts from four more conversations and to note down the news in each one.

1 Robyn and Steve are getting married.
2 Jeff is leaving the team.
3 Katy's going to pay for the damages.
4 The boss is going to give them a Christmas bonus.

🌐 2.39

1
A: *Have you heard? Robyn and Steve are getting married.*
B: *Really? No kidding? That's great news.*

2
A: *So, what do you think to the news?*
B: *What news?*
A: *Jeff is leaving the team.*
B: *What? But that can't be right! I mean, they just made him captain.*

3
A: *Katy says she's going to pay for the damages.*
B: *Yeah, yeah, pull the other one!*
A: *No, honestly, she is. She told me so herself.*
B: *Yeah? Well, I'll believe that when I see it.*

4
A: *So, anyway, Rik reckons the boss is going to give us an extra bonus at Christmas.*
B: *Yeah, and pigs might fly!*
A: *No, honestly, that's what everyone's saying. He's really happy with the way business is going and he wants to thank everyone for their hard work.*
B: *Okay, I'll take your word for it, though I won't be convinced until I've got the money in my hand.*

4

Play the recording again and ask the students to listen carefully and to note down any expressions of surprise or disbelief that they hear. You may need to pause the recording between extracts to allow them time to do this. When checking answers, you may need to explain some of the expressions. (See Language notes below.) Elicit any other expressions that the students know.

> 1 Really? No kidding?
> 2 But that can't be right!
> 3 pull the other one!, I'll believe that when I see it
> 4 and pigs might fly

Language notes

Vocabulary: idiomatic expressions

Pull the other one and *Pigs might fly*

- When you *pull someone's leg*, you're joking with someone by saying something that isn't true. You can respond with the expression *Pull the other one, it's got bells on it*. This expression is commonly shortened to *Pull the other one*.

- The expression *Pigs might fly* means that you think something is very unlikely to happen.

- Both idiomatic expressions are used to say you don't believe what someone is telling you. Note that the intonation is important when using both these expressions. They only work if the speaker says them in a tone of complete disbelief.

5

Pairwork. Ask the students to take turns to break a piece of news and respond to it. Make sure everyone understands the pieces of news in the list before they begin. Go round as they work, making sure that they're using a variety of expressions to denote surprise or disbelief. Also check that they're using an appropriate tone of surprise/disbelief.

Writing *Extra* (SB page 87)

News stories

1

Pairwork. Put the students into pairs and ask them to decide who will read which story. Encourage them to tell each other the details of their story rather than simply reading the other one. Get them to work out which one was published first.

> Text b was published first. (The poster at High Wycombe was put up as a result of the action taken at Warrington Bank Quay.)

2

- Pairwork. Ask both students in each pair to read both texts. Then ask them to look back at the newspaper articles in Exercise 1 and decide what kind of newspaper each one appeared in.

- When checking answers, ask them for examples of features that helped them decide. If you have access to British tabloid newspapers, take a few examples to class to give a clearer idea of the style of the popular press.

> popular press – text a   quality press – text b

3

Ask the students to match the phrases. Point out that those one the left (a–d) are more informal than those on the right (1–4). Then ask the students to find more examples of differences in style between the two stories.

> a) 4   b) 3   c) 2   d) 1
>
> *Suggested answers:*
> Use of quotations to break up text in text A; use of hedging in text B (is believed to be)

4

Pairwork. Ask the students to work together to rewrite article b in the style of a popular newspaper. You could display the finished articles in the classroom for everyone to read and enjoy.

Further practice material

Need more writing practice?

→ Workbook page 51
- Writing a short report.

Need more classroom practice activities?

→ Photocopiable resource materials pages 180 to 182
  Grammar: *Modals and meanings*
  Vocabulary: *Thick as thieves*
  Communication: *Legal matters*
→ The top 10 activities pages xv to xx

Need DVD material?

→ DVD – Programme 8: *The barrister*

Need progress tests?

→ Test CD – *Test Unit 8*

Need more on important teaching concepts?

→ Key concepts in *New Inside Out* pages xxii to xxxv

Need student self-study practice?

→ CD-ROM – Unit 8: *Law*

Need student CEF self-evaluation?

→ CEF Checklists pages xxxvii to xliv

Need more information and more ideas?

→ www.insideout.net

9 Night Overview

Section & Aims	What the students are doing
Reading & Speaking SB page 88 Reading for detail Fluency practice	Doing a quiz on energy patterns. Discussing the meaning of the expressions in the quiz. Talking about their own energy patterns and those of family and friends.
Vocabulary & Speaking SB page 89 Times of day and night Fluency practice	Putting times of day in chronological order. Matching expressions to times of day. Talking about different times of day and night.
Listening SB page 89 Listening for detail	Listening to a radio show about the body clock and circadian rhythms. Identifying true and false statements.
Reading SB page 90 Reading for gist and detail	Reading profiles from a sleep website. Answering questions on the people profiled and giving advice on sleep.
Grammar SB page 91 Concessive clauses and adverbials	Studying concessive clauses and adverbials. Completing a website posting. Writing a similar posting on a given problem.
Listening & Pronunciation SB page 92 Listening for detail Adverbs	Listening to people talking about staying up all night and taking notes. Completing extracts with adverbs and identifying the function of the adverbs. Counting syllables in adverbs.
Speaking: anecdote SB page 92 Fluency practice	Talking about a time they stayed up late or stayed up all night.
Speaking SB page 93 Fluency practice	Matching halves of proverbs about night. Discussing proverbs and creating their own proverbs.
Vocabulary SB page 93 Expressions with *night*	Completing sentences with expressions with *night*. Discussing questions.
Reading SB page 95 Reading for detail	Reading a text about the northern lights. Matching topic sentences to paragraphs. Finding evidence in the text to support statements.
Listening & Grammar SB page 95 Listening for detail Regrets and past conditionals	Listening to an account of a trip and answering questions. Completing sentences about regrets. Writing past conditional sentences using prompts.
Useful phrases SB page 96 Useful conversational phrases for making and responding to invitations	Listening to conversations and improving on people's responses. Examining formal and informal responses to an invitation. Completing a conversation with useful phrases. Taking turns making and responding to invitations.
Vocabulary *Extra* SB page 97 Phrasal verbs	Studying phrasal verbs and their meanings. Writing sentences with phrasal verbs. Completing sentences with particles.
Writing WB page 57	Writing an essay.

9 Night *Teacher's notes*

Warm up

Write the word *night* in the centre of the board. Ask the students to suggest words and expressions that they associate with *night*. Make a word diagram with their suggestions. Have one section for compound nouns such as *nightmare, night flight, night bus*, etc.

Reading & Speaking (SB page 88)

1

Focus attention on the title of the quiz and ask the students if they know what a lark and an owl are. (See Language notes below.) Ask the students to do the quiz. When they've finished, ask them to turn to page 132 to check their answers and read the analysis. Find out if they agree with the results.

Language note

Vocabulary: *lark* and *owl*
A lark and an owl are both types of bird. A lark, which has a sweet singing voice, has a reputation for getting up early in the morning; an owl is a nocturnal bird which sleeps during the day and hunts at night. The terms *lark* and *owl* refer to people who are at their best in the morning and those who come alive at night and stay up late.

2

Pairwork. Ask the students to discuss the meaning of the highlighted words and phrases. Encourage them to paraphrase but allow them to use dictionaries if necessary.

> goes off = rings
> doze = sleep for a short time
> sleep in = continue sleeping after the time you normally wake up
> wind down = relax after a period of activity, excitement or worry
> tucked up = comfortable and covered up in bed
> call it a night = decide that you have finished your activity for the night
> have an early night = go to bed earlier than usual
> going strong = still full of energy

3

Groupwork. Put the students into small groups. Ask them to compare their answers to the quiz and talk about whether they're larks or owls, extending the discussion to how they compare with their family and friends.

Vocabulary & Speaking (SB page 89)

1

Pairwork. Ask the students to work in pairs and put the expressions in the box into chronological order. Explain that *dawn* is when the first glimmer of light appears in the sky in the morning and *dusk* is the time after the sun goes down, when it's still not completely dark.

> at dawn, at sunrise, mid-morning, at midday,
> mid-afternoon, at sunset, at dusk, at midnight

2

Pairwork. Ask the students to work in pairs and decide what the expressions mean and which words are literary in style. Note: you may need to explain that *wee* means tiny.

> at noon – midday
> at twilight – dusk (literary)
> at daybreak – dawn (literary)
> at nightfall – dusk (literary)
> in the middle of the night– around two to four o'clock, when people are usually asleep
> at the crack of dawn – very early, when the first light appears
> in the wee small hours – in the hours just after midnight
> first thing in the morning – as soon as you get up
> last thing at night – just before you go to bed

3

Pairwork. Ask the students to discuss the different times and then to report back to the class on their discussions.

Listening (SB page 89)

1 🌐 3.01

- Groupwork. Put the students into small groups to discuss what the words in the box might mean. Encourage them to speculate rather than look the words up in a dictionary.
- Then ask them to listen to the recording to check.

> body clock – a mechanism in the body that regulates our circadian rhythms
> circadian rhythms – the changes that occur in our brain and body over the course of a day: the daily cycle of sleeping and waking

jet lag – a condition that occurs when people fly across time zones and their body clock is out of sync with the time at their destination
nocturnal creatures – animals that are active during the night and sleep during the day
diurnal creatures – animals that are active during the day and sleep during the night

🌐 3.01 (A = Anne Kramer; S = Dr Simon Holmes)

A: *Well, a very good morning to you and welcome to this week's edition of* Science Matters *with me, Anne Kramer. Today we have in our studio Dr Simon Holmes, who is an expert on body clocks, circadian rhythms and all things sleep-related, and who's going to tell us a little bit more about what it all means. Simon, a very warm welcome to the programme.*

S: *Thank you.*

A: *So, first of all, tell us, what exactly are circadian rhythms?*

S: *Well, Anne, circadian rhythms are essentially the changes that occur in our brain and in our body over the course of a day – our daily cycle of sleeping and waking if you like. In fact 'circadian' is a Latin word meaning 'around a day'. In other words, we operate in cycles of just over twenty-four hours, broadly in tune with the cycles of nature. And all animals and most plants live according to these rhythms. But in the animal kingdom, the rhythms vary according to whether an animal is a diurnal or nocturnal creature.*

A: *Diurnal or nocturnal? What's that exactly?*

S: *Well, basically that refers to whether the animal is awake during the day or during the night. As you know, we humans are diurnal, not nocturnal creatures. That means that we are active during the day and sleep during the night. Whereas some animals, such as bats or owls or foxes, are largely nocturnal – they sleep by day and hunt by night.*

A: *I see. And how exactly does that tie in with our body clock? And what is a body clock, in fact?*

S: *Well, a body clock is actually just as it sounds, it's, it's a mechanism in the body that works a bit like a clock and that regulates our circadian rhythms. Nobody knows exactly how it does this, but we do know that it interacts with signals, such as variations in sunlight and environmental activity, noise and so on, and then it, if you like, fine-tunes our feelings of sleepiness and wakefulness to keep them in sync with the external cycle of dark and light.*

A: *I see. So, is that why we tend to wake up earlier in summer and need more sleep in winter, for example?*

S: *Exactly. But research has shown that the normal circadian rhythm for most people is, as I say, roughly twenty-four hours – twenty-four hours and eleven to fifteen minutes to be precise, that's according to some research, though other scientists have put it slightly higher, at more like twenty-five hours.*

A: *Ah, that's interesting, Simon, because you say that humans are diurnal not nocturnal creatures, but that's not true of everyone, is it? Is it not the case that some people are owls and other people are larks – by nature, perhaps? What does science have to say about that?*

S: *Well, you're quite right, and it's important to stress that there is actually quite a lot of individual genetic variation in the pattern of circadian rhythms. It does seem that some people are genetically larkish and others genetically owlish, if you like. And these rhythms also fluctuate with age. Young children tend to be larks and then, sometime around the onset of puberty, it all changes. Adolescents start needing a lot more sleep, and shift to waking and performing better later in the day. And then, around the age of twenty or so, it all changes. And then, in later stages of life, it shifts again, and elderly people tend to become increasingly larkish.*

A: *So, does that explain why most teenagers seem to be physically incapable of getting out of bed at a sensible time in the morning? Like my nephew, for example, who never surfaces until it's time for lunch?*

S: *Well, you could be right!*

A: *So, I can tell my sister that my nephew will just grow out of it then, in due course?*

S: *Well, yes, he may do! Or he may just be one of nature's owls, I suppose.*

A: *And what happens, Simon, when these circadian rhythms get disrupted? Say, if we cross over to a different time zone, or have to work night shifts? How does our body clock adapt?*

S: *Well, obviously, if we cross over several time zones all at once, as on a long international flight, for example, our body struggles to adapt to the change, and that's when we suffer from what's known as jet lag.*

A: *Ah, yes.*

S: *Now, jet lag is a condition that affects us when our body clock is out of sync with our destination time, and the body's natural rhythms are upset. And it manifests itself in all sorts of symptoms, such as fatigue, insomnia, irritability, nausea, loss of appetite and even mild depression.*

A: *And what about night workers?*

S: *Yes, night workers, people who work on a night shift, are also prone to all sorts of physical and psychological problems, especially if they aren't able to catch up with their sleep during the day.*

A: *And moving on now to sleep patterns, there are a number of interesting questions …*

2

- Encourage the students to do as much as they can from their memory of their first hearing of the recording. Allow them to work in pairs or small groups.
- Play the recording again for the students to check their answers. You may need to pause the recording at strategic places or replay certain sections to help them.
- Have a class discussion of whether they find any of the information surprising.

a) False. It is just over 24 hours.
b) False. All animals and most plants live according to these rhythms, although the rhythms vary according to whether a creature is nocturnal or diurnal.
c) True. It interacts with signals such as variations in sunlight and environmental activity, noise, and so on.
d) True. It fine-tunes our feelings of sleepiness and wakefulness.
e) True. There is actually quite a lot of individual genetic variation in the pattern of circadian rhythms. It does seem that some people are genetically larkish and others genetically owlish.
f) False. Adolescents start needing a lot more sleep.
g) False. Elderly people tend to become increasingly larkish.
h) False. Jet lag is a condition that affects us when our body clock is out of sync with our destination time, and the body's natural rhythms are upset.

Reading (SB page 90)

1
- Explain that the four people in the photos have posted accounts of their sleep patterns on a sleep website. Ask the students to read what they say.
- Ask the students to say if they're like any of the people on the website and encourage them to talk about their own sleep habits.

2
Go through the items on the list with the class, then ask them to match them to the people.

a) Pete, Penny	e) Pete
b) Penny	f) Penny, Joe
c) Amy	g) Penny, Joe
d) Joe	h) Amy

3
Draw attention to the highlighted words in the text and ask the students to use them to complete the glossary. Students can then use the words in the glossary in sentences of their own.

a) recharge my batteries	f) a light sleeper
b) didn't get a wink of sleep	g) drop off
c) power naps	h) go out like a light
d) alert	i) groggy
e) sleeps like a log	j) wind down

4
- Pairwork. Ask the students work together to think of advice that they could give the people. When they've finished, put them in small groups to pool their ideas.
- Have a class feedback session and make a list on the board of pieces of advice. Find out if any of the students have their own ways of getting to sleep.

Grammar (SB page 91)
Concessive clauses and adverbials

1
Read the example sentences aloud to the class or ask several students to read them. Have a class discussion of whether they're the same or different in meaning and draw the students' attention on the information on concessive clauses and adverbials in the margin. (See Language notes below.)

The same

Language notes
Grammar: concessive clauses and adverbials
- A concessive clause is a subordinate clause which can start with *Although* or any of the other words and phrases in this section, and contains a fact or idea that seems to oppose the information in the rest of the sentence. In the sentence *Although I tried hard, I couldn't get to sleep* we know the outcome will be negative because *Although (I tried hard)* tells us that the second half of the sentence is going to contrast with the first part.
- *Although*, *Even though*, *Try as I might*, *Strange as it may seem* are all followed by subject + verb (*Even though I tried hard …*)
- *Despite* and *In spite of* are followed by noun or gerund (*In spite of my best efforts, … Despite asking him several times, …*)
- *Even so*, *Yet*, *However* and *That said* all appear at the beginning of a sentence, which presents the contrastive consequence or outcome relating to the previous sentence. *I tried hard. Even so, I couldn't sleep.*

2
Ask the students to look back at the text on page 90 and to find eight more clauses or adverbials that convey a similar contrast. Then check answers with the class and ask them to identify the two more formal examples.

<u>That said</u>, I find the only way … (line 11)
I usually drop off straight away – <u>even so</u>, I can generally only get away with … (line 13)
But <u>try as I might</u> to get off to sleep, I'll invariably be tossing and turning for ages. (line 24)
… but <u>even though</u> the sleeping pills have some effect, I'm wary of … (line 32)
<u>All the same</u>, I need a good eight hours' sleep … (line 49)
… <u>in spite of my efforts</u>, none of it has done any good. (line 66)
… I'm not convinced it will make any difference, <u>though</u>. (line 68)
<u>Much as I'd like</u> to stop snoring … (line 69)
More formal expressions:
try as I might, Much as I'd like

3

Do the first one with the class as an example, then ask the students to rewrite the remaining sentences. As they do this, go round making sure they're using concessive clauses and adverbials correctly. Then check answers by having several students reading out their sentences to the class.

> a) Even though I went to bed early, I was still groggy the next day.
> b) (Even) though I don't usually oversleep, I prefer to set the alarm clock. / I don't usually oversleep. I prefer to set the alarm clock, though.
> c) In spite of the fact that the bed was very uncomfortable, I slept like a log. / In spite of the uncomfortable bed, I slept like a log.
> d) Much as I'd like to get by on six hours a night, I can't manage on less than seven.
> e) I'm normally an early riser. That said, I like to have a lie-in on Sundays.

4

Ask the students to put the words in the right order. Allow them to compare in pairs before checking with the class.

> a) Exhausted as I was …
> b) Strange as it may seem …
> c) Hard as it may be …
> d) Try as I might …

5

- Ask the students to read the text and identify the writer's problem. Then ask them to complete it with appropriate words or phrases.

- Check answers with the class before initiating a class discussion on whether they've ever been in a similar situation, what they did and what advice they'd give.

> The problem is noisy neighbours.
> 1 Despite / In spite of
> 2 however / though
> 3 However / Even so / Nevertheless / All the same / That said
> 4 as (*though* is also possible)

6

- Pairwork. Ask the students to work together to choose a problem and write a posting for it. As they work, go round making sure they're including concessive clauses and that these are being used appropriately.

- When they've finished, ask them to swap their posting with another pair and to take turns offering advice.

7 Grammar *Extra* 9, Part 1

Ask the students to turn to *Grammar Extra* 9, Part 1 on page 142 of the Student's Book. Here they'll find an explanation of the grammar they've been studying and a further exercise to practise it.

1

> 1 a) Although I'm usually a really heavy sleeper, that night every single noise and movement seemed to wake me up.
> b) I'm usually a really heavy sleeper, even so, that night every single noise and movement seemed to wake me up.
> c) Despite usually being a really heavy sleeper, that night every single noise and movement seemed to wake me up.
> 2 a) In spite of their reassurances and offers of kind advice, I was still worried about the situation and couldn't sleep a wink.
> b) They reassured me and offered me kind advice. But I was still worried about the situation and, try as I might, I couldn't sleep a wink.
> c) They reassured me and offered me kind advice, even so, I was still worried about the situation and couldn't sleep a wink.
> 3 a) Even though I went to bed tired and depressed, I woke refreshed and ready to face the day.
> b) I went to bed tired and depressed. However, I woke refreshed and ready to face the day.

Listening & Pronunciation
(SB page 92)

1 🌐 3.02–3.04

- Focus the students' attention on the photos and tell them that they're going to hear these people talking about their experiences of staying up all night. Go through the questions before you play the recording.

- Check answers with the class, then put the students into pairs to discuss which of the nights described they'd most and least like to have shared and why. They then report back to the class on their conclusions.

> 1
> a) In the Himalayas, in Nepal, in the jungle below the snow line
> b) They watched the moon, talked about the sky, watched the shooting stars fly past.
> c) It was unforgettable, amazing, brilliant.
> 2
> a) Glastonbury (a music festival)
> b) They went out and went dancing and stuff and then mooched about some fields and sat on top of a hill and watched the sun come up.
> c) It was great, just completely manic, just completely crazy, amazing.
> 3
> a) London, on the South Bank (of the River Thames)
> b) They camped out to try to get tickets to see a show with an American talk show host. They didn't sleep and didn't get tickets because they were in the standby line.
> c) It was an absolute nightmare. They were very cold and really upset about not getting tickets.

3.02 (M = Mark; J = James)

James

M: You've been to the Himalayas, haven't you?

J: Yeah, I had this one unforgettable night up in the mountains, in Nepal, it was actually, and it was a full moon and we were up in the mountains. So we were in the jungle, below the snow line – we could see the snow line up in the mountains up ahead, but as the moon rose – because it was a very big, low, pale moon and we watched it come up through the mountains. We just couldn't take our eyes off it and the hours just passed, you know, just conversing about the sky, basically, as you watched the moon rise and change colour (Wow!). It lit up the whole valley (Amazing!) of the Himalayas and the snow, and it was just beautiful, and of course, then you'd choose a little area of the sky – we had binoculars and microscope – no, not microscope, (Telescope.) thank you, and we just concentrated on a square and watched the shooting stars as they would fly past, and you could be guaranteed, within about five minutes, to see a shooting star.

M: Amazing.

J: And it just took all night. We had a little fire dug in the ground keeping us warm, and some food, and the next minute the sun is coming up.

M: Brilliant.

3.03 (R = Rosie; M = Matt)

Rosie

R: I went to Glastonbury festival and it's great. It's just completely manic. The whole experience is crazy, but I was really lucky because I was there when it was sunny and so there was no rain (oh, great!) and I think it's crucial when you're at Glastonbury, to have at least one morning when you see the sun come up, so there's clearly no point in going to bed because everyone's up anyway and it's really noisy. So, we just went out and went dancing and stuff, and then sort of just mooched about some fields and sat on top of this hill and watched the sun come up, and it was amazing, and it was quite hard to stay awake all that time, but it was definitely, definitely worth it.

M: And how was the next day?

R: The next day was … A lot of sleeping was involved in the next day, which is a difficult thing to achieve in Glastonbury.

3.04 (P = Phillip; F = Flic)

Phillip

P: A few years ago there was an American talk show host that come over to do one show in London and me and my friends are massive fans, so we really wanted to see the show. So, we went to the South Bank where they were filming the night before, and camped out to try and get tickets and, unbelievably, there were about, I think, about twenty people there in front of us but we thought, oh, that's fine, we'll camp out, that will be great and we spent the whole night on the South Bank and obviously just didn't sleep. It was an absolute nightmare. It was so cold and we felt awful the next day, but the thing that kept us going was that we were going to see this show – literally our hero, and go and see this talk show host. The next day, when they were about to film the show, they called the people in and had a line, and we didn't realise we were the standby line, and they had twenty tickets and there were twenty people in front of us, and so we slept out the whole night, and spent the whole night there and didn't even get to see the show, unfortunately. We were really upset.

F: That's awful. Did you see it on the TV when they showed it?

P: Yeah, we did, but it wasn't the same.

2 3.05

- Ask the students to look through the gapped extracts before you play the recording so they know what information to listen out for.

- Play the recording, pausing and repeating if necessary to allow the students to complete the gaps.

a) actually	b) basically	c) completely
d) clearly	e) definitely	f) unbelievably
g) literally	h) unfortunately	i) really

3

Ask the students to match the adverbs in Exercise 2 to their functions.

1 completely, definitely, really	4 unbelievably
2 unfortunately	5 basically
3 clearly	6 literally
	7 actually

4 3.06

Ask the students to say the adverbs aloud and count the syllables. Check answers and then ask them to practise saying the adverbs. Make sure they do this with the correct number of syllables and that they put the stress in the right place.

actually – 3	ironically – 4
basically – 3	literally – 3
especially – 4	particularly – 5
eventually – 4	practically – 3
generally – 3	usually – 3

Language note

Pronunciation: syllable patterns in adverbs

In most of the adverbs in this section, the stress comes on the third syllable from the end (literally, eventually, ironically). Note how some of the vowel sounds disappear in the middle of many of the words (actually /ˈæktʃəli/, literally /ˈlɪtrəli/, generally /ˈdʒenrəli/, etc.

5

Ask the students to write their sentences. Put the students into pair to take turns reading their sentences aloud. Go round making sure they are pronouncing the adverbs correctly.

Speaking: anecdote (SB page 92)

For more information about how to set up, monitor and repeat Anecdotes, see page xx in the Introduction.

- Go through the instructions and the questions with the class. Give the students a minute or two to decide which occasion they're going to talk about. Then ask them to look at the questions and think about their answers to them. Allow them to make notes of what they're going to say and how they're going to say it, but discourage them from writing a paragraph that they can simply read out. Go round, monitoring and giving help where necessary.

- Pairwork. Put the students in pairs and ask them to take turns to tell their partner about a time they stayed up late or stayed up all night. Encourage them to ask each other follow-up questions to get further information. Ask some pairs to report back to the class on what they found out.

Speaking (SB page 93)

1

- Focus the students' attention on the proverbs. Point out that they're all about night, but come from different countries (some have been translated into English).

- Ask the students to match up the two halves of each proverb and discuss their results in pairs.

> a) 5   b) 6   c) 9   d) 7   e) 8   f) 1   g) 3
> h) 4   i) 2

2

Pairwork. Ask the students to discuss the questions in pairs. Get them to report back to the class on their conclusions.

> *Possible interpretations of the proverbs:*
> a) Don't judge things too quickly.
> b) Beware of bad people; they'll eventually be true to their nature even if at times they appear friendly.
> c) Bad things won't go on for ever. There's always hope that they'll come to an end.
> d) If the sky is red at night, the weather will be good the next day. If the sky is red in the morning, the weather will be bad that day.
> e) Don't make hasty decisions: if you have a problem, sleep on it and you may have a better idea of what is right in the morning.
> f) Someone who can overcome difficulties will also be successful when times are good and is, therefore, someone to be trusted.
> g) Don't judge by appearances. Things and people can appear different in different circumstances.

> h) It's when circumstances are confusing that people are tempted to do bad things. It's much easier to do the right thing when situations are clear, as there are fewer temptations.
> i) Although we cannot see the world around us when it is dark, by compensation we can see the stars and thus a much wider perspective. Perhaps by implication, something that seems bad or confusing at first may actually turn out to be extremely good or important.

3

- Discuss with the class the essential nature of proverbs. (They impart some kind of wisdom about life, often through imagery or metaphor of some kind and usually in a single sentence of relatively few words.)

- Pairwork. Ask the students to work in pairs to complete the proverbs in any way they want. Then get them to compare with other pairs around the class. Have a class vote on the best ones.

Vocabulary (SB page 93)

1

- Pairwork. Ask the students to work together to complete the sentences. Point out that the answers are all either compounds formed with *night* or collocations with *night*.

- When you check answers, get the students to say what the italicised expressions mean.

> a) all night long – throughout the night.
> b) a nightcap – an alcoholic drink that you have just before you go to bed.
> c) a night on the town – an evening's entertainment at clubs, theatres, bars, restaurants, etc.
> d) overnight sleeper – a train with beds travelling throughout the night.
> e) hen night – a celebration for a woman who is about to get married, with only her female friends present; stag night – a celebration for a man who is about to get married, with only his male friends present.

2

Pairwork. Put the students into pairs and ask them to choose one of the questions to discuss. Make sure that each question is discussed by at least one pair. Get the pairs to report back to the class on their discussions.

Reading (SB page 95)

1

Focus the students' attention on the background photo on page 94 and ask them what they can see. If no one recognises the aurora borealis (Northern Lights) explain what they are and ask if they know where than can see them. Ask the students to read the text and say whether the writer's trip was worthwhile or not, and why.

> Yes, the writer eventually sees the Northern Lights.

2

Tell the students to read the article again decide which sentence best fits with each paragraph. Allow them to compare answers in pairs before checking with the class.

1 d)	2 b)	3 a)	4 e)	5 c)

3

Go through the statements with the class, then tell the students to read the article again and find evidence in it to support them. Allow them to compare answers in pairs before checking with the class. Explain any difficult expressions. For example, *in days of yore* is a literary expression meaning in the far distant past.

a) In days of yore … (people) would see warriors with burning swords, shimmering shoals of fish and the spirits of the dead playing football with a walrus skull. Our modern eyes can't help but see more contemporary likenesses.

b) the aurora is … in duplicate … above Alaska, northern Canada, Iceland, Arctic Scandinavia and the north coast of Siberia – with a mirror image, the aurora australis, looping over Antarctica.

c) A week can pass without a flicker … seeing the aurora is a beguiling marriage of sheer luck and the effort you make to be in the best place at the optimum time … sightings are not guaranteed.

d) … the clear, dark skies that are ideal conditions for a sensational sighting. Travelling close to the Arctic Circle in the winter months holds the key, preferably on dates when there isn't a full moon (a rival light source) and to locations beneath the auroral oval that are not only far from light pollution but also blessed with good weather.

e) It is a brief encounter none of us will forget, sparking feelings of humility and euphoria.

4

Ask the students to complete the glossary on page 94 with words from the text. Allow them to compare answers in pairs before checking with the class.

a) fickle	d) celestial	g) rule of thumb
b) shimmering	e) galling	h) pristine
c) fleeting	f) apocalyptic	i) beguiling

5

Discuss the questions with the class and see how much agreement there is.

Listening & Grammar (SB page 95)

Regrets and past conditionals

1 🌐 **3.07**

• Focus the students' attention on the photos and tell them that they're going to hear Kieran talking about his trip to Machu Picchu, an ancient ruined city high up in the Peruvian Andes.

• Play the recording and ask the students to note down what was disappointing and what was rewarding about the experience.

Disappointing:
It was packed with tourists which meant that you couldn't really get a proper feel for the atmosphere of the place.
The altitude was a problem. He started suffering form altitude sickness as soon as he arrived.
He was exhausted so he slept right through his alarm and missed seeing the sunrise over the ruins.
Then the next day it was pouring with rain so there was no sunrise and he only had two days there so there wasn't another chance to see it.
It was raining so hard that his camera got soaked and his photos didn't come out.
Rewarding:
Seeing the ruins was really awe-inspiring, and the setting was magical.

🌐 **3.07** (K = Kieran; F = Fiona)

K: *Have I told you about my holiday in Peru?*

F: *No, I don't think so. Where did you go?*

K: *Um, I went to Machu Picchu, which was somewhere I'd always wanted to go.*

F: *Oh wow, that must have been amazing.*

K: *Yes, it was fantastic in many ways – seeing the ruins is really awe-inspiring, and the setting is magical, right in the middle of the jungle – but in other ways it was a bit disappointing.*

F: *Oh, what do you mean?*

K: *Well, for a start, it was packed with tourists, which meant that you couldn't really get a proper feel for the atmosphere of the place. I'd have liked to have gone there in the low season, when there are fewer visitors but, unfortunately, I couldn't get time off work then.*

F: *Oh, right, that's a shame.*

K: *And another problem was the altitude. I started suffering from altitude sickness as soon as I arrived, so I just went straight to bed. I think if I'd taken those altitude pills, I would have been okay.*

F: *Yeah, I heard about that. They say it takes a couple of days to acclimatise …*

K: *That's right, yeah … I'd also been planning to get up early the next day to see the sun rise over the ruins but, unfortunately, I was just too exhausted – I slept right through the alarm. Then the next day it was pouring with rain so obviously there was no sunrise. And then it was time to leave, which was a shame. I only had two days there. It's a pity I couldn't have gone for longer.*

F: *Oh well, at least you got some good photos hopefully?*

K: *No, that was another problem. It was raining so hard that my camera got soaked and the photos didn't actually come out.*

F: *Oh no! Still, at least you've got your memories?*

K: *Yeah. I don't regret going, not in the least. But I think I'd like to go again with more time and maybe read a bit more about the history beforehand so I could understand more about what I was seeing, and it would all be more meaningful. And perhaps not go on my own next time, either. Um, maybe you'd like to come with me?*

F: *Ah, we'll see …*

2 🌐 3.08

- Ask the students to read through the gapped sentences and think about how they might be completed. Then play the recording and ask them to complete the extracts.

- Focus attention on the ways of talking about past regrets and past conditionals in the margin.

> a) 'd have liked to have gone
> b) I'd taken, would have been
> c) I couldn't have gone

3

Ask the students to read the sentences and think about which alternatives are correct. Point out that more than one alternative may be correct in each sentence.

> a) 'd gone, could have gone
> b) not taking / not having taken
> c) 'd come, 'd have been / might have been
> d) If I'd been / Had I been, 'd / could
> e) But for / If it hadn't been for, 'd have

4

Ask the students to use the prompts to write sentences with similar meaning to the originals. Do the first one as an example, then ask them to complete the rest. Allow them to compare their sentences in pairs before checking answers with the class.

> a) I wish I'd gone / I could have gone in the low season.
> b) I regret not being able / not having been able to go with you.
> c) I would have liked to see / to have seen the sunrise.
> d) If it hadn't been packed with tourists, I'd have / I could have got a feel for the atmosphere.
> e) It's a pity I didn't take any good photos!
> f) But for my altitude sickness, I'd have / I could have got up to see the sunrise.
> g) If it hadn't been such a great experience, I wouldn't want to go again.

5

Pairwork. Put the students into pairs and ask them to tell each other about a holiday they've been on. Encourage them to include some details of things they regret or are glad about. Go round, giving help and encouragement. If you hear any particularly interesting accounts, ask the students to repeat them for the class.

6 Grammar *Extra* 9, Part 2

Ask the students to turn to *Grammar Extra* 9, Part 2 on page 142 of the Student's Book. Here they'll find an explanation of the grammar they've been studying and a further exercise to practise it.

2

> a) I'd stayed / 'd have found out
> b) had gone / wouldn't be
> c) I'd paid / was
> d) 'd taken part
> e) hadn't been talking / 'd have heard
> f) Had I told
> g) staying (having stayed)
> h) to have seen (to see)
> i) didn't meet

Useful phrases (SB page 96)

1

Ask the students to read the four short conversations and identify the problem with B's responses each time.

> They are too brief, do not invite the conversation to continue and may sound uninterested or rude.

2

Ask the students to decide where they can use the useful phrases to improve B's responses in Exercise 1. Don't provide answers yet.

3 🌐 3.09

Play the recording for the students to compare their answers to Exercise 2. Then put the students into pairs to practise the exchanges.

> 🌐 3.09
>
> 1
> *A: What are you up to tomorrow night?*
> *B: Nothing special – why do you ask?*
> 2
> *A: Are you doing anything tonight?*
> *B: No, what did you have in mind?*
> 3
> *A: Do you fancy coming to a jazz concert tonight?*
> *B: That's really kind of you but to be honest, I'm not very keen on jazz.*
> 4
> *A: I was wondering if you'd like to come round for a bite to eat this evening?*
> *B: That sounds great! I'd love to! Thanks.*

4

Read the invitation aloud and go through all the responses. Ask the students to identify the one that's more formal.

> Response c) is more formal.

5 🌐 3.10

- Ask the students to read the conversations and decide how best to complete the gaps.

- Play the recording for the students to check their answers. They then practise the conversations in pairs.

```
1  A: are you up to
   B: my eyes
   A: a shame
   B: would have been, anyway.
   A: other time
2  A: getting together
   B: Sounds
   A: a good time
   B: Actually
   A: fine
   B: then
3  A: fancy coming along
   B: Can I
   A: bring along
   B: forward
```

6

Pairwork. Put the students into pairs and ask them to take turns making and responding to an invitation. Encourage them to ask for details, to use as many useful phrases as the can and to make clear arrangements to meet where an invitation is accepted. Get some pairs to perform their dialogues for the class.

Vocabulary *Extra* (SB page 97)

Phrasal verbs

1

- Remind the students that phrasal verbs consist of a verb plus one or more particles. Ask them to read the sentences and identify the verb and the particle in the phrasal verbs

- Check answers and then establish the general meaning of *up* and *off* in phrasal verbs. Note: there's no fixed way of working out the meaning of phrasal verbs, but a knowledge of the general meaning of some of the particles goes a long way towards narrowing down their meaning.

```
a) You're still (up) and wide awake well after
   midnight.
b) What time do you plan to get (up)?
c) Can you remember a time when you stayed
   (up) all night?
d) I am (up) all night until I eventually feel tired
   enough to drop (off).
e) I generally start nodding (off) at about nine
   o'clock.

up = not in bed
off = falling asleep
```

2

Pairwork. Ask the students to match the phrasal verbs in bold in the sentences with the dictionary extracts. Check answers with the class before asking the students to take turns asking their partner the questions.

```
a) 5    b) 3    c) 4    d) 1    e) 2
```

3

Ask the students to choose three more phrasal verbs and write true sentences. Then ask them to compare their sentences with a partner.

4

Explain that in each case, the same particle is needed to complete both sentences in the pair. Check answers before asking the students to discuss in pairs whether the sentences are true for them.

```
a) out    b) on    c) off    d) down    e) in
```

5

Pairwork. Ask the students to work together to complete the sentences with the particles. Ask them to use the general meaning of the particles to help them.

```
a) up    b) out    c) down    d) up    e) on
```

6

Ask the students to check the meanings of the particles in their dictionaries and to choose three uses with different verbs to learn. Encourage them to write example sentences with the verbs they've chosen.

Further practice material

Need more writing practice?

→ Workbook page 57
- Writing an essay.

Need more classroom practice activities?

→ Photocopiable resource materials pages 183 to 185
   Grammar: *The teenage years*
   Vocabulary: *Brushing up your phrasal verbs*
   Communication: *Things that go bump in the night*
→ The top 10 activities pages xv to xx

Need DVD material?

→ DVD – Programme 9: *Regrets*

Need progress tests?

→ Test CD – *Test Unit 9*

Need more on important teaching concepts?

→ Key concepts in *New Inside Out* pages xxii to xxxv

Need student self-study practice?

→ CD-ROM – Unit 9: *Night*

Need student CEF self-evaluation?

→ CEF Checklists pages xxxvii to xliv

Need more information and more ideas?

→ www.insideout.net

Review C *Teacher's notes*

These exercises act as a check of the grammar and vocabulary that the students have learnt in Units 7–9. Use them to find any problems that students are having, or anything that they haven't understood and which will need further work.

Grammar (SB page 98)

Remind the students of the grammar explanations they read and the exercises they did in the *Grammar Extra* on pages 140 to 143.

1

This exercise reviews complex sentences from Unit 7. Point out that they're given the number of single clause sentences that each one can be broken up into. Check answers before asking the students to write their own complex sentence about what they like to do to relax. Put them into pairs to compare their sentences.

> *Suggested answers:*
> a) I had had a particularly stressful day at work. I got home. I switched on the TV. I promptly fell asleep.
> b) I really enjoy taking time out. I buy a newspaper. I find a quiet café. I order a coffee. I spend an hour or so quietly catching up with the news.
> c) After a long day of intensive study, I always try to do some sport. It clears my mind. It renews my energy levels.
> d) Going to the cinema really helps me unwind. It takes my mind off my problems. It lets me escape into another world for at least a couple of hours.
> e) Some people say that shopping is relaxing. I just think it's another source of stress. It often leads to over-spending. Over-spending can cause financial problems.

2

Pairwork. This exercise reviews modals for speculating about the future from Unit 7. Put the students into pairs to discuss the ideas first and decide which they think are likely to happen in the next ten years, which may happen sometime in the future, and which will probably never happen. When they have made their decisions, ask them to write sentences summarising their discussion. Check answers by having several students read their answers out to the class.

> (Students' own answers.)

3

This exercise reviews *paraphrasing* from Unit 8. Check answers before asking the students to discuss what happened next and to write the next three sentences of the story. Get the pairs to read out their sentences to the class.

> a) I was contacted by a man.
> b) The strange thing was that he refused to tell me his name.
> c) What he did tell me was that he was an old friend of the family and that he had a message for me.
> d) It was a message from my father, who had disappeared five years ago.
> e) In order to give it to me personally, he asked me to meet him outside the church at 6 o'clock.
> f) As I arrived at the church, the clock struck six. / As the clock struck six, I arrived at the church.
> g) A dark figure was standing in the doorway.
> h) My father was the dark figure!

4

Pairwork. This exercise reviews modals for talking about the past from Unit 8. Ask the students to work in pairs and to complete the sentences with their theories.

> (Students' own answers.)

5

This exercise reviews concessive clauses and adverbials from Unit 9. Check answers before asking the students to say which sentence best describes how they slept last night.

> a) even though   d) However,
> b) Despite having   e) in spite of
> c) Try as I might   f) Even so

6

This exercise reviews regrets and past conditionals from Unit 9.

> (Students' own answers.)

Vocabulary (SB page 99)

1

- This exercise reviews compound nouns from Unit 7. Check answers with the class and then get the students to match the compound nouns to the objects in the pictures.
- When you have checked that they have done this correctly, put them into pairs and ask them to think of five more compound nouns associated with objects or gadgets we use in daily life.

> cellular coverage
> earpiece
> keypad
> music player
> touch screen
> voice recognition
>
> a) (none shown)
> b) mobile phone – (cellular coverage not shown but implied), earpiece, keypad
> c) ticket machine – touch screen
> d) computer: voice recognition, music player

2

This exercise reviews words from Unit 7. Remind the students that they'll have to modify some of the words to make them fit the gaps. Check answers before asking the students to discuss whether or not they would like to have a digital coffee maker.

> 1 wowed   4 slick
> 2 going digital   5 sold
> 3 hype   6 trashed

3

This exercise reviews expressions to do with crime and the law from Unit 8. Make sure the students can explain why the incorrect words don't fit.

> a) probation (all the others are crimes; *probation* is a sentencing option)
> b) arson (all the others are people involved in a court case; *arson* is a crime)
> c) speeding (all the others are legal processes; *speeding* is a crime)
> d) to sentence (all the others are punishments; to sentence is a legal process)

4

This exercise reviews collocations with *law* from Unit 8. Check answers before putting the students into pairs to discuss whether they know anyone who matches the descriptions.

> a) above   d) take
> b) abiding   e) down
> c) trouble   f) word

5

This exercise reviews times of day and night from Unit 9.

> (Students' own answers.)

Pronunciation (SB page 99)

1

Remind the students that the boxes show the syllables of a word and the large boxes indicate the stressed syllables. Here they are being asked to classify words according to how many syllables they have and where the main stress falls. Encourage them to say each word aloud to get a feeling for what sounds right.

> (See answers in Exercise 2.)

2 🌐 3.11

Ask the students to underline the stressed syllables in the words in the table. Then play the recording for them to check their answers. Play it a second time for them to listen and repeat.

1 and 2

A: ■□□	B: □■□	C: □■□□	D: □□■□
<u>ba</u>rrister	at<u>tor</u>ney	em<u>be</u>zzlement	ado<u>le</u>scent
<u>di</u>gital	de<u>ci</u>sion	pe<u>de</u>strian	depri<u>va</u>tion
<u>man</u>slaughter	noc<u>tur</u>nal	sen<u>sa</u>tional	enter<u>tain</u>ment
<u>pro</u>minent	pro<u>ba</u>tion	te<u>le</u>pathy	situ<u>a</u>tion

Further practice material

Need more classroom practice activities?
→ Photocopiable resource materials page 186
   Board game: *Word jigsaw*
→ The top 10 activities pages xv to xx

Need progress tests?
→ Test CD – *Test Review C*

Need more on important teaching concepts?
→ Key concepts in *New Inside Out* pages xxii to xxxv

Need student self-study practice?
→ CD-ROM – *Review C*

Need more information and more ideas?
→ www.insideout.net

Section & Aims	What the students are doing
Reading & Speaking SB page 100 Reading for gist; fluency practice	Reading and completing a text. Discussing the issue of carbon and ecological footprints.
Vocabulary & Speaking SB page 101 Ecological expressions Fluency practice	Doing a lifestyle quiz. Making collocations describing eco-friendly lifestyles. Discussing eco-friendly activities.
Listening SB page 101 Listening for detail	Listening to a conversation and noting down facts that support arguments. Discussing their thoughts about reducing their carbon footprint.
Reading SB page 102 Reading for specific information	Reading about the world's oldest footprints and answering questions. Choosing the correct alternatives to complete sentences.
Grammar SB page 103 Passive structures	Comparing active and passive structures. Then rewriting a text. Combining sentences to include reduced passive clauses.
Listening & Speaking SB page 104 Listening for gist and for detail Fluency practice	Listening to someone talking about barefoot hiking. Making notes to answer questions. Discussing what it would be like to walk barefoot in certain situations.
Pronunciation SB page 104 Reading aloud	Identifying pauses in a story and predicting where they'll occur. Practising reading a passage aloud.
Speaking: anecdote SB page 105 Fluency practice	Talking about a walk they've been on.
Vocabulary SB page 105 Expressions with *foot* or *feet*	Completing sentences with *foot* or *feet*. Discussing the meaning of expressions with *foot* and *feet*.
Listening SB page 106 Listening for specific information	Matching speakers to the shoes they talk about and making notes. Discussing their own shoes.
Reading & Speaking SB page 106 Reading for gist and for detail Fluency practice	Reading two articles about men's and women's shoes. Identifying true and false statements. Discussing the link between personality and shoes.
Vocabulary & Writing SB page 107 Different types of shoes Writing a description	Categorising shoes according to gender. Identifying which shoes are being described by a psychologist. Writing a description of the owner of a pair of shoes.
Grammar SB page 107 Comparative structures	Studying ways of talking about differences. Writing sentences comparing a famous person with other people.
Useful phrases SB page 108 Useful conversational phrases for persuasion and responding to persuasion	Listening to people persuading others to do things and identifying the activities and the outcomes. Completing useful phrases from the conversation. Then writing a new conversation.
Writing *Extra* SB page 109 Report	Reading and discussing a report on students' travel habits. Identifying the use of the passive in the report. Matching quantity expressions to percentages. Interviewing other students and writing a report on their findings.
Writing WB page 63	Writing an email recommending places to visit.

10 Footprints *Teacher's Notes*

Focus attention on the title of the unit and ask the students if they know any proverbs or quotations about footprints in English or in their own language. If not, write some examples on the board and see if they can work out what they mean. For example:

Before you love, learn to run through the snow leaving no footprint. (Turkish proverb)

Someone who walks in another person's tracks leaves no footprints.

Don't tell me the sky is the limit: there are footprints on the moon!

Reading & Speaking (SB page 100)

1

Ask the students to look at the quotations and photo and to identify the theme.

> They're connected with footprints.

2

- Ask the students to read the two descriptions and say what the difference is between them.

- Then ask them to complete the descriptions with the words and phrases in the box.

> A carbon footprint is a way of measuring the environmental impact of human activities.
> An ecological footprint is a way of measuring the amount of land, water and other resources needed to sustain the current lifestyle of an individual or country.
>
> | | | |
> |---|---|---|
> | 1 impact | 6 citizen |
> | 2 greenhouse emissions | 7 resources |
> | 3 fossil fuels | 8 atmosphere |
> | 4 consumption | 9 lifestyle |
> | 5 household appliances | 10 developing country |

3

Pairwork. Go through the questions with the class and make sure they understand them. Then put the students into pairs and ask them to discuss the questions. In a class feedback session, encourage the students to share their ideas.

Vocabulary & Speaking (SB page 101)

1

Focus the students' attention on the quiz and explain *eco-friendly* if necessary (something that's eco-friendly inflicts little or no harm on the environment). Ask them to work individually to choose their answers.

2

Pairwork. Ask the students to discuss their scores. They could decide who has the most eco-friendly lifestyle. Ask them to report back to the class on which activities they think are the most important and the least important for reducing a person's carbon footprint.

> b) There may be some discussion on this, but generally speaking the most important activities in reducing a person's footprint are related to transport, because of CO_2 emissions: *I avoid flying where possible.* And also perhaps: *I walk, cycle or use public transport to go to work or college.* However, when it comes to flying, the students may argue that the flight will take place anyway, regardless of whether or not they are on it, whereas a personal choice not to drive a car to work does mean that there is one less polluting vehicle on the road.

3

- Remind the students that it's helpful to say words aloud to see what sounds right. Ask them to decide which words do not collocate with those in column A.

- Check answers before discussing the questions with the class.

> | | | |
> |---|---|---|
> | a) meat | d) central heating | g) food |
> | b) paper | e) glass | |
> | c) emissions | f) light bulbs | |

Listening (SB page 101)

1 3.12

- Focus attention on the photo. Explain that the students are going to hear Chloe and her mother, Barbara, discussing eco-friendly lifestyle choices. Go through the questions before you play the recording. Tell them to tick the items in the quiz that they mention and make a note of their different attitudes.

- Check answers with the class before playing the recording again. Ask the students to note down the facts that Chloe mentions to support her arguments.

a) Chloe is keen to reduce her family's carbon footprint, but her mother is less enthusiastic.
b) They mention turning off lights when leaving a room, leaving household appliances on standby, leaving the tap running, spending more than two minutes in the shower, recycling paper and glass, reusing plastic bags, cycling to work instead of taking the car, and avoiding flying.

Facts:

If her mother spent two minutes in the shower instead of five she would save 7,000 litres of water and over £30 a year in water heating costs. And she would have three extra minutes a day as well, that's 12 more hours per year.

The average car produces three tonnes of CO_2 a year. If everyone in this country went to work by bike instead of taking the car, that's a million tonnes of CO_2.

Planes are the major contributor to climate change. If you go by train you cut back on emissions by 90% on every trip.

The icecaps are melting and the polar bears are dying.

🌐 **3.12** (C = Chloe; M = Mother)

C: *Mum! You left the lights on again.*

M: *Sorry?*

C: *You left the lights on again. When I came downstairs this morning, all the lights were on. And the computer and the printer were plugged in, and the television was still on standby. Just think how much energy that was consuming.*

M: *Oh, this isn't going to turn into another carbon footprint lecture is it? It was bad enough you coming into the bathroom this morning and turning off the tap while I was still brushing my teeth …*

C: *Well, someone's got to think about our carbon footprint, haven't they? You'd already been in the shower five minutes before that. You could easily have a shower in two minutes instead of five.*

M: *Chloe, I hardly think that one person cutting down their shower by three minutes a day is going to have a massive effect on reducing our carbon footprint.*

C: *Yes, Mum, but if everyone said that, nothing would change. We've all got to do our bit to combat climate change. If you spent two minutes in the shower instead of five, you'd save 7,000 litres of water a year. And you'd have three extra minutes a day as well, that's 18 more hours per year you'd gain. Just think what you could do with all that extra time!*

M: *Chloe, I'm all for doing my bit. I put out my paper and glass to be recycled. I get biodegradable plastic bags when I go shopping at the supermarket. And I even reuse them sometimes.*

C: *Yes, Mum, but that's all you do. That's just a drop in the ocean. You're not going to save the planet unless you make some major changes in your lifestyle.*

M: *Like what, for example?*

C: *Like cycling to work instead of taking the car. Did you know that the average car produces three tonnes of CO_2 a year? If everyone in this country went to work by bike instead of taking the car, that's a million tonnes of CO_2 a year we'd save.*

M: *I hate to mention this, Chloe, but I don't seem to recall your refusing any lifts recently. And I also seem to recall your being overjoyed when I turned up in the car to pick you up from Sam's the other night when it was pouring with rain…*

C: *Okay, then … yeah … well … but when are you going to stop flying everywhere? You do know, don't you, that planes are the major contributor to climate change? If you go by train, you cut back on emissions by ninety percent on every trip.*

M: *Ah, so planes are the bad guys, are they? I seem to remember parting with a considerable amount of money to pay for a certain round-the-world ticket for a certain person's gap year. And quite honestly, I can't see the point in giving up flying when the rest of the population are quite happily going everywhere by plane. Why be so eco-friendly that you make yourself miserable?*

C: *Honestly! You are so selfish. The icecaps are melting and the polar bears are dying, and all you can think about is your own comfort.*

M: *Well, I'm afraid I'm not going to give up my holidays abroad just to make a couple of polar bears happy. Now, if the lecture's over, I'm going to make myself a cup of tea and have my breakfast. I have a busy day ahead.*

C: *Mum! You filled the kettle right up to the top! You only need to put in a tiny bit of water if you're only making one cup of tea. And as well as that, …*

2

Pairwork. Ask the students to discuss the questions and then to report back to the class on their conclusions.

Reading (SB page 102)

1

Pairwork. Focus the students' attention on the headline and the photos. Then put the students into pairs and ask them to discuss the questions. Encourage them to speculate where they don't know the answers, rather than going straight to the text to find out. Then have a class feedback session to find out what the students think and how similar their ideas are.

2

Give the students plenty of time to read the text and find the answers to the questions in Exercise 1. Find out how accurate their guesses were.

a) A short, small-brained species of apeman known as Australopithicus afarensis, an ancestor of modern human beings.
b) Laetoli in Northern Tanzania, about 3.6 million years ago.

c) They might have been preserved because they were pressed into volcanic ash. After their discovery by scientists, they were preserved by a special protective coating and reburied.

3

Ask the students to choose the correct alternatives. Then allow them to compare their sentences in pairs before checking answers with the class.

a) scientists
b) a female apeman
c) when humans started to walk
d) storm erosion
e) preserved

4

Pairwork. Ask the students to discuss what they think the highlighted words might mean. Remind them to look at the context, identify any prefixes or suffixes which might give a clue to meaning (e.g. the *ir* of *irreparable* suggests a negative, the *ologists* of *palaeontologists* suggests some kind of scientist or researcher), note any similarity to words they already know and identify the part of speech. Dictionaries should be used as a last resort here.

upright – straight and tall; vertical
late – dead (euphemistic, formal)
make out – see with difficulty
glanced – looked quickly and then looked away
irreparable /ɪˈreprəbəl/ – unable to be repaired
Palaeontologists /peɪlɪɒnˈtɒlədʒɪsts/ – people who study the history of the earth using fossils
degradation – the process of change into a worse condition
doomed – certain to fail or be destroyed

5

Pairwork. Ask the students to discuss the questions. Then ask them to talk about their own visits to historical sites. Remind them to ask their partners questions to elicit as much detail as they can about the places described and their impressions.

Grammar (SB page 103)
Passive structures

1

Focus attention on the information in the margin and remind the students of the structure and use of the passive. Then read out the sentences that are underlined in the text on page 102. Have a class discussion of which two sentences include the agent of the verb and why it is mentioned in these sentences and not the others. Ask them to look back at the sentences in the first section of the margin and say why some of these have the agent and some don't.

The Laetoli steps were discovered in 1976 by a team of scientists.
They found a couple of prints that had been exposed by the wind.
The agent is used here because it's important information. In the other sentences:
A study presented at an international conference … (the agent is obviously scientists but their exact identity is unknown)
… unless urgent action is taken, the site will suffer … (the agent is less important than the action)
Palaeontologists agree that something must be done … (the agent is less important than the action)

Grammar: passive structures
You use the passive when the person, people or thing that does an action (the agent) isn't known, isn't important or is less important than the action itself. Admittedly, the passive sounds more formal, but it sounds more appropriate. The most common passive structure is: subject + *is (being) / was (being) / are (being) / were (being) / has been / (may) have been / is/are going to be* + past participle.

2

• Give the students time to look at the photo and read the text. Ask them to say what problems the ruins are facing and what is being done.

• Have a class discussion on whether the verb structures in the text are active or passive and whether the active or passive is more natural in a text like this.

The ruins are under threat from sea erosion. We may lose them forever. An organisation called SCAPE is monitoring the situation.
The verbs are in the active voice. It would be more natural to use the passive, as a) it is a formal written report b) the focus is more on the actions than on the agents.

3

Ask the students to rewrite the text in Exercise 2 in the passive. Remind them to omit the agent of the verb if this isn't known, irrelevant or obvious. As they work, go round giving help where needed. Check answers with the class.

The prehistoric ruins at Jarlshof are being threatened by storms and rising sea levels. The settlement may have been built as long as 9,000 years ago. The island's coastline is being eroded by the sea and much of it has already been destroyed. The remains of this community could be lost for ever. Experts are alarmed by this potential loss. The situation is being monitored by an organisation called SCAPE. SCAPE was set up to protect ancient shoreline sites. So far, 30% of Scotland's sites have been surveyed including 3,500 which are judged to be at risk. The results of the survey are going to be published shortly.

4

Focus attention on the examples of reduced passive clauses in the margin. Ask them to find and underline the relative clause and the reduced passive clause in the two sentences in the exercise. Elicit the difference between them.

> a) Jarlshof is the site of a settlement <u>which was inhabited from the Bronze Age until the nineteenth century</u>. (relative clause)
> b) Jarlshof is the site of a settlement <u>inhabited from the Bronze Age until the nineteenth century</u>. (reduced passive clause)
> (The relative pronoun and the verb *to be* have been omitted in the reduced passive clause.)

Language note

Grammar: reduced passive clause

A reduced passive clause, also known as a reduced relative clause, is a clause where the relative clause and the verb *be* can be left out. Compare *They are a set of footprints **which were pressed** into volcanic ash.* with *They are a set of footprints **pressed** into volcanic ash.* The second sentence is more concise.

5

Do the first one as an example for the class, then ask the students to combine the remaining sentences using reduced passive clauses. As they work, go round reminding the students to omit the agent where appropriate and change other verbs from active to passive.

> a) Remains of a stone wall uncovered by a storm revealed evidence of the settlement.
> b) Tools and artefacts excavated by archaeologists have shed light on life in prehistoric times.
> c) Archaeologists are restoring some of the artefacts eroded by the sea.
> d) They have found buildings thought to date back nearly 2,500 years.
> e) The artefacts displayed by/in the Jarlshof museum provide insight into a unique way of life.

6

Pairwork. Put the students in pairs. Ask them to turn to the pages indicated and make notes. Encourage them to take turns talking about their sites using only their notes. Remind them to use passive structure where possible.

> *Possible answers:*
> **Lascaux caves, Dordogne, France**
> Prehistoric paintings are being threatened by bacterial and fungal infection. The caves have been closed to tourists. They are being monitored. They need to be preserved.
> **Wadi Mathendous rock art, Libya**
> Ancient cliff carvings are being threatened by tourism and vibrations from oil-drilling. Animals

and other symbols were drawn on the dry riverbed by prehistoric people. The rocks are climbed on and the pictures are being defaced by tourists. The oil-drilling must be stopped.

7 Grammar *Extra* 10, Part 1

Ask the students to turn to *Grammar Extra* 10, Part 1 on page 142 of the Student's Book. Here they'll find an explanation of the grammar they've been studying and a further exercise to practise it.

> 1
> 1 Plans were still being finalised.
> 2 Contact was first established.
> 3 The information was only made public.
> 4 It had been confirmed by a team of international experts.
> 5 Daily bulletins are being issued by the ETF.
> 6 It has been reported …
> 7 The exact location and date of the meeting are still to be confirmed.
> 8 A visit is expected.
> 9 No information has been released on this point.

Listening & Speaking (SB page 104)

1 🌐 **3.13**

Focus attention on the photos and ask the students to say what they show. Tell the students that they're going to hear an American man describing his experiences of barefoot hiking (hiking without shoes). Ask them first to say what they think the problems and good points of this might be. Then play the recording and ask the students to say whether the man describes it overall as a positive or negative experience.

> Positive (The man says that since this experience he has tried to hike barefoot as often as he can.)

> 🌐 **3.13**
>
> *Two years ago my family camped amidst the California redwoods. During a hike, my younger son decided to take his nap. Kicking off my shoes, I got comfortable under a redwood and let my son nap in my lap while my wife and elder son went on ahead. Upon their return, we had lunch and headed back to our campsite. On a whim, I decided not to put my shoes back on and walked back barefoot.*
>
> *The trail felt soft and cool; the cover of pine needles cushioned my footsteps. Normally, the return trip of a hike ends up being faster but, in this case, I was slowed down for two reasons. Since my feet were not hardened to the outdoors, I had to look down and deliberate every step to avoid stepping on potentially painful objects, such as sharp rocks. In addition, every time I wanted to see a tree, a cloud, or a hill, I had to stop. Normally, with hiking boots, I can walk while looking all around, but in this case I could not do both at the same time. I had to separate the two activities of hiking and of admiring the surroundings.*

A few side-effects made me very happy with my decision. Since I was focused on looking down, I noticed many more things on the forest floor; banana slugs, beetles, caterpillars, ants, leaves and cones, among others. Since my footprint was much smaller, softer and flexible, and I was focused on where my next step was landing, I believe I was more nonviolent. Since my son and I fell way behind, we saw different things. We saw a coyote. We noticed and took a side trail going down a rocky cliff that took me a good extra half-hour to traverse. But it was at the pace my son loved. And, of course, we saw many questioning smiles from passing hikers who doubtlessly had a good discussion later about a barefoot hiker carrying his boots.

Since then, I have tried to hike barefoot as often as I can, through as many terrains as possible (and I must admit that it has not been injury-free – I have to live with cuts and bruises). I enjoy the ability to walk through water or sit with my feet dangling in cold streams. I appreciate the sensations that my feet send to me – cold, heat, pain, pleasure. I feel more grounded and allow my feet to explore the different materials that they encounter. Just as my fingers are happy playing with sand, holding a piece of bark, or touching a petal, my toes enjoy wiggling in a puddle, scraping against a textured rock, pressing on a bed of pine needles, or rolling over a cone.

Last but not least, I found that hiking slowly opens up more possibilities. Once, hiking with a large group, I fell behind. Suddenly the park rangers closed the park to cut down an ailing giant redwood. People inside could not leave until this was complete. My friends waited outside in the parking lot while I saw a rare sight, a giant redwood crashing down causing a small cascade of falling trees. An earth-shattering, deafening, beautiful and sad event that I was lucky to experience, only because I decided to hike barefoot and slow down.

2

Go through the headings with the class, then ask the students to listen again and make notes. Play the recording again for them to check their answers.

> *Suggested answers:*
> a) They were hiking amidst the California redwoods.
> b) He took his shoes off to rest while his son had a nap and then decided on a whim not to put them back on.
> c) Since his feet were not hardened to the outdoors he had to look down and think about every step he took so that he didn't hurt his feet on sharp rocks. In addition, every time he wanted to look at something, such as a tree, a cloud or a hill, he had to stop.
> d) He noticed many more things on the forest floor. He saw different things because he was looking down most of the time. He didn't kill any insects by treading on them so he regards it as more non-violent. He and his son were behind the others so they saw different things. His young son enjoyed the pace they were travelling at.

e) He saw banana slugs, beetles, caterpillars, ants, leaves and cones, amongst other things.
f) The feeling of walking through water or sitting with his feet dangling in cold streams. He mentions cold, heat, pain and pleasure; wiggling his toes in a puddle, scraping his toes against a textured rock, pressing on a bed of pine needles, and rolling over a cone.
g) A giant redwood tree felled by the park rangers crashing down and causing a small cascade of falling trees.

3

Pairwork. You might need to do some preliminary work with vocabulary for expressing physical sensations and textures to give the students ideas and help in their discussion. Put the students into pairs and ask them to discuss the questions. Encourage them to report back to the class on their conclusions.

Pronunciation (SB page 104)

1

Pairwork. Put the students into pairs and ask them to discuss the questions. Then, in a class feedback session, find out how often and on what occasions the students might read aloud. These could range from being asked to do so at school to reading out an amusing fact or story from a newspaper to someone over breakfast.

> **Language note**
>
> **Pronunciation: preparing to read aloud**
> This may be a good time to remind your students about punctuation. It's like a set of road signs and it's there to guide them through a text. It will help them to recognise when to pause briefly, when to pause for longer, when to use rising intonation and when to use a falling intonation.

2

Ask the students to read the extract from the transcript of the recording and discuss what they think the slashes are for.

> The slashes represent where the speaker pauses in natural speech.

3 ⊕ 3.14

- Point out the two pauses marked by double slashes in the text in Exercise 2. Ask the students to listen to the recording and mark the other places where the speaker pauses. Allow them to compare notes with another pair before checking with the class.
- Play the recording again and ask them to underline the stressed words in each chunk.
- When you've checked answers, ask them to practise reading the passage aloud to each other.

> Two years ago // my family camped amidst the California redwoods. //During a hike, // my younger son decided to take his nap. / /Kicking off my shoes, // I got comfortable under a redwood //and let my son nap in my lap // while my wife and elder son went on ahead.// Upon their return // we had lunch // and headed back to our campsite. // On a whim, // I decided not to put my shoes back on // and walked back barefoot.

4 🌐 **3.15**

- Pairwork. Ask the students to work together to decide where the pauses are likely to occur. Encourage them to read the words aloud as they do this so that they get a feel for where pauses will come naturally. Remind them that the punctuation is there to give a clue about where pauses occur.

- Play the recording for the students to check their answers. Play it several times for them to practise reading at the same time as the speaker. Then ask them to read the passage aloud without the recording.

> The trail felt soft and cool; // the cover of pine needles cushioned my footsteps. // Normally, // the return trip of a hike ends up being faster, // but in this case // I was slowed down for two reasons. // Since my feet were not hardened to the outdoors, // I had to look down and deliberate every step // to avoid stepping on potentially painful objects, // such as sharp rocks. In addition, // every time I wanted to see a tree, // a cloud, // or a hill, // I had to stop. // Normally // with hiking boots // I can walk while looking all around, // but in this case // I could not do both at the same time. // I had to separate the two activities // of hiking and of admiring the surroundings.

Speaking: anecdote (SB page 105)

For more information about how to set up, monitor and repeat Anecdotes, see page xx in the Introduction.

- Go through the instructions and the questions with the class. Give the students a minute or two to decide which walking experience they're going to talk about. Then ask them to look at the questions and think about their answers to them. Allow them to make notes of what they're going to say and how they're going to say it, but discourage them from writing a paragraph that they can simply read out. Go round, monitoring and giving help where necessary.

- Pairwork. Put the students in pairs and ask them to take turns to tell their partner about a walk they've been on. Encourage them to ask each other follow-up questions to get further information. Ask some pairs to report back to the class about what they found out.

Vocabulary (SB page 105)

1

Ask the students to decide whether each gap should be filled with *foot* or *feet*. Then check answers with the class.

a) feet, foot, feet	c) foot, feet, feet, feet
b) foot, foot	d) foot, foot, feet

2

- Pairwork. Ask the students to discuss the meanings of the expressions in pairs. Encourage them to speculate and make guesses based on the context of each one. Allow them to use dictionaries to check, but insist that they make a decision on each one first.

- Have a class discussion of whether there are any similar expressions in their own language(s).

> get/have itchy feet = want to travel or make a change in your life
> put your foot down = firmly insist on doing or not doing something
> put your feet up = sit down and relax
> shoot yourself in the foot = say or do something stupid which ruins your chances of something
> get/have a foot in the door = get a chance to start working somewhere
> not put a foot wrong = not make any mistakes
> have feet of clay = have faults or imperfections that get you into trouble
> have two left feet = be a terrible dancer
> get/have cold feet = suddenly feel uncertain about going through with a plan
> put your foot in it = accidentally say something that annoys or embarrasses someone (derived from the expression *to put your foot in your mouth*, which has the same meaning)
> wait on someone hand and foot = do everything for someone
> stand on your own two feet = behave independently

3

Pairwork. Ask the students to work in pairs to discuss the questions. Encourage them to report back to the class on what they found out.

Listening (SB page 106)

1

Have a class discussion of these questions and let the students share their thoughts on shoes.

2 🌐 **3.16**

- Focus attention on the photos. Ask the students to describe the shoes. Tell them that they're going to hear four people talking about their shoes. Ask them to listen and match their descriptions to the photos.

- Play the recording again for the students to note down the answers to the questions.

1 d)   2 a)   3 b)   4 c)

Speaker 1
a) She needs sensible low-heeled shoes that are going to be hard-wearing because she's on her feet all day.
b) She mainly wears them for work.
c) They're sensible and low-heeled, but a bit scuffed and they could do with a bit of a polish.

Speaker 2
a) He tried on lots of pairs in the shop, but bought these because the others were not as comfortable.
b) He wears them all the time (day in day out).
c) They are probably not the trendiest style and now they are a bit worn out.

Speaker 3
a) He saw the shoes in a sale and couldn't resist buying them. He is a difficult size and finds it hard to get shoes that fit properly and look good, so he was pleased to find them.
b) He wears them on special occasions when he needs to look smart.
c) They are size 46 and a wide fitting. They are classic lace-up brogues and reasonably stylish.

Speaker 4
a) She bought them for her sister's wedding, to go with a red outfit.
b) She took them off several times during the wedding and has hardly worn them since.
c) They are expensive elegant designer shoes, but not very comfortable. They have little pointy toes and high heels.

🔘 **3.16**

1

I wear these shoes mainly for work. I'm on my feet all day so I really need sensible low-heeled shoes that are going to be hard-wearing. They're a bit scuffed and they could do with a bit of a polish, but actually no-one looks at my feet so I reckon I can generally get away with it.

2

I've had these trainers for about three years now and to tell you the truth I wear them day in, day out. They're probably not the trendiest style out but I tried on loads of pairs in the shop, and the others were nowhere near as comfortable as these. They're a bit worn out now, but I hate buying shoes so I always make mine last longer than they probably should.

3

I saw these shoes in a sale and I couldn't resist buying them. I take a size 46 and I need a wide fitting too, so sometimes it's hard to get shoes that fit properly and look good as well. I mean, they're just classic lace-up brogues but I think they're reasonably stylish and they're good for wearing on special occasions when I need to look smart.

4

I got these shoes for my sister's wedding, to go with a red outfit. There's a matching handbag too. They're designer shoes, and they're by far the most extravagant ones I've ever bought, they cost an arm and a leg. And they're not the most comfortable of shoes either – I had to take them off after the ceremony and again after all the photographs because my feet were killing me and to be honest, I've hardly worn them since. But I love the little pointy toes and I think they make me look quite elegant, even though I tend to wobble a bit on the high heels.

3

Pairwork. Ask the students to take turns to talk about their own shoes. Tell them to discuss where they bought them and why, how often they wear them, what they look like and how comfortable they are. The listening partner asks questions to elicit more information.

Reading & Speaking (SB page 106)

1

Give the students plenty of time to read the two articles and find the answers. Then check answers and elicit the students' initial reactions to the texts.

Text 1 c)   Text 2 a)

2

Go through the sentences with the class, then ask the students to read the articles again and decide whether they're true or false. Then you could ask them to find evidence for their choices in the article.

a) True. (in the centuries since the first cavemen wrapped their feet in animal skins to protect their dainty toes from the elements, men have continued to make bizarre choices when it comes to footwear)
b) False. (is it really fair that we hold his penchant for crocodile-hide cowboy boots against him?)
c) False. ('If they're down at heel, and in need of repair then he might not have the money to have them mended, which is okay,' she says.)
d) True. (… your shoes say a lot about who a person is … splashing out can make sense)
e) False. (there may be some grain of truth in the claim that shoe style preferences are linked with your actual personality)
f) False. (ankle boots are … judged to be elegant and feminine by some, the wearers are not seen to have the same dynamic drive that a woman wearing knee-high boots has)

3

Ask the students to look at the highlighted adjectives in the article and complete the glossary. Then ask them to discuss whether they know anyone who matches these definitions with a partner.

a) abrasive	e) scruffy
b) obsessive	f) lackadaisical
c) dainty	g) coy
d) sloppy	h) fastidious

4

Pairwork. Ask the students to discuss the questions in pairs. Encourage them to report back to the class on their conclusions.

Vocabulary & Writing (SB page 107)

1

Go through the list of words describing types of shoes in the box. Make sure everyone understands these. Then ask the students to divide the words into two groups: those which are not normally worn by men and those which are. Also ask them to decide which words can be used to describe the shoes in the photos.

> Not normally worn by men: clogs, court shoes, sling-backs, wedges, stilettos
>
> 1 clogs   2 stilettos   3 slip-ons   4 flip flops
> 5 Doc Martins®   6 court shoes

2 ⊕ 3.17

Pairwork. Ask the students to listen to the recording and with their partner decide which shoes the psychologist is talking about and who they belong to.

> Melanie – 1   Judith – 3
> Poppy – 2   Saffron – 4

> ⊕ 3.17 (P = Presenter; M = Margaret Banks)
>
> P: *Welcome back. Now, as promised, I'm joined in the studio by psychologist Margaret Banks who has written a brilliant book called* Let your shoes do the talking, *which promises to help us discover what people's shoes really say about them. Margaret, welcome.*
> M: *Hello, Poppy.*
> P: *Now, we've asked some of our audience today to bring in their favourite pair of shoes. Margaret, would you care to take a look at them? What kind of person do you think would wear these, for example?*
> M: *Hmm, well, I'd say that these shoes certainly suggest someone who is creative and idealistic, who perhaps has an alternative, slightly hippy lifestyle. The shoes are designed to be comfortable and good for your feet. And the vibrant colour to me indicates someone who is pretty self-assured and comfortable with herself.*
> P: *Great! Well, we'll be finding out soon if your predictions about the wearer are correct. In the mean time, would you mind taking a look at these shoes?*

> M: *Oh yes. These shoes tell me that their owner is fashion-conscious and glamorous. She's certainly no shrinking violet, but probably a bit more flirtatious and feminine, and less domineering than someone who might wear boots, for instance. They're really for a woman who's looking to make a red carpet entrance.*
> P: *I see. Very interesting… And how about these ones?*
> M: *Right, these shoes probably belong to someone who is somewhat older than the other women, and perhaps rather quiet, conservative and conventional. She is a follower rather than a leader, and perhaps not very dynamic.*
> P: *Oh, I see. Um…. okay, finally, what about these?*
> M: *Right. Well, clearly the owner is young and perhaps quite trendy, and someone with a carefree and rather casual approach to life. The shoes give off a playful, fun vibe. They say, 'I don't care about expensive designer fashions, there are so many other things that are far more interesting!'*
> P: *Fantastic! Right, thank you so much Margaret, for your assessments. Now it's time to reveal how accurate your predictions were …*

3

- Pairwork. Ask the students to pick another pair of shoes from the picture and write their own description of what sort of person they think the owner might be.
- When the descriptions are ready, ask the students to swap with another pair and try to guess which shoes the description they've received refers to.

Grammar (SB page 107)

Comparative structures

1

Get several students to read the sentences aloud. Draw their attention to the expressions in bold and ask the students to say what kind of difference they refer to. When you've checked answers, draw their attention to the further example sentences in the margin.

> a) c, e, f   b) b 4   c) a   d) d

Language note

Grammar: comparative structures
At this level it's important for your students to be familiar the intensifiers which go with comparative structures. For example:

(1) *Those are more interesting.*
*Those are **a bit** more interesting / Those are **a little** more interesting / Those are **far** more interesting / Those are **a lot** more interesting.*

(2) *These are as comfortable as the others.*
*These are **almost** as comfortable as the others / These are **just** as comfortable as the others / These are **nowhere near** as comfortable as the others / These are **nothing like** as comfortable as the others.*

2

Ask the students to match the words in the box with those in bold in Exercise 1 which have a similar meaning. When checking answers, get the students to put the new words in the sentences in Exercise 1 so that they hear them in context. Point out that there is no word in the box to replace *just* in sentence d).

a) a bit – a little, slightly
b) somewhat – rather
c) far – a lot, considerably, infinitely, much, way
e) by far – far and away
f) nowhere near – nothing like

3

Pairwork. Ask the students to choose a famous person and write three sentences comparing this person with other people. Go round, making sure they use comparative structures and adjectives correctly and that they don't include the person's name in their sentences. When they're ready, ask the students to read their description to another pair who try to guess who the person is.

4 Grammar *Extra* 10, Part 2

Ask the students to turn to *Grammar Extra* 10, Part 2 on page 142 of the Student's Book. Here they'll find an explanation of the grammar they've been studying and a further exercise to practise it.

2
a) He's <u>considerably</u> more patient …
b) … I suppose this one is just <u>slightly</u> more attractive.
c) She's <u>no</u> better than the last one …
d) … this year's holiday was <u>just</u> as good …
e) This is <u>by far</u> the worst film I've ever seen!
f) … just as outrageous, just <u>as</u> violent.
g) … your job is far <u>less</u> stressful compared to Randy's. …
h) This novel is far <u>more</u> challenging …

Useful phrases (SB page 108)

1

• Begin by brainstorming the language that the students already know for making invitations and persuading (and also expressing unwillingness).

• Pairwork. Ask the students to take turns being the person doing the inviting and the one who's tired.

2 🌐 3.18–3.21

• Go through the instructions with the class. Then play the recording for the students to listen and note down the two items for each conversation.

• Check answers before playing the recording again and asking the students to note down the reasons used to persuade the other person.

1 to sign a petition to save the rainforests – The man agrees to sign.
2 to buy shoes for her sister's wedding – Sally agrees to buy them.

3 to apply for the job of fitness trainer at the Carlton Health Centre – Tom agrees to apply.
4 to go sailing next summer – Jess agrees to go.

1 If they get several thousand signatures, people will take notice and the message will start to get home.
2 It's for her sister's wedding, which is once in a lifetime. She'll regret it if she doesn't buy them.
3 It's worth trying and sending in an application. He has the right qualifications and he may get shortlisted for an interview.
4 It's a fantastic opportunity and she'll really enjoy it.

🌐 **3.18** (Y= Young woman; M = Man)
1
Y: *Excuse me, sir. Can you sign this petition to save the rainforests?*
M: *Well, um, it's a good cause but I can't honestly see the point in signing a petition. No-one's ever going to take any notice of a few signatures.*
Y: *Oh, I disagree. I think it's well worth making our voice heard. If we get several thousand signatures, I think people will sit up and listen, and then our message will start to get home.*
M: *Well, okay then, but I don't honestly think it'll make any difference.*

🌐 **3.19** (K= Kathy; S = Sally)
2
K: *Oh, Sally, they look gorgeous! You should get them.*
S: *Yes, but they're so expensive. What's the point spending so much money on shoes you're only going to wear once?*
K: *Oh, go on! It's your sister's wedding, it's once in a lifetime. Treat yourself! You'll regret it if you don't buy them.*
S: *Well, it's a lot of money, but … okay then. If you really think so.*

🌐 **3.20** (M= Matt; T = Tom)
3
M: *Hey, Tom, have you seen this advert for a fitness trainer at the Carlton Health Centre? You should apply.*
T: *What's the use of applying? They're bound to get loads of applications, from people far more experienced than me.*
M: *Oh, come on, nothing ventured, nothing gained. You might as well try. You never know, you may get shortlisted for an interview.*
T: *Yes, but even if I got an interview, I wouldn't get the job. I'm hopeless in interviews.*
M: *Oh, come on, don't be defeatist! You're a qualified trainer. Just send in an application! It's worth giving it a go.*
T: *Well, okay then, if it'll make you happy. But I think it's a waste of time, quite frankly.*

4

J: *Hey, guess what? Sarah and are Ruth are going sailing next summer and they want me to go with them.*

M: *Jess, what a fantastic opportunity! You must go.*

J: *Hmm, I'm not sure. I've never done any sailing before. What if I get seasick? And what if I don't like sailing?*

M: *Well, you should cross that bridge when you come to it. I think you should go for it. You'll really enjoy it.*

J: *Well, maybe you're right. Maybe I should give it a try.*

3

Ask the students to complete as many gaps as possible before listening to the recording again. Check answers with the class and deal with any difficulties.

Trying to persuade someone:	Expressing doubts or reservations:
1 well worth	1 see the point in
2 yourself	2 the point of
3 ventured	3 What's the use of
4 gained	4 What if
5 as well	
6 defeatist	*Agreeing:*
7 when you come to it	1 you really
8 go	2 it'll make you
	3 a waste of
	4 a try

Language notes

Vocabulary

* *Nothing ventured, nothing gained*
  This is a proverb which means that if you don't take risks, you won't receive any rewards.

* *Defeatist*
  A defeatist is someone who never tries anything because they're already convinced that they will fail.

* *You should cross that bridge when you come to it*
  This means that you shouldn't worry about potential difficulties until they actually occur.

4 🌐 3.22

Tell the students that they're going to listen to another conversation. Tell them to identify what the woman is trying to persuade her friend to do.

> She's trying to persuade her to go into the sea.

S: *Come on, you know you want to, really.*

P: *No, absolutely not! It's out of the question! I'll freeze!*

S: *No, you won't. You'll love it, really. Go on, just for me! Mary went in last week, you know. She loved it.*

P: *Honestly, I'm not in the mood and I haven't got a costume anyway.*

S: *I told you, I've got an extra one. You can borrow it. Look.*

P: *Hah, you must be joking! That's hideous! I'm not putting that on.*

S: *Okay, okay, you can have this one. It's brand new!*

P: *Hmm, well, … I'm still not sure I feel like it, really.*

S: *Go on, it'll do you good. Just think how much better you'll feel when you come out!*

P: *Hmm … Oh, alright. You've twisted my arm. But I get to use the towel first when we get out.*

S: *Fair enough! Let's go.*

5

* Go through the list of expressions with the class. Ask the students to listen again and correct one of the words in the sentences so that they match the expressions used in the recordings.

* Students then say which ones are used to persuade, to refuse or to agree.

a) ~~in~~ on	e) ~~mad~~ joking
b) ~~blue~~ question	f) ~~for~~ like
c) ~~with~~ for	g) ~~make~~ do
d) ~~way~~ mood	h) ~~leg~~ arm

a) persuade: a, c, g
b) refuse: b, d, e, f
c) agree: h

6

* Pairwork. Go through the instructions with the class and ask each pair to choose one of the situations. Tell them that they'll perform their conversation for another pair who have to guess the situation, so they shouldn't give too many obvious clues. As they write their conversations, go round helping and encouraging them to use as many of the useful phrases for persuading, expressing reservations and agreeing as possible.

* Put each pair with another pair. Make sure that they have chosen different situations. Ask them to take turns performing their conversation and guessing the situation.

Writing *Extra* (SB page 109)

Report

1

Ask the students to read the report and match the headings to the paragraphs. Then have a class feedback session, encouraging discussion of different customs and habits.

> 1 b)   2 c)   3 a)

2

- Pairwork. Go through the questions with the class. Then put the students into pairs to discuss them.
- Check answers with the class. Encourage them to paraphrase rather than quote directly from the text.

> a) To investigate whether current public transport facilities are meeting students' needs, to encourage more students to travel in by bicycle or on foot and discourage the use of private cars.

3

- Ask the students to find the highlighted words in the text and to match them to words in the box with similar meaning.
- Check answers by asking the students to read sentences from the text with the new words in place.
- Ask the students to underline all the passive structures in the text. Ask them to say whether it's clear who wrote the report or not.

> carried out – conducted
> establish – determine
> minimise – reduce
> found – discovered
> cited – mentioned
> questioned – asked
> centred around – focused on
> proposed – suggested
> initiated – started
> issued – distributed
>
> 1 An investigation <u>was carried out</u> into the means of transport currently <u>used</u> by students to travel into college. …
> 2 <u>It was found that</u> just over half the students (53%), … <u>When questioned</u> about whether they would consider cycling, …
> 3 In the light of the findings, the following measures <u>are proposed</u>:
> - Negotiations <u>should be initiated</u> with local bus companies to …
> - The City Council <u>should be encouraged</u> to improve existing cycle tracks …
> - Cycle storage facilities <u>should be increased</u> on college premises.
> - Parking spaces <u>should be reduced</u> and a limited number of parking permits <u>should be issued.</u>
> - The success of the measures <u>should be monitored and evaluated</u> a year after implementation.
>
> It isn't clear who wrote the report. The writer isn't mentioned as this information is not important – the focus is on the content.

4

Ask the students to match the quantity expressions to the percentages. Allow them to compare their answers in pairs before checking with the class.

> The vast majority of – 90%
> just over a third of – 35%
> exactly a quarter of – 25%
> a little under half – 47%
> The overwhelming majority of – 99%
> one in ten – 10%
> A tiny percentage of – 1%
> virtually no – 0.1%
> a sizeable minority of – 28%

5

- Pairwork. Go through the topics with the class. Then put the students into pairs to choose one of them.
- As the students prepare their lists of questions, go round helping where necessary.
- Allow plenty of time for the interviewing and report writing. Remind the students to make appropriate use of formal language, including formal vocabulary and passive structures. Point out that the example report in Exercise 1 is divided up into sections with headings. Encourage them to do the same in their reports. Suggest that they use bullet points for their recommendations as in the example.

Further practice material

Need more writing practice?

→ Workbook page 63
- Writing an email recommending places to visit.

Need more classroom practice activities?

→ Photocopiable resource materials pages 187 to 189
  Grammar: *Divine Chocolate*
  Vocabulary: *Use your head*
  Communication: *Pink dolphins*
→ The top 10 activities pages xv to xx

Need DVD material?

→ DVD – Programme 10: *Family Affairs*

Need progress tests?

→ Test CD – *Test Unit 10*

Need more on important teaching concepts?

→ Key concepts in *New Inside Out* pages xxii to xxxv

Need student self-study practice?

→ CD-ROM – Unit 10: *Footprints*

Need student CEF self-evaluation?

→ CEF Checklists pages xxxvii to xliv

Need more information and more ideas?

→ www.insideout.net

11 Words *Overview*

Section & Aims	What the students are doing
Speaking & Listening **SB page 110** Fluency practice Listening for detail	Matching words to descriptions. Talking about English words. Listening to people discussing words in English. Discussing the use of English words in other languages.
Vocabulary **SB page 111** New words	Matching titles and photos to opening paragraphs of articles. Studying words which are new to English. Guessing meaning from context. Talking about the relevance of new words to their lifestyle.
Speaking **SB page 112** Fluency practice	Discussing the things they write and the frequency in which they write them. Discussing a quotation about writing in the digital age.
Reading & Vocabulary **SB page 112** Reading for detail Words and phrases for expressing yourself	Deciding on useful tips to improve writing and comparing them with the ones given. Matching tips to paragraphs in a blog on successful writing. Completing a glossary. Completing sentences with words from the glossary, then discussing their own writing style.
Grammar **SB page 114** Avoiding repetition	Identifying referents in a text. Using substitution and ellipsis to improve texts. Identifying which words can be left out of sentences and why. Making a conversation as short as possible, using substitution and ellipsis.
Speaking **SB page 115** Fluency practice	Discussing English spelling. Reading and discussing a text on how English spelling could be improved.
Pronunciation **SB page 115** Differences in spelling and pronunciation	Identifying silent letters in sentences. Identifying silent letters in place names. Reading a limerick aloud and correcting misspellings.
Useful phrases **SB page 116** Useful conversational phrases for getting your point across	Listening to two people talking about socialising online. Identifying the point someone is making and saying if they agree. Listening and replacing words with useful phrases. Writing a conversation. Using the useful phrases to respond to statements.
Vocabulary *Extra* **SB page 117** Origins of new words	Explaining the meaning of words. Matching words to their origins. Matching words to categories. Discussing the introduction of new words to a language. Seeing how dictionaries show information about sources of new words.
Writing **WB page 67**	Writing a cover letter.

Words *Teacher's notes*

Warm up

Ask the students to open their books at the first page of the unit and to look at the three quotations around the photos at the top. Ask them to discuss which they prefer and why, and to say if they know any other quotations or sayings about words.

Speaking & Listening (SB page 110)

1

- Pairwork. Explain that the focus here is not so much on the meanings of words as their form and origin. Ask the students to look at the words in the box and use them to complete the sentences.

- Allow the pairs to compare their results with other pairs before checking with the class. When you've finished, make sure everyone understands all the words. (Note: *facetious* is usually used to describe something someone said, which was intended to be humorous but came across as silly or inappropriate, e.g. *He's always making facetious comments.*) A word like *madam*, which can be read forwards or backwards is called a *palindrome*. Words like *brunch* and *smog* which are formed by combining other words are called *portmanteau* words (from the French for *suitcase*).

> a) madam
> b) brunch
> c) smoke, fog
> d) choice
> e) facetious
> f) feedback
> g) shampoo, penguin (note *pen gwyn* means white head in Welsh)
> h) weird, peculiar. Weird, peculiar

2

- Groupwork. Put the students into small groups and ask them to discuss the questions. Explain that *newly-coined* means recently invented.

- Ask the groups to compare their answers with another group and then report back to the class on their conclusions.

3 🖸 3.23–3.26

- Ask the students to listen to the four conversations on the recording and tick the questions in Exercise 2 that the people discuss.

- Play the recording again for them to note down the words they talk about. Pause the recording after each section to allow them to identify the words and write them down. Then discuss the questions with the class.

> 1 d   2 a   3 c   4 a
>
> 1 blogging, online, surfing, online surfing
> 2 mellifluous, impostor syndrome
> 3 download, lunch
> 4 sidewalk

> 🖸 **3.23** (G = Gillian; K = Kevin)
>
> 1
> G: *Gosh, there are loads, aren't there? Like blogging.*
> K: *Oh, yeah.*
> G: *Anything to do with …*
> K: *Anything internet-wise, yeah.*
> G: *Yeah, absolutely. World Wide Web.*
> K: *Even online. I mean, it's two words that would have existed, but put them together and suddenly it's a whole new …*
> G: *Yeah, completely, I think, you know blogging.*
> K: *Surfing.*
> G: *Online surfing.*
> K: *Surfing, which again would have existed but is different now. It's amazing.*
>
> 🖸 **3.24** (T = Trudy; S = Sue)
>
> 2
> T: *Yes. Mellifluous. Isn't it lovely? It was used to describe an actor's voice of mellow, sweet sounding, flowing – I just thought it was beautiful. How about you?*
> S: *Well, I heard this thing called impostor syndrome, which is something that apparently we, well, a lot of us feel, which is that we don't really have the skills that we say we have, or we feel inadequate about those – you know, about a certain job we are doing, which*
> *I thought was really interesting.*
>
> 🖸 **3.25** (C = Carolina)
>
> 3
> C: *Well, I think there's a lot of words in English that are currently in Spanish. A lot to do with technology – for instance, we say download, which is not a Spanish word, it's English. We also – we say lunch – it's very bad because, of course, it's comida in Spanish but now we've inherited this word – lunch.*

> **3.26** (C = Carolina; M = Mike)
>
> 4
> C: It was, I think, sidewalk.
> M: Really?
> C: Yes, it's very strange for me, you know, because
>   I thought it was pavement (right), like the thing
>   that you walk on when you are off the road.
> M: And how did you learn that?
> C: I was in New York and they said to me, you have
>   to cross onto the other sidewalk. I didn't know
>   what he said, 'what are you talking about?', you
>   know, but yes, so that I learnt. It was great.

4

Ask the students to decide what they think about the statements before you have a class discussion. Find out who agrees most with which statement.

Vocabulary (SB page 111)

1

Go through the titles with the class and elicit what the topics of the articles might be about. Point out that headlines often contain words with more than one meaning. For example, *matters* in the second title might just mean 'things' or 'affairs', or it could mean 'is important'. *Time out* has several meanings, ranging from a brief suspension of play during a sports match to a leisure period or even the automatic switching off of a machine because a set period of time has elapsed with no activity from the operator. Accept any reasonable answers: the point here is to get the students to speculate.

2

* Ask the students to read the opening paragraphs of the articles and match them to the titles.

* When you've checked answers, ask the students to match the articles to the photos and to say which article interests them most and why.

> 1 Money matters – photo c
> 2 Life online – photo b
> 3 Time out – photo a

3

* Ask the students to look at the bold words in the paragraphs and categorise them according to whether they know them, have seen them or have never seen them.

* Pairwork. Put the students into pairs and ask them to compare their answers. They should teach each other any words that they do know and that their partner doesn't. Then ask them to focus on categories b) and c) and to try to guess their meaning from the context. The words in the sidebar are not exactly the same but are words which have been created in a similar way and may give them some clues.

4

Check students' answers with the ones listed below or ask students to check online: www.insideout.net. Then discuss the questions with the class.

> credit crunch = A financial situation where it is difficult to borrow money from banks
> rightsizing = Politically correct term for downsizing (making employees redundant so that a company can save money and survive/make a larger profit)
> upskill = To learn a new skill that will improve your chances of getting a job
> conspicuous consumerism = spending a lot of money on luxury goods
> lipstick economy = Describing consumer trends when people prefer to spend on small luxuries, like cosmetics, rather than buy more expensive goods
> recessionistas = People who reinvent fashion looks using second hand clothes and cheap accessories
> lifecasting = Posting short thoughts or ideas on a website using a mobile phone or IM service
> microblogging = Writing after the minute details of their day to day lives on blogs
> phoneography = A combination of iphone and photography, used to talk about images captured by mobile phones
> twitterverse = A combination of twitter and universe, referring to the community of people who use the service
> status = what you are doing at the moment
> netspeak = the style of writing used in internet chatroom and in instant messages, characterised by the use of emoticons, abbreviations and acronyms
> RL = Real life as opposed to virtual life, where people meet and communicate online
> always on, always connected = always online and available, either by email, IM or mobile phone and also always being updated and informed about what's happening in the world.
> digital down time = Time spent relaxing without the use of technological gadgets
> unplugging = switching off all digital appliances and especially mobile phones and the internet
> face time = Spending time with people face to face, in the same room
> IM = instant messaging: an internet service which allows users to exchange short text messages in real time
> joy-to-stuff ratio = The balance between being happy and buying new goods.

Language notes

Vocabulary: new words
It's always worth trying to guess words from context as new words enter the lexicon on a daily basis. Many 'new' words are conflated words, i.e. two words fused together to form a new one. They often turn out to be short-lived. Newly created words like *twitterverse* require us to be familiar with the social networking service Twitter and the word *universe*. This new word may exist long enough to make it into our dictionaries.

Similarly, *lifecasting* (life + broadcasting), *microblogging* (a short weblog) and *recessionista* (recession + fashionista) can all be worked out if familiar with the composite parts. And if you can't work a word out from it's context or the composite parts of a word, and it isn't in your dictionary (yet!), there's only one course of action left: Google it!

Speaking (SB page 112)

1

Groupwork. Put the students into small groups and ask them to discuss the questions. Ask a spokesperson from each group to report back to the class on their discussions.

2

Read the quotation aloud or ask a student to read it. Then ask the students to think about their own answers to the questions. Give them time to formulate their opinions before starting a class discussion. Encourage the students to give reasons for their answers.

Reading & Vocabulary (SB page 112)

1

Pairwork. Put the students into pairs and ask them to close their books and to come up with five tips they could give someone to improve their writing. Suggest that they think back to the early days of their language learning and consider what they've learnt about writing since then. Also ask them to think about pieces of writing that they've read in their own language which they found unsatisfactory and decide what could have been done to improve them. Ask the pairs to read their tips to the class.

2

- Ask the students to open their books and compare their tips with those in the list. Find out how many are the same as theirs.
- Have a class discussion of what the writer might have said about each tip and to speculate on how each tip could be explained or elaborated.

3

Give the students plenty of time to read the blog on page 113. Then ask them to match the tips in Exercise 2 to the paragraphs of the text. Then ask them to compare answers with a partner and to discuss whether they predicted correctly what was said about each one.

1 d)	2 a)	3 e)	4 f)	5 c)	6 g)	7 b)

4

Pairwork. Put the students into pairs to discuss the questions. Then ask each pair to report back to the class on their opinions.

5

Pairwork. Put the students into pairs and ask them to find the highlighted words in the article and to discuss their possible meanings. Remind them to look at the context, think about words they know which are similar in structure, identify the part of speech, etc. When they've looked at each of the words, ask them to complete the glossary.

a) favour	f) put your point
b) glean	across
c) go around the houses	g) rambling
d) hit the right note	h) sink in
e) preamble	i) tangent

6

- Ask the students to use the words in the glossary to complete the sentences. Remind them to make any modifications that are necessary. Check answers by getting individual students to read out sentences so that they hear the words in context.
- Then ask the students to say whether or not the sentences are true for them and why.

a) rambling	e) glean
b) preambles	f) sinks in
c) go around the houses	g) hit the right note
d) put my point across	

Grammar (SB page 114)
Avoiding repetition

1

- Pairwork. Focus attention on the text and ask the students to read it and decide what the words in bold refer to. You could ask them to underline these words.
- Go through the examples in the margin with the students about substitution and check answers with the class. Point out that the phrases in bold have been used to avoid repetition. You could read the text to the class with the repetition put back in to show them how tedious it would be, e.g. *The most important question to ask is what response do I want to get? The answer to the question what response do I want to get? obviously depends on what you're writing.*

> That = the questions, what response do I want to get?
> It = what you're writing
> that case = It may be a memo at work
> It = what you're writing
> them = your readers
> either = punctuation and paragraphs
> Their = punctuation and paragraphs

2

Go through the instructions with the class, then ask them to decide which words in the box can be used to substitute the sections in bold in the tip. Ask them to compare answers in pairs and then to think of suitable headings for the tip.

1 It	4 They	7 them
2 Either way	5 their overuse	
3 To do so	6 they	

Headings for the two tips:
a) Use discourse markers to link sentences together
b) Use personal examples and anecdotes appropriately

Language note

Grammar: avoiding repetition (substitution)
In order to avoid repetition you can substitute nouns or noun phrases with pronouns or possessive adjectives. To substitute a verb phrase, use *so* or *not*: *Do you know what you want to say? If* **so** (= you know what you want to say), *just come out and say it. If* **not** (= if you don't know what you want to say), *keep quiet.*

3 🌐 **3.27**

• Pairwork. Remind the class that another way of avoiding repetition in texts is to use ellipsis (omitting words). Ask the students to work in pairs to decide which words could be cut from the sections in bold without losing the meaning.

• Play the recording for them to check their answers. Ask the students which words were cut and why.

> a) know what you want to say; know what you're saying
> b) repeat it
> c) they don't show this (replace with *not*)
> d) that you
>
> The words were cut to avoid unnecessary repetition.

> 🌐 **3.27**
>
> a) *If you're going around the houses, it's probably because you're not really sure yourself of exactly what you want to say. And if you don't, your readers definitely won't.*
> b) *You may feel that a point needs stressing, and that you therefore want to repeat it just to make sure it sinks in. Don't.*
> c) *Do the paragraphs show where you take a breath and when you start out on a new idea? If not, put them in.*
> d) *Also make sure you've included the right attachments and are sending it to the right recipients.*

Language notes

Grammar: avoiding repetition (ellipses)
• To avoid repetition, you can leave words out of a sentence, as long as the meaning isn't lost. *Make sure ~~that~~ you are doing it for the right reasons and not just because he wants you to ~~do it~~.*

• Both substitution and ellipsis, together with the use of time (*first, then, after that*), causal (*because*) and contrastive (*but, however*) linkers, and referencing, form the basis of cohesion – a linguistic term for the relationship between parts of a text that hold it together and give it meaning.

• Note: anaphoric reference refers back to something: *When I first met Jem,* **he** *was dressed as a farmer.* (The pronoun *he* refers back to the noun *Jem*); cataphoric reference refers forward to something: *When I first met* **him**, *Jem was dressed as a farmer.* (The pronoun *him* refers forward to the noun *Jem*).

4 🌐 **3.28**

• Pairwork. Get a couple of students to read out the conversation to the class. Then put them into pairs and ask them to try to make it as short as possible without losing any of the meaning.

• Play the recording for them to check their answers. Then have a class discussion on whether or not they agree with the speakers.

> A Do you do a lot of writing?
> B I used to do a lot of writing ~~at school~~, but now I don't ~~write~~ at all.
> A What about writing text messages? Don't you ever write ~~text messages~~ *them*?
> B Yes, of course, ~~I write text messages~~ every day! But I don't really think of ~~writing text messages~~ *that* as writing. Do you ~~think of it as writing~~?
> A No, I suppose *not* ~~I don't think of it as writing~~. But I do write a lot of emails at work. I think ~~emails~~ *that* counts as writing.
> B Yes, I suppose ~~that what you say is true~~ *so*. But I was thinking more about essays and reports ... now ~~essays and reports are~~ *that's* what I call real writing.

4 Grammar *Extra* 11

Ask the students to turn to *Grammar Extra* 11 on page 144 of the Student's Book. Here they'll find an explanation of the grammar they've been studying and further exercises to practise it.

> **1**
> 1 a) 2 a) 3 a) 4 a) 5 a) 6 b) 7 b)
> **2**
> | | |
> |---|---|
> | 1 them | 6 ~~it gave her more time~~ |
> | 2 it | 7 ~~it gave her time~~ |
> | 3 is this so | 8 them |
> | 4 them | 9 what |
> | 5 that was so | 10 ~~of what you have said~~ |

Speaking (SB page 115)

1

Pairwork. Put the students into pairs and ask them to discuss the questions. Encourage them to report back to the class and find out how many pairs chose the same words for b).

2

- Draw the students' attention to the photo of Mark Twain and the information about him in the margin. Then ask them to work in pairs and to read the article aloud. They could take one paragraph each. The second student may find the task more difficult as Twain's suggested spelling changes are implemented and the words become less and less recognisable.

- Get the students' reaction to the text and ask them if they think Twain was serious about wanting to improve English spelling in this way. (Probably not. As this text demonstrates, trying to simplify English spelling might make it much more difficult to read words correctly, rather than easier.) Ask if there are any suggestions in the text that they think would be good.

Pronunciation (SB page 115)

1

Go through the instructions with the class, then ask the students to decide which letters are silent and to cross them out. Encourage them to read the sentences aloud to get a feel for what sounds right. Then check answers with the class and get several students to read the sentences aloud correctly.

a) Knowing how to pronounce English words correctly is important but there's no doubt that it is one of the hardest things to learn.
b) Keep your receipt if you want to return a purchase, otherwise there's no guarantee you'll get your money back.
c) I had a really bad case of pneumonia earlier this year. Even watching the TV was tiring, so I spent most days just listening to the radio.
d) Psychiatrists can be very vague. They'll rarely give you a direct answer to a question.
e) During the flight the plane will climb to 10,000 metres above sea level.

Language note

Pronunciation: differences in spelling and pronunciation

As a general rule, 'k' is silent before 'n' (*knock, know, knife*); 'b' is silent before 't' (*doubt, debt*) or after 'm' (*comb, lamb, bomb, climb*); 'p' is silent before 's' (*psychiatrist*) or 'n' (*pneumatic*); and when a word ends in 'ue', it usually isn't pronounced, although in one syllable words it can lengthen the vowel that precedes it. For example: *plague* and *vogue* are pronounced /pleɪg/ and /vəʊg/, not /plæg/ and /vɒg/.

2 ⊕ 3.29

- Ask the students if they've ever been to any of these places and if they know the correct pronunciation. If they do, get them to say them aloud. Get several students to make guesses about how the others should be pronounced. Ask them to cross the silent letters out in pencil so that they can correct this later.

- Play the recording for them to check their answers. Then get them to listen again and repeat the names.

a) Gloucester	d) Brighton
b) Leicester	e) Greenwich
c) Grosvenor Square	f) Guildford

3

- Pairwork. Explain that a limerick is a humorous five-line poem which follows a set rhyme pattern and often begins with the line *There was an old/a young [person] from [place].* The first and second lines have to rhyme, as do the third and fourth lines. The fifth line always ends with a word that is either the same as or rhymes with the last word of the first line.

- Ask the students to work in pairs and to decide how this limerick should be read. Point out that some words are misspelled. Encourage them to say the limerick aloud as they decide how the words should be pronounced. Then get several pairs to read their versions to the class.

4 ⊕ 3.30

Play the recording for the students to listen and check. You might like to play it again, pausing after each line for them to repeat. Then ask them to work in their pairs to correct the misspelled words.

There was a young lady from Gloucester,
Whose parents thought they had lost her.
From the fridge came a sigh,
'Let me out or I'll die!'
But the problem was how to defrost her.

Useful phrases (SB page 116)

1 ⊕ 3.31

Tell the students that they're going to listen to two people discussing socialising online. First ask if they have any friends that they only 'talk' to online and how popular online socialising is amongst their circle of friends. Then play the recording and ask if the speakers think online socialising is a good thing to do, and why or why not.

The woman is worried that it can be dangerous. The man questions her position and seems to think that it's a good thing, and that it is actually safer than talking to strangers face to face.

🔘 3.31 (M = Matt; S = Sue)

M: *So, are you saying that people who socialise online are all freaks and weirdos?*

S: *No, you know I didn't say that! You're deliberately misconstruing my words! My point was, that it can be a problem, you know, you don't know who you're talking to … and they could be … yes, I suppose, they could be weirdos or something … I mean, you never know, do you?*

M: *So, what are you implying? That we should all stop using chatrooms and networking sites and whatever?*

S: *No, that's not my point … and you know it … what I want to say is that we need to be careful, that's all … you know, don't give away too many personal details … don't make yourself vulnerable …*

M: *But surely it's much safer to talk to someone at a distance than to talk to a stranger in a club or a bar …*

S: *You just don't understand … I'm not saying that it's dangerous to chat with people online … my point is that you have to be really careful when it comes to arranging to meet them in real life … you just don't know who they are, or what they want …*

2

- Ask the students to read through the transcript and to say exactly what Sue's point is. Remind them of the work they did on paraphrasing in Unit 8 and encourage them to restate her argument in their own words rather than quoting chunks of the text verbatim.

- Check answers with the class. Then point out that there are differences between the written transcript and the recording. Ask them to replace the highlighted words with what the speakers actually said.

> It can be dangerous to give out personal information online, or to arrange to meet people in real life who you've only ever met online.
>
> 1 I didn't say that!
> 2 You're deliberately misconstruing my words!
> 3 My point was
> 4 So, what are you implying?
> 5 that's not my point
> 6 what I want to say is
> 7 You just don't understand
> 8 my point is

3 🔘 3.32

Ask the students to listen to the useful phrases and to mark the main stress. Then check answers before playing the recording again for them to practise saying the phrases.

> a) I didn't <u>say</u> that!
> b) You're de<u>li</u>berately misconstruing my words!
> c) That's <u>not</u> what I meant!
> d) You're <u>twisting</u> my words!
> e) So, what <u>are</u> you implying?
> f) That's <u>not</u> what I'm saying!
> g) You're <u>missing</u> the point!

4

- Pairwork. Go through the flow chart with the class to make sure everyone understands the pattern their conversations should take. Then put the students into pairs and ask them to write the conversation. Remind them to include as many of the useful phrases as they can. When they've finished, get them to practise their conversations.

- Ask the pairs to read their conversations to the class.

5

Groupwork. Ask the students in each group to take turns to respond to each of the statements. They should put their points across clearly and challenge each other with questions like *So what are you saying?*

Vocabulary *Extra* (SB page 117)
Origins of new words

1

Pairwork. Put the students into pairs and ask them to discuss what they think the highlighted words mean. Remind them to look for clues such as the part of speech, the context, similarities to words they already know, etc. Encourage them to report back to the class.

> a) biro – a ballpoint pen
> b) demo – a demonstration
> c) guesstimate – giving a rough estimate based on guesswork
> d) google – to find information using the online search engine Google
> e) laser – light amplification by stimulated emission of radiation
> f) paparazzi – newspaper reporters and photographers who follow celebrities around
> g) tsunamis – tidal waves
> h) wannabe – an adjective describing people who want to be something but aren't

2

Ask the students to try to match the words in Exercise 1 with their origins. Then to check their answers in the dictionary entry.

> 1 f (Italian), g (Japanese)
> 2 a (the inventor of the ballpoint pen was a Hungarian called Lazlo Biro)
> 3 d)   4 h)   5 c)   6 e)   7 b)

3 🔘 3.33

- Ask the students to look at the words in the box. Ask them to say what the words mean and to match them to the categories in the dictionary entry.

- Play the recording for the students to check their answers. You might like to point out that one of the seven speakers talks about two of the words.

decaf – decaffeinated (clipping)
facebook (v) – to communicate with people using the social network Facebook (conversion)
fuggedaboutit – forget about it (respelling)
kosher – okay, acceptable (a borrowing from Hebrew)
Kleenex – a paper handkerchief (eponym)
lol – laugh out loud; also *lots of love* (acronym)
scuba – self-contained underwater breathing apparatus (acronym)
stalkerazzi – paparazzi who continually follow the same celebrity wherever they go (blending; also borrowing)

🌐 3.33

1
This is another one of those names that's become a verb, you know like google and skype. We can now ask questions like, 'Do you facebook?' Or complain that we've been facebooking all day.

2
I like this one. It's a kind of extreme paparazzi. One that hones in on one celeb in particular and just follows them round all day and all night – like a stalker. That's where it comes from, 'stalker' plus 'paparazzi'.

3
I honestly didn't know that people actually say this, I thought it was just one of those netspeak, texting abbreviations, and if they did say it in real life, I'd expect them to say 'laugh out loud', but apparently people do actually say 'lol' – a lot! And a lot of people use it sarcastically – to say that something is not funny.

4
I love this word, it's become a kind of exclamation, you know like, 'Lend you some money, fuggedaboutit!' It hasn't really changed its meaning, it's like 'gonna' or 'dunno', it's just that when you see it written down like that, you can't help but say it with a New York mobster accent.

5
Did you know that this word is actually an acronym? It stands for Self-Contained Underwater Breathing Apparatus. I didn't know that. I thought maybe it was a brand name or something, you know like Jacuzzi – or Kleenex – I mean, who says, paper hankie anymore?

6
This is one of those words that's really strayed quite far from its origins. I mean, it's kept its basic meaning, but you can use it for absolutely anything now … you know, it started out as the Hebrew term, being used strictly to describe Jewish dietary requirements, but now people use it for absolutely anything, you know like, 'Hey, is everything kosher?' Meaning is everything okay?

7
Yeah, it's one of those ubiquitous abbreviations – I mean, everything is shortened these days isn't it? You know 'goss' instead of 'gossip', or 'demo' instead of 'demonstration' – and I reckon you'd sound really pretentious if you went into a café and ordered a 'decaffeinated coffee' … absolutely no-one says that anymore!

4

Pairwork. Put the students into pairs and ask them to discuss the questions. Encourage them to report back to the class on their conclusions.

5

Ask the students to look in their own dictionaries and find out how they show information about the sources of new words. If they have different dictionaries, get them to compare the different methods.

Further practice material
Need more writing practice?
➔ Workbook page 67
• Writing a cover letter.

Need more classroom practice activities?
➔ Photocopiable resource materials pages 190 to 192
Grammar: *5 reasons to get an e-book*
Vocabulary: *Ode to the spell checker*
Communication: *Hidden word*
➔ The top 10 activities pages xv to xx

Need DVD material?
➔ DVD – Programme 11: *Accents*

Need progress tests?
➔ Test CD – *Test Unit 11*

Need more on important teaching concepts?
➔ Key concepts in *New Inside Out* pages xxii to xxxv

Need student self-study practice?
➔ CD-ROM – Unit 11: *Words*

Need student CEF self-evaluation?
➔ CEF Checklists pages xxxvii to xliv

Need more information and more ideas?
➔ www.insideout.net

12 Conscience *Overview*

Section & Aims	What the students are doing
Speaking & Listening SB page 118 Fluency practice Listening for detail	Discussing giving money to people in the street. Listening to people talking about who they give money to and matching speakers to the people they're talking about and their attitudes towards them. Talking about their own attitudes to people asking for money.
Vocabulary SB page 118 Describing street people	Categorising words according to register and formality. Discussing helping people who ask for money.
Grammar SB page 119 Special uses of the past simple	Completing sentences from the listening text. Identifying the meaning of past verb forms. Completing sentences with special uses of the past simple.
Reading SB page 120 Reading for gist and detail	Reading a text and identifying the connection between football and homelessness. Doing a jigsaw reading on the Homeless World Cup. Discussing statements and finding supporting evidence. Writing a tag-line for an advertising campaign.
Vocabulary SB page 121 Verb/Noun collocations	Studying verb/noun collocations. Rewriting sentences using the verbs given. Putting criteria for a happy and fulfilled life in order.
Reading & Speaking SB page 122 Reading for detail Fluency practice	Reading and answering a quiz about guilt. Discussing what kind of people would give certain answers in the quiz.
Listening SB page 123 Listening for gist and detail	Listening to a conversation to establish the link between four cartoons. Answering questions about what they heard. Identifying words which are omitted in speech.
Vocabulary SB page 123 Expressions with conscience	Completing sentences with expressions with conscience. Discussing actions that would give them a guilty conscience. Talking about a time they felt guilty and tried to make amends.
Useful phrases SB page 124 Useful conversational phrases for apologising	Listening to conversations and identifying what people are apologising for. Completing extracts from the conversations with useful phrases. Matching apologies to responses. Acting out situations where someone has to apologise. Matching *sorry* to various functions. Discussing apologies and apologising.
Writing Extra SB page 125 Responding to a complaint	Listening to a conversation to identify the problem and the advice given. Reading two responses to a letter of complaint and analysing them. Identifying features of a letter. Reading a letter of complaint and identifying the nature of the complaint. Using notes to write a reply.
Writing WB page 71	Writing a promotional flyer.

Conscience *Teacher's notes*

Ask the students to keep their books closed and in groups to brainstorm the type of people who might ask you for money on the street. Give them a time limit of two to three minutes. Then ask them to pool their ideas as a class.

Ask the students to open their books and see if the photos show people included in their lists.

Speaking & Listening (SB page 118)

1

Focus attention on the photos and elicit the answer to question a). Get the students to discuss the other questions in pairs and then to report back to the class.

> a) The charity collector because they're asking for money for someone other than themselves.
> b) and c) (Students' own answers.)

2 🌐 3.34–3.39

Go through the lists of people and attitudes before you play the recording. Ask the students to match the speakers to people they're talking about and their attitudes to them. When checking answers, you may need to explain that someone who is *work shy* avoids doing any kind of work, even though they are capable of working.

> 1 homeless people – it's better to give something other than money
> 2 charity collectors – you should only give to charity collectors
> 3 beggars in general – beggars are all work-shy
> 4 street performers – it's okay if they do something to earn it
> 5 charities in general – it's important to know where the money is going
> 6 people who clean our windows – the government should do something to stop them

🌐 3.34

1

Well, I don't think it's such a good idea to give money because, er, well, I'd be really worried that somebody would spend it on alcohol rather than something

nourishing or, you know, because they always say, like, 'penny for a cup of tea' or whatever. Um, so what I think I might do is, um, buy a sandwich, or hot drink, or something in winter or … and give it to them there, or maybe find some old clothes.

🌐 3.35

2

Yes, I usually put a couple of coins in a donation box, um, I mean, obviously if it's, if I'm not in a hurry and if it's easy to get at the change. Um, the thing I don't do is I don't believe in giving money to beggars.

🌐 3.36

3

Well, I never give any money to anybody. As far as I'm concerned, it just encourages them. You know, I pay my taxes so the state will look after these people. I mean, that's what we're paying all these high taxes for and you know what, quite frankly, I just think it's sheer laziness. I mean, I think they could get up off their bums and get a job if they really wanted to. It's just that they don't want to work.

🌐 3.37

4

Well, I don't mind giving money to people who are doing something to earn it, I mean, you know, I'd rather they actually did something to earn the money, you know, like, like street artists or, or buskers. I mean, I think someone who is actually playing music, it puts people in a good mood on the way to work, so you know, I usually give those people something. A few pennies.

🌐 3.38

5

Yeah, I never give money on the street any more. Um, I, um, I do give money through my bank, um, to charities that, um, I'm particularly concerned about. Once a month they get money from my bank. And that way I find I know where it's going and it also means that you're giving extra money because of tax relief.

🌐 3.39

6

Oh, it really annoys me. These people with their squeegies. I don't see why I should give money for cleaning my windscreen. I haven't, I haven't asked them. I think it's high time that the government did something about it because it really is annoying. No, I never give them anything.

3

Play the recording again and ask the students to think about which speaker they sympathise with most and least. Ask them to compare their answers and give reasons for their opinions.

Vocabulary (SB page 118)

1

Go through the instructions with the class and discuss the meaning and implications of the words and expressions in the box.

> a) neutral: busker, homeless person, street performer, street person, street vendor
> b) potentially offensive: bag lady, beggar, down-and-out, squeegee merchant, tramp, vagrant, wino
> a) formal: homeless person, street performer, street person, street vendor, vagrant
> b) spoken/informal: bag lady, beggar, down-and-out, squeegee merchant, tramp, wino

Language note

Vocabulary: register
When learning a word, it's important the students have an understanding of whether the register of the word is formal, colloquial or neutral. This section looks at the register of some words and phrases, highlighting the potential for offence that the wrong choice of word can cause.

2

Groupwork. Put the students into small groups and ask them to discuss the questions. Go round giving help where needed and ask a spokesperson from each group to report their conclusions to the class.

Grammar (SB page 119)

Special uses of the past simple

1 🔘 3.40

- Go through the instructions with the class and give them a minute or two to decide how the sentences should be completed.

- When they've made a guess at each sentence, ask them to listen to the recording to see if they were correct. Then identify the tense and why it has been used with the whole class. Go through the example sentences in the margin and point out that the past simple is used after certain expressions, including *it's time*, *I'd rather*, *suppose* and *imagine*.

> a) did   b) did
>
> The tense used is the past simple – although the sentences are referring to the present, the past simple is used with *I'd rather* and *it's high time* to show disapproval of the present situation.

Language notes

Grammar: special uses of the past simple
- In many cases use of the past simple, while referring to the present or future, establishes a notional distance between what you are saying and reality at the moment of saying it. For example, conditional sentences (*Suppose you had ...*, *Imagine we were ...*, etc.) refer to the present and use the past simple to show that the person is talking about a hypothetical situation. The past simple can be used to report what someone has said. Even if what the person has said remains true, the past simple is used to put a notional distance between when it was first said and when it was reported.

- There are some expressions like *I'd rather* (+ subject + past simple) and *It's high time* (+ subject + past simple) which contain a criticism of a present situation and offer an alternative in a couched manner. Compare *I want him to go* with *I'd rather he went* and *Go to bed!* with *It's high time you were in bed.*

2

Do this exercise with the class, identifying whether or not the expressions and sentences are actions in the past and discussing how the same ideas would be expressed in their language(s).

> None of them refer to the past except for f).

3

- Ask the students to complete the sentences, then allow them to compare with a partner before checking with the class.

- Ask the students to decide which sentences they agree with and to compare with a partner.

> *Suggested answers:*
> a) stopped   d) did
> b) started   e) gave/offered
> c) gave/helped   f) spent

4

Do this with the class, first giving them time to have a good look at the cartoons, then ask them to complete the punch lines with the correct expressions. Finally, ask them to write their own sentences with these expressions.

> a) It's about time you had a shave
> b) I'd rather you didn't speak with your mouth full

5 Grammar *Extra* 12

Ask the students to turn to *Grammar Extra* 12 on page 144 of the Student's Book. Here they'll find an explanation of the grammar they've been studying and further exercises to practise it.

1

a) If I _had_ more time, …

b) No change.

c) No change. (Also possible: 'that they _had_ done everything in their power …')

d) No change. (Also possible: 'warned that homelessness _was_ not a problem …')

e) I think it's about time we all _stopped_ thinking about shopping as if it _was_ some sort of sport or national pastime.

f) No change.

g) It's high time somebody _did_ something about …

h) I'd rather the government _spent_ money on providing …

2

(Students' own answers.)

Reading (SB page 120)

1

Focus attention on the cover of the DVD. Ask what is unusual about the football pictured (it's old and tatty, but the pattern of the scuffed leather forms a globe). Ask them to read the blurb (cover copy) and say what the link is between homelessness and football. Check answers and find out if anyone has heard of the Homeless World Cup before.

> Since 2006, homeless people from across the world have taken part in an international football championship called the Homeless World Cup.

2

- Pairwork. Put the students into pairs and ask them to decide who will be A and who B. Tell them to read their respective articles and to answer the questions.

- Then ask the students to take turns telling each other about their texts and comparing their answers.

> a) It encourages homeless people to work together, to create a routine, to believe in themselves and to develop their self-esteem. This in turn gives them the confidence and the social network to be able to help themselves to improve their conditions.
>
> b) The competition was founded by two businessmen, Mel Young, a social entrepreneur and Harald Schmied, editor of a newspaper sold by street people in Austria.

3

- Pairwork. Ask the students to work together to find the correct answers and then get them to underline the parts of the texts that provide the evidence.

- If any of your students are taking the Cambridge ESOL CAE exam, this task is good preparation for the reading task in Paper 1.

> a) 4 (There are an estimated one billion homeless people in the world. That's roughly the same number of football fans who watched the 2006 World Cup.
>
> b) 3 (an annual five-a-side football tournament … 48 countries … represented by men and women living in temporary accommodation or on the streets) Note: for the non-football minded, the official World Cup is held once every four years, there are 11 players in a team, and there is a separate competition for women's teams.
>
> c) 3 (92% of players have a new motivation for life; 73% of players change their lives for the better …)

4

Pairwork. Ask the students to complete the sentences based on information in the text they read. Make it clear that one must be true and the other false. Then ask them to show their sentences to their partner and try to identify the true ones.

5

- Pairwork. Draw the students' attention to the information in the margin and point out the tag line on the DVD box at the top of the page (_a ball can change your life_). Go through the instructions with the class and ask them if they can improve on this tag line in 15 words. As they work on their tag lines, go round giving help where needed.

- In a class feedback session, have all the tag lines read out and vote on the best one.

Vocabulary (SB page 121)

1

Ask the students to decide which verbs go with which nouns and noun phrases. Point out that many of these collocations were used in the texts on the Homeless World Cup, which they read in the previous section. Allow them to discuss this in pairs before checking with the class. Suggest that they try putting them into sentences to test out whether their combinations work or not.

> a) address a problem
> b) boost your self-esteem
> c) persue an education
> d) represent your country
> e) reunite families
> f) secure employment

2

- Ask the students to use the collocations they made in Exercise 1 to complete the sentences. Remind them that they may need to modify the verbs to make them fit the sentences grammatically.

a) reunited, families
b) securing employment
c) pursue, education
d) address a, problem / address, problems
e) represent, country
f) boost, self-esteem

3

• Go through the example with the class and make sure they understand that the verbs given can be used to make sentences with the same meaning as those in Exercise 2. Ask the students to rewrite the remaining sentences.

• Check answers by having several students read out their sentences to the class. Then ask them which version is more formal and which verbs were used in the articles they read.

a) Many of the players have got back together with their families.
b) Some have succeeded in getting jobs and have started working regularly for the first time in their lives.
c) Others have decided to do a course at night school or even university.
d) The majority have managed to deal with major problems such as drug addiction.
e) They're all proud to be playing for their country.
f) The Homeless World Cup helps players feel better about themselves.

The version in Exercise 2 is more formal. Mainly it was the more formal verbs that were used in the articles.

4

Groupwork. Ask the students to work in small groups to put the items in the order that they think is most important in order to live a happy and fulfilled life. Ask them to discuss whether any of the four things can exist in isolation. Get a spokesperson from each group to report back to the class on their conclusions.

Reading & Speaking (SB page 122)

1

Pairwork. Make sure everyone understands *guilty feeling* (a feeling you have when you know that you've done something wrong and you regret doing it, or when you're aware that you aren't doing something that you should). Ask the students to work through the quiz in pairs but to keep a record of their individual answers. Go through any difficult vocabulary with the class.

Language notes
Vocabulary: *torn* and *dither*
• *Torn* here means the feeling that you don't know which of two possible courses of action to take, you're pulled in both directions.
• To *dither* is to hesitate and to be unable to make a firm decision.

2

• Ask the students to turn to page 133 and compare their answers with the analysis there. Get them to discuss what kind of person they think would always give A, B or C answers. In a class feedback session write any useful adjectives that they use to describe such people in a list on the board, and ask the students to say what they think the quiz says about them.

Listening (SB page 123)

1 🌐 3.41

Focus the students' attention on the cartoons and get them to say what they can see and to speculate about how the cartoons might be connected. Then play the recording and ask them to say what the link is.

Jay has been asked to look after her neighbour's cat (cartoon a) and to water her plants (cartoon b). Her friend Keira suggests asking her teenage cousin to do it (cartoon c) so that can go away for the weekend with her friends (cartoon d).

🌐 3.41 (K = Kiera; J = Jay)

K: *Hey, Jay, how you doing?*
J: *Not too bad. You?*
K: *Listen, we're planning a weekend away – we're going to Tom's grandparents' place in the country. Fancy coming?*
J: *Oh, I'd love to ... But I can't ...*
K: *Why?*
J: *I promised I'd look after my neighbour's cat. She's away on holiday. I have to go round and feed it every day – and I promised I'd water the plants and ...*
K: *Hey, the plants'll survive for a weekend without water, won't they ... ?*
J: *Yeah, I suppose so ...*
K: *And you can put some food out for the cat ... I mean, it's not like a dog, you don't have to take it out for walks or anything, do you?*
J: *No, but ... well, you know, I promised ... and, well ...*
K: *I know, you hate letting people down! You and your guilty conscience. You need to lighten up a bit! Hey – I've got an idea!*
J: *What?*
K: *You know my cousin Susie?*
J: *Yeah ...*
K: *Well, she doesn't live very far from you ... and she'd do anything, absolutely anything for a bit of extra money ... why don't you ask her to do it for you? Give her a couple of quid, you know ... you'll be doing both of you a favour ....*

J: *Well, I don't know ... I mean, she's only 15 ... what if something happened? What if she lost the key? Or ... or ....*

K: *Or what? Oh, you're such a worrier! What can possibly go wrong? Look, if it makes you feel better, give her your mobile number – then, if anything does go wrong, she can call you ... and if you really feel you need to, you can make an extra copy of the key and leave it with my mum or something ...*

J: *Yeah, I suppose so ...*

K: *And you can go away with a clear conscience ...*

J: *Yeah, but ...*

K: *No buts ... oh, and yes, forgot to tell you .... Paul's coming ...*

2

Pairwork. Ask the students to discuss the questions in pairs. Then get them to report back on their conclusions.

> a) If she goes away for the weekend, she'll be breaking her promise to her neighbour.
> b) She's going to ask Kiera's cousin to feed the cat and water the plants and she's going to give an extra key to Kiera's mum in case of emergencies.
> c) (Students' own answers.)

Language note

Vocabulary: *ease your conscience*
To *ease your conscience* is to do something that makes you feel less guilty about something you have or have not done.

3

- Ask the students if they can remember which words the speakers dropped. Get them to say the extracts aloud, missing out the words that they think were dropped to see if they sound right.
- Play the recording again for them to check their answers.

> a) How you doing?
> b) Not too bad. You?
> c) Fancy coming?
> d) You know my cousin, Susie?
> e) Forgot to tell you ...

4

Have a class discussion on who the students identify with most, Jay or Kiera. First, establish what sort of people they are. (Jay is the sort of person who feels guilty if she breaks a promise. She'll give up something she wants to do in order to avoid upsetting someone else. Kiera is less fixated on what is right. If she were in Jay's position, she wouldn't think twice about leaving some food for the cat and abandoning the plants for a few days. She's more pragmatic and looks for solutions that will enable her to do what she really wants to do.)

Vocabulary (SB page 123)

1

Focus the students' attention on the expressions with *conscience* in the box and ask them which ones they know and if anyone can explain them to the class. Ask the students to complete the sentences and then to compare them in pairs before you check answers with the class.

> a) on his conscience
> b) an easy/a clear conscience
> c) a guilty conscience
> d) eased my conscience
> e) in all conscience
> f) a clear/an easy conscience
>
> Note that *an easy conscience* and *a clear conscience* have similar meanings and are interchangeable in these sentences.

Language note

Vocabulary: *in all conscience*
In all conscience is an expression which means 'in fairness' and is often used to express the idea that one can't or shouldn't do something because it would be against one's moral judgement. You might want to demonstrate its use with further examples:
I can't in all conscience accept the prize because the work wasn't really mine.
Can you, in all conscience, tell them that you didn't cause the accident when you know that you did?

2

- Ask the students to decide which of the things on the list would give them a guilty conscience and to add three more. Go round giving help with vocabulary if needed.
- When they've finished, put them into pairs and ask them to discuss their list with their partner's list and to say which three things make them feel the guiltiest, and what they do to ease their conscience. Ask them to report back to the class on their ideas.

3

Refer the students to the photo in the margin and explain that to *make amends* means to do something for someone by way of apology for something bad you've done to them or in order to put something right. You could make amends for forgetting someone's birthday by buying them some flowers or by taking them out for dinner. Ask the students to discuss in pairs or small groups the times they've done things that made them feel guilty and what they did to make amends.

Useful phrases (SB page 124)

1 3.42–3.47

- Focus attention on the signs and ask what word occurs in each of them (*sorry*). Explain that this word is used to apologise to other people for things that we have done wrong.

- Ask the students to listen to the conversations and identify what the people are apologising for and who sounds most apologetic (most sincere in their apology).

- Check answers with the class. You might like to ask the students who sounds the least apologetic (the person in c) who has brought up a sensitive topic of conversation; this *sorry* isn't really an apology, more an indication that the person thinks the friend is being over-sensitive). One of the speakers doesn't use the word *sorry* at all. Ask the students if they can remember which one (the last one announcing the cancelled concert). Point out that this speaker says *We regret to inform you …* and *We apologise for …*, which are more formal ways of saying sorry.

---

1 forgetting to book a table at a restaurant
2 over-reacting to a comment made by his friend
3 bringing up a sensitive topic in the conversation
4 taking the wrong bag
5 missing a meeting
6 a cancelled concert

The man in 2 is the most apologetic.

 3.42

1

A: *Did you phone the restaurant?*
B: *Oh, I'm sorry, it totally slipped my mind! I'll do it right now.*
A: *Yeah, well don't leave it too late – there might not be any tables left!*

 3.43

2

A: *Oh, hi there.*
B: *Hello.*
A: *Look. I've been wanting to talk to you about the other night.*
B: *Oh.*
A: *Yeah, well, the thing is, I've been thinking about what you said and how I reacted and I think I owe you an apology. I overdid it.*
B: *You certainly did. You were completely out of order! All I said was that you played better before you started spending half your life in front of a computer screen.*
A: *Yeah, yeah, I know. I'm sorry. I completely over-reacted. Friends?*
B: *Yes – this time! Next round's on you though.*
A: *Okay, okay.*

 3.44

3

A: *Listen, I'd rather not talk about it if you don't mind.*
B: *Sorry! I had no idea you were so touchy today!*
A: *Can we just drop it, please? I'm not in the mood.*

 3.45

4

A: *Erm … excuse me … but I think that's my bag you've got.*
B: *Sorry? What did you say?*
A: *I think that's my bag.*
B: *What? Oh. Oh yes, oh dear. I'm so terribly sorry. I thought it was mine.*
A: *That's alright. Don't worry about it. Easily done.*

 3.46

5

A: *How did the meeting go yesterday? Sorry I wasn't there, by the way.*
B: *Sorry! Is that all you can say. I had to deal with all those people on my own and all you can say is sorry? It's just not good enough. You think you can apologise and everything's going to be okay? Well, it doesn't work that way.*
A: *Look, I really, really am very sorry. I know I left you to carry the can. But it won't happen again. I promise.*
B: *Yeah, well, it better hadn't!*

 3.47

6

We regret to inform you that tonight's concert has been cancelled due to circumstances beyond our control. We apologise for any inconvenience caused. All tickets will be refunded at the box office.

2

Ask the students to look at the useful phrases and think about how they should be completed. Play the recording again to help them complete the phrases.

---

a) sorry, slipped my mind
b) owe you an apology
c) Sorry, no idea
d) so terribly
e) am very sorry, won't happen
f) regret to inform you

3

Play the recording again. Ask the students to concentrate on the intonation and voice range, and to practise saying the useful phrases in the same way as the speakers.

Pronunciation: stress shift and meaning change
When apologising, the word *sorry* is usually stressed on the first syllable and expressed neutrally, but the intonation of the word can change according to the mood of the speaker. By changing the intonation it can mean *I'm not at all sorry* (if said uninterestedly), or even *I was trying to apologise sincerely but I've changed my mind because of your attitude!* This would normally be intoned at volume with both syllables of the word being stressed equally.

4

Read the responses aloud, or get some students to read them out. Ask the students to match them to the apologies in Exercise 2.

---

1 e)   2 a)   3 b)   4 d)   5 c)

Possible answers:
1   a couple
2   friends who play together in a team
3   good friends or a couple
4   two strangers – possibly in an airport baggage hall or at the checkout in a shop
5   two colleagues

In the last recording (6) it could be the manager of a theatre.

5

• Pairwork. Ask the students to read the situations and decide what they'd say in each of them, and how angry they think the other person would be.

• Ask them to choose one of the situations and act out a short conversation. Go round as they work, giving extra help if needed. Choose some pairs to perform their conversations to the class.

6 🌐 **3.48**

• Go through the list of functions of the word *sorry* and point out that *sorry* isn't only used for apologising. It can also be used, for example, to interrupt someone (*Sorry! I think you've dropped this*). Then play the recording and ask the students match each *sorry* to its use.

• Check answers with the class and then initiate a discussion on what words the students use for *sorry* in their own language(s) and whether the same expression would be used for all six uses listed here.

---

1 d)   2 c)   3 e)   4 f)   5 b)   6 a)

🌐 **3.48**
1   *Sorry, I'm getting off at this stop.*
2   *Sorry to hear about the driving test! Better luck next time.*
3   *Sorry, I didn't catch that...*
4   *Sorry ... do you know where the train station is?*
5   *Sorry, but you won't be able to join the team.*
6   *Sorry I'm late!*

7

Groupwork. Put the students into small groups and ask them to discuss the questions. Appoint a spokesperson from each group to report back to the class.

Writing *Extra* (SB page 125)
Responding to a complaint

1 🌐 **3.49**

Go through the questions with the class so that they know what information to listen out for. Then play the recording and ask the students for their answers. Find out if anyone has any sympathy for the check-out assistant, and ask how they feel when they're waiting at a check-out and someone ahead of them in the queue suddenly discovers that they haven't enough money to pay and must put some or all of the items back.

Kelly was spoken to rudely by the check-out assistant in a supermarket. Laura suggests she writes a letter of complaint.

🌐 **3.49** (K = Kelly; L = Laura)

K: You know, I was in the supermarket yesterday and the check-out assistant was really, really rude to me ...

L: Rude to you? What do you mean?

K: Yeah, well, she was ... I was in the queue, and she'd started ... started ringing stuff up ... and I didn't have a lot ... milk, some bread, you know ... and then I put my hand in my pocket. And it was ... it was ... so embarrassing ...

L: What?

K: I'd forgotten my purse, I mean, I had a ... a little bit of money on me, but not enough.

L: Oh, yeah, that happened to me the other day, too ...

K: ... and so I told the woman on the till, you know, I said, like, 'Sorry, I think I'm going to have to put some stuff back' ... nicely, you know, I wasn't rude or anything ...

L: Yeah?

K: Yeah ... and she just flew off the handle ... started going on and on at me ... 'Can't you check before you come in the shop? Can't you see you're wasting my time?' ... I suppose she must have been having a bad day or whatever ...

L: So what did you do?

K: Well, I was really embarrassed and I didn't know what to say, so I just said, 'Okay, forget it', and walked away ... maybe I should have tried to calm her down ... I ... I don't know ...

L: Yeah, but, I mean, she was shouting at you ...

K: Yeah, but the worst thing was that as I walked away I heard ... I heard her say ... say ... 'Stupid cow' ... or something like that, under her breath.

L: Woah!

K: Yeah, and well, it ... it got to me ... I turned round and said, like, 'Say that again? What did you say? Say it to my face!'

L: Good for you!

K: *Yeah … but by now everyone was looking … and I was going to ask her for an apology … or … I don't know … ask for … ask to speak to the manager or something … but I lost my cool … I just turned round and walked out … and now … well, now it's too late to do anything about it …*

L: *No, it isn't. Write to the manager. Go on, write and complain. I would.*

K: *Yeah, but, you know, she was probably just having a bad day …*

L: *Okay, so what? She really shouldn't have treated you like that … go on, get it off your chest …*

K: *I don't know …*

L: *Come on, I'll help you.*

2

- Ask the students to read the letter from the store manager. Have a class discussion of how they think Kelly reacted when she got it.

- Ask the students to read the reply again and to identify three mistakes the store manager made. Point out that these are not language mistakes, but mistakes in what he should and shouldn't have done in his letter.

Suggested answers:
She was probably very offended and angry. The letter is rude and aggressive.
The store manager (1) denied his own responsibility as manager, (2) denied the store's responsibility for the behaviour of their staff and (3) did not apologise for the incident.

3

- Ask the students to read the alterative reply from the store manager. Have a class discussion of how they think she'd react if received this letter.

- Ask the students to read the reply again and to identify the places where the manager says the things on the list.

She would probably be much happier – the tone is polite, the writer expresses sympathy and apologises for the incident, both personally and on behalf of the company. He takes responsibility for the incident and says that he will try to make sure it doesn't happen again.

a) Thank you for informing me of your experience. … I hope that you will have a better experience of our services in future, and will not hesitate to contact me personally with any suggestions as to how they might be improved.

b) Please accept my personal apologies, and those of the company.

c) Our organisation failed to provide you with the service you are entitled to expect.

d) The matter has been investigated, and steps have been taken to prevent a recurrence.

4

Ask the students to read the letter of complaint and identify the problem.

A taxi failed to turn up on time and the customer missed their flight.

5

Pairwork. Ask the students to work together to read the notes and respond to the letter. As they work, go round giving extra help where needed.

6

Ask the students to check their letters carefully to make sure all the points in the list have been addressed. You might like to display the finished letters in the classroom for everyone to read and enjoy.

Further practice material

Need more writing practice?
→ Workbook page 71
- Writing a promotional flyer.

Need more classroom practice activities?
→ Photocopiable resource materials pages 193 to 195
  Grammar: *The great debate*
  Vocabulary: *Word families*
  Communication: *Easy money*
→ The top 10 activities pages xv to xx

Need progress tests?
→ Test CD – *Test Unit 12*

Need more on important teaching concepts?
→ Key concepts in *New Inside Out* pages xxii to xxxv

Need student self-study practice?
→ CD-ROM – Unit 12: *Conscience*

Need student CEF self-evaluation?
→ CEF Checklists pages xxxvii to xliv

Need more information and more ideas?
→ www.insideout.net

Review D *Teacher's notes*

These exercises act as a check of the grammar and vocabulary that the students have learnt in Units 10–12. Use them to find any problems that students are having, or anything that they haven't understood and which will need further work.

Grammar (SB page 126)

Remind the students of the grammar explanations they read and the exercises they did in the *Grammar Extra* on pages 142 to 145.

1

This exercise reviews passive structures from Unit 10.

1 were worn	5 was used
2 were found	6 lived
3 date	7 was made
4 had	8 was made

2

- This exercise reviews reduced passive clauses from Unit 10. Remind the students that reduced passive clauses and relative clauses are both ways of conveying the same information.
- When they have written the reduced passive clauses as full relative clauses, ask them to match the descriptions to the photos.

> a) which were designed originally for use on boats
> b) They can even be teamed up with a smart skirt and blouse for the office.
> c) which was previously seen mainly on muddy lanes or farmyards.
>
> a) 2　　b) 3　　c) 1

3

This exercise reviews comparative structures from Unit 10. Check answers by getting the students to show the rest of the class their shoes and to read out their sentences.

> (Students' own answers.)

4

This exercise reviews substitution and ellipsis from Unit 11. Ask the students to read the whole conversation and think about what the topic might be. If they are really stuck, point out that there is a big clue in the last line. Ask them to say what the words in bold refer to.

> it – passed his/her driving test
> it – the driving test/passing his/her driving test
> it – his/her driving licence
> It – having a driving licence
> is – is pleased

5

This exercise reviews substitution and ellipsis from Unit 11.

> *Suggested answer:*
> What is crowdsourcing? Who takes part? Well, everyone and anyone. Taking part is part of the basic concept. The term was first used in 2006. It describes a process by which a company broadcasts a business problem online and issues an open call for solutions. These come from anyone who is online. The crowd offers solutions and they also sort through them and find the best ones. And the company doesn't have to pay a penny for the service!

6

- This exercise reviews special uses of the past simple from Unit 12. Put the students into pairs to decide on the correct form of the verbs in brackets.
- When you have checked answers, ask them to look at the sentences again and decide who is talking to whom and what the situation is. They can then compare their conclusions with another pair.

> | | |
> |---|---|
> | a) prefer | d) told |
> | b) made | e) didn't know |
> | c) faced | f) knew |

Vocabulary (SB page 127)

1

This exercise reviews ecological expressions from Unit 10. Check answers with the class and then get the students to say whether the statements are true for where they live or where they come from.

a) recycled
b) organic
c) locally-grown/organic
d) solar-powered
e) energy-efficient
f) sustainable/organic
g) renewable

2

This exercise reviews expressions with *foot* and *feet* from Unit 10. Check answers before asking the students to discuss in pairs whether or not any of these things have happened to them recently.

a) put your foot in it
b) put your feet up
c) put your foot down
d) shoot yourself in the foot
e) get a foot in the door
f) be waited on hand and foot
g) get itchy feet
h) get cold feet

3

This exercise reviews new words from Unit 11.

1	crunch	6	status
2	economy	7	always
3	consumerism/consumption	8	always
4	life	9	digital
5	micro	10	stuff

4

This exercise reviews words describing people who ask for money on the street from Unit 12. When they have solved the anagrams, ask the students to say which, if any, of these people they saw on the way to class. Encourage them to give details and say where they were and what they were doing.

a) bag lady
b) beggar
c) busker
d) tramp
e) vagrant
f) wino
g) down-and-out
h) homeless person
i) street vendor
j) squeegee merchant

5

This exercise reviews verb/noun collocations from Unit 12. Check answers before asking the students to try to think of people to match each sentence.

a) 4   b) 1   c) 6   d) 3   e) 2   f) 5

Pronunciation (SB page 127)

1

Remind the students that the boxes show the syllables of a word and the large boxes indicate the stressed syllables. Here they are being asked to classify words according to how many syllables they have and where the main stress falls. Encourage them to say each word aloud to get a feeling for what sounds right.

(See answers in Exercise 2.)

2 ⊕ 3.50

Ask the students to underline the stressed syllables in the words in the table. Then play the recording for them to check their answers. Play it a second time for them to listen and repeat.

1 and 2			
A: ▢□□	**B:** □▢□	**C:** □▢□□	**D:** □□▢□
<u>e</u>nergy	e<u>mi</u>ssions	cons<u>pi</u>cuous	infor<u>ma</u>tion
<u>fe</u>minine	fa<u>ce</u>tious	de<u>vel</u>opment	miscon<u>stru</u>ing
<u>ho</u>nestly	flir<u>ta</u>tious	re<u>ne</u>wable	punctu<u>a</u>tion
<u>se</u>ttlement	sti<u>le</u>ttos	sus<u>tai</u>nable	repe<u>ti</u>tion

Further practice material

Need more classroom practice activities?

→ Photocopiable resource materials page 196
   Speaking and listening: *Tell us about*
→ The top 10 activities pages xv to xx

Need progress tests?

→ Test CD – *Test Review D*

Need more on important teaching concepts?

→ Key concepts in *New Inside Out* pages xxii to xxxv

Need student self-study practice?

→ CD-ROM – *Review D*

Need more information and more ideas?

→ www.insideout.net

Resource materials

Worksheet	Activity and focus	What the students are doing
Unit 1		
1 Grammar *Do I know you?*	Pairwork: predicting information Revision of tense and aspect	Completing 'true' sentences about their partner and asking questions to check.
1 Vocabulary *Being a man*	Pair and groupwork: information gap Collocations and expressions from Unit 1	Completing opinions with correct collocations and checking with a partner.
1 Communication *Class Q & A*	Whole class: mingling Revision of question forms	Finding out interesting information about each other.
Unit 2		
2 Grammar *A bunch of partitives*	Pairwork: matching game Partitive-noun collocations	Drawing lines to connect partitives with a suitable noun collocate.
2 Vocabulary *Mineral or tap?*	Groupwork: dominoes game Collocations with food and drink	Playing dominoes to connect suitable adjectives and nouns.
2 Communication *Food for thought*	Pairwork: gapfill and discussion Review of vocabulary from Unit 2	Completing statements correctly and then discussing whether the statements are true for them.
Unit 3		
3 Grammar *Tale of two cities*	Pair and groupwork: re-ordering sentences Sentence inversion	Re-ordering sentences and trying to guess the name of the city they are describing.
3 Vocabulary *Sentence halves*	Pairwork: matching sentence halves Revision of verb-noun collocations	Matching sentence halves to make twelve dictionary examples.
3 Communication *City of dreams*	Pairwork: vocabulary revision and extended speaking Anecdote task	Categorising vocabulary and talking about their (least) favourite city.
Review A *Getting to know you inside out*	Groupwork: board game Revision of topics from Units 1–3	Playing a board game, asking and answering questions.
Unit 4		
4 Grammar *A memorable day*	Individual and groupwork: writing The future as seen from the past	Writing different sentences in a story.
4 Vocabulary *Finding synonyms*	Pair / groupwork: pelmanism game Revision of expressions from Unit 4	Matching and memorising expressions.
4 Communication *Revision story*	Groupwork: writing a story from cues Revision of vocabulary from Unit 4	Creating a written story incorporating key vocabulary.

Worksheet	Activity and focus	What the students are doing
Unit 5		
5 Grammar *Proverb auction*	Teamwork: auction game Revision of article use	Deciding whether some common proverbs are correctly written.
5 Vocabulary *Communicative crossword*	Pairwork: crossword Revision of vocabulary from Unit 5	Writing and exchanging clues to complete a crossword.
5 Communication *Money talks*	Groupwork: board game Revision of vocabulary from Unit 5	Speaking for 30 seconds about a topic on the board.
Unit 6		
6 Grammar *Stative or dynamic phrases?*	Pairwork: Sentence analysis Stative and dynamic verb use	Discussing correct verb forms for common verbs in common phrases.
6 Vocabulary *Ways of speaking and looking*	Pairwork: gapfill and discussion Other ways of saying *speak* and *look*	Completing sentences in two different ways. Discussing if the sentences are true.
6 Communication *Memories*	Pairwork: speaking Question forming	Guessing questions for answers.
Review B *Don't say it!*	Groupwork: speaking game Abstract nouns and vocabulary revision from Units 1–6	Word association. Defining and guessing nouns.
Unit 7		
7 Grammar *My future in a hat*	Whole class Revision of future forms	Completing sentences, drawing them out of a hat and finding out who wrote them.
7 Vocabulary *Give us a clue*	Group and pairwork: communicative crossword Vocabulary for communications and technology	Writing and exchanging clues to complete a crossword.
7 Communication *Planet news*	Groupwork: planning and writing articles Summarising Using *will* for predictions Using the passive	Reading and paraphrasing news articles. Planning and writing articles about the future for the front page of a newspaper.
Unit 8		
8 Grammar *Modals and meanings*	Pairwork: pelmanism game Revision of past modals	Matching past modal sentences with their exact meanings.
8 Vocabulary *Thick as thieves*	Pairwork: completion task Speculating and making deductions	Completing six amusing crime stories and checking with their partner.
8 Communication *Legal matters*	Whole class: speaking Questions about the law	Asking and answering questions about the law.

Worksheet	Activity and focus	What the students are doing

Unit 9

9 Grammar *The teenage years*	Whole class: speaking Expressing past regrets	Completing sentences about regrets and then discussing ones that are true for you.
9 Vocabulary *Brushing up on phrasal verbs*	Pairwork: pelmanism game 3-part phrasal verbs + collocations from Unit 9	Matching a 3-part phrasal verb with a strong collocate.
9 Communication *Things that go bump in the night*	Pairwork: mutual dictation Concessive clauses and adverbials	Completing a story by dictating missing parts to each other.
Review C *Word jigsaw*	Groupwork: board game Revision of vocabulary and grammar from Units 7–9	Making grammatically correct sentences by collecting words on the board.

Unit 10

10 Grammar *Divine Chocolate®*	Pairwork: improving text Passive structures	Using passive structures to improve a text.
10 Vocabulary *Use your head*	Pairwork: reading and speaking Idiomatic expressions	Completing expressions with parts of the body and using them in discussion.
10 Communication *Pink dolphins*	Pair and groupwork: presenting and preparing arguments Taking part in a meeting	Reading about and discussing the development of tourism in a beauty spot. Using roleplay to take part in a meeting.

Unit 11

11 Grammar *5 reasons to get an e-book*	Pairwork: discussion and reading Ellipsis and substitution	Using ellipsis and substitution to make text more concise.
11 Vocabulary *Ode to the spell-checker*	Pairwork: reading and writing Homophones	Correcting spellings to make a coherent poem.
11 Communication *Hidden word*	Individual and groupwork: speaking and listening Fluency practice	Speaking on a topic for one minute including a particular word which the others have to guess.

Unit 12

12 Grammar *The great debate*	Pairwork / whole class: special uses of the past simple	Correcting statements and then discussing them in the form of a debate.
12 Vocabulary *Word families*	Pair / group work: spelling and pronunciation Revision of vocabulary from Unit 12	Completing a table of word families and a table of pronunciation patterns.
12 Communication *Easy money*	Pairwork: reading and speaking Reading for re-telling	Reading and re-telling a story with a partner.
Review D *Tell us about*	Groupwork: speaking and listening Fluency and revision	Talking for one minute about a topic without repetition or hesitation.

Teacher's notes

1 Grammar Do I know you?

Page 157

Activity

Pairwork: speaking

Focus

Revision of tense and aspect

Preparation

Make one copy of the worksheet for each student in the class.

Procedure

- Divide the class into pairs and give each student a worksheet.
- Ask the students to write their partner's name in the space at the top of the worksheet.
- Explain that they are going to find out how well they know their partner. (If it is a completely new class then they will find out how intuitive they are.)
- Ask the students to complete what they think is a true sentence about their partner using the verb in brackets and an appropriate verb form. At this stage they mustn't ask their partner any questions.
- Check the students have written the correct forms.
- When they have completed all their sentences the students take it in turns to ask 'yes/no' questions to check whether their ideas were right. Note that whether the sentence is positive or negative, the question will be the same.
- They should put a tick or a cross in the column provided depending on whether they have guessed correctly or not. Encourage them to ask one or two follow up questions as well. For example:

  Student A: *Were you born near here?*
  Student B: *Yes, I was.*
  Student A: *I thought so. Whereabouts exactly?*
  Student B: *In the main hospital.*
  Student A: *Oh. So was I! When…*

- When the students have finished checking they should add up their total number of correct guesses and then read the score at the bottom of the worksheet.

Follow up

Get the students to form new pairs and tell each other about their previous partner.

Notes

In some sentences more than one combination of tense and aspect is possible. In such cases students might like to discuss how the choice they make affects the meaning.

1 Vocabulary Being a man

Page 158

Activity

Pair and groupwork: information gap

Focus

Common collocations and expressions, some taken from the texts on pages 6 and 7. Discussion of gender stereotypes.

Preparation

Make one copy of the worksheet for each pair of students in the class. Cut the copies into A and B.

Procedure

- Divide the class into two groups, Group A and Group B. Give each student in Group A a copy of sheet A and each member of Group B a copy of sheet B.
- Tell the students to read the eight people's comments and complete the text as appropriate. In each group the students can discuss and share ideas in order to complete the task.
- Regroup the students into pairs so that each pair has one student with sheet A and one student with sheet B.
- Ask them to take it in turns to read out the comments: their versions should be identical. Ask them to discuss any differences and decide if those differences are due to incorrect English or another acceptable way of saying the same thing.

> **Suggested answers**
> 1 tyre needs changing, middle of the night
> 2 mixed messages, share their feelings, can't win
> 3 pride themselves, straight to the point
> 4 real man
> 5 day and age, sign of weakness, in touch with our feelings, bringing up our children
> 6 serious illness, sore throat, take to their beds
> 7 spatial awareness, reading a map
> 8 sense of self, take themselves too seriously

Follow up

Get the students to discuss the comments and decide which ones they agree with, which ones they partly agree with and which ones they think are nonsense.

1 Communication Class Q & A

Page 159

Activity

Whole class: speaking

Focus

Revision of question forms

Preparation

Make one copy of the worksheet for each student in the class.

Procedure

- Give one copy of the worksheet to each student.
- Tell the students that they are going to find out more about each other and then complete some sentences with the information they have found out. Give them ten minutes to think about their own answers for each piece of information.
- Explain that they are going to walk around the classroom, asking and answering appropriate questions until they have completed the worksheet. For example:

  What's your greatest achievement?
  Which living person do you most admire?
  What's your favourite journey? etc.

- Students then write, for example:

  Peter's greatest achievement is overcoming his fear of spiders.
  The living person Magda most admires is her grandmother.
  Ana's favourite journey is the walk upstairs at bedtime.

- Encourage the students to move around and talk to as many different people as possible.
- When the students have completed their worksheets, divide the class into pairs or small groups and ask them to share the most interesting things they found out about each other.

Follow up

Ask students to write five further questions to find out more information. Get them to interview each other with their new questions and write up the answers as sentences.

2 Grammar A bunch of partitives

Page 160

Activity

Pairwork: Matching game

Focus

Partitive-noun collocations

Preparation

Make one copy of the worksheet for every pair of students in the class.

Procedure

- Write a few partitives on the board e.g. *a pair of / a slice of / a bunch of* and get them to brainstorm nouns that collocate with each partitive. See how many they can come up with in, say, a minute.
- Divide the class into pairs. Give each pair a copy of the worksheet and ask them each to use a different coloured pen. Explain that they are going to test their knowledge of partitives by playing a game.
- In each pair, the students take it in turns to draw a circle round a partitive followed by a line connecting it to the appropriate noun collocate, which they also circle. The aim of the game is to connect all the partitives and nouns correctly without crossing lines. The game continues, therefore, till one of the students either draws a line that has to cross an existing line or is challenged successfully about an incorrect connection. When this happens the other student is the winner.

> **Correct answers**
>
> | | |
> |---|---|
> | a pair of pliers | a herd of cattle |
> | a pack of wolves | a shoal of herring |
> | a set of guidelines | a slice of ham |
> | a pile of rubbish | a flock of sheep |
> | a bunch of daffodils | a series of events |
> | a drop of blood | a range of hills |
> | a swarm of bees | a packet of crisps |
> | a clump of trees | |

Follow up

Students could be asked to consult their dictionaries and find at least one other collocate for each partitive. Here are some possibilities:

> a pair of knickers / tweezers etc.
> a pack of hounds / lies etc.
> a set of scales / rules etc.
> a pile of dishes / papers etc.
> a bunch of roses / grapes etc.
> a drop of rain / milk etc.
> a swarm of ants / wasps etc.
> a clump of hair / earth etc.
> a herd of cattle / deer / elephants etc.
> a shoal of fish / mackerel etc.
> a slice of bread / life etc.
> a flock of geese / birds etc.
> a series of problems / setbacks etc.
> a range of mountains / ideas etc.
> a packet of biscuits / tea etc.

2 Vocabulary Mineral or tap?

Page 161

Activity

Groupwork: dominoes

Focus

Collocations with food and drink

Preparation

Make one copy of the worksheet for each group of three to four students in the class. Cut up the dominoes as indicated.

Procedure

- Explain that the students are going to play a game of dominoes in which they form types of food and drink. Elicit different ways food (e.g. meat, eggs) can be cooked and drinks (e.g. coffee, water) can be served.

- Divide the class into groups of three to four students and give each group a set of dominoes placed face down on the table.

- Ask the students to take five dominoes each and leave the rest in a pile, face down.

- Ask the students to take turns placing their dominoes, for example:

water	decaffeinated	coffee	potato	salad	fried

If they do not have a domino that works, they pick up a domino from the pile and miss a turn. Circulate, checking that the students have found the correct connections. The first student to get rid of all their dominoes wins. (Because of the crossover of different ways of cooking food, students may reach a stalemate situation towards the end where nobody can play. In this case, the student with the fewest dominoes wins.)

2 Communication Food for thought

Page 162

Activity

Pairwork: gap fill and discussion

Focus

Vocabulary from Unit 2

Preparation

Make one copy of the worksheet for each student in the class.

Procedure

- Divide the class into pairs and give one copy of the worksheet to each student.

- Ask the students to work together to complete the sentences with the correct word from the three given.

- Check that the students have completed the sentences correctly.

- Once students have finished, ask them to go back and read each statement and say whether it is true or not for them. Encourage the students to compare and discuss any differences they might have. You could refer them to the Student's Book pages 22 and 23 for expressions of agreement / disagreement they might use, or choose some to write up on the board as prompts during their discussion.

1 – a) tasty	8 – c) live
2 – b) oven	9 – c) spent
3 – a) exquisite	10 – b) acquired
4 – c) cook	11 – c) strong
5 – c) tasteless	12 – b) spicy
6 – b) seen	13 – a) idea
7 – a) order	14 – a) good

3 Grammar Tale of two cities

Page 163

Activity

Pair and groupwork: reordering sentences

Focus

Inversion

Preparation

Make one copy of the worksheet for each pair of students in the class. Cut the copies into A and B.

Procedure

- Divide the class into two groups. Give everyone in group A a copy of sheet A and everyone in group B a copy of sheet B.

- Tell the students to read and complete the descriptive sentences by re-ordering the sentence beginnings. In each group the students can discuss and share ideas in order to complete the task.

- Check the students' answers.

- Regroup the students back into pairs so that each pair has one student with sheet A and one student with sheet B. Ask them to take it in turns to read out the sentences one by one and ask their partner to guess which city is being described.

> **Student A**
> Seldom have I seen this metropolis
> The city does not only
> Only after you've experienced
> Under no circumstances should you try
> In no other city will you find
> Not only does the city have
> On no account should you leave the city
> Rarely will you find a local resident
>
> Student A = Sao Paulo, Brazil

3 **Vocabulary** Sentence halves

Page 164

Activity

Pairwork: matching sentence halves

Focus

Revision of verb-noun collocations from Units 1–3

Preparation

Make one copy of the worksheet for each pair of students in the class. Cut up the cards as indicated.

Procedure

- Divide the class into pairs and give each pair a set of cards. Ask the students to spread the cards face up on the table.

- Explain that there are twelve sentences altogether and each card contains half a sentence. Tell the students that the sentences are all examples from the Macmillan English Dictionary illustrating verb-noun collocations they have seen in Units 1–3. Ask the students to match the halves together to make correct sentences.

- Circulate and monitor, checking that the students have made the correct connections.

- Check the answers with the whole class. (The sentences are correctly matched as they appear on the worksheet.)

Follow up

As all dictionary examples come from vast corpora of 'real' written and spoken English, students may like to guess in what sort of context these sentences appeared: written or spoken, formal or informal? Ask them to choose three collocations and 'invent' a context by writing what came before and after the example sentence.

Alternatively, ask the students to choose six of the collocations and look them up in their own dictionary. Can they find them under the noun or the verb entry? What example sentence is given? Are there any other interesting expressions or phrases with the same noun or verb?

3 **Communication** City of dreams

Page 165

Activity

Pairwork: telling an anecdote

Focus

Describing cities, extended speaking

Preparation

Make one copy of the worksheet for each student in the class.

Procedure

- Write the headings 'City of my dreams' and 'City of my nightmares' on the board and brainstorm some ideas. Write a few suggestions under each heading.

- Give one copy of the worksheet to each student and ask them to put the words and phrases under the headings according to their own opinions. Most of the phrases appear in Unit 3 of the Student's Book so this activity is useful revision. Ask them to compare their opinions.

- The second part of this worksheet is an anecdote where the students are asked to talk about the best (or worst) city they have visited. For more information on how to set up, monitor and repeat anecdotes, see page xx in the Teacher's book introduction.

Follow up

The best follow up is to get the students to repeat the anecdote to a different partner at a later date. See page xx for more details.

Review A Getting to know you inside out

Page 166

Activity

Groupwork: board game

Focus

Revision of topics from *New Inside Out* Advanced Student's Book, Units 1–3

Preparation

Make one copy of the worksheet for each group of students. Enlarge the worksheet to A3 size if possible.

Procedure

Divide the class into groups of three or four students. Give each group a copy of the game and a dice and counters. Then explain the rules.

Rules of the game

1 Place your counters on the arrow marked START and throw the dice.

2 The first player to throw a six starts the game.

3 The first player throws the dice and moves their counter along the board according to the number on the dice.

4 When you land on a square, answer the question or ask somebody else, according to the instruction on the square. If you land on a square marked ASK ANY QUESTION! you can choose any question on the board and ask any other player. Alternatively, you can make up your own question and ask any other player.

5 Players then play in turns, moving round the board.

6 If a player doesn't want to answer a question, they are allowed to pass and miss a turn.

7 The game continues until the first player reaches the square marked FINISH.

4 Grammar A memorable day

Page 167

Activity

Individual and groupwork: writing a story

Focus

The future as seen from the past

Preparation

Make one copy of the worksheet for each student in the class.

Procedure

- Give one copy of the worksheet to each student. Explain that they are going to write a story about a memorable day.

- Give the students a few moments to look at the different stages of the story. Then ask them to complete the first sentence. Encourage the students to be imaginative and amusing.

- Ask the students to fold their worksheet over so that what they have written is hidden and the next unfinished sentence is visible. Then ask them to pass their worksheet to the student on their left.

- Give the students enough time to complete the sentence that is now at the top of the worksheet, fold their worksheet over and pass it to the student on their left as before. Repeat the same procedure until all the sentences have been completed. (If you feel that any students will take much longer than others you may want to state a time limit for the sentence completion, e.g. 60 seconds, to avoid a jam.)

- When the last sentence has been written, divide the class into groups of three or four, ask the students to open out the completed story and read it to the others in their group.

- Ask the students to choose the most interesting or amusing story in their group, which they then read out to the whole class. The class listens to the stories and votes on the best.

4 Vocabulary Finding synonyms

Page 168

Activity

Pair / groupwork: pelmanism game

Focus

Mixture of expressions from Unit 4

Preparation

Make one copy of the worksheet for each pair / small group of students in the class. Cut up the cards as indicated.

Procedure

- Divide the class into pairs / small groups and give each pair / small group a set of cards. Ask the students to place the cards face down on the desk.

- Explain to the students that there are twelve pairs of expressions. Each pair consists of an expression from Unit 4 and its synonym. The aim of the game is to match each expression with its synonym.

- Explain that they should take it in turns to turn over two cards, one at a time, and read aloud the expression on each card. If the expressions are synonyms, the student keeps the pair and gets another turn. If the expressions are not synonyms, the student turns the cards face down again and ends their turn.

- The game continues until all the pairs of cards have been won. The student with the most pairs is the winner.

- Check the answers with the whole class.

> It was staggering. / It was extremely surprising.
> It was electrifying. / It was extremely exciting.
> It was unprecedented. / It had never happened before.
> I was gutted. / I was very disappointed.
> I hunted high and low. / I looked everywhere.
> I was taken for a ride. / I was conned.
> It sounded fishy. / It didn't sound right.
> I was very naïve. / I was very gullible.
> I didn't fall for it. / I didn't believe it.
> It had me in stitches. / It was extremely funny.
> I refused point blank. / I said absolutely not.
> I could hardly contain myself. / I was very excited.

Follow up

Cut some large photos out of a magazine showing two people of any description who could be speaking to each other. Ask students in their pairs to choose one of the pictures and then to come up with a dialogue between the people, using at least three of the expressions from the cards. Explain that students don't need to use the expressions exactly as presented. Get the students to perform the dialogues and then vote for the best one.

4 Communication Revision story

Page 169

Activity

Groupwork: writing a story

Focus

Revision of vocabulary from Unit 4

Preparation

Make one copy of the worksheet for each group of six to eight students in the class. Cut the cards out as indicated.

Procedure

- Tell the students that they are going to write a short story using vocabulary from Unit 4.
- Ask the students to work in groups of six to eight.
- Give each group one copy of the worksheet cut into cards and ask them to divide out the cards equally between them.
- Now ask the students to work in pairs or small groups with other students from their group. Ask them to combine their cards.
- Tell the students that they have twenty minutes to write a story incorporating the words and phrases on their cards into the story. The story should be as coherent as possible, but tell the students not to worry too much about the quality of the story – the aim is to revise the vocabulary by putting it into correct contexts. It doesn't matter if the story is somewhat nonsensical!
- When the time is up, ask students to exchange stories and to check for mistakes.
- Then ask the students to take turns to read out their stories so that the class can either vote for the best one or guess which words and expressions were on their cards.

Follow up

Ask each pair or small group of students to transform their story into a cloze activity by blanking out some of the words in the text. These words can be either a) the words that were on the cards or b) every sixth or tenth word.

Ask the students to put the blanked out words in random order in a box above the text. Students then exchange texts and use the words in the box to fill in the blanks.

Variations

1) Ask students to work in small groups of 3 to 5 and instead of dividing out the cards, put them in a pile face down in the middle of the table. Ask students to take it in turns to take a card from the top of the pile and make a sentence including the word or phrase on the card. The next student should take a new card and continue the story by adding a sentence incorporating the word or phrase on his or her card. Continue until all the cards have been used up.

2) Instead of using the cards on the worksheet, ask the students to choose five or six of the most useful words and phrases they have noted down in the past week and use them in a similar activity. See The Top Ten Activities for Advanced Students on page xviii, 6 Five Favourites.

5 Grammar Proverb auction

Page 170

Activity

Team auction game

Focus

Articles

Preparation

Make one copy of the worksheet for each student.

Procedure

- Give one copy of the worksheet to each student in the class. Divide the class into teams. Explain that they are going to play a game in the style of an auction. Tell them that the proverbs on their worksheet are up for sale at a public auction. Some are written correctly and others are written incorrectly. (NB The mistakes are all due to the incorrect use of articles.)
- Each team must try and buy the proverbs they think are correct by bidding more money than the other teams. Each team has a total of £10,000 to spend at the auction. The teacher (or one of the students) takes the role of the auctioneer, reads out the proverb and opens up the bidding.
- The winner is the team that buys the highest number of correct proverbs.

> **Correct and corrected proverbs**
> ✗ ~~The~~ advice is cheap
> ✓ All that glitters is not gold
> ✓ Every cloud has a silver lining
> ✗ ~~The~~ knowledge is ~~the~~ power
> ✗ Make ~~the~~ hay while the sun shines
> ✓ Many hands make light work
> ✗ Money can't buy ~~the~~ happiness
> ✗ ~~The~~ necessity is the mother of invention
> ✓ Never bite the hand that feeds you
> ✗ The early bird catches ~~a~~ the worm
> ✓ Time is money
> ✓ Where there's a will, there's a way

Follow up

- Ask the students to try and work out a meaning for each proverb.

> **Suggested meanings:**
>
> Advice is cheap: it is easy to give advice but not always easy to take it or act on it.
>
> All that glitters is not gold: something may look very good on the outside or from a distance, but when you get it you find it is not worth very much.
>
> Every cloud has a silver lining: something good may result from a bad thing happening.
>
> Knowledge is power: the more you know the more you are in a position to change something.
>
> Make hay while the sun shines: do as much work as you can while your situation is good; save for hard times in the future.
>
> Many hands make light work: if lots of people help, the job won't seem so difficult.
>
> Money can't buy happiness: being rich does not guarantee a happy life.
>
> Necessity is the mother of invention: the creation of an invention is often started because you need something that doesn't exist.
>
> Never bite the hand that feeds you: if you rely on somebody, don't stop them giving you what you need.
>
> The early bird catches the worm: if you want something make sure you give yourself early opportunities to get it.
>
> Time is money: time spent doing something costs somebody money.
>
> Where there's a will there's a way: if you want something enough you will find a way of getting it.

- Ask the students to vote for their favourite proverb.
- Ask the students whether they have similar proverbs in their own language. Do they have other proverbs connected with money that they can translate?

Variations

This doesn't have to be done as an auction. You can simply get the students in pairs to look through the proverbs and discuss which ones they think are correct and which ones are incorrect. Then feed back. If any pair finishes early, you could give them extra proverbs:

A bird in the hand is worth two in the bush
A fool and his money are soon parted
A penny saved is a penny earned
Look after the pennies and the pounds will look after themselves
Money doesn't grow on trees
Nothing ventured, nothing gained
The love of money is the root of all evil
Waste not, want not

5 **Vocabulary** Communicative crossword

Page 171

Activity

Pairwork: write and exchange clues to complete a crossword

Focus

Revision of vocabulary and relative clauses from Unit 5

Preparation

Make one copy of the worksheet for each pair of students and cut it into two as indicated.

Procedure

- Divide the class into two groups : group A and group B. Explain that they are going to write crossword clues for each other.
- Give each member of group A a copy of Crossword A, and each member of group B a copy of Crossword B.
- Within each group, ask the students to work in pairs. Ask the pairs to write a crossword clue for each word. Group A write clues for all the Across words, and group B write clues for the Down words. They should write the clues on a separate piece of paper.
- If a vocabulary item consists of two or more words, students should indicate this at the end of the clue. For example, 3 down *low cost*: 'Something which is cheap, inexpensive. 2 words.'
- Circulate and monitor, helping with vocabulary and any other problems. Encourage students to find the words again in Unit 5 and, if necessary, check how they are used in context.
- When they have completed the clues, take the clues from the pairs in group A and give them to the pairs in group B, and vice versa. Students then complete the missing words on their crossword.
- If students are having difficulties with any of the clues, encourage them to look at the clues of the other students in their group.
- When they have finished, let them check their solutions.

5 **Communication** Money talks

Page 172

Activity

Groupwork: board game

Focus

Revision of topics and vocabulary from Unit 5

Preparation

Make one copy of the worksheet for each group of 3 or 4 students. Cut the answers off as indicated. You will also need dice and counters.

Procedure

- Divide the class into groups of three or four, and tell them that they are going to play a speaking game.

- Give each student a counter and each group a copy of the worksheet and a dice. Appoint one member of each group as the time-keeper and give a copy of the answers to this student.

- Explain the game:

  1 The students take turns to roll the dice, move along the board with their counter according to the number on the dice and talk about the topic on the square. They should talk for at least thirty seconds without stopping.

  2 The time-keeper ensures that the players talk for at least thirty seconds, and decides whether the student successfully spoke for the full thirty seconds without stopping. If successful, the student can play next time round. If not, he/she misses a turn.

  3 If a student lands of a square with a currency question, the time-keeper checks their answer. If they answer correctly, they can play next time round. If not, he/she misses a turn.

  4 The winner is the first person to reach the last square.

- When they have finished, ask the students to report to the class anything interesting they found out about each other.

6 Grammar Stative or dynamic phrases?

Page 173

Activity

Pairwork: speaking and writing

Focus

Stative and dynamic uses of common verbs

Preparation

Make one copy of the worksheet for each student in the class.

Procedure

- Explain that students are going to look at twenty common phrases with the verbs *be*, *feel*, *have*, *hear*, *know*, *look*, *see* and *think*. They have to decide whether a stative or dynamic use of the verb is more appropriate in each case.

- Give one copy of the worksheet to each student in the class and divide the class into pairs.

- Ask each pair to discuss whether they think the verb use should be stative or dynamic and why. Also, ask them to consider in what context they might hear or see these phrases.

> **Answers**
> 1 He~~'s just /~~ **'s just being** silly again – pay no attention.
> 2 I know that Sally **feels** / ~~is feeling~~ quite strongly about this issue.
> 3 I **feel** / ~~'m feeling~~ like a cup of coffee.
> 4 I ~~felt~~ / **was feeling** quite cheerful when we set out. *
> 5 I ~~don't have~~ / **'m not having** that kind of behaviour in my class. **
> 6 I **had** / ~~was having~~ the house all to myself last week.
> 7 I've **had** / ~~'ve been having~~ it up to here with Kevin – he never stops complaining.
> 8 I **have** / ~~'m having~~ a duty to report anything suspicious to the police.
> 9 He went to the door but there was no-one there. He must ~~hear~~ / **be hearing** things.
> 10 If he gets a date with Clare, we**'ll never hear** / ~~'ll never be hearing~~ the end of it.
> 11 He could be a murderer for all I **know** / ~~'m knowing~~.
> 12 Can I help you? ~ No thanks, I ~~just look~~ / **'m just looking**.
> 13 Do you think it **will look** / ~~will be looking~~ bad if I don't go and see him?
> 14 Do you know whether he ~~sees~~ / **'s seeing** anyone at the moment?
> 15 It's difficult for me because I can **see** / ~~be seeing~~ both sides.
> 16 Maybe now they**'ll see** / ~~'ll be seeing~~ reason and scrap the project.
> 17 If she **thinks** / ~~'thinking~~ I'll help her, she has another thing coming.
> 18 I'm sorry, I ~~just don't think~~ / **'m just not thinking** straight at the moment.
> 19 Sam ~~thinks~~ / **'s thinking** of buying our car.
> 20 Just who **do you think** / ~~are you thinking~~ you are?
> * Both are possible with not much change in meaning.
> ** Both are possible: stative use means 'I don't usually have that behaviour'. Dynamic use means 'I'm not going to have that behaviour now'.

Follow up

You might ask the students to choose five of the phrases to learn and invent their own example sentences.

6 Vocabulary Ways of speaking and looking

Page 174

Activity

Pairwork: gapfill and discussion

Focus

Other ways of saying *speak* and *look*

Preparation

Make one copy of the worksheet for each student in the class.

Procedure

- Divide the class into pairs and give one copy of the worksheet to each student.
- Ask the students to work together and decide which of the three alternatives cannot complete the sentence. Encourage them to use dictionaries if necessary.
- Once students have finished, ask them to go back and read each sentence and say whether it is true or not for them. Encourage the students to compare and discuss any differences they might have.

```
1 – express / communicate / converse
2 – ramble on / drone on / mutter
3 – argue / discuss / disagree
4 – sound off / exclaim / rant
5 – shouting / yelling / crying
6 – staring / gazing / glaring
7 – squinting / peering / winking
8 – glare / frown / blink
9 – a glimpse / sight / a glance
10 – performance / speech / talk
```

6 Communication Memories

Page 175

Activity

Pairwork: speaking

Focus

Questions

Preparation

Make a copy of the worksheet for each pair of students in the class. Cut up the worksheet as indicated.

Procedure

- Divide the class into pairs, A and B, and give each student the appropriate section of the worksheet. Tell the students not to show one another their worksheets.

- Ask the students to read their questions and write brief answers.
- When they have finished, ask the students to fold over their worksheets so that only their answers can be seen and then exchange worksheets with their partner.
- Explain that the students have to look at their partner's answers and try to guess what the questions were. Their partner should not tell them the questions right away if they are wrong but give clues to help them. For example:

  Student A (reading the answer 'Chamonix, France'): *Is this your first holiday destination?*
  Student B: *No, it isn't. But it's the place where I first saw something.*
  Student A: *Is this where you first saw snow?*
  Student B: *Yes, that's right.*

- Encourage the students to ask questions to find out more information about some of the situations; for example, *Did you like it? What did you speak about?* etc.
- Hold a class feedback session. Ask students to tell you which questions took them longer to answer than others. Invite some students to report to the class anything interesting they found out about their partner.

Review B Don't say it!

Page 176

Activity

Groupwork: speaking game

Focus

Vocabulary revision. Abstract nouns from *New Inside Out* Advanced Student's Book, Units 1–6

Preparation

Make one copy of the worksheet for every six to eight students in the class and cut them out as indicated. Keep set A and set B separated.

Procedure

- Ask the students to think of an abstract noun they have learnt recently and write it on the board. Ask them to give you words that they associate with this noun. For example *autonomy*: self, on your own, independent, individual, single, solitary etc. Then ask them to identify the three words they associate most strongly with the noun they have chosen. Finally, ask them to make a definition of the noun *without* using the three words they most associate with it.
- Explain that the students are going to play a game by giving definitions of words for other students to guess but that there will be some words they are not allowed to use in their definitions, in any form.
- Divide the class into groups of six to eight and then divide each group into Team A and Team B.

- Put the word cards face down in two piles, A and B, on a desk in between the two teams.
- Player A stands facing their team, Team A, picks up a card from the top of Team A's pile and holds it up so that Team B can see the words on the card. One player from Team B starts timing Player A for one minute.
- Player A describes the word at the top of the card to Team A, *without* using the other words on the card. If they use one of the words on the card, they take another card.

  If they do not know the word at the top of their card, they can put it back to the bottom of the pile and take another one.

  When team A have guessed the word, player A takes the next card from the top of the pile and repeats the activity.
- Player A continues to describe words to Team A for one minute. After one minute, count the number of words Team A have guessed and give one point for each correct guess.
- The game continues with teams and players taking it in turns to describe and guess words until all the cards have been used.
- The team with the highest score at the end of the game are the winners.

7 Grammar My future in a hat

Page 177

Activity

Whole class: writing, speaking

Focus

Ways of talking about the future

Preparation

Make one copy of the worksheet for each group of three students in the class and cut it up into ten pieces as indicated. You will need a hat or a container of some kind.

Procedure

- Choose one of the unfinished sentences from the worksheet and write it on the board. Elicit possible ways of completing the sentence.
- Ask the students to work in groups of three for the first part of this activity. Give one set of unfinished sentences to each group. Spread them out face down and ask each student in each group to take three.
- Ask them to complete their three sentences in any way they like. They should not write their names or let the students next to them see what they are writing. Give students a five-minute time limit for this.

- The students now all work together as a class. Put the hat (or container) in the middle of the room. Ask the students to fold up their completed sentences and put them in the hat.

  Mix up the folded sentences in the hat and then tell the students that they are going to stand up, take one sentence each and find out who wrote it. Demonstrate this by taking a piece of paper from the hat and reading the sentence out. For example:

  It's highly unlikely that I'll ever sing in a band.

  Elicit the type of question they will need to ask in order to find out who wrote the sentence. For example:

  Is it likely that you'll ever sing in a band?

  Make it clear that even though several students might say it's highly unlikely that they'll ever sing in a band, they are looking for the person that actually wrote the sentence.
- The students now stand up and do the activity. If they take one of their own sentences out of the hat then they should put it back and take another one. Each time they find the person who wrote the sentence, they should write the person's name on the piece of paper, keep it and take another one.
- The activity finishes when there are no more sentences in the hat. The 'winner' is the person who has collected the most sentences.

  You could then go round the class and get the students to report back on their findings.

7 Vocabulary Give us a clue

Page 178

Activity

Group and pairwork: communicative crossword

Focus

Vocabulary associated with computers, phones and the internet

Preparation

Make one copy of the worksheet, cut in half as indicated, for each pair of students in the class.

Procedure

- Write on the board: *It's a word that describes an electronic system that records and stores spoken messages.* Ask the students to guess the word (*voicemail*). Tell students they are going to write similar sentences as clues for a crossword.
- Divide the class into group A and group B. Give each student in each group a copy of the appropriate half-completed crossword and explain that they have to work together to write clues for the words written on their crossword.

- When they have finished writing their clues, students should work with a partner from the other group. They must not show each other the crossword. Ask them to sit facing each other and take it in turns to ask their partner for clues for the missing words on their crossword. At the end they can look to check their answers.

Suggested clues

1A (Across) voicemail: an electronic system that records and stores spoken messages

2D (Down) inbox: the place in your email program where you find your new e-mails

3D monitor: the computer screen

4D surf: to explore or look for things on the internet

5D webcam: like a video camera but it broadcasts images over the internet

6A scanner: a piece of equipment that copies images onto a computer

6D server: a central computer that controls or holds information for other computers in a network

7A browser: a program that allows you to look at and search through information on the internet

8D graphics: drawings or artwork

9D hard drive: the part of your computer that holds all the information

10D podcast: a multimedia file such as a radio programme or music video that can be downloaded from the internet

11D attachment: a file you add to an email

12A programmer: a person who writes software for a computer

13A text: to send a written message to someone using a mobile phone

14A modem: a piece of equipment that allows you to connect a computer to a telephone line

14D mouse: a small device that you move in order to do things on a computer screen

15D keyboard: the set of keys on a computer that you press in order to write words or do things

16A upgrade: to improve existing computer equipment

17D icon: a small picture on the computer screen that you can click on to open a program or edit things

18A delete: to remove text, date, files etc. from a computer

19A download: to transfer information to your computer from another computer system or the internet

20A bookmark: to add a website address to the favourites menu so that you can access it again easily

---

7 Communication Planet News

Page 179

Activity

Groupwork: planning and writing

Focus

Summarising a text; using *will* for predictions and the passive

Preparation

Make one copy of the worksheet for each student in the class.

Procedure

- Introduce the topic by asking the students to think of the big news stories of this decade (for example: climate change agreements, mapping human genes, credit crunch, etc.). Then ask the students to describe the breakthroughs predicted in the next hundred years.

- Divide the students into groups of three to four students and give each student a copy of the worksheet. Explain that the students are not going to read the entire page. Ask them to divide the page up so that each student reads one or two articles each. Tell them to be prepared to tell the rest of the group about their articles. Circulate, helping with vocabulary as necessary.

- When they have finished, ask the students to take turns to tell the rest of the group about the articles they read.

- Tell the students they are now going to produce their own front page of a newspaper of the future. Brainstorm a few ideas with the whole class and then give the groups plenty of time to come up with their own ideas, plan their articles and decide who will write what. Make sure all the students are involved in the writing stage.

- Ask the groups to write the articles and paste them together to produce the front page of their newspaper. Circulate and monitor, helping with vocabulary as necessary.

- When the groups have finished, display the newspapers on the classroom wall. Allow the students time to circulate and read the other newspapers.

8 Grammar Modals and meanings

Page 180

Activity

Pair / groupwork: pelmanism game

Focus

Revision of modals for talking about the past

Preparation

Make one copy of the worksheet for each pair / small group of students in the class. Cut up the cards as indicated.

Procedure

- Divide the class into pairs or small groups and give each group a set of cards. Ask the students to spread the cards face down on the table.

- Explain to the students that there are eleven sentences and that each one contains a different past modal. For each past modal sentence, there's a corresponding sentence describing the meaning of the past modals. The aim of the game is to match the sentences and their meanings.

- Explain that they should take it in turns to turn over two cards, one at a time, and read aloud the phrases on each card. If they think the two cards go together, the student keeps the pair and gets another turn. If the cards do not go together, the student turns the cards face down again and ends their turn.

- The game continues until all the pairs of cards have been won. The student with the most pairs is the winner.

- Check the answers with the whole class. (The sentences are correctly matched as they appear on the worksheet).

Follow up

Ask students to work in pairs and test one another. Students put the past modal sentences and meanings in the correct pairs. They then take it in turns to read out a meaning to their partner who gives the past modal sentence from memory.

8 **Vocabulary** Thick as thieves

Page 181

Activity

Pairwork: reading and speaking

Focus

Speculating and making deductions about crime stories

Preparation

Make one copy of the worksheet for each pair of students.

Procedure

- Explain that the students are going to read some true stories about failed robberies or about how robbers got caught. Explain that each story has a crucial piece of information missing. In most cases, the missing information is the action or event which resulted in their failures or in them getting caught.

- Divide the class into pairs and give each pair a copy of the worksheet. Explain that the worksheet title *Thick as thieves* is an idiomatic expression which

means to be very close or friendly, but in this case it is used as a play on words because the thief in each situation was thick (stupid).

- Ask the students to read the stories and speculate about or deduce from the context what the missing information could be.

- Conduct a class feedback session. Ask pairs to tell the class their ideas. Finish by confirming what the actual missing information was.

1	handed him over to the police	5	that his wallet had been taken by a pickpocket while he was shopping
2	he put it in his pocket and set off the alarm as he left the store	6	that the couple had unwittingly left their nine-month-old child behind
3	four hundred police officers gathered for an official ceremony with Rio's governor	7	that he didn't have any money to pay for his ticket, and not wanting to make a fuss
4	his business card fell unnoticed to the floor		

Follow up

Get the students to discuss which stories they think are the funniest / most bizarre.

8 **Communication** Legal matters

Page 182

Activity

Whole class: speaking

Focus

Asking and answering questions about the law

Preparation

Make one copy of the worksheet for each group of up to 12 students. Cut the cards out as indicated.

Procedure

- Tell the students that they are going to ask and answer questions about the law.

- If there are more than 12 students in the class, divide them into groups. Give one card to each student in the class.

- Tell the students that they are responsible for finding out the answer to the question on their own card by speaking to everybody in the class or group. Make sure each student knows how to ask their question correctly.

- Now ask the students to go round the class or group, asking and answering questions. Tell them that they can make notes on the back of their card if necessary. Encourage them to find out as much information as possible.

- When they have finished, they should sit down and take it in turns to report back to the class or group on what they found out.

Follow up

Ask the students to write up the information they have gathered as a poster to be displayed in the classroom.

Variations

You could brainstorm a few more law-related questions beginning 'How many…? FIND OUT' to make the activity more relevant or interesting to the particular class you are teaching. What do they want to find out? Simply get the students to fill out a few more blank cards with their own ideas and add them to the 12 cards you have or substitute them for some of the other photocopied cards.

9 Grammar The teenage years

Page 183

Activity

Whole class: speaking

Focus

Expressing past regrets

Preparation

Make one copy of the worksheet for each student in the class.

Procedure

- Give one copy of the worksheet to each student in the class. Get the students to work together in pairs and complete the sentences with the correct grammar. Remind them that these are past regrets about their teenage years (early teenage years if the class is young).

> If only I'd tried harder at school.
> I wish I'd studied something different.
> I wish I'd learned how to play an instrument.
> I wish I'd gone to a different school.
> If only I'd listened to my parents.
> If only I hadn't listened to my parents.
> I wish I'd been nicer to my parents.
> I'd love to have had an older sister or brother.
> I'd like to have known my great grandparents.
> I regret watching so much rubbish on television.
> I wish I'd gone out more.
> I wish I'd gone out less.
> I regret spending so much time online.
> If only I hadn't wasted so much money on clothes.
> If only I'd known then what I know now.

- Ask the students to read the list and choose three regrets that are true for them. Then ask them to stand up and go round the class looking for people who have chosen one of the same regrets as them.
- When they find someone who has chosen one of the same regrets they should ask and answer questions

to find out why they chose it. Encourage them to find out as much information as possible.

- When all the students have spoken to several different partners about their wishes, ask them to sit down in groups of three or four and report back any interesting things they found out.

9 Vocabulary Brushing up on phrasal verbs

Page 184

Activity

Pair / groupwork: pelmanism game

Focus

Revise and extend three-part phrasal verbs from Unit 9

Preparation

Make one copy of the worksheet for each pair / small group of students in the class. Cut the worksheet into cards as indicated.

Procedure

- Divide the class into pairs / small groups and give each pair / small group a set of cards. Ask the students to place the cards face down on the desk.
- Explain to the students that there are twelve three-part phrasal verbs and twelve corresponding object noun collocates. The aim of the game is to match each phrasal verb with a strong collocate.
- Explain that they should take it in turns to turn over two cards, one at a time, and read aloud the phrases on each card. If they think the two cards show a strong collocation, the student keeps the pair and gets another turn. If the cards do not go together, the student turns the cards face down again and ends their turn. Note: There are a few phrasal verbs that could potentially take more than one collocate eg. *stand up for the kids*. However, that would leave you with X*go on at your rights*X which is not possible. Students will discover this by process of elimination. It may be a useful discussion point as a follow-up.
- The game continues until all the pairs of cards have been won. The student with the most pairs is the winner.
- Check the answers open class.

> *come up against a problem* = to experience / encounter a problem
> *come up with a solution* = to think of a solution
> *face up to reality* = to accept / deal with reality
> *get away with murder* = to do something bad and not get punished or criticised for it
> *get out of the washing up* = to avoid doing something you promised
> *go down with the flu* = to become ill with a particular illness

Follow up

Cut some large photos out of a magazine showing two people of any description who could be speaking to each other. Ask students in their pairs to choose one of the pictures and then to come up with a dialogue between the people, using at least three of the phrasal verbs. They can use these collocates or explore other possibilities. Get the students to perform the dialogues and then vote for the best one.

9 **Communication** Things that go bump in the night

Page 185

Activity

Pairwork: mutual dictation

Focus

Concessive clauses and adverbials

Preparation

Make one copy of the worksheet for each pair of students and cut it in half as indicated.

Procedure

- Tell the students that they are going to read about a haunted hotel. Point out that there is some information missing from the text that you are going to give them.
- Ask them to work in pairs: Student A and Student B.
- Give one copy of text A to each student A and one copy of text B to each student B. Tell them not to show their part of the story to their partner. Explain that their partner has the part of the story which is missing from their own version.

  Note: You may need to explain the meaning of *outlaws* if students are not familiar with it.

- Ask the students to take turns dictating lines of the story and write them down in the spaces provided on their worksheets. They should spell difficult words and mention punctuation.
- When they have finished, ask them to compare completed texts (which should be identical).

Follow up

As students whether they know of places that are supposed to be haunted, or whether anybody has actually seen a ghost.

Review C Word jigsaw

Page 186

Activity

Groupwork: revision

Focus

Revision of vocabulary and grammar from *New Inside Out* Advanced Student's Book, Units 7–9

Preparation

Make one copy of the worksheet (enlarged to A3 size if possible) for each group of four students in the class. You will need one dice per group and one counter per student.

Procedure

- Divide the class into groups of four students and give each group a copy of the worksheet.
- Explain that the aim of the game is to collect as many points as possible by making grammatically correct sentences.
- Look at the board game with the class. Explain the rules:
  1 Students take turns to throw the dice and move round the board. When they land on a square they choose one of the words in the square and write it down in their notebooks. Students then cross out the word they chose on the board so that it cannot be used again.
  2 Each time a student passes 'Go' he/she has to write a sentence containing the words he/she collected going around the board that time. (Verb forms can be changed, e.g. *be* can be changed to *being, is, are, was, were, been* and nouns can be singular or plural.)
  3 Students read out their sentences and the rest of the group adds up their score. Students score one point for each word used and lose one point for each word not used. Circulate and monitor, making notes of any errors to correct at the end.
  4 Students each go around the board twice, and they cannot use any of the words they or anybody else in the group have already crossed out. (As the game progresses, students will find that squares have no available words.)
- At the end of the game the winner is the player with the most points.
- Conduct a class feedback session. Invite individual students to read aloud some of their sentences.

10 Grammar Divine Chocolate®

Page 187

Activity

Pairwork

Focus

Passive structures

Preparation

Make one copy of the worksheet for every pair of students in the class and cut in half as indicated.

Procedure

- Tell the students that they are going to read about a brand of Fairtrade chocolate called 'Divine'. See www.fairtrade.org.uk for information about Fairtrade products.
- Divide the class into two groups. Give each student in group A a copy of text A, and each student in group B a copy of text B.
- Firstly, ask the students to read their text through once and ask you about any language they do not understand.
- After that, ask the students to work with another partner from the same group. Draw their attention to the parts of their text which are circled and ask them to notice that the circled words are the objects of active verbs.
- Ask them to re-write these parts of their text using the circled words as subjects of passive structures. They should use 'by' if necessary.
- When they have done this, ask them to change partners and work with a student from the other group.
- Ask the students to compare their texts and check that their passive structures are correct. Text A and Text B should be identical.
- Ask the students to decide whether they think the text is more natural with passive structures in place.

10 Vocabulary Use your head

Page 188

Activity

Pairwork: reading and speaking

Focus

Idiomatic expressions with parts of the body

Preparation

Make one copy of the worksheet for each student. Cut the worksheet into two sections as indicated.

Procedure

- Divide the class into pairs and give each student a copy of the top section of the worksheet.
- Ask the students, in pairs, to complete the expressions by choosing the correct alternative. Encourage them to think of any similar expressions in their own language and ask them to make calculated guesses if necessary. You may wish to allow the students to use a dictionary.
- Check the answers with the whole class.

1b	2a	3c	4c	5b	6a	7c	8a	9b	10c

- Give each student a copy of the discussion section of the worksheet. Ask them to read through and think about the situations or people. Then get the students to talk to each other about each situation. Encourage them to ask questions and find out as much as possible.
- Ask the students to report back anything interesting from their discussions.

Follow up

- Ask the students to find five more expressions with five different parts of the body.
- Ask students to think about expressions in their own language that include parts of the body and try to translate them or find equivalent expressions in English.

10 Communication Pink dolphins

Page 189

Activity

Pair and groupwork: preparing and presenting arguments

Focus

Taking part in a meeting

Preparation

Make one copy of the worksheet for each student in the class.

Procedure

- Introduce the topic by asking the students to think of any natural unspoilt beauty spots in their country. Does the tourist industry in their country protect or alter these natural beauty spots for commercial or other purposes? How do the students feel about this?
- Before reading the text, find out how many students in the class would like to go to the Amazon rainforest on holiday. Give each student a copy of the worksheet and allow them five minutes to read the article. In pairs or small groups, ask the students to discuss whether they have changed their minds after reading the text.

- Ask the students to read the information about developing tourism at Lake Tarapoto and the instructions for the task. Check that the students understand what they have to do. Divide the class into groups of five and assign a role to each student.
- Allow the students time to prepare their arguments. Circulate and monitor, helping with vocabulary as necessary.
- Ask the students to hold a meeting in their groups to discuss the issue. Before starting their meetings, ask each group to nominate a chairperson and a person to take the minutes. Set a fifteen-minute time limit for the meetings.
- Allow the groups another five minutes to discuss and finalise the minutes.
- Ask each group to present their decisions to the class. Hold a class discussion on the outcomes.

11 **Grammar** 5 reasons to get an e-book

Page 190

Activity
Re-writing a text to make it more concise

Focus
Using ellipsis and substitution to avoid repetition

Preparation
Make one copy of the worksheet for each student in the class.

Procedure
- Find out how many students in the class have an e-book or have read anything on an e-book. Ask the class to brainstorm the advantages of e-books over paper books.
- Give one copy of the worksheet to each student in the class and ask them to read through to find out how many of the advantages they thought of are mentioned in the text.
- Ask the students to read the text again, and to cross out any words or phrases that are not necessary, without changing the meaning of the text, or substitute words and phrases with other words such as *it, they, this, that* or *either way*. Remind the students that the aim is to avoid unnecessary repetition and to make their writing more concise.
- Ask students to compare their new versions of the text.

Suggested answer

1 **It's compact**
   Whether you're a student or someone who travels a lot, the e-book is a godsend. Either way, you probably need to take a stack of books, and this is a huge burden. Thanks to the e-book, you can not only save loads of space in your bag but also in your home. My shelves are full of books, and so are my office and basement. I usually have to give books away to make space for new ones. But no longer – with the e-book, the problem has been solved.

2 **It's always open**
   When I'm reading, I tend to get really absorbed. This means that I carry my book around the house, reading it while I eat breakfast, brush my teeth, chop vegetables, etc. The problem with a paper book is that I always have to find a way to keep it open and this usually means putting something heavy across it. Of course, this tends to obscure part of the page, which is a nuisance. With an e-book, it's always flat.

3 **It has an excellent catalogue**
   Almost any book you would ever want to read is already available on most e-books, and thousands more are being added on a regular basis.

4 **It's green**
   E-books are good for the planet. They help to save trees – none are used to make an e-book.

5 **It's the future**
   Sorry, but it is. E-books are what we'll be reading while we rocket to Mars in 2050 – either that, or our personal robots will be reading them to us.

Follow up
Ask the students to brainstorm all the disadvantages of e-books and get them to write a text entitled '5 reasons not to buy an e-book'.

11 **Vocabulary** Ode to the spell checker

Page 191

Activity
Pairwork: reading and writing

Focus
Homophones

Preparation
Make one copy of the worksheet for each pair of students in the class.

Procedure

- Read the poem aloud to the students and elicit from them what it is about. (It's a poem about a computer spell checker, a supposedly reliable resource for locating spelling errors in a document.) Explain the meaning of any unfamiliar words.

- Divide the class into pairs and give each pair a copy of the worksheet. Ask the students to read the poem and to say why it contains so many incorrect spellings. Then ask them to rewrite the poem with the correct spellings. Circulate and monitor, helping as necessary.

- When they have finished, ask pairs to compare their answers with another pair.

- Check the answers with the whole class. Either invite individual students to write a line of the poem on the board, or hand out a photocopy of the correct version of the poem.

> I have a spelling checker
> It came with my PC.
> It clearly marks for my review
> Mistakes I cannot see.
>
> I strike a key and type a word
> And wait for it to say
> Whether I am wrong or I am right
> It shows me straight away.
>
> As soon as a mistake is made
> It knows before too long,
> And I can put the error right
> It's rarely ever wrong.
>
> I have run this poem through it,
> I am sure you're pleased to know,
> It's letter perfect all the way –
> My checker told me so.

11 **Communication** Hidden word

Page 192

Activity

Individual and groupwork: speaking and listening

Focus

Fluency

Preparation

Make one copy of the worksheet for each group of three to five students in the class. Cut up the cards as indicated. Each group needs a watch with a second hand.

Procedure

- Divide the class into groups of three to five students and give each group a set of cards placed face down on the table.

- Explain that the students are going to take turns to pick up one of the cards (without showing it to the rest of the group) and speak for one minute on a topic. The topic is not what is written on the card but one chosen by the rest of the group; for example, the weather, shopping, British food, films, etc. The object is to subtly include the word on the card in the speech. At the end of the minute, each student in the group guesses what the word was. If a student correctly guesses the word, he/she scores a point. If nobody guesses, the speaker scores the point. The student with the most points at the end of the game is the winner.

- While the students are playing the game, circulate and monitor, noting down any errors which can be used for a correction activity at a later stage.

Follow-up

Prepare a *Spot the mistake* or *Grammar auction* activity using the errors which you wrote down while students were playing.

Notes and comments

This activity is based on an idea by Paul Jones. *Hidden word* can be used to recycle vocabulary that students have recently learned.

12 **Grammar** The great debate

Page 193

Activity

Pairwork: grammar and speaking

Focus

Special uses of the past simple

Preparation

Make one copy of the worksheet for each student in the class.

Procedure

- Divide the class into pairs and give each student a copy of the worksheet.

- Ask the students to complete the statements with the correct form of one of the verbs given.

- Check the answers with the whole class.

> **1** was **2** was **3** had **4** was **5** stopped
> **6** were **7** stopped **8** was **9** took

- Ask the students to read the statements again and put a tick ✓ if they agree, a cross ✗ if they disagree or a question mark ? if they're not sure either way. Then ask the students to discuss the statements with their partner and see how many points they agree or disagree on.

Follow up

You might ask your students to use the same frames – i.e. 'It's about time …' / 'People would rather …' / If + past simple – to write their own topics for debate.

Variations

If there are widely differing views on some of the topics, you might want to throw the second part open to the whole class. You could set up a more formal debate with one team speaking 'for' the motion and one team speaking 'against'. You might want to remind the students of some useful language for discussion:

Strong agreement	Absolutely. I couldn't agree more. I totally agree.
Conceding a point	Perhaps you're right. Okay, you win. You've convinced me.
Qualified agreement	That's partly true. On the whole, yes. I'd go along with that.
Hedging	I take your point, but … Yes, but …
Strong disagreement	I don't agree. On the contrary, … I totally disagree.

12 Vocabulary Word families

Page 194

Activity

Individual/pair/groupwork: spelling and pronunciation

Focus

Revision of vocabulary from *New Inside Out* Advanced Student's Book Unit 12

Preparation

Make one copy of the worksheet for each student in the class.

Procedure

- Give a copy of the worksheet to each student and ask them to complete the first stage by adding the correct endings to the words in Table A. Explain that there may be more than one form of a word. In pairs, students check their answers. Make sure the students are aware that *dependent* (person) ends in -ent while *dependant* (adjective) ends in -ant. Also, note the -or endings for *competitor, educator, investigator* and -er endings for *employer, worrier and organise*r. *Organiser* can also be spelt with an 'z'.

- Ask the students to complete Table B by transferring the words from Table A into columns according to their stress patterns. Note: *employed* does not fit any of the patterns given: (oO).

- If you want to add an element of competition, give one point for each correct spelling, and one point for each correct pronunciation. The student or pair of students with the highest number of points are the winners.

A

NOUN / SUBJECT	PERSON	ADJECTIVE
addiction	addict	addictive / addicted
competition	competitor	competitive
charity	charity worker	charitable
dependence / dependency	dependant	dependent / dependable
education	educator	educational / educated
employment	employer	employable / employed
homelessness	homeless person	homeless
information	informer / informant	informative
investigation	investigator	investigative
organisation	organiser	organised organising
representation	representative	representative
worry	worrier	worrying / worried

B

□□	□□□	□□□
addict homeless person worker worry worried	addiction addictive addicted dependant dependent dependence employment employer informer informant	charity homelessness organised worrier worrying
□□□□	□□□□	□□□□
competition education information	competitor competitive dependency dependable employable informative	charitable educator organiser organising
□□□□□	□□□□□	□□□□□
educational representative	organisation investigation representation	investigator investigative

Follow up

Call out a collocate of a word in the table and ask the students to identify the word from the table which collocates with it.

For example:

drug, TV, computer *addict / addiction*

highly *addictive*

charitable **organisation / institution**

highly / fiercely *competitive*

alcohol / drug *dependence*

dependent **on something** (not 'of')

private, adult, continuing, further, higher, physical *education*

proportional, legal *representation*

highly *organised*

organised **crime**

a mine of / freedom of *information*

information **overload / superhighway**

conduct, demand, launch, order, require, undertake *an investigation*

12 Communication Easy money

Page 195

Activity

Pairwork: reading and re-telling

Focus

Reading for detail

Preparation

Make one copy of the worksheet for each pair of students in the class. Cut up the worksheet as indicated.

Procedure

- Divide the class into pairs, A and B, and give each student the appropriate section of the worksheet. Explain that one story on the worksheet is true and the other is made up. Tell the students not to show each other their stories.

- Ask the students to read their stories. Circulate, helping with vocabulary as necessary.

- Then collect in the worksheets and ask the students to retell their stories to their partner.

- Now ask the students, in their pairs, to discuss which story they think is true and why. Encourage them to think of as many reasons as they can for their choice.

- Conduct a class feedback session. Invite pairs to tell the class why they think Story A or B is true. Have a class vote before you tell the class that Story B is in fact the true story.

Review D Tell us about ...

Page 196

Activity

Groupwork: speaking and listening

Focus

Fluency

Preparation

Make one copy of the worksheet for each group of three to four students in the class. Each group needs one dice and a watch with a second hand and each student needs a counter.

Procedure

- Divide the class into groups of three to four students and give each group a copy of the worksheet.

- Look at the board game with the class and explain how to play:

  1 Each student places his/her counter anywhere on the board.

  2 Students take turns throwing the dice, move the appropriate number of squares, read the prompt in the square and talk continuously about that topic for one minute.

  3 If a player lands on a *Tell us about…* square, the other students in the group choose a topic for him/her to talk about.

  4 If a student manages to talk for sixty seconds, he/she gets a point. However, if the student hesitates too often, repeats information or does not manage to talk for the full sixty seconds, he/she does not get a point.

  5 The winner in each group is the first student to get five points.

- While the students are playing the game, circulate and monitor, noting down any common errors which can be used for correction at a later stage.

Follow up

Prepare a *Correct the mistake* activity using the errors that you noted down while the students were playing.

1 Grammar

Do I know you?

Guess the right information about your partner. Write 12 'true' sentences using an appropriate verb form: simple, continuous, perfect, perfect continuous, affirmative or negative.

Partner's name:	✓ = I was right ✗ = I was wrong
(be born) _____ near here.	
(always live) _____ at the same address.	
(do) _____ the same job this time last year.	
(learn) _____ English for more than ten years.	
(go) _____ to Ireland.	
(read) _____ all the Harry Potter books by the age of 15.	
(meet up) _____ with a friend this evening.	
(read) _____ a really good book at the moment.	
(always have) _____ the same mobile phone number.	
(work) _____ in an office.	
(enjoy) _____ meeting new people.	
(stay in) _____ last night.	

How well do you know your partner? Score one point for each tick.

0–4   You've got some serious 'getting to know you' to do!

5–8   You know quite a bit but you could always find out more.

9–12   You know lots of things. Sit next to somebody else!

1 Vocabulary

Being a man

A

1
I hate it when people say men are redundant. Tell us that men are redundant when your _____ needs changing, or there's something climbing through your bedroom window in the middle of the _____ !

♂

2
It must be confusing to be a man nowadays. There are so many _____ messages. On the one hand, they're expected to be sensitive and share their _____ . But then you hear women saying they love a 'bad man'. They _____ win really, can they?

♀

3
Men _____ themselves on having telephone conversations that last less than a minute. Unlike women, they get straight to the _____ . 'All right? Lunch? Pick you up at one. Bye.' Job done.

♂

4
Being a man means being brave and fearless. If you're frightened of spiders or mice, you're not a _____ man.

♀

5
I'm glad I'm a man in this day and _____ rather than when our grandparents were young. In the past, if a man showed his emotions, it was perceived as a sign of _____ . Now we're more in _____ with our feelings than ever before, more involved in bringing up our _____ .

♂

6
While women suffer from colds, men get the far more _____ illness, man-flu. The symptoms of both ailments are the same: runny nose, sore _____ and a slight temperature. Most women ignore colds. Men with man-flu tend to _____ to their beds for a week!

♀

7
There are lots of things men are better at than women – anything that requires physical strength or spatial _____ . Opening jars, for example, or _____ a map.

♂

8
A man's sense of _____ is defined by his ability to create results and achieve goals. Women, however, prefer men who don't _____ themselves too seriously.

♀

B

1
I hate it when people say men are redundant. Tell us that men are redundant when your tyre needs _____ , or there's something climbing through your bedroom window in the _____ of the night!

♂

2
It must be confusing to be a man nowadays. There are so many mixed _____ . On the one hand, they're expected to be sensitive and _____ their feelings. But then you hear women saying they love a 'bad man'. They can't _____ really, can they?

♀

3
Men pride _____ on having telephone conversations that last less than a minute. Unlike women, they get _____ to the point. 'All right? Lunch? Pick you up at one. Bye.' Job done.

♂

4
Being a man means being brave and fearless. If you're frightened of spiders or mice, you're not a real _____ .

♀

5
I'm glad I'm a man in this _____ and age rather than when our grandparents were young. In the past, if a man showed his emotions, it was perceived as a _____ of weakness. Now we're more in touch with our _____ than ever before, more involved in _____ up our children.

♂

6
While women suffer from colds, men get the far more serious _____ , man-flu. The symptoms of both ailments are the same: runny nose, _____ throat and a slight temperature. Most women ignore colds. Men with man-flu tend to take to their _____ for a week!

♀

7
There are lots of things men are better at than women – anything that requires physical strength or _____ awareness. Opening jars, for example, or reading _____ .

♂

8
A man's _____ of self is defined by his ability to create results and achieve goals. Women, however, prefer men who don't take themselves too _____ .

♀

 New Inside Out Advanced Teacher's Book © Macmillan Publishers Limited 2010

1 Communication

Class Q & A

1 _____'s greatest achievement is _____

2 The living person _____ most admires is _____

3 _____'s favourite journey is _____

4 The best decision _____ has ever made was _____

5 The worst decision _____ has ever made was _____

6 _____'s most treasured possession is _____

7 The single best moment of _____'s life was _____

8 A word that sums up _____ is _____

9 One of _____'s negative characteristics is _____

10 The most amazing place _____ has ever visited is _____

11 _____'s idea of perfect happiness is _____

12 _____ is learning English because _____

13 The talent _____ would most like to have is _____

14 Something _____ really objects to is _____

15 A characteristic _____ really admires in people is _____

16 A characteristic _____ really dislikes in people is _____

17 _____'s greatest ambition is _____

18 _____ wishes he / she were more _____

2 Grammar

A bunch of partitives

(a pair of) daffodils blood

events ham a set of

cattle a pack of a shoal of

rubbish hills a swarm of

a flock of bees sheep

a clump of a series of a bunch of

a drop of (pliers) crisps

a packet of a range of trees

wolves herring guidelines

a slice of a pile of a herd of

2 Vocabulary

Mineral or tap?

potatoes	black	coffee	roast
potatoes	house	wine	fried
eggs	Caeser	salad	sparkling
wine	baked	fish	mineral
water	decaffeinated	coffee	potato
salad	fried	fish	red
wine	tap	water	fruit
salad	roast	beef	white
wine	hard-boiled	eggs	mashed
potatoes	steamed	fish	green
salad	sparkling	water	white
coffee	scrambled	eggs	baked

2 Communication

Food for thought

1 I fancy a nice _____ bowl of home-made soup for dinner this evening.
   a) tasty   b) tasteful   c) tasteless

2 French breakfasts are the best in the world – freshly-baked croissants and crispy baguettes straight out of the _____ . Lovely!
   a) furnace   b) oven   c) cooker

3 Only Italians can make _____ pizzas.
   a) exquisite   b) experienced   c) extremely

4 My mother's an excellent _____ .
   a) cooker   b) chef   c) cook

5 I don't like vegetables – they're completely _____ .
   a) untasty   b) without taste   c) tasteless

6 Restaurants are places where children should be _____ and not heard.
   a) quiet   b) seen   c) absent

7 Gone are the days when you could _____ a simple cup of coffee. Nowadays there's just too much choice: latte, cappuccino, Americano, espresso ... !
   a) order   b) command   c) demand

8 Personally, I don't eat to live, I _____ to eat. Mealtimes are the highlight of my day.
   a) exist   b) die   c) live

9 Many a time have I _____ a fortune on a meal in a restaurant and then wished I'd eaten at home.
   a) paid   b) lost   c) spent

10 I hate whisky – it's definitely an _____ taste.
   a) enquired   b) acquired   c) required

11 The first thing I have in the morning is a nice _____ cup of tea.
   a) forceful   b) strengthened   c) strong

12 I couldn't live without _____ food.
   a) spiceful   b) spicy   c) spiced

13 Why people are so negative about fast-food I have no _____ . It's quick, it's delicious and it's cheap.
   a) idea   b) clue   c) reason

14 A glass of red wine a day is _____ for you.
   a) good   b) healthy   c) positive

 New Inside Out Advanced Teacher's Book © Macmillan Publishers Limited 2010

3 Grammar

Tale of two cities

A

seen   I   metropolis   have   seldom   this

1 _____ on a list of the most attractive cities in the world, but what the city lacks in natural beauty, it makes up for in cultural attractions.

the   only   city   does   not

2 _____ boast some of the finest museums in the Southern Hemisphere, but it also hosts around 90,000 cultural events each year.

experienced   you've   after   only

3 _____ the amazing nightlife and multi-cultural vibe of the city will you understand the attraction of this concrete jungle.

you   should   no   under   try   circumstances

4 _____ to go out clubbing in your jeans and trainers – people dress up before heading out into the chic bars and trendy dance locations.

find   you   no   city   in   will   other

5 _____ such a mix of cultures living side by side.

city   the   have   only   not   does

6 _____ the world's third largest population of Italians outside Italy, but it also has the largest population of Japanese outside Japan.

account   should   city   the   no   on   you leave

7 _____ without going to the top of the Italia building in the downtown area – the view is spectacular.

find   rarely   you   local   a   resident   will

8 _____ , or *Paulista*, who would dream of living anywhere else.

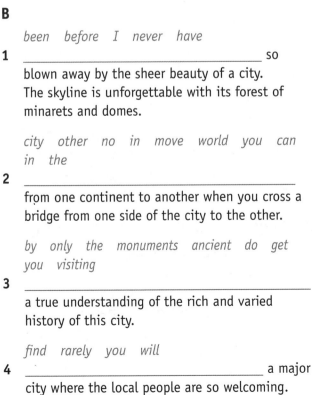

- ✂

B

been   before   I   never   have

1 _____ so blown away by the sheer beauty of a city. The skyline is unforgettable with its forest of minarets and domes.

city   other   no   in   move   world   you   can in   the

2 _____ from one continent to another when you cross a bridge from one side of the city to the other.

by   only   the   monuments   ancient   do   get you   visiting

3 _____ a true understanding of the rich and varied history of this city.

find   rarely   you   will

4 _____ a major city where the local people are so welcoming.

should   pay   no   on   account   you

5 _____ the asking price for purchases made in any of the huge bustling markets – you'll be expected to haggle, and vendors will be offended if you don't.

experienced   before   I   a   never   have   city

6 _____ of such contrasts: ancient and modern, religious and secular, Asia and Europe, mystical and earthly.

account   leave   city   on   you   no   should   this

7 _____ without watching the sunset over the Bosphorus.

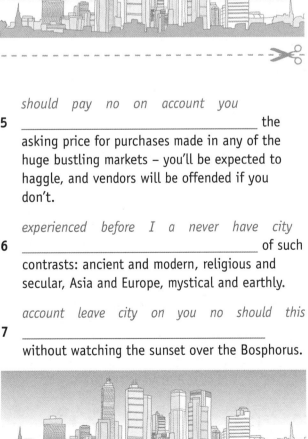

3 Vocabulary

Sentence halves

Portman urged the government to come	to its senses and stop nuclear testing.
We have to try and get in without drawing	attention to ourselves.
The refugees fell	prey to criminal gangs.
He flies	off the handle every time the mail is late.
They began to offer takeaway food, and other restaurants followed	suit.
I hope you'll give	our conversation some thought.
Shall we leave	a tip for the waiter?
We were asked to make	way for the bride and groom.
I paid	good money for those shoes and you've only worn them twice.
I can't put	my finger on it but something about this deal really smells.
I'll leave you to take	care of the refreshments.
He began to work	his magic on the crowd.

 New Inside Out Advanced Teacher's Book © Macmillan Publishers Limited 2010

3 Communication

City of dreams

1   Look at some words and phrases to do with cities. Put them under the headings according to your personal preferences. Compare your ideas with a partner.

buskers   **bustling markets**   *crowded city centre*   **elegant parks**

family-run restaurants   fashionable clubs   haphazard modern development

historic buildings   **hordes of tourists**   narrow cobbled streets   *noise pollution*

overhead expressways   *pavement cafés*   pedestrianised areas   *quaint backstreets*

quiet residential areas   soaring office blocks   sprawling suburbs   **street vendors**

traffic congestion   *tree-lined avenues*   *trendy shops*

City of my dreams	City of my nightmares

2   **You're going to tell your partner about the best (or worst) city you have visited.**

- Ask yourself the questions below.
- Think about *what* to say and *how* to say it.
- Tell your partner about the best (or worst) city you have visited.

a) What's the name of the city and where is it?

b) When did you first go there and why?

c) How did you get there?

d) Who did you go with?

e) What did you know about the city before you went?

f) What was your first impression?

g) How long did you stay there and what did you do?

h) How many times have you visited the city?

i) When was the last time?

j) What do you most (least) like about it?

k) Would you like to live there? Why? Why not?

Review A

Getting to know you inside out

START

ANSWER! What's the best meal you've ever had?

ASK SOMEBODY! How would you describe the way you dance?

ANSWER! When did you last laugh until you cried?

ASK SOMEBODY! What's the best chat-up line you know?

ASK ANY QUESTION!

ANSWER! What TV show did you never miss as a child?

ASK SOMEBODY! What's the ugliest town or city you've ever been to?

ANSWER! What is your favourite meal of the day?

ASK SOMEBODY! Who's the best conversationalist you know?

ASK ANY QUESTION!

ANSWER! What's the worst thing about travelling by air?

ASK SOMEBODY! In what ways are you like your mum or dad?

ANSWER! How would you describe a perfect weekend?

ASK SOMEBODY! What are you really good at?

ASK ANY QUESTION!

ANSWER! When did you last feel annoyed and why?

ASK SOMEBODY! What's the most dangerous thing you've ever done?

ANSWER! When did you last take a taxi and where were you going?

ASK SOMEBODY! What's the weirdest thing you've ever eaten?

ASK ANY QUESTION!

ANSWER! What would you miss most about your country if you lived abroad?

ASK SOMEBODY! How do you relax?

ANSWER! What are you most looking forward to this week?

ASK SOMEBODY! What sort of music are you listening to these days?

FINISH

4 Grammar

A memorable day

Complete one part of the story of a memorable day. Then fold the paper over and pass it to the person on your left.

It was to be a special day, because I was celebrating ... *(What were you celebrating?)*

- FOLD -

To mark the occasion, I was planning to spend the day with my friends doing something different. *(What were you planning to do?)*

- FOLD -

But things started to go wrong from the moment I woke up. I had been hoping to look my best, but when I looked in the mirror I was horrified to see ... *(What was wrong with your appearance and what did you do about it?)*

- FOLD -

I had been planning to dress to impress! *(Describe the outfit you were going to wear.)*

- FOLD -

But to my dismay, when I took it out of the wardrobe... *(What had happened to the outfit? What did you decide to wear instead?)*

- FOLD -

Finally, I left the house. I was due to meet my friends in my favourite place. *(Describe your favourite place.)*

- FOLD -

But on the way, something happened that made me very late. *(What happened?)*

- FOLD -

By the time I arrived at the meeting place, my friends had left. I was on the verge of leaving, when I heard someone call my name. I looked round, and couldn't believe my eyes. *(Who did you see and what were they doing?)*

It was the perfect end to a memorable day.

4 Vocabulary

Finding synonyms

It was staggering.	It was extremely surprising.	It was electrifying.
It was extremely exciting.	It was unprecedented.	It had never happened before.
I was gutted.	I was very disappointed.	I hunted high and low.
I looked everywhere.	I was taken for a ride.	I was conned.
It sounded fishy.	It didn't sound right.	I was very naïve.
I was very gullible.	I didn't fall for it.	I didn't believe it.
It had me in stitches.	It was extremely funny.	I refused point blank.
I said absolutely not.	I could hardly contain myself.	I was very excited.

 New Inside Out Advanced Teacher's Book © Macmillan Publishers Limited 2010

4 Communication

Revision story

time heals	live up to	plastic surgery	young at heart
known as	ill health	slick	categorically denied
erratic behaviour	reclusive	was planning to	on the verge of
about to	the scene of the crime	deception	to cut a long story short
gullible	unscrupulous	taken for a ride	fall for
strictly speaking	in other words	that is to say	a huge parcel
trip over	clutching	refuse point blank	sprawled

Proverb auction

The advice is cheap.

All that glitters is not gold.

Every cloud has a silver lining.

The knowledge is the power.

What am I bid? £4,000 ... £4,500 ... £5,000. Any advance on £5,000? Do I hear £5,500? Going ... going ... gone! For £5,000.

Make the hay while the sun shines.

Many hands make light work.

Money can't buy the happiness.

The necessity is the mother of invention.

Never bite the hand that feeds you.

The early bird catches a worm.

Time is money.

Where there's a will there's a way.

Communicative crossword

A Write clues for the words 1, 5, 7, 9, 10, 11, 12, 14 and 15 across.

1 DISCOUNTED
5 UNSCRUPULOUS
7 UPMARKET
8 ET
9 LAVISH
10 NIFTY
11 BUDGET
12 RIP-OFF
14 FAD
15 CHEAPSKATE

B Write clues for the words 1, 2, 3, 4, 6, 8 and 13 down.

1 DAYLIGHT ROBBERY
2 SURPLUS
3 LOW COST
4 SPLASH OUT
5 U
6 GET RID OF
7
8 EXORBITANT
9
10
11 B
12 I-
13 SOFA
14 A
15

5 Communication

Money talks

START

1 IN WHICH COUNTRY IS THE CURRENCY CALLED THE RIAL?

2 someone you know who lives beyond their means

3 the last present you bought

7 WHAT IS THE CURRENCY OF ARGENTINA?

6 the last item you bought online

5 your last expensive night out

4 something you're saving up for

8 the most extravagant person you know

9 the last time you splashed out on an expensive purchase

10 the most expensive item you own

11 a time when you paid over the odds for something

15 the most generous person you know

14 your favourite shop

13 IN WHICH COUNTRY IS THE CURRENCY CALLED THE DONG?

12 where the upmarket shops are in your town or city

16 the last luxury item you bought

17 the place where you buy your basic necessities

18 someone you know who lives frugally

19 WHAT IS THE CURRENCY OF THAILAND?

23 your opinion of no-frills airlines

22 something you think is a waste of money

21 something you've bought second-hand

20 a restaurant in your town or city that's beyond your means

24 a time when you've haggled

25 IN WHICH COUNTRY IS THE CURRENCY CALLED THE RAND?

26 a time when you've been ripped off

27 someone you know who is really tight-fisted

31 WHAT IS THE CURRENCY OF DENMARK?

30 something you wouldn't buy online

29 a profession you think is worth a high salary

28 your favourite brands

Answers: 1 Brazil 7 peso 13 Vietnam 19 baht 25 South Africa 31 krone

New Inside Out Advanced Teacher's Book © Macmillan Publishers Limited 2010

6 Grammar

Stative or dynamic phrases?

1 Look at these example phrases from the *Macmillan English Dictionary*. In each case:
Choose the most appropriate verb form. Is the verb use stative or dynamic?
Think about the meaning. In what context might you hear (or see) these phrases?

1   He**'s just / 's just being** silly again – pay no attention.

2   I know that Sally **feels / is feeling** quite strongly about this issue.

3   I **feel / 'm feeling** like a cup of coffee.

4   I **felt / was feeling** quite cheerful when we set out.

5   I **don't have / 'm not having** that kind of behaviour in my class.

6   I **had / was having** the house all to myself last week.

7   **I've had / 've been having** it up to here with Kevin – he never stops complaining.

8   I **have / 'm having** a duty to report anything suspicious to the police.

9   He went to the door but there was no-one there. He must **hear / be hearing** things.

10 If he gets a date with Clare, we**'ll never hear / 'll never be hearing** the end of it.

11 He could be a murderer for all I **know / 'm knowing**.

12 Can I help you? No thanks, I **just look / 'm just looking**.

13 Do you think it **will look / will be looking** bad if I don't go and see him?

14 Do you know whether he **sees / 's seeing** anyone at the moment?

15 It's difficult for me because I can **see / be seeing** both sides.

16 Maybe now they**'ll see / 'll be seeing** reason and scrap the project.

17 If she **thinks / 's thinking** I'll help her, she has another thing coming.

18 I'm sorry, I **just don't think / 'm just not thinking** straight at the moment.

19 Sam **thinks / 's thinking** of buying a new car.

20 Just who **do you think / are you thinking** you are?

2 Now choose five phrases to learn and write your own examples.

6 Vocabulary

Ways of speaking and looking

1 I can *express / communicate / converse* confidently in three languages.

2 I had a teacher at school who would *ramble on / drone on / mutter* for hours about a subject and it was so boring that the lesson would go very slowly.

3 I used to *argue / discuss / disagree* about everything with my parents, but we get on much better now.

4 If I'm angry about something, I can't keep it in – I have to *sound off / exclaim / rant* about it to anybody who'll listen, and then I feel better once it's off my chest.

5 My grandfather is a bit deaf, and he has an embarrassing habit of making personal comments about people in a loud voice. Because he's deaf, he doesn't realize he's *shouting / yelling / crying*.

6 I often go window-shopping and spend hours *staring / gazing / glaring* at all the expensive things I want but can't afford.

7 I wish my mum would wear her glasses when we go shopping. It's embarrassing to see her *squinting / peering / winking* at the prices because she can't focus properly.

8 I hate it when people have long, loud phone conversations on the train. I *glare / frown / blink* at them and hope they'll get the message. They usually just ignore me and carry on with their conversation.

9 I remember, when we used to go on family holidays to the seaside, how exciting it was to catch *a glimpse / sight / a glance* of the sea.

10 I'd hate to give a *performance / speech / talk* in front of a big audience. I'd be terrified.

    New Inside Out Advanced Teacher's Book © Macmillan Publishers Limited 2010

6 Communication

Memories

A

1 What was the last phone number you dialled?

2 What did you have for breakfast this morning?

3 How long did it take you to fall asleep last night?

4 What was your last conversation in English about?

5 What used to make you embarrassed as a teenager?

6 How did you celebrate your tenth birthday?

7 Where were you when you first saw snow?

8 What was your favourite TV programme as a child?

FOLD

B

1 Who was the first person you spoke to this morning?

2 What was the last item of clothing you bought?

3 What was the last book you read from start to finish?

4 When did you last go to the dentist?

5 What was your last argument about?

6 What was your first English teacher's name?

7 What was your favourite game as a child?

8 What used to make you frightened?

FOLD

Review B

Don't say it!

✂

A

autonomy	behaviour	challenge	compliment	eavesdropping	efficiency
independent	behave	determination	nice	conversation	effective
self	react	difficult	praise	listen	good
individual	act	fight	positive	overhear	results

energy	enthusiasm	evidence	humour	nightmare	opinion
power	interested	facts	funny	dream	attitude
effort	excited	prove	laugh	scary	believe
electricity	bubbly	crime	sense	bad	think

plot	recommendation	romance	speculation	support	technology
story	suggestion	love	idea	help	scientific
happen	advice	feeling	guess	kindness	advance
film	problem	mood	wonder	approve	machine

✂

B

bargain	celebration	chat	cooperation	eccentricity	emotion
price	party	conversation	help	strange	feeling
cost	event	talk	together	behaviour	experience
low	birthday	message	assistance	unusual	love

entertainment	environment	harmony	myth	observation	opportunity
performance	place	music	story	watch	chance
enjoy	conditions	peace	magic	comment	possibility
music	world	happy	Greek	notice	easy

policy	relationship	skill	stress	tale	tension
plans	connection	ability	worry	story	nervous
rules	involve	training	nervous	anecdote	relax
ideas	friend	experience	pressure	tell	frightening

 New Inside Out Advanced Teacher's Book © Macmillan Publishers Limited 2010

7 Grammar

My future in a hat

It's highly unlikely that I'll ever _____	Knowing me, before long I'm bound to _____
In the next ten years, I may very well _____	Before the end of the year I'll probably _____
I doubt whether I'll ever _____	One of these days, I'll almost certainly _____
In the not too distant future, I may _____	In the next five years, I'll definitely _____
It's unlikely, but one day I might _____	If I'm lucky, I'll _____

7 Vocabulary

Give us a clue

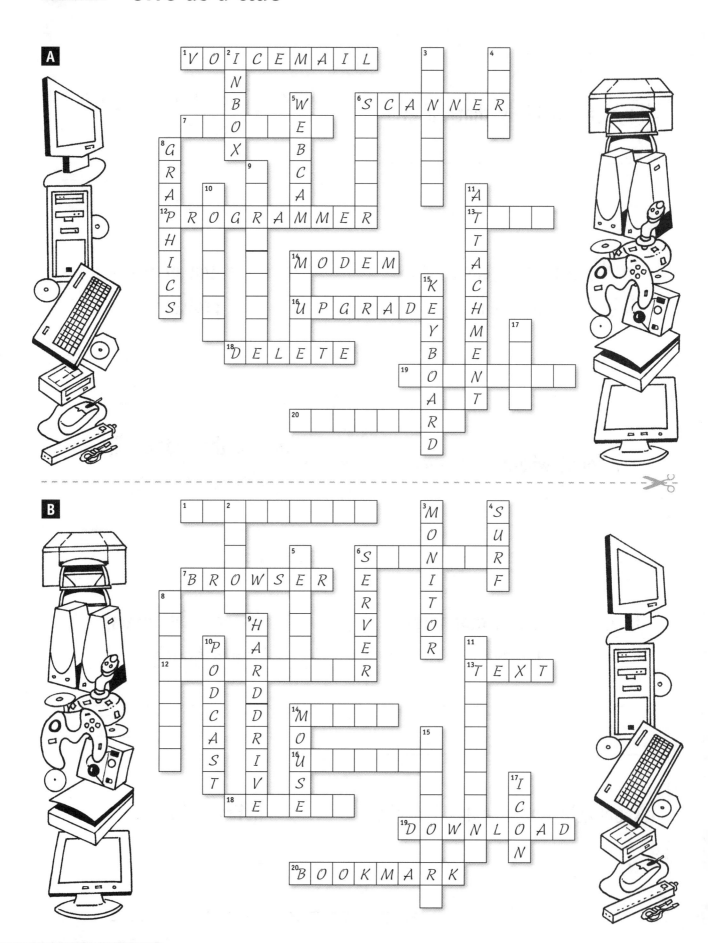

7 Communication

Planet News

Earth meets its match

Yet further messages have been received from star 42 in the constellation Ursa Major. Messages from the newly-named "Planet Eden" were first received last month by the Space Council's Planet Finder Mission and a team of the world's top scientists, linguists and computers have been analyzing the recordings twenty-four hours a day since then. The messages are yet to be fully understood, but the Space Council's chief scientific officer, Marta Fernandez, said yesterday that patterns in the signals were beginning to emerge. She went on to say that even though the signals were originally transmitted thirty-five million years ago, this was absolute proof of the existence of extra-terrestrial, intelligent life. She described the discovery as the most exciting and important ever made. She added that because they'd sent messages to us, it was likely that they could also be on their way to visit.

The big sleep

Three men who "died" thirty years ago were this morning having breakfast after being revived at midnight last night. Professor Scott Bowyer, who has headed the 'Eternal Life Project' since it began in 2069, announced the breakthrough this morning, saying that humans had at last conquered death. The three volunteers were frozen while they were still alive and have spent the last thirty years in capsules in Beijing University's cryogenics department. The three are currently undergoing a series of neuroscans and are having their mental and emotional states assessed. They will then have their brains uploaded with the major news and cultural stories of the past three decades.

150 years young

Vanessa Amilhat today became the first person to celebrate a 150th birthday. Born in Paris in 1949, she puts her longevity down to not worrying about money, walking a kilometre a day, and a careful diet of vaccine and protein-enhanced food and drink. Madame Amilhat told reporters this morning that she didn't feel a day over a hundred and that she was looking forward to celebrating her 200th birthday in 2149.

From here to paternity

He's American, 6 ft. tall, works out regularly at the gym, and he's having a baby. David Venus, now seven months pregnant, was finally revealed to the world at the Earth Fertility Convention in New York yesterday. "I'm glad the sickness has stopped," Mr Venus told the conference while rubbing his swollen belly, adding "I'm feeling on top of the world, and now I'm just looking forward to being a father."

First woman trillionaire

The publication of this year's "World Rich List" has for the first time revealed more women than men among the world's hundred richest people. Dr. Hillary Spencer, chief executive of GECL Industries, heads the list with an estimated worth of just over 2.2 trillion dollars. GECL, the world's largest company, employing over one million people worldwide, produces genetically engineered foods containing therapeutic proteins and vaccines and claims that if we eat carefully, we need never become ill again.

William Dawes, founder of EyeCom, which ten years ago developed the contact lens computer screen, is the world's richest man with an estimated fortune of 1.6 trillion dollars.

Others new to the list include Sam Smith, founder of NetSafe, the Internet security company, Linda Thomas, head of cosmetic laser-surgery company Biocos, and Amber Arrows, pop singer, actress, and politician.

Brazil crash out

In last night's World Premier Championship semifinals, Southeast Asia defeated Brazil by twelve goals to five and Saudi Arabia drew 4–4 with Scandinavia. Brazil's defeat means that Saudi Arabia is now favourite to win for the second year in a row.

8 Grammar

Modals and meanings

He must have gone.	I'm sure he's gone.
He might have gone.	It's possible that he's gone.
He can't have gone.	I'm sure he hasn't gone.
He should have gone.	He didn't go and I disapprove.
He needn't have gone.	There was no obligation for him to go.
He couldn't go.	He was unable to go.
He may not have gone.	It's possible that he didn't go.
He ought not to have gone.	He went, and I disapprove.
He wouldn't go.	He refused to go.
He ought to be going.	I think it's time he went.
He had to go.	He went because it was an obligation.

 New Inside Out Advanced Teacher's Book © Macmillan Publishers Limited 2010

8 Vocabulary

Thick as thieves

In Linz in Austria, a nineteen-year-old youth held up a store with an air rifle and took $200. A few days later, he saw a photofit picture in the local press and complained to his mother that it was a terrible likeness. She (1) *handed him over to the police,* and he was immediately arrested.

In Camarillo, California, a man went into a department store and took several suits into a dressing room. He carefully snipped off the security tag from one suit and then put it on under his clothes. Rather than leave the security tag behind, thinking it would be found and used as evidence, (2) _____ _____ _____. He was grabbed by a store employee as he stepped out of the store.

In January, a man was jailed for two years at Kingston Crown Court in England for the burglary of an apartment three months before. He had left behind his wallet containing his passport. He insisted he was innocent of the crime claiming(5) _____ _____ earlier in the day.

After robbing bus passengers in Rio de Janeiro of more than $800 last month, the robber jumped off the bus right in front of (3) _____ _____ _____. The commanding general of the military police himself abandoned the podium to give chase. The felon was eventually captured after a gun battle.

A couple and their sleeping baby shared a table with a Spanish tourist outside the Museum of Modern Art in New York. A few minutes after the couple left, the tourist realized that her handbag had been taken. The woman, noticing (6) ____ _____ _____, phoned the police and calmly waited for the thieves to return. They did indeed return ten minutes later and were promptly arrested.

A man entered the World Savings Bank in Plantation, Florida last month and demanded money. The teller said there were no envelopes to put the money in, so the robber pulled one from his pocket. As he did so, (4) _____ _____ _____. The police telephoned him at work the next day and he was arrested five minutes later.

An armed robber was sentenced to eight years' imprisonment last week after being caught getting off a bus. The robber had attempted to hold up the Co-op Pioneer supermarket in Penzance, England but fled empty-handed when told that the tills were empty. He ran out of the store and straight onto a passing bus. Realizing (7) _____ _____, he got off the bus and was arrested by the police.

How many people have had something stolen from their car?

FIND OUT

How many people know someone who's in the police force?

FIND OUT

How many people have had something stolen from their house?

FIND OUT

How many people have seen a crime movie recently?

FIND OUT

How many people have been robbed in the street?

FIND OUT

How many people have read a crime novel recently?

FIND OUT

How many people have been fined for speeding?

FIND OUT

How many people have been victims of identity theft?

FIND OUT

How many people have had a parking fine?

FIND OUT

How many people think their neighbourhood is safer than it was ten years ago?

FIND OUT

How many people know someone who's a lawyer?

FIND OUT

How many people think the country has an effective legal system?

FIND OUT

9 Grammar

The teenage years

If only I _____ harder at school. (try)

I wish I _____ something different. (study)

I wish I _____ how to play an instrument. (learn)

I wish I _____ to a different school. (go)

If only I _____ to my parents. (listen)

If only I _____ to my parents. (not listen)

I wish I _____ nicer to my parents. (be)

I'd love to _____ an older sister or brother. (have)

I'd like to _____ my great grandparents. (know)

I regret _____ so much rubbish on television. (watch)

I wish I _____ more. (go out)

I wish I _____ less. (go out)

I regret _____ so much time online. (spend)

If only I _____ so much money on clothes. (not waste)

If only I _____ then what I know now. (know)

9 Vocabulary

Brushing up on phrasal verbs

come up against	a problem	come up with
a solution	face up to	reality
get away with	murder	get out of
the washing up	go down with	the flu
go on at	the kids	look forward to
the summer holidays	make up for	lost time
put up with	that awful noise	run out of
petrol	stand up for	your rights

 New Inside Out Advanced Teacher's Book © Macmillan Publishers Limited 2010

9 Communication

Things that go bump in the night

A

Built in 1837, St James Hotel is situated on the Alabama River overlooking the picturesque city of Selma.

_____

_____

_____

Over the years, it has been a popular destination for businessmen, plantation owners and soldiers, as well as a few unsavoury characters. The notorious outlaws Frank and Jesse James frequented the hotel during the 1880s.

_____

_____

_____

Strange as it may seem, when the hotel reopened in 1997, it became apparent that old customers were still enjoying their favourite hotel.

_____

_____

_____

A ghost named Lucinda is supposedly Jesse's girlfriend. She is described as a beautiful, tall, black-haired woman, smelling of lavender. She sits in the courtyard and watches the living.

_____

_____

_____

When a team of paranormal investigators were brought in, they set up recording equipment to find out what was going on.

_____

_____

However, when playing the tape back later on, they heard several voices, and in particular the deep voice of a man saying very clearly, 'Well, that's a stupid question.'

_____

_____

_____

B

_____

_____

_____

Although it was completely renovated and refurbished in the late 1990s, the original features and old Southern American charm have been preserved.

_____

_____

_____

The St. James became well known for its dining room and drinking room, which were popular with locals. But despite its popularity, the hotel closed in 1892 for over 100 years.

_____

_____

_____

Passers-by reported seeing a white orb floating around the window of Room 301. Legend says the ghost of Jesse James stands at the window, watching for the law.

Hotel guests have seen and heard all sorts of strange things: the barking of a phantom dog, curtains moving spontaneously, lights flashing on and off and glasses clinking behind the bar when nobody was there.

_____

They sat very still in the middle of the room and asked the question "Is there anybody there?" Despite their best efforts, they got no reply.

_____

_____

If you're not afraid of things that go bump in the night, you can stay in Room 301 at the St James, but if you do, you may not be alone.

Review C

Word jigsaw

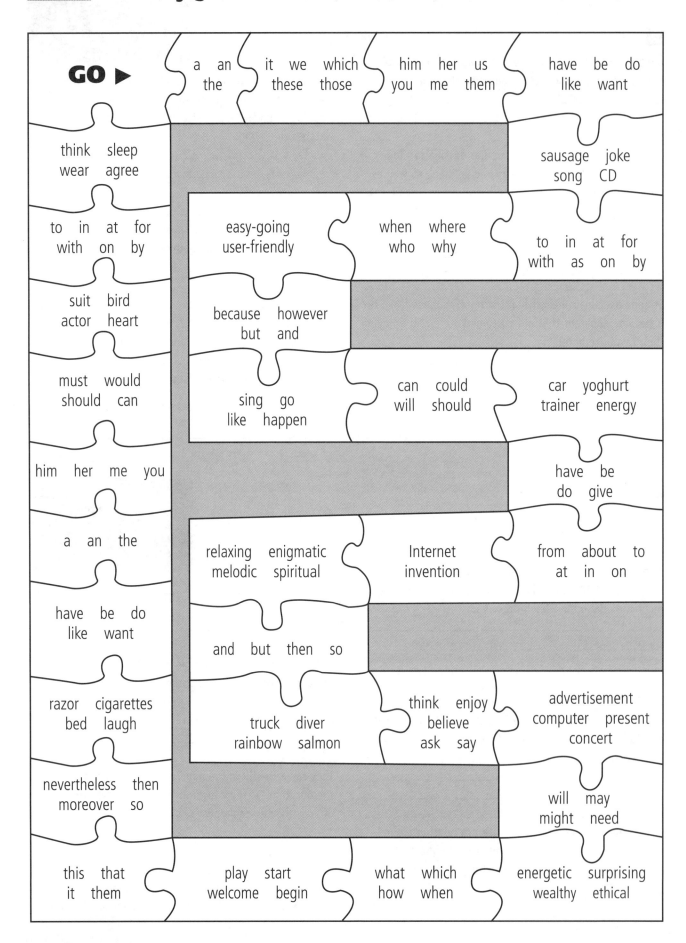

GO ▶

a an the | it we which these those | him her us you me them | have be do like want

think sleep wear agree | | | sausage joke song CD

to in at for with on by | easy-going user-friendly | when where who why | to in at for with as on by

suit bird actor heart | because however but and | |

must would should can | sing go like happen | can could will should | car yoghurt trainer energy

him her me you | | | have be do give

a an the | relaxing enigmatic melodic spiritual | Internet invention | from about to at in on

have be do like want | and but then so | |

razor cigarettes bed laugh | truck diver rainbow salmon | think enjoy believe ask say | advertisement computer present concert

nevertheless then moreover so | | | will may might need

this that it them | play start welcome begin | what which how when | energetic surprising wealthy ethical

New Inside Out Advanced Teacher's Book © Macmillan Publishers Limited 2010

10 Grammar

Divine Chocolate®

The story of Divine Chocolate® begins in 1993 when a cocoa farmers' cooperative, Kuapa Kokoo, was set up in Ghana to run a democratic organization to ensure that the farmers themselves benefit directly from the sale of the cocoa they produce.

In 1998, Kuapa Kokoo started working with a group of British organisations who care about getting cocoa farmers a better deal. The Day Chocolate Company was formed and they created **the Divine chocolate bar** . Since then, variations such as Divine white chocolate, dark chocolate and drinking chocolate have been added to the company's list.

Day Chocolate's mission is to work towards fairer trade with developing countries, and to ensure people buy **more cocoa** at the Fairtrade price. Almost half of the company's shares are owned by the farmers, which means they also have a say in how they produce and sell **the chocolate** .

Divine has been developed with the British public in mind. British people eat the most chocolate per capita of anyone in the world, making the UK an important market for the cocoa farmers.

They grow **cocoa for Divine chocolate** in the southern regions of Ghana. In Ghana cocoa is usually grown on family farms on small plots of land, although in parts of Asia some companies are establishing **larger plantations** .

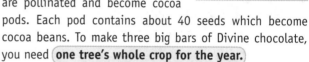

Cocoa trees grow up to 15 metres high, and the flowers only appear 3–4 years later. Roughly 10,000 blossoms are produced by each tree, but only a very few are pollinated and become cocoa pods. Each pod contains about 40 seeds which become cocoa beans. To make three big bars of Divine chocolate, you need **one tree's whole crop for the year.**

The cocoa pods are harvested 5 to 6 months after pollination. This is a very labour intensive stage of the process. First, the farmers cut **the pods** from the trees. Great care must be taken not to damage the rest of the tree. After that, they split **the pods** open with big sharp knives and the pulp is extracted.

After harvesting, they ferment and dry **the beans** . The beans are then brought into Europe by a Dutch importer. From there they take **the dry cocoa beans** and transform them into delicious, creamy chocolate.

- ✂

The story of Divine Chocolate® begins in 1993 when a cocoa farmers' cooperative, Kuapa Kokoo, was set up in Ghana to run a democratic organization to ensure that the farmers themselves benefit directly from the sale of the cocoa they produce.

In 1998, Kuapa Kokoo started working with a group of British organisations who care about getting cocoa farmers a better deal. They formed **the Day Chocolate Company** , and the Divine chocolate bar was created. Since then, they have added **variations such as Divine white chocolate, dark chocolate and drinking chocolate** to the company's list.

Day Chocolate's mission is to work towards fairer trade with developing countries, and to ensure more cocoa is bought at the Fairtrade price. The farmers own **almost half of the company's shares** which means they also have a say in how the chocolate is produced and sold.

They have developed **Divine** with the British public in mind. British people eat the most chocolate per capita of anyone in the world, making the UK an important market for the cocoa farmers.

Cocoa for Divine chocolate is grown in the southern regions of Ghana. In Ghana they usually grow **the cocoa** on family farms on small plots of land, although in parts of Asia larger plantations are being established by some companies.

Cocoa trees grow up to 12 and 15 metres high, and the flowers only appear 3–4 years later. Each tree produces roughly **10,000 blossoms** , but only a very few are pollinated and become cocoa pods. Each pod contains about 40 seeds which become cocoa beans. To make three big bars of Divine chocolate, one tree's whole crop for the year is needed.

They harvest **the cocoa pods** 5 to 6 months after pollination. This is a very labour intensive stage of the process. First, the pods are cut from the trees by the farmers. They must take **great care** not to damage the rest of the tree. After that, the pods are split open with big sharp knives and they extract **the pulp** .

After harvesting, the beans are dried and fermented. A Dutch importer then brings **the beans** into Europe. From there the dry cocoa beans are taken and transformed into delicious, creamy chocolate.

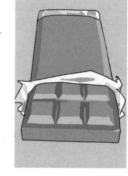

10 Vocabulary

Use your head

1 Choose the correct alternative to complete these common expressions.

1 I realise that by telling Alice about her surprise party I've really put my _____ in it.
   a) hand   b) foot   c) head

2 When we go on holiday, we always ask our neighbour to keep an _____ on things while we're away.
   a) eye   b) ear   c) arm

3 Now that I've gone on to a three-day week, I've got so much more time on my _____ .
   a) feet   b) shoulders   c) hands

4 At school our English teacher used make us learn long passages of poetry off by _____ . I can still remember some of them.
   a) head   b) mind   c) heart

5 Once Anna's set her _____ on getting something, there's no stopping her.
   a) teeth   b) mind   c) head

6 They met in 2005 and fell _____ over _____ in love. They've been inseparable ever since.
   a) head / heels b) nose / toes   c) face / feet

7 It was a relief to tell her about my doubts. It was good to get it off my _____ .
   a) stomach   b) shoulders   c) chest

8 I should have told him that we didn't like his proposal but I just didn't have the _____ for it.
   a) stomach   b) hair   c) head

9 Members of this political party have to _____ the line or they are expelled.
   a) finger   b) toe   c) eye

10 I'm sorry but I'll deal with it as soon as I can. I'm up to my _____ in work at the moment.
   a) elbows   b) shoulders   c) eyes

- ✂ - -

2 Tell your partner about ...

1 a time when you really put your foot in it.

2 the person you'd ask to keep an eye on your house if you went away.

3 a time in your life when you felt you had a lot of time on your hands.

4 a song or a poem that you know off by heart.

5 a time when you set your mind on doing something. What happened?

6 a couple you know who are head over heels in love.

7 a time you got something off your chest.

8 a time you didn't have the stomach to do something.

9 a time when you've had to toe the line.

10 a time when you were up to your eyes in work.

 New Inside Out **Advanced Teacher's Book** © **Macmillan Publishers Limited 2010**

10 Communication

Pink dolphins

Hidden deep within the Amazon rainforest in the south of Colombia is Lake Tarapoto, home to a rare and almost mythical species: *Inia geoffrensis* or pink river dolphin. Thought by some to be extinct, this fresh-water dolphin had simply been forgotten, and in 1987 a Colombian biologist, Fernando Trujillo, made it his life mission to study and protect it.

It wasn't easy for him. Not only had he to understand the local Indian culture, but he also had to deal with a corrupt local bureaucracy, a far from eco-friendly fishing lobby, and the vested interests of the logging and industrial sectors, which were busy polluting the river close to the lake. And then there was the rainforest itself, where the delicately balanced ecosystem is at odds with every aspect of the modern world.

Trujillo began a study of flowers growing near the lake after he heard an old myth that fish are created from the falling petals of a magical tree. It was an enchanting explanation for what turned out to be a biological truth. Many of the fish in the lake relied upon these petals for food. Any deforestation would therefore help to deplete an important source of food for the fish.

Trujillo has come to see the dolphins as part of the wider, carefully balanced ecosystem and has encouraged the local Ticuna tribe to rediscover traditional fishing methods. The use of spears for fishing might not be as effective in the short-term as nets, but they are preferable when fish stocks have been reduced to a non-sustainable level. It has been revealed that, until recently, nearly thirty dolphins died every year after being caught in fishermen's nets. Now the number of deaths is down to two or three a year.

Roleplay: developing tourism

As a means of boosting the local economy, the Colombian government is considering developing tourism at Lake Tarapoto. As well as those from the business world who are in favour of such a development, there is some resistance from local community members, who feel that this place of natural beauty could be irreparably damaged.

In groups of five, each choose a role card for a debate. Read your role card and take notes on what you are going to say. Be prepared to state your case either for or against the development and be able to justify your reasons. Then, in your group, hold a meeting to discuss the plan.

Rolecards

Local Ticuna Indian

You are concerned that your peaceful village life close to the lake will be adversely affected by the arrival of tourists. This feeling is shared by most of the local community. On the other hand, you believe that your knowledge of the area might enable you to get a job as a tour guide. You want assurances that, should development go ahead, tourist numbers will be restricted and for only two months of the year.

Local government official

You feel that promoting tourism at Lake Tarapoto would be a good way to generate much-needed money for the local community. You are insistent that the profits generated from any tourist activity should be used locally to improve the standard of living of local people and not go into the pockets of a few business entrepreneurs. You want a long-term, sustainable, and equitable solution to tourist development in the area.

Fernando Trujillo

You are against turning Lake Tarapoto into a tourist resort. You are concerned that the natural habitat of many species, including that of the pink river dolphin, will be irreparably damaged and that the delicately balanced ecosystems will be ruined for ever. You want the lake and its environs to be given special protected status and for there to be no development whatsoever. You have the backing of most of the local community.

Business entrepreneur

You are desperate to turn Lake Tarapoto into a tourist attraction and are seeking permission to build a hotel close to the lake. You have future plans to develop even more hotels and associated facilities. You would also like local transportation to be improved to ease access to the resort. This would mean cutting through the rainforest to build a new road. You would also like boat trips to be made available to tourists at the resort.

Independent advisor to the government

You are truly independent on this issue. You must listen to all the participants, ask questions as necessary, and finally make a decision whether to proceed with the development.

5 reasons to get an e-book

1 It's compact

Whether you're a student or whether you're someone who travels a lot, the e-book is a godsend. If you're a student or someone who travels a lot, you probably need to carry a stack of books, and carrying a stack of books is a huge burden. Thanks to the e-book, you can not only save loads of space in your bag, but you can also save space in your home. My shelves are full of books, and my office and my basement are also full of books. I usually have to give books away to make space for new books. But I no longer have to give books away to make space for new books – with the e-book, the problem has been solved.

2 It's always open

When I'm reading, I tend to get really absorbed. The fact that I'm really absorbed means that I carry my book around the house, reading my book while I eat breakfast, reading my book while I brush my teeth, while I chop vegetables, etc. The problem with a paper book is that I always have to find a way to keep a paper book open, and keeping it open usually means putting something heavy across the book. Of course, putting something heavy across the book tends to obscure part of the page, which is a nuisance. With an e-book, it's always flat.

3 It has an excellent catalogue

Almost any book you would ever want to read is already available on most e-books and thousands more books are being added on a regular basis.

4 It's green

E-books are good for the planet. E-books help to save trees – no trees are used to make an e-book.

5 It's the future

Sorry, but it is the future. E-books are what we'll be reading while we rocket to Mars in 2050 – either we'll be reading e-books, or our personal robots will be reading e-books to us.

   New Inside Out **Advanced Teacher's Book** © Macmillan Publishers Limited 2010

11 Vocabulary

Ode to the spell checker

Rewrite the poem with the correct spellings.

Eye have a spelling checker
It came with my pea see.
It clearly marks four my revue
Miss takes eye cannot sea.

Eye strike a key and type a word
And weight fore it too say
Weather eye am wrong or eye am right.
It shows me strait a weigh.

As soon as a mist ache is maid
It nose be four two long,
And eye can putt the error rite
Its rare lea ever wrong.

Eye have run this poem threw it,
I am sure your pleased two no,
Its letter perfect all the weigh –
My checker told me sew.

11 Communication

Hidden word

monkey	tennis racket	taxi driver	wedding ring
shop assistant	armchair	giraffe	passport
newspaper	London bus	trousers	spaghetti
umbrella	pilot	guitar	bicycle
dictionary	ice hockey	dolphin	chewing gum
cornflakes	bananas	ashtray	identity card
iPod	The Beatles	footballer	underwear

 New Inside Out Advanced Teacher's Book © Macmillan Publishers Limited 2010

12 Grammar

The great debate

1 **Complete the statements with the correct form of *be*, *have*, *stop* or *take*.**

1 It's about time single-sex education _____ made illegal – it's just not natural.

2 Most people would rather smoking _____ banned in all public spaces – inside and out.

3 If every couple _____ a joint bank account, there would be fewer arguments about money.

4 If the voting age _____ reduced to 16, young people would become more interested in politics.

5 It's high time women _____ complaining about being second-class citizens.

6 If there _____ more women in positions of power, the world would be a better place.

7 It's about time we _____ keeping animals in zoos.

8 It's high time the physical punishment of children by parents _____ outlawed throughout the world.

9 It's high time the government _____ climate change more seriously.

2 **Read each statement again. Put a tick (✓) if you agree, a cross (✗) if you disagree or a question mark (?) if you're not sure either way. Discuss your opinions with a partner.**

12 Vocabulary

Word families

A

NOUN/SUBJECT	PERSON	ADJECTIVE
addict_____	addict	addict_____ / addict_____
competit_____	competit_____	competit_____
charity	charity worker	charit_____
depend_____ / depend_____	depend_____	depend_____ / depend_____
educat_____	educat_____	educat_____ / educat_____
employ_____	employ_____	employ_____ / employ_____
homeless_____	homeless person	homeless
informat_____	inform_____ / inform_____	informat_____
investigat_____	investigat_____	investigat_____
organisa_____	organis_____	organis_____ / organis_____
representat_____	representat_____	representat_____
worry	worr_____	worry_____ / worr_____

B

   New Inside Out Advanced Teacher's Book © Macmillan Publishers Limited 2010

12 Communication

Easy money

Story A

It was a normal Saturday morning. John Blake woke up, made some coffee and then sat down to read the mail. One particular letter caught his attention. It was addressed to him with "urgent" printed on the front and looked rather official. He opened it. It read: *Dear Mr Blake, first the BBT Lottery congratulates you and your family on your big win. The money has been deposited in your account and will be immediately available for withdrawal. You will be required to sign the enclosed forms and we would also like to advise you that our specialized financial advisors can help you to invest your money wisely and make a real success of your lottery winnings.*

John was confused. He had never played a lottery in his life. Questions were running through his head. How much money was involved? What had happened? What type of mistake was this? He quickly looked through all the other pieces of paper; among them was the one he had to sign. He began reading it through but his eyes were quickly attracted to a sentence in the corner. It read: *In receipt of $1,001,250 paid into City Central Bank, Boston, Account No. 34562 PY980.* He read it and read it again. This couldn't be true. Things like this just didn't happen in real life.

The next two days were the longest in John's life. On Monday morning he went into the City Central Bank in Boston and requested his credit situation. The teller took a piece of paper, wrote a number on a piece of paper and calmly handed it to John. It read: *The city bank would like to inform you that your current account is $1,009,000 in credit. Have a nice day.*

John left the money in his account for over six months. Then he took legal advice and had the money transferred into an off-shore account. It wasn't until the end of the financial year that the BBT Lottery realised its mistake. The legal battle that took place lasted over two years.

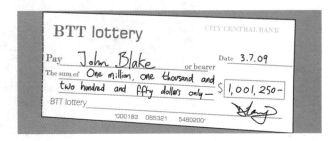

Story B

It was one of those stupid junk mails, you know, the promotional letters that you get sent to your house nearly every morning. You get them every day. *Patrick Combs, you have won $95,093.* There was a cheque for the same amount. The cheque was very real looking, but in the corner was written "non-negotiable for cash". Patrick Combs read the rest of the advertisement. It told him that he could be earning real cheques just like this one if he did what they said. He looked at the cheque again. Real, he thought, this looks pretty real to me.

Of course he knew it was an advertisement, but something in his head told him to try it. He thought it would make a funny story to tell his friends. Imagine saying 'Guess what! I put one of those advertising cheques in my bank account and the stupid bank accepted it.'

So on Monday morning on his way to work, he dropped into his local bank and deposited the cheque. The teller never asked anything. She simply took the cheque, stamped it, and gave him a receipt for the money. He wasn't that surprised. He knew that this didn't actually mean that he had been credited with the money. He knew that within three days he would receive a letter from the bank saying the cheque was invalid and hadn't been cleared.

Three days passed and no such letter arrived. A week later and still no letter. He went down to his nearest cash machine, popped in his card, and requested his balance. The machine printed out on the screen: *Your balance is $104,889. Thank you for banking with Interstate Bank.*

He couldn't believe his eyes. It had been a joke. He had never expected them to accept the cheque, but even more he had never expected the cheque to come from a real account with real money in it. The cheque was an advertisement: how could they be so stupid as to print a cheque that had a real bank account number on it?

The bank did eventually realize their mistake, but by then Patrick Combs had already made plans to protect his money. The story went to national television, the *Wall Street Journal* and an amazingly complex legal battle with the bank in question.

New Inside Out Advanced Teacher's Book © Macmillan Publishers Limited 2010   PHOTOCOPIABLE   **195**

Review D

Tell us about …

My favourite gadget is…	*By the end of the year, I'll have…*	In the third millenium, we…	*If I could no longer use a computer, …*	**Tell us about …**
Tell us about …				I've never been able to…
I often feel guilty about…				*My favourite computer game is…*
It's high time I…	*A charity I support is…*		*The worst crimes are…*	I generally use the internet to…
	Some English words used in my language are…		It's OK to break the law if…	
A charity I support is…	**Tell us about …**		**Tell us about …**	*My country's press is…*
A traditional story from my country is…				I'll never forget the first time I…
A story I remember from my childhood is…	I once won…	**Tell us about …**	The main differences between my first language and English are…	*It's always been an ambition of mine to…*

 New Inside Out Advanced Teacher's Book © Macmillan Publishers Limited 2010